Abandoning Dead Metaphors

Abandoning Dead Metaphors

The Caribbean Phase of Derek Walcott's Poetry

Patricia Ismond

UNIVERSITY OF THE WEST INDIES PRESS

Barbados • Jamaica • Trinidad and Tobago

University of the West Indies Press
1A Aqueduct Flats   Mona
Kingston 7   Jamaica   W I

©2001 by The University of the West Indies Press
All rights reserved. Published 2001

05 04 03 02 01   5 4 3 2 1

CATALOGUING IN PUBLICATION DATA

Ismond, Patricia
Abandoning dead metaphors : the Caribbean phase of
Derek Walcott's poetry / Patricia Ismond

p. cm.

Includes bibliographical references and index.
ISBN: 976-640-107-1

1. Walcott, Derek – Criticism and interpretation.
2. West Indies – In literature. I. Title.

PR9272.9.W3Z694 2001   811.54

Set in Plantin Light 10/14 x 27
Book and cover design by Robert Harris
E-mail: roberth@cwjamaica.com
Printed in Canada

Cover illustration: Derek Walcott, *Causeway, Pigeon Island*. The
Project Helen Collection, St Lucia National Trust, Castries, St Lucia.

In memory of my mother, Lilin, and Papa

Contents

Acknowledgements

Thanks are due to Derek Walcott and his publishers, Farrar, Straus and Giroux, and Faber and Faber, for quotes from Walcott's books and essays; to Wilson Harris and his publishers, for use of material from *The Guyana Quartet,* and to *Caribbean Quarterly* for quotes from Harris's "History, Fable and Myth"; to Professor Edward Baugh, for the use of some of his sources in *Memory as Vision: Another Life;* to Stewart Brown, editor of *The Art of Derek Walcott,* and his publisher for several references made to and quotes from that book; to Rei Terada and publisher, for use of material in her *Derek Walcott's Poetry: American Mimicry,* in my engagement with her critical perspective in that book; and to John Thieme and his publisher, for a similar use of material from his *Derek Walcott;* to Robert Hamner, for his quite comprehensive Walcott bibliography in *Critical Perspectives on Derek Walcott,* which proved invaluable. I am indebted to Walcott, again, and his family, for providing me with relevant background information over the years.

I am also grateful to the Stanford Humanities Center of Stanford University for the fellowship that enabled me to begin this work; and to the University of the West Indies, St Augustine, my workplace, for the sensitive response of its administration to the problems and setbacks that sometimes interrupted its progress.

I am especially happy to express my gratitude to the following persons who read the manuscript and contributed to its improvement in various ways: Professor Gordon Rohleher, my colleague and friend, who picked out the gaps in the manuscript in its early stages and gave generously of his breadth of knowledge; Professor Mervyn Morris, for his sensitive and most encouraging reading of the manuscript; Dr Pamela Collins, my friend, who extends so easily from her own area of expertise in agriculture to embrace the arts of language and literature; and Rawle Gibbons, who also contributed to the closing of some of the gaps in the work.

I am eternally grateful to the special friends whose encouragement and faith in the effort helped me bring it to completion: Trevor Prevatt, Dr Pamela Collins and Lawrence Scott.

I remain forever indebted to my sister Esther, whose love sustained and steadied me through it all.

Abbreviations

Works frequently cited in the text have been identified by the following abbreviations.

AL	*Another Life*
CP	*Collected Poems 1948–1984*
Dream	*Dream on Monkey Mountain and Other Plays*
FT	*The Fortunate Traveller*
Green Night	*In a Green Night*
"Muse"	"The Muse of History"
SG	*Sea Grapes*
SAK	*The Star-Apple Kingdom*
Ti-Jean	*Ti-Jean and His Brothers*
"Twilight"	"What the Twilight Says" (essay)
Twilight	*What the Twilight Says* (collection)

CHAPTER ONE

Introduction

The Caribbean Focus

This book deals with the Caribbean phase of Walcott's poetry, as represented by the volumes produced from 1948 to 1979, an output extending from the juvenilia (*25 Poems* [1948], *Poems* [1951], and *Epitaph for the Young* [1949]) to *The Star-Apple Kingdom* (1979). The Caribbean phase coincides, effectively, with the period of Walcott's residence in the Caribbean, and ends with his change to residence in the United States – or more accurately, to what may be called either his itinerant status as commuter between, or his dual residency in, the Caribbean and the United States. In this context, *The Star-Apple Kingdom* presents itself as the last fully Caribbean volume, *The Fortunate Traveller* (1982), which follows, being a transitional work of the change to dual residency. The present work concentrates on this Caribbean phase of the poetry as an important one concerned with Caribbean identity and self-definition.

Walcott has gone on to become, since this earlier part of his career, a writer of phenomenal world stature; and the consensus, especially among metropolitan critics, is that the Walcott who has come into his own voice and authority is the later one (usually dated from *The Star-Apple Kingdom*).[1] The earlier

Walcott, even including *Another Life* (1973), is generally regarded as lacking the innovative freedom of language characteristic of the later. However, a proper appreciation of this earlier, distinctly Caribbean phase of his career proves necessary for important reasons. First, this is the formative phase of the entire Walcott achievement – the place where he pursues the revolutionary effort native to his purpose as a writer of colonial origins, to arrive at the maturity of definitions of self and identity. As such, it has a completeness and integrity of its own. The other, equally vital, significance follows from the first. The meanings and definitions achieved in this phase are foundational to the total Walcott: they constitute the very groundings from which he proceeds to bridge newer and older worlds, and the quality of the syncretism that has established itself as a hallmark of his genius since *Omeros* (1990).

Several of the many critical commentaries on Walcott have dealt with the revolutionary effort central to this phase, and have identified such salient aspects of this effort as the anticolonial quest for identity on the one hand, Walcott's close attachment to the Western tradition on the other, and the tensions between the two. *Abandoning Dead Metaphors* uncovers the revolutionary effort in a particular, distinct route that has so far remained largely unobserved. Its reading of that effort is as follows: Walcott's anticolonial, revolutionary route turns primarily on a counter-discourse with the dominant mode of thought of the colonizer's tradition, against which he pursues an alternative, liberating order of values and meanings, generated from the different time and place of his Caribbean, New World ground. The engagement with the colonizer's tradition is, effectively, a dialectical one, and it subserves the purpose of exploring and defining his native world. Of equal importance is the fact that this interfacing of older tradition and native world is engaged through metaphor: a dialectical, subversive argument with the Old World European tradition of metaphors, and the generation of fresh ones from his New World setting. Metaphor appears as a major term of reference throughout Walcott, as pervasive during this phase as in his later works. Directly pertinent to our context are a number of references expressive of his perspectives on his early venture. In "Crusoe's Journal" he speaks of his Caribbean setting as "a green world, one without metaphors" *CP*, 92);[2] and he uses the term "borrowed metaphors", echoed in "borrowed ancestors" ("Homecoming, Anse La Raye", *CP*, 127) to describe his relationship to the Western tradition. The revolutionary effort, then, is routed through a metaphorical enterprise. To understand the poetics of this metaphorical enterprise, and what it aims at in revolutionary terms, we need at this point to consider some of the peculiar emphases in Walcott's concept of metaphor.

Walcott's concept of metaphor is a strictly poetic one, and comprehends figuration in the widest, generic sense – as Rei Terada puts it perceptively: "metaphor functions, as usual, [in Walcott] as a figure for figuration".[3] Ideas and images in Walcott have shifting, even revers(ing) emphases, and metaphor is no exception. At one point in *Another Life*, where metaphor is central to his theme, he equates it with "metamorphosis" to argue against an older, classical metaphysics that projected metaphor as an ideal of higher transformation. But there is a recurring usage which points to its core significance for him. It is his identification of *naming* – a seminal and quite familiar concept in his work – with metaphor and the metaphorical. As early as the essay "The Figure of Crusoe" (1965), he makes this identification and gives an explanation of the anthropomorphic psychology that links the two: "That given a virgin world, a paradise, any sound, any act of naming something, like Adam baptising the creatures, because that action is anthropomorphic, that is like the pathetic fallacy, it projects itself by a sound onto something else, such a sound is not really prose, but poetry, is not simile, but metaphor."[4] In his Nobel lecture, *The Antilles: Fragments of Epic Memory* (1992), he returns to this idea of metaphoric naming, relating it to a Caribbean diasporic necessity of finding new metaphors: "The original language dissolves from the exhaustion of distance like fog trying to cross an ocean, but this process of renaming, of finding new metaphors is the same process that the poet faces every morning."[5] In an interview with Edward Hirsch (1977), he speaks of the metaphoric principle that goes into the task of language creation/naming, at primal, root sources. He cites from the native French creole of St Lucia the original naming of a bird *ciseau la mer* (scissors of the sea), and comments thus: "It was the experience of a whole race renaming something that had been named by someone else and giving that object its own metaphoric power. That was the privilege of being born in what is usually called an underprivileged, backward, and underdeveloped society."[6] It is relevant that Walcott attributes this capacity for metaphoric naming to a people in the "Adamic" – early – phase of its culture: he situates both himself and the grassroots creators of the native French creole in that metaphoric capacity.

What are the constitutive elements and significance of metaphor as focused in this concept of the metaphoric principle of naming/language creation? One of his major later poems, "The Light of the World" (*The Arkansas Testament*,

1987) gives some insight into this. Walcott is reflecting on the metaphoric, analogic structure of an expression, again from St Lucian French creole. The expression comes from a woman trying to get onto a bus.

> She said to the driver: "*Pas quitter moi a terre.*"
> which is in her patois: "Don't leave me stranded",
> which is in her history and that of her people:
> "Don't leave me on earth", or, by a shift of stress:
> "Don't leave me the earth" [for an inheritance];
> "*Pas quitter moi a terre*, Heavenly transport,
> "Don't leave me on earth, I've had enough of it."

Walcott probes the "literal" signified – "Don't leave me stranded" – through embedded, interconnecting layers of reference: through the reality of the day-to-day condition, always sociohistorically determined; to the existential reaches of human desire (for deliverance).[7] In the metaphoric, image-making principle at work in the signified, the existential world of desire and fear comes into play. Originating in the anthropomorphic factor described by Walcott in the passage from "The Figure of Crusoe", the metaphoric principle also engages, at its deepest reaches, the impulse to relate physical, experienced worlds to metaphysical, imagined ones. The final import of these intimations of "leav[ing] on earth" is that the metaphoric act of language/naming partakes of human intelligence, inward knowing and being, as this enters into and shapes our way of relating to our world. This core of meaning remains constant in Walcott's concept of metaphor, which he views as the very element of poetry; and indeed, of Imagination itself.

When Walcott speaks of worlds with or without metaphors, he is thinking in terms of the aggregate of metaphors in a culture, metaphors that connect together in a mainstream to carry the prevailing mode of the deeper intelligence of that culture – in other words, the special ethos of its desire, its higher imagining of itself. (Thus a variant of this idea of worlds with versus without metaphors occurs in the image of older, named worlds "forested with titles", versus undiscovered ones that "wait for names", in "Guyana V".) One must stress from the outset that Walcott does distinguish between this aggregate and the singular, divergent or iconoclastic elements that stray from it. But he is also focusing, as a distinct reality, a mainstream of metaphors that serve as a repository of that culture's dominant mode of intelligence and tradition. Octavio Paz expresses a similar idea when, discussing the unity of poetry and history, he states: "Therefore, man's true history is the history of his images:

his mythology."[8] Further, such a mainstream of metaphors as Walcott is concerned with is also, accordingly, the vehicle of the muse of its dominant tradition. The term *muse* itself features prominently in Walcott's discourse during this period, as is highlighted in the seminal essay "The Muse of History",[9] and belongs in the complex of ideas on metaphored and unmetaphored worlds. In Walcott's thinking, the muse of a tradition and its dominant mode of intelligence are its moving spirit, motive force, responsible for directing the course of its action, that is, history. Thus, in his dialectical, counter-discursive engagement with the colonizer's mainstream tradition of metaphors, he targets head-on the epic-heroic and cumulative muse of history enshrined in these metaphors – an effort that is concentrated and fully articulated in *Another Life* (1973), the major definitional work of the phase (chapter 5). Ultimately – and we come here to the confluence of the complex of ideas we have been considering – Walcott is zeroing in on this question: What is the "concept man"/humankind ("Guyana I"), harboured and operative in that muse, that has directed the course of western European civilization in its making of history? In effect, Walcott is intent on reading a civilization's muse of humanity as it is carried and enacted in its muse of history. What this means is that his revolutionary route, undertaken through this metaphorical enterprise, is definitively a philosophical and epistemological one; and its substantive, countering mission – the search for fresh metaphors from his newer, different ground – is the search for an alternative, "another light" of humanist intelligence.

The revolutionary purpose under consideration, its metaphorical modality, unfolds as a primary movement and dominant discourse through the poetry of this Caribbean phase. The pattern can be traced, through the successive volumes, in poems that comprise the canon of the period. It begins in an apprenticeship which, committed to the cause of a native art, is dominated by the colonial's overdependence on the metaphors of the colonizer, a relationship particularly acute in Walcott's case. In this very situation lies the problematic which sets the terms of the counteractive, revolutionary effort (chapter 2, "Apprenticeship: Juvenilia to *In a Green Night*"). Walcott awakens from the contradictions and incongruities of this apprenticeship to a keen confrontation with the question of identity, especially as it comes to bear on the diasporic crisis of historylessness, what he termed "history as amnesia"[10] (the starting point of many of the first generation of Caribbean anticolonials). Africa is a major component in this amnesia, featuring primarily as an area of loss, the anguish of a "far cry" ("Laventille", "A Far Cry from Africa"). For him, though, the historylessness stares mainly from the gap between these borrowed metaphors of the colonizer's world, and the emptiness/virgin state of his unmetaphored green world. Thus the earliest, most original promptings of his revolutionary purpose, presaged by this privation, find expression in the will to "abandon dead metaphors" ("The Castaway") – urging the imperative of exploring fresh metaphors of his "unnamed", virgin world, its dual condition of negation and possibility. Following on from his apprenticeship, this movement runs from *The Castaway* (1965) to *The Gulf* (1969) (chapter 3: "Abandoning Dead Metaphors").

The underlying crisis of amnesiac history/historylessness constitutes the core, formative conflict of the Caribbean phase, determining the dialectic of the metaphorical enterprise discussed above. It is what propels him into the major inquiry into the muse of Old World Western imperial history – the largest single theme in the discourse of the period. The importance of the theme of history in Walcott is well represented in his several discursive pieces on the subject (we have already noted the outstanding "Muse of History"). It has also been generally well recognized in the criticism, notably in Edward Baugh's "The West Indian Writer and His Quarrel with History", which deals, in Walcott's case, with the relationship between his sense of the region's history as negation, and his concern with the larger idea of history.[11] The nature of Walcott's concern with history, and the extent to which it shapes his thought and credo, comes into definitive perspective in the context of the dialectical discourse of abandoning dead metaphors of the Old World Western tradition, and generating fresh ones in his newer world. This concern with history and its muse is most fully represented in *Another Life,* where the entire trajectory of the revolutionary effort being focused in the present work is comprehended.

Another Life is, accordingly, the centrepiece of this study. A work arguably equal in power to *Omeros* (1992), it receives extensive treatment here (chapter 5: "Alter/native Metaphors in Fulfilment"). It is in this work that the philosophical intention of Walcott's revolutionary route, its engagement through muse-carrying metaphors, emerges most clearly, to penetrate his final aim of finding an alternative order of humanist intelligence. That order of humanist intelligence is one revisioned and altered in the light of the history that has happened to give rise to new worlds out of old. An integral access of this alternative purpose comes into full view here: the metaphoric naming/discovery of his Caribbean landscape through the elementals of its virgin condition.

The "Guyana" sequence (chapter 3, "Abandoning Dead Metaphors") stands out as a first milestone in this effort. The engagement with elementals extends into a recovery of the aboriginal and pre-Columbian history, their traces and continuing presence on native ground. The latter – pre-Columbian history and the aboriginal – constitute an important factor entering into the exploration of the muse of history. Thus, in the consciousness shaped out of this landscape and its sociohistorical environment, prehistory and recorded empirical history interface and intersect each other to enable a liberating hold on history-in-time. (One of the areas singled out in the commendations of the Nobel committee was Walcott's "historical imagination".) That consciousness means for Walcott a more liberating concept/image of humankind, vis-à-vis the older image harboured in the muse that runs from epic-heroic to dominion-minded, imperialistic man. Walcott grounds his definitions of Caribbean New World possibility in the philosophical underpinnings and spiritual meanings and principles of this thought. James Livingston, a critic with a sure grasp on a lasting source of Walcott's power, puts it this way: "What finally constitutes Walcott's proper claim to the New World, what finally delivers him from colonial servitude into independent consciousness, is the forging of a language that goes beyond mimicry to an elemental naming of things with epiphanic power."[12] At the same time, it should be observed, these groundings of Caribbean identity in Walcott leave the way open for the intercourse and interconnections between "here" and "elsewhere" which are characteristic of his later work (*The Arkansas Testament*).

Throughout the poetry of this Caribbean phase, Walcott is also urgently concerned with the issues of politics and ideologies of identity in Caribbean society, at a time when these issues are paramount in the emergent, anti-imperialist world (the 1960s and 1970s). His approaches to this public sphere are strictly congruent with the deeper concerns of the philosophically oriented revolutionary effort outlined above. Examining two major statement essays ("What the Twilight Says"[13] and "The Muse of History"), and the "public" poems of the *Castaway–Gulf* period, the present study attempts to isolate and theorize Walcott's revolutionary creed, with particular reference to his views on race, ancestry and politics (chapter 4: "Revolutionary Creed, Race, Politics and Society"). The volumes following *Another Life* show a keen concentration on sociopolitical and ideological issues in the post-independence Caribbean. Exploring case histories of these issues in two outstanding long poems, Walcott extends his own vision of the ideological directions and quality of consciousness necessary for a meaningful Caribbean selfhood (chapter 6: "Society and Nationhood in the Caribbean: Towards Another Life"). It is an outlook closely shaped by the values and meanings culminating in *Another Life,* making his statement in these poems a fitting conclusion to the revolutionary effort of this phase. The public consciousness and the main revolutionary effort, then, set alongside each other in this way, together underscore the intensity and integrity of Walcott's commitment to Caribbean definition during this phase of his career.

✖

Generally speaking, criticism has not adequately explored Walcott's Caribbean discourse as an important part of his overall achievement; and, in addition, has understated or missed his concern with Caribbean definition. As earlier indicated, many critical pieces (essays, articles) have dealt with isolated aspects of the achievement examined in the present book,[14] but none have given these the kind of intensive treatment that is possible within an extended study. To date, there are four book-length studies of Walcott: Edward Baugh's monograph on *Another Life,* entitled *Memory as Vision* (1978), Robert Hamner's *Derek Walcott* (1981, updated edition 1993), Rei Terada's *American Mimicry* (1992), and John Thieme's *Derek Walcott* (Contemporary World Writers, 1999). Hamner's book is a general survey of Walcott's career, and, given this scope, it does not accommodate any one defining perspective on the writer. Terada and Thieme explore distinct perspectives on Walcott's artistic achievement – the former on Walcott's poetry, the latter on the poetry and the drama. The present review will begin with these two, and conclude with Baugh's monograph.

Terada approaches Walcott through a complex theory of mimicry. In that theory, mimicry – simulation, as distinguished from mimesis – represents the principle and process of repetition through which cultures and civilizations come into being, a process manifesting itself in the chain of infinite correspondences, infinite differences by which present relates to past. For her, Walcott's work presents a paradigm of that principle of mimicry by which the New World of the Americas creates itself in relation to the Old World of European tradition. It is a thesis which comes to bear, especially given her postmodernist emphases, on Walcott's relationship to the European poetic past. Thieme examines an achievement centred on Walcott's cross-culturalism and hybridism, which work toward the dismantling of Manichaean opposites. Thieme's exposition, though, stresses the creolization of European intertexts as the main agency of this cross-culturalism. Essentially, both these critics start from a Walcott who embodies the continuum from European to newer worlds – the assimilative Walcott, whose relationship with the European tradition and its "influences" remains unbroken from the earliest to the latest stages of his career. Both Terada's and Thieme's are viable and important perspectives and, in each case, well executed. But, given this angle, in both these critics the Caribbean context and its peculiar achievement are underrepresented or subordinated.

Terada's theme is mediated through postmodernist and poststructuralist ideas that open up fresh areas in Walcott criticism, and she has been rightly commended for that contribution. These postmodernist ideas, however, pertain especially to the Walcott of *Omeros* and *The Arkansas Testament,* and she clearly reads Walcott backward from these texts. Thus, her exploration of the theme of mimicry includes such important and pertinent emphases as the concern with art as representation of the object world, and the analytic concern with the linguistics of verbal representation. One of the most valuable contributions in her study is the exposition of Walcott's "creole poetics" in the chapter entitled "The Pain of History Words Contain".[15] She analyses Walcott's language as a mixture of creoles, to project from this the idea of his linguistic hybridism as a model of all language – a "creole of creoles". On the other hand, her focus on Walcott's preoccupation with art as representation makes for certain limitations in her reading of *Another Life.* According to Terada's reading, the main subject in this poem is the relationship between object/material world and figuration – crystallized in the poem's discourse on painting, the more purely representational mode of art – with attendant questions about the stability and permanence of perception. It is a focus that necessarily excludes the Caribbean context and cause prominent in *Another Life,* which has been described as "unequivocally Caribbean".[16]

Primarily concerned with the European poetic continuum as it is, Terada's exposition of her theme of "the potentially infinite regression of mimicries"[17] tends to privilege textuality at the expense of context. Her reading of the poem "The Sea Is History" (*SAK*) provides a striking example of the kind of blurring or neutralizing of context characteristic of this approach. In the present study, this important poem serves as a classic model[18] of the dialectical counter-discourse with the traditional idea of history through which Walcott moves to an alternative definition. That alternative definition answers particularly to the charge of Caribbean historylessness, an issue which Walcott has resolved by the time of *Another Life*. Terada's reading presents significant contrasts to our own in this book.[19] Both readings agree that the "no history" charge frames the argument of the poem; but her reading does not see its polemic as being levelled at the traditional idea of history as cumulative, epic-heroic achievement – the concept behind the verdict of Froude, and of Naipaul after him. As will be argued in chapter 3, Walcott, refuting the "no history" charge, uncovers and (re)instates a denied Caribbean selfhood in terms that achieve a transvaluation of the traditional idea of history. He employs the following strategy for the purpose: for each episode in the Judaeo-Christian biblical narrative, he finds parallels/equivalents in the Caribbean story. Thus the "lantern of a caravel" heralded the dread Genesis of its people in the slave trade; their Exodus was experienced in the brute horrors of the middle passage; their Lamentations endured in the grinding mills of plantation slavery; and, as well, their will to resistance and deliverance found expression in the creativity of their Songs of Babylonian bondage – the tradition of black music/spirituals.

In these equivalents, Walcott valorizes the inner capacities and principles that have gone into the experience of the particular crucible of that history – the struggle against desolation and despair, faith rooted in the will to deliverance, and, no less than these, a people's own self-betrayal in latter times of political independence, deferring the dream of liberation. It is an integral part of his argument that these capacities and principles are a "natural inheritance", innate human elementals, which he has also defined as "first principles"; and that they are the substance of which real history consists. It is in these, he contends as a distinct answer to the "no history" charge, that Caribbean self-achievement consists, though invisible from the perspectives of epic "greatness" and its trappings. Terada misses this purpose of delineating and claiming a Caribbean self in Walcott's careful enunciation of these equivalents – missing the urgency of the motive of historylessness, which penetrates back to his own starting point in the angst of amnesiac history. She gives precedence to the generic idea of the interpenetration of nature and culture/history, the genealogy of whose textuality harks back to Shakespeare: "over that art, / Which you say adds to nature, is an art / That nature makes."[20] In these terms, Walcott's concern to find and name the inscape of a people's self/soul in the particular substance of their history thins away. Recognizing the question of a Caribbean history addressed by the poem, her conclusions on the meanings and answers it offers are, first, that the history of the Caribbean people is preserved in the nature/memory of the body; and next, that the poem finally locates history, beginning in the organic, in the realm of the future, the realm of "the amorphous and ambivalent".[21] These are resolutions which do not get a local habitation and a name, as, the present study suggests, Walcott does intend.

Thieme's book is valuable and timely as the most sustained exploration of cross-culturalism and hybridization/syncretism in Walcott's work – features widely regarded as the distinctive aspects of his international achievement. He explores, as the primary modality of this cross-culturalism, a creolization aptly defined by his alternate designation "poetics of migration"; and concentrates on the migrating intertexts of the European tradition. The representative protagonists of these interests feature as major, creolized metaphors in Walcott's work: Adam, Crusoe, Don Juan, Odysseus. One might observe that there are also a number of prominent intertexts from Caribbean and South American writers in this phase of his career: from Wilson Harris, Brathwaite, Borges, Carpentier, Césaire, all dealt with in the present study. Thieme is, however, generally more sensitive to the Caribbean context than is Terada, especially via its more immediate access in the drama. He makes constant reference to Walcott's search for a Caribbean tradition and aesthetic; but, given the approach described above, the Caribbean context remains, in the main, understated in his case. More precisely, he fails to adequately identify or account for the distinct Caribbean factor at work in Walcott's hybridism. Projecting Caribbean culture as a product of mixtures and juxtapositions of earlier ones, he does not deal with the realities of sociohistorical environment and place – they are subsumed in his word "specifics" – in which that hybridization is produced; or the particular Caribbean mode of being (a phrase he uses) and sensibility that comes out of the whole matrix.

Thieme's reading of the Caribbean context in Walcott accordingly sidelines the issue of amnesiac history/historylessness and the larger questions of the muse of history central in this phase of Walcott's career. Missing these, he also misses Walcott's route through subversive argument with the "dead metaphors" of the mainstream tradition of Old World Europe, a route that leads to the dismantling of the Manichaean order he underscores. His views on *Another Life* are especially interesting in this respect. He is aware of and makes a strong statement on an aspect of the poem central to our own reading in the present study: "And this is exactly how *Another Life* works, with potent images of the local landscape gradually supplanting those of European litera-ture."[22] For him, though, this is only illustrative of how European originals, "stolen" and assimilated by the colonial, work referentially to lead to local counterparts. This fundamental aspect of the poem remains, in fact, unex-plored, and the poetics of migrating texts informs his focus on it. His view is that *Another Life*, mediating autobiography through intertexts, suggests in the end that "fictions of self are original, but derivative reworkings of received fictions".[23]

Since it appeared in 1978, Baugh's *Memory as Vision* has been the only authoritative study on *Another Life*, a poem which has not really received the critical attention it deserves. Baugh combines two related objectives in this monograph: providing the background information indispensable in a poem that belongs so fully in the St Lucian setting; and the exposition of his interpretive theme, memory as vision, which centres an important dimension of a poem about Walcott's return to his native land. Baugh's theme is that in *Another Life*, memory transmutes experience into art; a theme which unfolds, in his exploration, into the poem's concern with the relationship between art and the actual, and the accesses of perception in the meanings that reside within that relationship (see his commentary on Anna as early love in the poem, 53–56).

As in the two critics examined above, the concern with the nature of art emerges as a prominent theme in Baugh's reading of *Another Life*. Baugh knows, however, beyond postmodernist definitions, that Walcott believes in and seeks out Imagination as the thing itself, the faculty behind figuration; believes in it as the progenitor of that "other life" held within "the common life outside" ("For the Altarpiece of the Roseau Valley Church, Saint Lucia", *CP*, 319), which makes an otherwise inchoate world "real". (It is a dimension inherent in Walcott's peculiar concept of metaphor, examined earlier in this chapter.) There is a more immediate and substantive difference between Baugh and these two metropolitan critics: his exposition of this theme never loses sight of the experienced Caribbean context, even as it transcends the particular. The discourse on the nature of art in *Another Life* is not perceived as referential to tradition (Thieme's "received fictions"), or treated as a meditation on representation of a decontextualized object world (Terada). Inevitably carried in the focus on memory, the Caribbean context is fully represented in Baugh. Thus Baugh foregrounds the combined themes of colonial history and the muse of history. He also pays attention, importantly, to the poem's concern with the issue of Walcott's dividedness between allegiance to European tradition and commitment to native culture. The significant and fundamental difference between Baugh's study and the present one, however, occurs in the reading of this matter of Walcott's dividedness between the two worlds. Baugh's reading sees dichotomy and settles on its tensions. From the perspective of the present work, however, *Another Life* is the very place where Walcott confronts and seeks to resolve the dichotomy. Finally, Baugh does not see in this dividedness the cause and locus of a revolutionary effort – the deconstruction and dismantling of an older order of meanings, the search for a newer order – through which the poem achieves its main purpose as a work of Caribbean, New World definition.

On the whole, criticism has not really addressed or appreciated the main aspects of Walcott's Caribbean achievement explored in this book. Above all, the subversive counter-discourse with the European tradition of metaphors and its muse has remained unnoticed. A recognition of this area of his effort should help to put the problematic question of Walcott's relationship to the European tradition into wider perspective. This relationship is not, as is generally assumed, a homogeneous, symmetrical, unbroken affair, progressing from overdependence to creolization of the European legacy. It is instead quite complex, many-sided, and finally eclectic: in Walcott's practice, it ranges over correspondences and parallels, rebuttals, acts of communion and of subversion, continuities and discontinuities. (There is a logic and integrity behind this range, but this is a subject outside our scope.) The subversive inquiry into its dominant mode of intelligence, as focused in this work, represents a critical turning-point within that relationship, necessitated by the imperative of defining a self denied and submerged by the imperialistic constructs of that mode of intelligence. What makes the difference is the expansiveness and depth of this route to self-definition – namely, the philosophical and epistemological intention contained in the dialectic of setting a newer world against the old. It directs him to what are core factors in the shaping of his consciousness: as discussed above, the metaphoric naming of the elementals of his virgin landscape; and, continuous with this naming, a sense (a surviving presence) of prehistory as it interfaces and intersects with a burdened empirical history in that landscape. It is worth noting here that Antonio Benítez-Rojo, among the foremost theorists of Caribbean culture, cites this intersection as a distinguishing characteristic of Caribbean discourse:

> The Antilles are an island bridge connecting "in a certain way" South and North
> America, that is, a machine of spume that links the narrative of the search for
> El Dorado with the narrative of the finding of El Dorado; or, if you like, the
> discourse of myth with the discourse of history . . .[24]

It is, in fact, from these reaches of a consciousness in vital contact with the elemental and mythic that Walcott is liberated and reoriented into the sources of a more mature and wider kinship, not only with Europe, but with all the ancestors – Africa, Asia, and Indoamerica. "[M]aturity is the assimilation of the features of every ancestor", he says in "The Muse of History" (*Twilight*, 36). This is one of the key points of our claim that the Caribbean achievement remains foundational to the total Walcott. Walcott finds, in this incidence of the elemental and mythic – and he resembles Wilson Harris in this – the groundings of the syncretic fusions, the gateway to the place where these ancestors, their legacy of Old World "fragments", meet and cross each other. Thus, in the narratives of *Omeros*, Homer the arch myth-maker/griot of European literary tradition, African griot, Amerindian shaman, and Seven-Seas, the Caribbean island-diasporic-wanderer and encompasser of all myths, meet and cross each other. These culminations in the later, world-embracing Walcott are those of Walcott the mature product of the Caribbean phase. There are, of course, predating these syncretic fusions of the later Walcott, the assimilations and "borrowed" metaphors of the European literary tradition that survive through his entire career. These lasting assimilations, which Thieme identifies as migrating, creolized metaphors, all show his instinct for archetypes. They comprise, significantly, arch-namers/inventors and arch-rebels – Adam the namer/inventor, Crusoe as castaway/inventor, Don Juan as arch-rebel, and Odysseus as arch-wanderer. The instinct for the archetypical and prototypical shown in these earliest and lasting assimilations is all of a piece with the elemental/mythic groundings we have been considering.

In our discussion of the Caribbean achievement so far, several key aspects of the significance of landscape have emerged. The focus of this study brings into full view the prominence of landscape in the Walcott credo and aesthetic. The physical/naturalistic landscape – which naturally incorporates sea(scape) par excellence in Walcott – is a major ground of exploration. The nature and quality of his engagement with landscape during this phase is, along with the other features identified above, the source of the lasting lyricism in his work. That lyricism takes its peculiar spirit from a faith which Walcott sees as an inherent possibility of the newness of the diasporic Caribbean world in its landscape. He expresses it thus in "The Muse of History":

> the possibility of the individual Caribbean man, African, European, or Asian in ancestry, the enormous, gently opening morning of his possibility, his body touched with dew, his nerves as subtilized to sensation as the mimosa, his memory, whether of grandeur or of pain, gradually erasing itself as recurrent drizzles cleanse the ancestral or tribal markings from the coral skull, the possibility of a man and his language waking to wonder here. (*Twilight*, 53)

The sentiment still resonates in "Fragments of Epic Memory" twenty years later. Infused with the spirit of that faith – and indeed its very vehicle – Walcott's lyricism, epiphanic and numinous, is much more than a matter of "nature poetry", the term used by Thieme to describe it.[25] The spirit of that lyricism carries over into his readings of other landscapes in his later poetry, permeating and suffusing that poetry to elicit the response of an otherwise sceptical Helen Vendler that the lyrical Walcott is unassailable.[26]

Finally, the Caribbean focus, as deployed in this book, highlights another area integral to Walcott's achievement in this phase. It brings into the foreground the fund of fresh, original metaphors and images generated from Walcott's native ground – fresh metaphors and images that have remained up to now less visible than those of the European tradition and their creolizations. Prominent among these is Walcott's encircling sea metaphor and its many facets: the Atlantic of the earliest Walcott as image of the amnesiac middle passage and the loss of Africa ("Laventille", chapter 3); the seas of the region as image of the collective Caribbean unconscious with its submerged terrors of historical calamity ("The Schooner *Flight*", chapter 6, and amplified in *Omeros*); and, comprehending all, the "sea is history" conceit, where the sea becomes the locus of the intersection of the temporal/empirical and the timeless, of the simultaneity of endings and beginnings ("The Sea Is History", chapter 3, and "The Schooner *Flight*", chapter 6). There are also metaphors of the elementals of forest settings in Harrisian journeys through the interior ("Guyana" sequence, chapter 3). The fund also includes outstanding meta-phoric portraits such as the muse of revolution, embodiment of the ideology of retaliatory violence threatening in militant times to overtake the region ("The Star-Apple Kingdom", chapter 6); and the personification of colonial history in the figure of the colonizer surviving in an old, anachronistic "parchment [white] creole", such as one might meet in any of the islands ("The Schooner *Flight*", chapter 6). In Walcott's practice, metaphoric principle runs into and is coincident with myth – as in the mythologizing of the rustic Trinidadian village of Rampanalgas, scene of a revisioned and reinscribed muse of history-in-time (*AL*, chapter 5); and the epiphanic apprehension of the story of the leaping Caribs of Grenada as an ancestral, mythic "leap into light" (*AL*, chapter 5). These, and many others, attest to the power of a native talent that achieves its own authority, and also brings fresh leases of life to tradition.

CHAPTER TWO

Apprenticeship

Juvenilia to *In a Green Night*

In *Another Life,* where he returns to his beginnings in St Lucia to search the roots of his creative endeavour, Walcott characterizes the initial phase of his career as a "divided childhood", and clearly identifies the source of this dividedness in his deep attachment to the "borrowed metaphors" of the Western tradition. What has crystallized in memory captures the most impor-tant truths about that beginning: the reality of a young talent strongly fired with the ambition of being among the first pioneers of a West Indian art, and at the same time, deeply drawn to the artistic achievements of the colonizer's world. He had, however, given direct utterance to this underlying dilemma in the well-known poem "A Far Cry from Africa", written at the early stages of his career. Responding to the shock of the Mau-Mau crisis in Kenya (early to mid-1950s), the extreme violence of that racial collision between British colonizer and native African, Walcott had been moved to express his own sense of conflicting allegiance between a victimized Africa and "the English tongue I love":

> I who am poisoned with the blood of both,
> Where shall I turn, divided to the vein?

> I who have cursed
> The drunken officer of British rule, how choose
> Between this Africa and the English tongue I love?
> . . . .
> How can I face such slaughter and be cool?
> How can I turn from Africa and live?

(CP, 18)

Walcott's *cri de coeur* was immediately recognized as a classic expression of the psychological dimension of the crisis faced by the colonized in those early stages of anticolonial militancy. But it is important to pay attention to the particular terms in which this dilemma is registered in his case. As a descendant of Africa, he reacts from a strong atavistic sense of racial kinship against its victimization. The opposite pull is equally powerful – it is to "the English tongue I love". While he distinctly repudiates the yoke of its imperial regime, represented by "the drunken officer of British rule", his love of and claim to the English tongue are as natural as the bond of kinship with Africa.

This love of and claim to the English language as a historical legacy – and he was to give it the force of a polemical declaration[1] – is not only significant as his point of departure. It underlies his entire achievement. While pertinent for all West Indian writers, this question of the colonizer's language as heritage bears a special emphasis in Walcott's individual case. The essential Walcott problematic – and its resolution – devolves to a large extent onto his engagement of what came first as "the language of the master". In effect, his revolutionary struggle has been waged mainly within this arena. He is sensitive from the outset to the levels of servitude and indentureship to the colonizer's Word/world that complicates his love of the latter. His original, formative struggle has been to free himself of that servitude and to find fresh reaches of inventiveness in exploiting it to explore the "new waters" of his own world. He has achieved, in the process, a genuine revitalization and extension of this language.

In a Green Night (1962) marks the true launching of Walcott's career as a poet, but one must return to his earliest poetic efforts in the juvenilia for a true appreciation of the nature and bearings of this point of departure. The three books which comprise the juvenilia – *25 Poems* (1948), *Epitaph for the Young* (1949), and *Poems* (1951) – are separated from *Green Night* by some ten years. The period covers his university career (1950–53), and six years of settling down to a career as a West Indian artist in Trinidad, including a one-year stint studying theatre in America (1957–58).[2] There are significant changes and advances in his poetry over this period, but the juvenilia form an integral background to *Green Night*. This is immediately evident from an examination of the content of *Green Night*. Both *25 Poems* and *Poems* provide a number of the important poems in that volume, *Epitaph* being one long poem. From *25 Poems* come "Prelude", "As John to Patmos", "A City's Death by Fire", "Elegy", "The Harbour", "To a Painter in England"; from *Poems,* a much weaker volume, comes "A Country Club Romance" ("Margaret Verlieu Dies" in *Poems*).

Further, and at a more substantial level, a survey of the content of these volumes shows dominant concerns and themes common to the juvenilia and *Green Night*. They begin, in both cases, with the pledge of artistic vocation dedicated to the service of a new landscape ("I With Legs Crossed Along the Daylight Watch"/"Prelude"); and include a self-conscious preoccupation with the risks and potentially tragic fate of the artist (*Epitaph,* "The Fishermen Rowing Homeward in the Dusk"/"The Harbour"), and the twin preoccupations with the crisis of belief and art as belief (*Epitaph,* "Return to D'Ennery, Rain", and "In a Green Night"). A number of poems in *Green Night* are also concerned with giving lyrical presence to his landscape, fulfilling the pledge made in "As John to Patmos", and culminating in the prize-winning poem "A Sea-Chantey".[3] The links are also registered on another less obvious but very important level. Imitativeness and literariness are major characteristics of the juvenilia, as was immediately noted by the reviews, even while they responded to the young poet's considerable promise. By the time *Green Night* appears, the charge of imitativeness has given way to an appreciation of voices and influences more judiciously accommodated to his regional content.[4] There is, however, an underlying dimension of continuity from the imitativeness to the voices and influences, signalling, as do the continuity of concerns cited above, a single initial phase in Walcott's career. It is a phase which describes, in its orientation and characteristic achievements, a period of apprenticeship. This chapter will deal with the peculiar aspects of this period of apprenticeship.

Epitaph for the Young

Walcott begins, like any aspiring young poet, with an excessive dependence on models and influences from the tradition. But the prodigious range and scale of these influences – classical, traditional, and modernistic – draw attention from the outset. The original objectives and spirit with which he sets out, however, stand out clearly amid the derivative pieces. They are expressed with striking clarity and integrity in one of his earliest pieces, "I With Legs Crossed Along the Daylight Watch", the poem which was to serve as his introductory "Prelude" in *Green Night*. The poem enacts and celebrates the arrival of his artistic vocation as a promise of liberation, of arousal from what has so far been a condition of dearth and stasis, which is as much his as that of his island. The opening image of tropical proneness and inertia subsumes and identifies the plight of his island in his own:

> I, with legs crossed along the daylight, watch
> The variegated fists of clouds that gather over
> The uncouth features of this, my prone island
>
> . . . .
> Until from all I turn to think how,
> In the middle of the journey through my life,
> O how I came upon you, my
> Reluctant leopard of the slow eyes.

(CP, 3–4)

So that the envisioned possibility, the sombre note of elation with which he greets this promise, is as much his island's as his own – a subtly internalized pledge of his future as an artist to his landscape. "As John to Patmos", a poem of the same period, reaffirmed this pledge. *Epitaph for the Young*, and the majority of the poems in *25 Poems* and *Poems* are, however, primarily about the prospects and risks of the artistic calling, the problem of religious belief, and extending from this, quasi-philosophical reflections on transience and death. What this suggests is that Walcott's deepest angst concerns his prospects and prognosis for what he regards as an unprecedented and awesome venture. This is reflected in the inward, often self-regarding postures and attitudes which characterize his treatment of these themes. In effect, the genuine impulse to serve the landscape is subordinated to this preoccupation with his role and destiny as artist. The landscape is engaged and refracted mainly from that core reality.

It is in *Epitaph for the Young* that we get the clearest illustration of these features. *Epitaph* presents in twelve cantos the personal odyssey of Walcott as the young questing poet. Written concurrently with *25 Poems* (1946–49), it represented an autobiographical outlet for the early Walcott. It contains, therefore, a record of his closest motivations and leanings at this initial stage. The other and most prominent feature of *Epitaph* is its sheer literariness, a literariness that almost masks content. The poem comes through as a panoply of voices and forms from the masters of the Western literary tradition – classical, traditional and contemporary. It has the advantage of gathering into one place the range and extent of Walcott's attachment to the literary tradition of the master. To examine the content of the poem is to get a clear picture of the salient aspects of his apprenticeship, and its seminal sources at both the personal and cultural levels.

Walcott goes to the classic form of the Homeric sea odyssey for the basic framework of his quest, also invoking such modern antecedents as Joyce and Pound. Eliot's modernistic treatment of the interior monologue provides his dominant narrative technique, while the canto format sustains the underlying lyrical intention, harking back through Pound to Dante. The protagonist is the persona of Walcott as young artist, following the first call of the artistic imagination to search for a meaningful order of belief, against a world of disillusionment and doubt. The search for belief precipitates a head-on religious-cum-metaphysical argument, which often runs into blasphemous confrontation with the Christian God. It is, of course, in the guise of Joyce's Stephen, his then current hero,[5] that Walcott undertakes this quest, and the clearly discernible intention of the poem is to describe, like Stephen, his portrait as a young artist. The characteristic posture of Walcott/Stephen in this effort is caught in this passage:

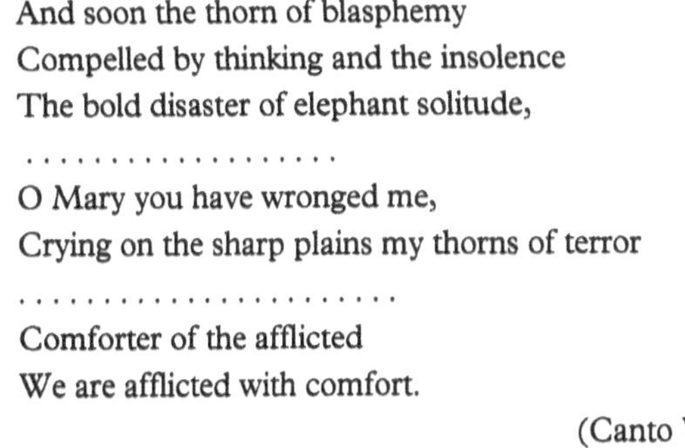

> And soon the thorn of blasphemy
> Compelled by thinking and the insolence
> The bold disaster of elephant solitude,
>
> . . . .
> O Mary you have wronged me,
> Crying on the sharp plains my thorns of terror
>
> . . . .
> Comforter of the afflicted
> We are afflicted with comfort.
>
> (Canto V, 13–14)

As dispossessed son pursuing, through shipwreck and doubt, the mythic quest for the father (*Ulysses*), Stephen serves as a truly inclusive medium for all the literary analogues that Walcott aims to encompass in this work. The quest thus retraces a mythic route which invokes such prototypes as Hamlet and Telemachus, to merge with counterparts in the Christian myth of Dante, one of the most direct and strongly echoed voices in *Epitaph*:

> I made out as I were dreaming, my father's spirit in arms.
> And when the old mystery had ascertained that it
> Was he whose face I sought through life
> And whom no filial memory could aid me by I said
> Bending my face to his
>
> > "Are you here, Ser Brunetto?"
>
> . . . .
>
> And he, "If Thou observe the Star that guides the mariner
> Beyond the dubious haven of the promontory, you will please our Father . . .
>
> > (Canto VIII, 24)

Beneath the welter of voices and allusions, however, there is one clear and consistent focus in this quest for belief. While he looks to emulate the "brilliance of Stephen's reasoning", the emphases in his dialectic are not exactly those of Joyce's hero. The exclusive concern here is with the contradictions of the doctrine of sin and redemption, the bondage of flesh versus the doctrine of perfectibility. The crux of the argument is with a God who has made "imperfect piety with his perfect pardon". In the end, the iconoclastic spirit seeks grace and reconciliation, resolving to desist from mysterious probings in the manner of Prospero (Canto XII). This particular slant has its direct and deep-seated roots in Walcott's religious upbringing. He grew up in a household where his mother, living with the twin concerns of caring for her children and the early loss of their father[6] – what he describes as "my father's yearly dying"[7] – was devoted to the pieties of her Methodist faith, in an island whose culture was dominated by religion. The religious strain in Walcott's sensibility goes back to these tenacious roots. They also account for his early linking of the questions of art, death and belief, which finds its clearest, early expression in "Elegy", written in memory of his father.[8]

If the religious concern is original and authentic, what is equally clear from the literary affinities examined above is that it is being mediated through the art of the classical and religious masters of the tradition, from the Hellenic through the Judaeo-Christian tradition. A significant pattern emerges from this movement through the great myths of the Western tradition. In rebelling against the orthodox and conventional faiths of his setting, the young Walcott cultivates art as a higher order of truth and knowledge. He identifies imaginative art with the exercise and freedom of the individual intellect, its very element and space. It is the original point of his identification with the rebellion of Stephen. There are personal factors, over and above the idealisms and philosophical precociousness of the young apprentice, which account for the particular weight this carries in his case. Canto IV, where he makes his fullest excursion from the literary to the immediate realities of his environment, paints this picture of the bleak future the island had to offer its native sons on leaving school:

> They left school and soon became,
> *Magna cum laude*,
> Companions of inanity, knights of the order of rotgut,
> Others, desiring the unguent of fame,
> The sick ego, posturing to be applauded,
>
> . . . .
> They too succumbed in the wavering season
> Between forty and dying.
> Died most as Suppressor of His Majesty's Conscience in the Colonies,
> Inspector of Civil Service lavatories
>
> . . . .
> Attaché to the Assistant Attaché
> Requiescat in papier.
>
> (Canto IV, 11)

This had been the fate of his father before him, and of his father's generation. The situation is spelt out again in "Leaving School", where he describes the sole alternative of a life in the civil service which awaited those who did not escape through the single annual Island Scholarship.[9] The choice and ambition of a career in art was therefore a bold and virtually unprecedented step, an asylum and major escape route. He was, of course, acutely aware of the anxieties and insecurities with which this choice was fraught. As earlier noted, these anxieties represent a prominent theme throughout the juvenilia, a number of poems affecting the Baudelairean mask of the doomed poet. It is most pervasive in *Epitaph*, where the Icarus motif recurs as a twin aspect of the rebellion of the Stephen Dedalus/Walcott persona. The title of his poem thus signals both the blight of his generation, from which he hopes to escape, and his own fears lest his prove an ill-fated choice. Finally, he enacts in *Epitaph* the positive through which he hopes to counter the odds: the exercise, through art, of Imagination, with which he equates freedom and energy, against the constrictions of his immediate setting.

Capacity for thought, equated with art as a higher religion, has a serious, transcendent value for the early Walcott. A closer scrutiny of his extensive borrowings from the masters becomes necessary at this point, since his main accesses to this speculative effort are through these masters. What characteristic features do these borrowings present and what is their underlying import; what do they reflect of the propensities and psychology directing Walcott's early efforts? As *Epitaph* shows, the imitation consists first of all in a close reproduction of the metaphoric contexts of the masters, extending to the effort to capture voices and methods intact. The vast composite of metaphors includes Homer's odyssey in the *Iliad* and *Odyssey*, its Christian counterpart in Dante's metaphor of quest/journey in *The Divine Comedy*, Shakespeare's Renaissance variant in the fictions of *Hamlet* and *The Tempest*, the redeployment of these classical/Christian configurations in Eliot's wasteland metaphor, in Baudelaire's iconoclastic "fleurs du mal", and the Stephen Dedalus metaphor in Joyce, Walcott's most representative point of entry. These are all, essentially, variant metaphors of the one Word of the Western metaphysic, anchored in the conception of existence in terms of the antinomies of humanity and divinity.

What emerges clearly from this level of engagement and its peculiar intensity is of critical importance: the young Walcott assumes a heritage in that tradition, and aspires to fellowship in and admission to its pieties. This is the first and original level of his "love of the English tongue", and what, above all, gives his apprenticeship its characteristic stamp. It is to prove the most testing. There is nothing unusual in this beginner's dependence on the classical heritage of a tradition. Further, as Walcott himself points out in both "Meanings"[10] and "Twilight", the classical inheritance was quite inevitable even for a colonial talent, given the content of colonial education in his day. It becomes a remarkable and critical feature, however, when seen in the context of the implicit revolutionary purpose of his pioneering ambition. From that standpoint, it underscores the peculiar force of his filial attachment to that tradition, testifying to this primary aspect of his apprenticeship. Nothing captures the potency of that faith in the Word of the master more acutely than the longing which still echoes, after some thirty years, from these lines in *Another Life*: "O / mirror, where a generation yearned / for whiteness, for candour, unreturned" (*CP*, 146).

Carried along on the currents of this strong pull to the Western literary tradition, however, Walcott is far from insensitive to the discrepancies, the

strains and the stresses of his position as a not-quite-legitimate son.
Addressing the problem that "there is not a West Indian literature" in Canto
IV, he faces the basic contradiction of his effort in *Epitaph*:

> A classical alas,
> For naked pickaninnies, pygmies, pigs and poverty,
> Veiling your inheritance you kneel before
> The sessile invocation of the thrush, the sibilant yew trees,
> By broken and flaked languages, near a drying river,
> You practise the pieties of your conquerors,
>
> (*Epitaph*, 10)

This canto also expresses a good deal of social bitterness in exposing the
conditions of a destitute and degraded environment against the false image of
an exotic paradise, a perspective which predominates during this period.[11]
When closely examined, however, the substance of Walcott's incipient protest
is most closely associated with his sense of being excluded from the master's
culture. It is a reflex of the yearning to be adopted, to cite his phrase in "What
the Twilight Says".[12] This finds expression in a bitter, defensive preoccupation with skin/colour as the barrier which excludes him from that legacy.
In numerous images scattered throughout the juvenilia, talent and destiny
appear to be "cabined, cribbed, confined" by skin colour. Thus, there are
the famous lines from *Epitaph*: "You in the castle of your skin, / I the
swineherd" (Canto III, 6);[13] "the will numbs remembering the paralysis of
complexion" (*Epitaph*); phrases like "Narcissus in his skin", "tunnel of your
skin" (*Poems*). Another early poem entitled "Sambo Agonistes" sounds the
same theme in these telling lines: "For a nigger poet is twice the world's
joke."[14] Walcott sums up the prevailing attitudes and psychology of this
apprenticeship when he returns in *Another Life* to this portrait of himself
as young aspirant: "a prodigy of the wrong race and colour" (*CP*, 145).

The salient aspects of Walcott's beginning all derive, ultimately, from his
genuine apprenticeship to the Western Word/imagination. This apprenticeship comprises a willing tutelage at the hands of the masters, based on the
assumption of a truth upheld by its metaphors. Confusion and ambivalence
about race and colour, already inherent in the colonial condition, take their
peculiar bias from here. Thus he begins this early[15] to explore his racial
hang-ups in terms of the sexual/love encounter with a white woman, a motif
which survives into his later work.[16] It is equally important at this juncture,
however, not to lose sight of the fact that this attachment to the colonizer's

cultural tradition coexists with the no less sincere desire to pioneer a new and native art. "As John to Patmos" and "A City's Death by Fire" are being written about the same time as *Epitaph*. Seen in this context, the burden of this apprenticeship is a critical starting point of the struggle for self-liberation on the part of the colonized, and Walcott's case is an ultimate paradigm – the instinctive rebellion against the domination of the imperial power while continuing in unconscious acquiescence to its mind; the disavowal of the political bond while still succumbing to the claims of its spiritual legacy. Returning to this period in *Another Life,* Walcott defines it as a period of servitude, the stealing of "the houseboy" (*CP,* 219). But at that time it represented a genuine faith and "dream of reason",[17] to cite his more accurate description (*CP,* 145).

Still to be examined, though, is the question of how this adherence to the metaphors of the Western tradition relates to his efforts to discharge his commitment to his landscape. To shift away from *Epitaph* to *Green Night* is to come to a clear and concentrated engagement with landscape, extending, as already seen, from a number of the stronger, localized pieces from the juvenilia. What changes appear between the mode of *Epitaph* and this more regional effort? How far has Walcott moved beyond the basic terms of this apprenticeship in the characteristic achievements of *Green Night* ?

In a Green Night

In a Green Night was hailed by two authoritative voices – those of C.L.R. James, a founding genius of black and Third World nationalism, and Robert Graves, the then "grand old man" of English letters. James responded to this feature: "What is the world that he is seeing? It is the West Indies, islands, the sea that surrounds them, and the people, noticeably often, fishermen. . . . I have a curious feeling that most of what he will have to say will be found in these waters."[18] From Robert Graves came the notice repeated in the blurbs of many subsequent volumes: "Derek Walcott handles English with a closer under- standing of its inner magic than most (if not any) of his English born contemporaries."[19] The two comments highlight immediately striking features of this volume. There is, first, the strong presence of the West Indian landscape; and second, the remarkable degree of competence in handling the verbal and rhythmic resources of the language, which prompted Graves's response to its "inner magic". A survey of the volume shows a concentration on rendering the postures of the islands both in the better poems carried over from the juvenilia and in those written later in the period, for example, "A City's Death by Fire" and "Tales of the Islands" respectively. The other equally prominent feature is that he works within a range of traditional forms and voices, and attains considerable lyric power in technical mastery of these forms. Out of the unique convergence of the two comes the prizewinning "Sea Chantey", a poem whose elation is at once the elation of craft and the elation of celebrating landscape. These features point to the essential dynamic of the volume. Walcott's effort in this collection is centred on two related things: concentration on craft through technical mastery of a range of traditional forms; and the concern to adapt and appropriate these forms in the service of his landscape. In the course of this effort, a pattern emerges as he gravitates towards areas of imitation congenial to his predilections and needs. In effect, the basic working framework here remains one of imitation, and Walcott is the apprentice learning the rudiments of his craft and finding his own accesses of confidence within the traditional medium. We turn to the poetry to examine the nature and levels of his achievement in this effort.

At a primary level, the imitation is represented in the range of traditional forms with which he is working. Among these are the sonnet, especially in the Elizabethan and seventeenth-century tradition, which predominates during the period ("A City's Death by Fire", "The Harbour", and "Tales of the Islands"); and a range of traditional stanzaic modes in iambic pentameter and four-foot measures. The latter include the Elizabethan love-lyric, almost as prominent as the sonnet ("Pays Natal", "En Mi-Carême"); the Miltonic elegy ("Steersman, My Brother"); and speculative pieces in the seventeenth-century mode ("A Lesson for this Sunday", "Orient and Immortal Wheat"). He also works with techniques and elements from particular poets and literary styles. In the area of traditional poetry, the metaphoric modes of the Metaphysicals are prominent, reflected in the use of such motifs as "in a green night" from Marvell's "Bermudas", and "manor of thy friend's" from Donne's "For Whom the Bell Tolls". The modern period features especially strongly in elements from Eliot's style, and the singular influence of Dylan Thomas, considerable throughout the juvenilia.

The much-anthologized poem "A City's Death by Fire" provides a remarkable introduction to the specific aspects and bearings of the kind of effort prevailing in *Green Night*. It was early recognized as a poem of considerable merit, both in terms of native content, and for its high level of technical accomplishment, behind which the influence of Dylan Thomas was immediately obvious. The poem records Walcott's response to the devastation of his native town of Castries by fire in 1948. The impact of that fire made it one of the truly historic and emblematic landmarks in his early biography.[20] The young Walcott is here inspired to rise beyond the shock and trauma of the holocaust to the hope and prayer of a possibility of renewal. In that hope, the fire becomes an earnest of his own incipient ideal and faith in the emergence of a new and better society. The experience of the poem is couched in strong religious terms, which originate, as already seen, in his personal background. The fire takes the image of a "hot gospeller" dealing a death which is a ritual "baptism by fire".

Dylan Thomas, whose *25 Poems* provided Walcott with the title for his first book of poems, serves as a genuine catalyst in this poem. There is the echo of his theme of life-renewing death in "A Refusal to Mourn the Death, by Fire, of a Child in London".[21] But it is Thomas's method which is paramount here. Walcott attempts to adopt the model of Thomas's innovative treatment of language, especially as it pivots on the technique of metaphoric transference and identification. The transferences of the candle image in "Light Breaks Where no Sun Shines" have inspired his own use of the candle image in "A City's Death by Fire". He explores his ideas in the poem through a network of references extended from that image. It is, first of all, candle as flame/light, the "eye" by which the artist is guided to read and record his city's death by fire ("Under a candle's eye, . . . I / Wanted to tell . . ."). The candle/flame image also provides the fire/smoke reference, from which the poem evokes its symbolic intimations of the consuming fire that refines. The physical detail of melting candle wax links with the burning down of the material/wooden world, to lead to the disavowal of tears, which the melting wax resembles, shed for the merely material loss ("why / Should a man wax tears, when his wooden world fails?"), and to conclude with the affirmation of faith in a higher spiritual renewal.

Walcott has closely adapted Thomas's techniques of extracting and combining the multiple associations and figurations of the word as image. But in his hands, the technique serves a mode of perception quite different from Thomas's. Metaphoric identification and transference in Thomas come out of his visionary faith in the continuum of the life force through all forms. In Walcott's poem the technique works to apprehend the relations and correspondences between orders of reality, outer and inner, physical and metaphysical. Walcott's correspondences engage the faculty of reasoning, where Thomas's depend more on the intuitional. The modality in Walcott resembles the metaphysical conceit which is to prove, as we shall see, a model close to his own genius. What he has taken, finally, from Thomas is the latter's engagement with the full figural possibilities of the word-image – the linguistic phenomenon itself. With this he has assimilated an outstanding related feature – the music of Thomas's fusion of the figural and the phonic in his sheer joy of the image. Craft in the poem also concentrates on links of sound, through a close pattern of such devices as consonance, alliteration and internal rhyming, as in the following examples: "tale by tallow", "the hills were a flock of faiths", "bird-rocked sky". Walcott moved early enough beyond the overly studied acrobatics of his imitation of Thomas in this poem. But it served as a truly liberating influence in pointing towards the metaphoric and phonic properties of language as a primary area of his talent.

"A City's Death by Fire" displays an underlying pattern of Walcott's craft, mediated through the principles of imitation, and some of its significant early characteristics. "Tales of the Islands", the outstanding sonnet sequence in the volume, presents a considerable advance in this effort and its achievements. He undertakes some original experiments with the sonnet form, and these experiments are an integral part of his purpose to accommodate the form to serve native content in a series of portraits of the islands. Concentration on crafting of the sonnet form itself is intense. He described his aims as follows: "What I have been trying to do with them over the last five years is to get a certain factual, biographical plainness about them . . . to dislocate the traditional idea of the sonnet as a fourteen-line piece of music. The idea is the same as in prose; dispassionate observation."[22]

Before proceeding to the formal aspect emphasized in his statement, we need to begin with a look at content. The sequence represents his most sustained overview of the peculiar ills and problems of society in the region so far, and is indeed the very first to do so in verse. It surveys the issues of race, religion, culture, manners and mores in the environment. A number of portraits of individual case histories, most of which are authentic, capture and document these issues. They tell of the delusions and absurd effects of racial pride among the small class of white creoles in St Lucia, as in the case of Cosimo de Chrétien, who, in a life committed to maintaining the purity of his blood, ends up a victim of arrested growth, his abnormality reminiscent of the imbecile Quasimodo in *The Hunchback of Notre Dame* (chapter II);

of darkness and obscurantism in the religious environment of the island, where belief in the mysterious power of obeah exists side by side with practices and attitudes of Christian piety (chapter IX); of the younger educated generation, his own, caught in a "fête" culture devoid of angst and of direction; of a setting whose stagnation is conducive to decadence and exile, as in the experience of the Conradian expatriate figure in chapter VII. The cumulative plight and distress of West Indian society unfolds from the sequence. Behind it lies the spectre of history. Though most of the tales are based in St Lucia, Walcott ranges through the entire region for this first sustained expression of the pain of landscape. (Jamaica is the setting in chapter IV, and Trinidad is represented by its idiolect and fête culture in chapter VI.)

Walcott shows technical inventiveness in redeploying the basic resources and elements of the sonnet form, traditionally lyric and reflective, for the narrative and descriptive modes of these portraits. The main structural resource of the sonnet, the break between the octet and sestet, provides his key functional device. It becomes the ironic twist of the concluding section of each tale, pointing to the moral of the tragic contradictions of these case histories. He thus draws fully on a characteristic feature of the sonnet: the activity of the reflective intellect in the turning movement (sestet), which yields further, unexpected insights. It serves to highlight the anomalies of his environment. The centring irony enables him to achieve the objective of detached observation, of letting the tales speak for themselves. Within the narrative/descriptive format, however, he works to maintain the sonnet form's lyrical, musical character, adhering meticulously to a regular metre and rhyme-scheme. This formal structure and its music give his "tragic twists" the kind of aphoristic impact typical of the sonnet.

Chapter II, one of the most finished pieces in the sequence, will serve as a good illustration of the various aspects of Walcott's technical crafting and general aesthetic goals in the sequence. It tells the tragedy of Cosimo de Chrétien, of French noble lineage, who must remain isolated from the black current of life in the island to maintain his white pedigree. The first ten lines, corresponding to the octet, present the portrait of Cosimo isolated in his setting, amid the decor and bric-à-brac of No. 13, Rue St Louis:

> Cosimo de Chrétien controlled a boardinghouse.
> His maman managed him. No. 13.
> Rue St Louis. It had a court, with rails,
> A perroquet, a curio-shop where you

> Saw black dolls and an old French barquentine
> Anchored in glass. Upstairs, the family sword,

(CP, 22)

The assorted heirlooms and relics of his distant pedigree establish Cosimo and the cause to which his life has been devoted: "never to bring the lineage to disgrace". The concluding section (the last four lines, corresponding to the sestet) turns to reflect on the deep irony of time which keeps that white blood pure, but at a heavy cost. Cosimo ends up as something of a halfwit, himself a local curiosity as the shadow figure restricted to "peering from balconies" for his sole contact with life. The dialectical force of that irony is enhanced by introducing the turning movement with the echo of Shakespeare's line, "Devouring Time, which blunts the Lion's claws" (Sonnet 19). The rhyme scheme is skilfully aimed at underlining the message of this irony. Thus the *fggfg* scheme of lines 6–10 rhymes *withered race, pride of place, disgrace,* and echoes that rhyme in the assonance of *chaste, whist,* and *twist* in the last three lines. Another effective feature is the blending in of French words such as *maman, perroquet* and *barquentine.* Here Walcott prefers standard French, to capture the formal atmosphere of Cosimo's class. (He draws on several West Indian creole forms in some of the other "Tales", as will be discussed below.) Finally, the technique of metaphoric correspondence we met in "A City's Death by Fire" also features here, helping to structure the central irony. Thus the poem deliberately invokes an analogy between the "rusting icons" of the curio shop "anchored in glass", and Cosimo who appears, himself, as a curio shut in behind the balconies and "court with rails" of No. 13, Rue St Louis.

Chapter II is a model of Walcott's aesthetic achievement in crafting the formal literary resources of the sonnet for narrative/descriptive purposes. Another immediately striking area of his craft in the sequence is the attempt to represent, along with standard usage, the dialect and creole forms native to the region. Elements from the creoles and dialects are blended into the standardized usage as local(izing) effects: this is the basic method in the overall scheme of the sequence. In some places, however, Walcott concentrates exclusively on experimenting with creole and dialect usage. Chapters IV and VI are the classic examples. In his very fine study entitled "Some Subtleties of the Isle", John Figueroa focuses on the variation and flexibility of language usage in the "Tales", and gives a full appreciation of what he rightly identifies as Walcott's effective use of the West Indian linguistic continuum from standard through vernacular forms.[23]

The original impetus behind the experiment with creole and native forms is the localizing effort itself. He is intent on reproducing the actual voice and tone of the native setting, especially in direct dramatizations of scenes. Chapter VI, where he tries to capture his own emergent generation in the act of "fêting", West Indian style, is written exclusively in dialect and creole forms. To compare an earlier version with the final version appearing in *Green Night* is to appreciate how carefully and patiently, over some ten years, he worked towards capturing the native tongue. We will quote the first ten lines of the versions appearing in *Bim*[24] and in *Green Night* respectively, for a look at the emendations. Emendations are indicated by underlines in each case:

1. *Bim* version – Chapter VI

"my country 'tis of thee"

Garçon, that was fete – I mean they had
Free whisky and they had some fellows beating
Steel from one of the bands in Trinidad,
And everywhere you turn people was eating
Or drinking and so on and I think
They catch two guys with his wife on the bench,
But "there will be nothing like Keats, each
Generation has its angst, and we have none,"
And he wouldn't let a comma in edgewise
(Black writer, you know, one of them Oxford guys),

2. *Green Night* version – Chapter VI

Poopa, da' was a fete! I mean it had
Free rum free whisky and some fellars beating
Pan from one of them band in Trinidad
And everywhere you turn was people eating
And drinking and don't name me but I think
They catch his wife with two tests up the beach
While he drunk quoting Shelley with "Each
Generation has its angst, but we has none"
And wouldn't let a comma in edgewise.
(Black writer chap, one of them Oxbridge guys).

Most of the emendations are from standard to creole and dialect usage, covering the areas of grammar, vocabulary, and idiomatic and colloquial expression. Thus in line 1 we have changes from standard to dialect usage in *that* → *da'*, *they had* → *it had*. Standard vocabulary is replaced by colloquial usage, for example *fellows* → *fellars* in line 2, *steel* → *pan* in line 3, and *guys* → *tests* in line 6. Most effective for conveying both the spirit of the occasion and its local character is the complete change from formal grammatical expression to an idiomatic style in lines 7 and 8. *While he drunk* strikes a typically West Indian posture, and sets the tone for the supremely eloquent change from *we have none* to *we has none* in line 8. The grammatical lapse is effective as an ironic comment on the pseudointellectual tone of the occasion. These changes are all geared towards reproducing as fully as possible the tone, accent and spirit of the West Indian setting, modelled especially on that of fête-loving Trinidad.

The use of the West Indian linguistic continuum represents a major area of innovation in the "Tales". It is clear, though, when we look at the ones not written in creole, that he seeks an inclusive linguistic flexibility. Chapter V provides an interesting example. It dramatizes his response to a ritual cere-mony of an African-based religious cult, known as *kélé*, in a rustic district of St Lucia.[25] Walcott, showing his early scepticism about the meaningful survival of African religions in the region, expresses his sense of the fraudu-lence of its rites of animal sacrifice and drumming: "The whole thing was more like a bloody picnic." He makes use, in this tale, of a select vocabulary, diction and syntax specially calculated to achieve his tone of sceptical rejection. A prime target of his scepticism is the foreign anthropologist, here British, who comes to observe the scene: "The fête took place one morning in the heights / For the approval of some anthropologist" (*CP*, 24). Thus, there is the irreverence of British slang and idiomatic usage, for example, "bloody", "Great stuff, old boy"; the unceremonious coarseness of phrases like "chop off", and "tie up" to describe the rituals of animal sacrifice; and the irony of the mock rhythmic flow of "dancing with absolutely natural grace", pivoting on the felicitous metrical placing of "absolutely" in that line – an irony which has been missed by several commentators.[26]

While the local content is integral, then, this inclusiveness in the crafting of language is part of a wider goal of verbal resourcefulness and aesthetic completeness. This is, in fact, all of a piece with the deep structure of the sequence. When closely observed, the sequence reveals an underlying adher-ence to the aesthetic discipline and formal structure of the sonnet, despite Walcott's considerable adventurousness. The innovations are contained within the given structure. Significantly, the sequence is framed between the strictly traditional form of the first and last sonnet, where the poet-narrator appears in his own person, as Figueroa points out in his article.[27] This feature – the underlying commitment to the formal structure – is significant for what it reflects of the balance between the concern with technical competence and the engagement with the pain of landscape. It is obvious from "Tales" that the concern with the native predicament is beginning to press seriously against Walcott's consciousness. But the elation of craft seems to have a balancing effect. It is an aspect of his apprenticeship to which we will return later on in the chapter.

It is, in fact, the elation of craft which gives the volume its characteristic spirit. It inspires and is at one with a lyrical celebration of landscape, which is perhaps more pervasive than the painful strains sounded in "Tales". "A Sea Chantey", as earlier mentioned, is the most accomplished product of this marriage of joy of craft and landscape. The poem stands out for the musicality and original freshness with which it renders the Caribbean sea setting. The pastoral joy of landscape first sung in "As John to Patmos" had found expression in a number of poems closely patterned on the tradition of the Elizabethan love lyric – poems, for example, like "Pays Natal", "Brise Marine", "En Mi-Carême". "A Sea Chantey" breaks out of this imitative mould to give the landscape lyrical presence, creating a native "marine pastoral" out of the particular features of its sea setting. Walcott's technical strategy is a well-chosen and closely focused one; he sets out to echo the liquid sounds of water in the phonics of the poem, and thereby to distil "sea-music". These liquid notes are rung from the sounds that name the distinct features of the setting. There is a dalliance of sound reminiscent of Thomas, as in the skilful play of alliteration, assonance and rhyme in this opening sequence, which "recites" the names/sounds of features, places, and persons in the setting:

> Anguilla, Adina,
> Antigua, Canelles,
> Andreuille, all the l's
> Voyelles, of the liquid Antilles,
> The names tremble like needles

> (*CP*, 44)

Through a series of sound pictures, the poem evokes the peculiar fragrance of the setting in its characteristic aspect of "anchored frigates" in "ports of calm coral". The three-beat measure moves to the tune of litanic recitation, giving these "ports of calm coral" an atmosphere of stillness in motion. Walcott handles this rhythm with mastery, to sound now the lighter notes of cheer and freedom, now the more solemn strains of praise and benediction. The setting thus sustains its "luxe, calme, et volupté", and is able, through deft modulations, to hint at the deeper strains of labour and life struggles in these waters ("Quiet, the fury of their ropes", "the blue heave of leviathan"), suggesting a world, a totality of experience, contained within that "calme".

Behind this picture of peace and plenitude lies the echo of Marvell's "a holy and a cheerful note" in "Bermudas", a poem which strongly influenced Walcott during this period, as is evident from both the title and the title poem of this volume. But he could not go much further with this celebration of his own "paradisal sea". His line "the elation can be useless and empty" ("Allegre") is an implicit admission of this. There are, however, a few places where he makes a genuine breakthrough to his own areas of strength and individual voice – poems which achieve a true originality and maturity of expression. They stand out amid what had been, up to that point, primarily a matter of technical accomplishment. Two poems represent this classic achievement in *Green Night*: chapter X of "Tales", and "A Letter from Brooklyn". Both of these poems, significantly, come out of the depth of personal sentiment, and are concerned with circumstances of utmost importance in his private life at this stage. "Tales, Chapter X" deals with his departure from St Lucia for university in Jamaica.[28] Walcott knew intuitively that this leave-taking meant the probability of a final break with his island (the sense of a prodigal betrayal stays with him to this day), and he extends it in the poem as a valedictory experience. In "A Letter from Brooklyn" he responds to the touching tribute of a frail old woman moved to write to him about a reality he holds most sacred: the memory of his father and his vocation as an artist. Both poems, one might note from the outset, reflect the strong religious upbringing so much in the foreground in the early Walcott.

"Tales, Chapter X" remains one of the most fully realized poems in the entire Walcott corpus.[29] It is an early achievement of perfect coordination between serious content and execution. The inner content and intensity of the experience of separation unfolds dramatically from the actual experience of leaving the island by air.[30] The authentic and artistic appeal of the poem combine in this live enactment of the flight. We apprehend the visual reality of the contours and features of the receding island and its coastline, following, with photographic accuracy, the gradual process of its final disappearance:

> I watched the island narrowing the fine
> Writing of foam around the precipices, then
> The roads as small and casual as twine
> Thrown on its mountains; I watched till the plane
> Turned to the final north and turned above
> The open channel with the grey sea between
> The fishermen's islets until all that I love
> Folded in cloud; . . .

(*CP*, 27)

The core meaning of the poem is contained within that climaxing image "all that I love / Folded in cloud". Its implications and resonances give the poem its depth of thought and emotion. We move through that image to higher planes of separation: from the immediate and graphic to the cosmic, with intimations of the existential in the allusion to the principle of finitude in human destiny (signalled in the clouds' enfolding of all that he loved). The advance towards this recognition traces the process of a gradual surrender to the burden of departure, a wisdom in acceptance and reconciliation of its painful conflicts. Importantly, the aesthetic pattern of metaphoric correspondences is integral to the intellectual process of realization. The organic, sequential growth of correspondences, from one image to the next, creates an effective whole. Walcott exercises his usual technical concentration to underline this movement of thought and emotion. The repetition of "I watched", for example, captures the gradual pace of the island's disappearance from view; and the rising pace of his accurate iambics conveys the tone of controlled dignity in his surrender to separation as destiny. Finally, there is the absolute rightness of the concluding line, which underscores the reality of a world left behind even as it registers the immediate, ordinary reality of the other setting (Barbados) in which the plane alights: "When we set down at Seawell it had rained."

In chapter X, the microcosmic, personal experience of breaking ties with his native land becomes the medium of a further perception of the macrocosmic reality of space, time and finitude. In effect, the concrete transmutes into metaphor to mediate between physical and metaphysical levels, outer and inner worlds. "A Letter from Brooklyn" comes out of the same essential dynamic. The emotive power of the poem comes from the extent of his empathy with the frail old woman who writes in memory and appreciation of his father's gift as a painter. Walcott is truly touched by the quality of sensibility that enables her to see art as a sacred gift. His act of empathy begins with a powerful opening conceit: he sees in her "spidery" handwriting, now wavering, now lucid, an image of her thought processes; the image penetrates to a further level of correspondence between the old woman's effort of expression and that of artistic creation itself:

> An old lady writes me in a spidery style,
> Each character trembling, and I see a veined hand
> Pellucid as paper, travelling on a skein
> Of such frail thoughts its thread is often broken;
> Or else the filament from which a phrase is hung
> Dims to my sense, but caught, it shines like steel,
> As touch a line, and the whole web will feel.

(CP, 41)

The image enables a true insight and sensitivity to the faith and spiritual strength of the old woman. The culminating recognition is caught in this line: "The strength of one frail hand in a dim room". The line is itself a metaphor pregnant with these final meanings. Walcott comes to see humanity and creative struggle reaffirmed in Mable Rawlins's gesture, especially in her simple association of art with heaven ("Heaven is to her the place where painters go"). He draws strength from her example to renew his "sacred duty to the Word".

The metaphoric modality of these two original poems bears strong resemblances to the style of the Metaphysicals, and is essentially the same in principle. This brings us to what is an outstanding and, finally, most significant feature in *Green Night*: the prominence of the seventeenth-century period in general, and particularly of the Metaphysicals, in this collection. The seventeenth century dominates in *Green Night* as the source of Walcott's most serious and extensive borrowings from the metaphors of the Western tradition. The borrowings are conspicuous in a number of important poems. At the head stands the image from Marvell's "Bermudas" which provides him with the title and title poem of the volume, a testament to his aspiration and outlook in this first phase of his endeavour: "He hangs in shades the orange bright / Like golden lamps in a green night." An analogue from Donne's timeless poem on the theme of a shared human destiny serves as a reference point in his first serious confrontation with the evil of slavery and colonialism – "as well as if a manor of thy friend's".[31] An epigraph taken from Sir Thomas Browne accentuates his focus in the same poem: "it cannot be long before we lie down in darkness, and have our light in ashes" ("Urn Burial"). He takes his cue from Traherne's "The corn was orient and immortal wheat", in his poem "Orient and Immortal Wheat", for his ironic reflections on the anthropomorphic origins of our visions of heaven and hell.[32]

What is the source of this strong appeal exerted by the Metaphysicals and the seventeenth-century mystics? What elements and aspects of their artistic world account for the fact that they are virtually his main mentors during this period? It is striking, first of all, that all the borrowings cited are metaphoric formulations, ideas and perceptions coded in expressive imagery. Moreover, these metaphors all function in the context of Christian religious belief and cosmology. In Marvell's poem the image of the bright orange against its shadowy green setting is, "like golden lamps in a green night", an earthly reflection of the divine sphere of eternal light, and the Bermudas seem a portion of God's earth specially reserved for a manifestation of His light. Joan Bennet, echoing a motif pervasive in the work of the Metaphysicals, captures the essence of this religious figuration in the following description: "Metaphysical poetry is poetry written by men for whom the light of day is God's shadow."[33]

If these metaphors all mirror a higher, transcendent order – and it should be stressed that all those borrowed by Walcott do – their distinctive "metaphysical method" is also an integral part of their content, and responsible for their particular structure of meaning. In his essay on Walcott's apprenticeship, Stewart Brown comments on the strong influence of the metaphoric mode of the Metaphysicals thus: "It was the Metaphysicals' technique of using metaphor as the prime vehicle of shape and meaning in their poetry that seems to have so greatly impressed Walcott . . . ."[34] The underlying principle throughout is that of the metaphysical conceit, reproduced in the formulation by Bennet cited above. The technique of the metaphysical conceit works to produce striking analogies and correspondences. It is especially dependent on the exercise of intellect, and therefore involves an element of conceptual thought. Joan Bennet emphasizes the intellectual factor called into play: "The peculiarity of the Metaphysical poets is not that they relate, but that the relations they perceive are more often logical than sensuous or emotional, and they constantly connect the abstract with the concrete, the remote with the near, and the sublime with the commonplace."[35] The principle is most strikingly illustrated in Donne, whose analogies generate and structure his argumentation. "A manor of thy friend's", in which Walcott finds an analogy with the ruins of the great house of the slave plantations, is one of the analogies through which he speculates on the truth that "each man's death diminishes me" ("For Whom the Bell Tolls").

The image drawn from Marvell's "Bermudas" seems primarily sensuous and pictorial in its appeal, but the exercise of logic is also there in the act of perception which selects and converts "forest" into night/shadow, and "oranges" into divine light defined against shadow. Interestingly, Walcott's title poem takes its model but departs in meaning from Marvell's. Instead of Marvell's perpetual light against shadow ("eternal spring"), the orange tree in that setting presents to Walcott's eye a picture of "various light": the variations from green to gold to darkening/aging become a manifestation of mutability as reflected in the wider pattern of the changing seasons and their "cyclic chemistry". Through this configuration he perceives the way to a circumspection that must offset his own anxieties about the future, especially the possibility of "darkening" change in his endeavour:

> By such strange, cyclic chemistry
> That dooms and glories her at once
> As green yet aging orange tree,
> The mind enspheres all circumstance.
>
> . . . .
> Or if Time's fires seem to blight
> The nature ripening into art,
> Not the fierce noon or lampless night
> Can quail the comprehending heart.

(CP, 50–51)

Significant here is the fact that the exercise of logic remains vital in Walcott's reworking of the image. This helps to underline the true nature of his affinity with the Metaphysicals. He is deeply immersed in their thought, but it is precisely the intrinsic unity between that thought (religiously informed) and its original method which constitutes its final appeal for him. The combination represents what could be described as a "reasoned metaphysics". He was to retain the technique of the conceit, with its inherent principle of conception, even when he moved out of the religious context. But at this stage, he responds fully to the appeal of their "reasoned metaphysics".

It is in this specific area of his close affinity with the Metaphysicals that Walcott remains most firmly bound to the faith and "light" of the Western tradition at this stage. This area signs and underlines his apprenticeship to its thought and metaphors, and gives the volume its final outlook. In *Green Night,* the Christian order prevails as the immediate context of that bond to the tradition. It is there in "A City's Death by Fire", in "A Letter from Brooklyn", and explicit in a number of important poems of belief, such as "Steersman, My Brother", "Orient and Immortal Wheat", and "A Lesson for this Sunday". As earlier seen, Walcott has strongly internalized this religious bond from his upbringing. The creative redeployment of the Christian tradition has two culminating points in the literature – Dante in the medieval period, and the Metaphysicals in the Renaissance. His apprenticeship to the Word shows an essential continuity from Dante, as the most inclusive voice in *Epitaph,* to the Metaphysicals in this volume.

The poem which most clearly demonstrates the reality of this apprentice-ship and its wider implications is "Ruins of a Great House". "Ruins of a Great House" is an important position poem. Walcott takes his first naked look at the violations and injustices of the slave past and is provoked to strong outrage, and to condemnation of its surviving ills. In this first engagement of the quarrel with history, however, he finds the way to a genuine reconciliation in the light of the Renaissance humanism of the Metaphysicals. This first live encounter with the past is occasioned by a visit to the ruins of one of the great houses which, as the abode of the white master or overseer, dominated the plantations during slavery. The visit occurred during Walcott's undergraduate days in Jamaica. Actually, a quite interesting biographical context surrounds this poem. The ruins to which he had been exposed in St Lucia thus far comprised memorials of the great admirals and imperial battles of the eighteenth century, upholding the image of an epic history.[36] The visit to these ruins in Jamaica,[37] where slavery and its imprints were much stronger, would have been his first encounter with the physical memorials of the depredations of the slave past. Furthermore, while that reality was held at a certain remove by the literature that dominated his youthful beginnings, university education brought him into closer contact with it.[38] The poem gives us this sense of a rude awakening to the shocking actualities evoked in memory by that site:

> and pacing, I thought next
> Of men like Hawkins, Walter Raleigh, Drake,
> Ancestral murderers and poets, more perplexed
> In memory now by every ulcerous crime.
>
> (*CP*, 20)

The emotional core of the poem is located in this sense of outrage and revulsion, even bewilderment, at the extent of imperial guilt and corruption. The real sting comes from an anomaly to which Walcott is especially sensitive: that the literature and crimes of the empire were produced from one and the same source, that a Raleigh could be at once artistic purveyor of its idealism, and criminal adventurer. Walcott wrestles in this poem with personal pain and perplexity in trying to reconcile the great ethos of humanistic idealism that characterized the seventeenth century with the extreme violations of its colonizing venture. This keen sense of disillusionment lies behind his indictment of the period: "The world's green age then was a rotting lime / whose stench became the charnel galleon's text" (*CP*, 20). Donne's famous testament in "For Whom the Bell Tolls" comes most appropriately to mind at this point: it seems but a classic expression of the same hoax, provoking even greater anger. Thus: "My eyes burned from the ashen prose of Donne." In the tug between that recriminatory anger on the one hand, and the truth content of Donne's metaphysical argument that "every man's death diminishes me", it is the latter which prevails. Walcott's too methodically measured analogies in the following lines are not quite effective in conveying that turning current in his feeling:

> Ablaze with rage, I thought
> Some slave is rotting in this manorial lake,
> And still the coal of my compassion fought:

(CP, 20)

These lines remain a residual area of weakness in the poem. But there is no doubt that he is authentically inspired by Donne's vision of a shared human destiny to see the "vain expense / of bitter faction" as the common lot of peoples and nations, suffered by Britain itself before his own region. In this conviction of a deeper bond between victors and victims, masters and slaves, his movement beyond anger to compassion is a genuine affirmation.

"Ruins of a Great House" highlights the underlying ambiguity of Walcott's apprenticeship to the Western tradition in this first phase of his endeavour. He sets out with a strong revolutionary commitment to the cause and upliftment of his landscape, but it is in the light of the European mind and its spiritual tradition that the native image must find this upliftment. This harks back to the basic situation we saw in "A Far Cry from Africa". The imperial system of domination ("the drunken officer of British rule") is repudiated outright; but there is still a claim to kinship with the western European tradition of thought. The lines from *Another Life* quoted earlier yield their full personal significance at this point: "O / mirror, where a generation yearned / for whiteness, for candour, unreturned" (*CP*, 146). That yearning might be termed "the last infirmity of the anticolonial mind".

The net effect and final consequence of this bond is that there is not yet, in this "green" phase, a serious engagement with identity as an issue. The question of identity is virtually delayed, held in abeyance during this phase. The grievances and frustrations do press strongly against his consciousness, as we saw in the "Tales", but they are, with few exceptions, formally contained, and even sublimated. In effect, his concentration on technical mastery in the appropriation of traditional forms also fits into this prevailing orientation. While it does serve to build a solid technical foundation, it represents a tacit adherence to the inherited order and modes of perception enshrined in these forms. Walcott's own acknowledgement in "What the Twilight Says" sums it all up: "Imitation was pure belief."[39]

CHAPTER THREE

Abandoning Dead Metaphors

The Castaway and *The Gulf*

Indigenizing the Crusoe Metaphor

Walcott's next volume of poetry, *The Castaway,* comes out of a period of important changes and developments in his personal life and career. After a year studying theatre in America (1957–58), he had returned to Trinidad to make that island his home and base as an artist. He founded the Theatre Workshop in 1959, and settled down to a full-time career as an artist, divided between his work in developing the workshop, and his writing (plays and poetry). He also settled down to family life with Trinidadian Margaret Maillard, whom he married in 1962. With youth and adolescence well behind him, he was entering an adult phase distinguished by a deliberate and full responsibility to work as an artist in the region. It was the beginning of a phase which, lasting some twenty years, would prove the most seminal and productive. It remains the true backbone of his career and achievement.

The Castaway introduces a pervasive mood of negation, which contrasts strongly with the elation and affirmative spirit of the earlier phase. This mood of negation extends into *The Gulf* and finds expression in the recurring themes of void, of a personal crisis of belief, and of exile as an artist – themes which stand out in major poems like "The Castaway" and "The Gulf", and "Homecoming: Anse La Raye". The incipient, underlying sources of this negation had, in fact, already been sounded in "Return to D'Ennery", one of the later poems of the *Green Night* collection. In this poem, which struck a note of hopelessness and desolation uncommon in *Green Night,* Walcott expressed a keen sense of remorse at the loss of religious faith, and at a deepening crisis of spiritual exile which he attributes to his inability to arrive at fulfilment of "a general passion, a personal need". What directly precipitates this crisis in the poem is the abject condition of one of the poverty-stricken coastal villages in St Lucia, Dennery; a place which, with its culture of "poverty, pigs and prayers", "seemed born for being buried there" (*CP*, 28). There is, in effect, a direct connection between the condition of Dennery, his sense of the futility of his artistic pledge, and this abnegation of faith. Curiously, he ends up seeing the poor of Dennery as better off than himself for having retained that religious faith. The contradiction, though, does serve to emphasize the intensity of this crisis of belief, which seems to harden as he settles further into his career. Thus: "the heart / Is circled by sorrows, by its horror / And bitter devotion to home" (*CP*, 29). This experience in Dennery points obliquely to an underlying source of Walcott's spiritual malaise – his growing awareness of the gap between those incipient faiths which had fed his earlier artistic aspirations, and the irremediable, intransigent condition of the native landscape. The implications are also there in the lines "blurring each boast / your craft has made".

The opening poem of the volume, "The Castaway", gives concentrated expression to these sentiments of void and negation, putting them in their wider context. A crucial title poem, "The Castaway" functions as a genuine prospectus of the focal areas and directions of Walcott's creative endeavour in what turns out to be a vital new departure. It makes its statements through a complex process which can be fully decoded only in relation to the peculiar form in which it is presented. Walcott is engaged in a self-dramatization of his own persona as a castaway figure deliberately modelled on Defoe's Robinson Crusoe.[1] In effect, he is wearing, to cite his own definition, the mask of Crusoe.[2] Within that fictional framework, which invokes significant parallels with the original Crusoe, the poem dramatizes the psychological process of Walcott experiencing the negations of his native landscape as a Crusoe/castaway figure. He is isolated on a deserted beach (representative of a landscape whose physical particulars resemble that of the original *Crusoe*), and oppressed by a sense of the nothingness and the desolate condition of his surroundings. Barely discernible, meaningless motions of natural objects and features in that setting – the seaweed in the shallows, the buzzing sandfly – seem to echo his own sense of futility and its chafing, visceral effects.

> The salt green vine with yellow trumpet-flower,
> A net, inches across nothing.
> Nothing: the rage with which the sandfly's head is filled.
>
> (CP, 57)

The extremity of his situation points to the need to initiate some scheme of action to meet the necessity of survival – as did the original Crusoe. This will to survive finds its own peculiar terms and process in his case as an artist/castaway: his course lies through contemplative observation of the processes of the elemental world before him, which include signals from nature in decay, as well as nature regenerating and creating itself:

> In the sun, the dog's feces
> Crusts, whitens like coral.
> We end in earth, from earth began.
> In our own entrails, genesis.
>
> If I listen I can hear the polyp build,
>
> (CP, 57–58)

The dog's faeces which, whitened by the purifying heat of the sun, resemble coral; the infinitesimal action of the coral-building polyp out at sea – both provide cues to the human potential for a similar creative process and for the poet's own urge towards an autonomous self-creation. In this lies the possibility of survival. The recognition compels this radical, highly significant resolve:

> God-like, annihilating godhead, art
> And self, I abandon
> Dead metaphors . . .
>
> (CP, 58)

It inspires his will to explore his innate human powers to make and unmake worlds. The latter comes to rest on the express purpose of "abandoning / Dead metaphors". An independent, regenerative effort at survival must begin, therefore, in this abandonment of dead metaphors. That goal of abandonment echoes what he described in "Twilight" as "the annihilation of what is known".[3] Definitively to be abandoned are the older values, concepts, order – all of what has so far defined the concept man/humanity – enshrined in the traditional, inherited metaphors. This is the first articulation of what will prove the core determination of the castaway in response to his crisis of negation. At this stage, however, the will to autonomous creation remains overwhelmed by the oppressive weight of negation, compounded by these dead metaphors. The poem proceeds to distinctly identify these dead metaphors with the iconography of Christianity, representative of the Western Word/world. The concluding movement of the poem presents the poet's psyche haunted by the tracings of these foundered metaphors, their wreckage in his setting, in which the figurations of a dismembered, crucified Christ are discernible:

> That green wine bottle's gospel choked with sand,
> Labelled, a wrecked ship,
> Clenched sea-wood nailed and white as a man's hand.
>
> (CP, 58)

This is, admittedly, one of the more difficult early poems, to which Walcott was referring when he spoke of having a "nostalgia for obscurity".[4] But the key points of its content are accessible, and its statement reducible. As dramatized here, the castaway mask is Walcott's way of experiencing his landscape at this stage, and this experience leads to a deep sense of void and negation. However, this presages an equally strong urge to find a regenerative route out of the negation. For him the effort must begin in unburdening himself – especially given his own peculiar adherence – of the metaphors of the Western tradition of belief, the foundering of which is certainly manifest in the ills which disfigure the landscape. Most importantly, the purpose of abandoning dead metaphors carries the intrinsic, necessary counterpart of discovery and creation of new metaphors, originating in perceptions of his native ground. A line from "Crusoe's Journal" (*The Castaway*) makes reference to the recognition of this need, on Walcott's part, for native metaphors: "In a green world, one without metaphors" (*CP*, 93). These two interactive aspects of his purpose – the abandoning of old metaphors, and the generating of indigenous ones – define one dynamic, and represent the unifying motive of what is most fundamental to his creative effort from *The Castaway* to *The Gulf*. The purpose of abandoning dead metaphors is, accordingly, a radical new departure from his apprenticeship, and marks the true beginning of his quest for identity.

To enter into an appreciation of these new directions, one must begin with a close examination of the use to which Walcott puts the story of the original Crusoe, and the complex of meanings it carries for him. One might note from the outset that the Crusoe theme, developed during this period, retains a lasting hold on his imagination. It reappears in *Pantomime,* an important play of the 1980s, reviewing the changing relations between former colonizer and colonized peoples. In addition, in an interview with Bill Moyers, that paradigm is used again to focus his perspectives on the interdependence of neo-imperial powers (like America) and the developing world.[5] This persistence of the Crusoe–Friday motif over time is a measure of how deeply Walcott internalized the Crusoe–Friday theme, beginning from this period of his career. In effect, Defoe's Crusoe replaces Joyce's Stephen Dedalus as "his current hero". The identification with the Crusoe narrative is, however, so conscious and eclectic that he succeeds in transposing it to his own situation, to make it the vehicle of an authentic perspective anchored in his own ground. It amounts to a virtual indigenization of the Crusoe narrative.

The core of Walcott's identification with Defoe's hero rests on two main parallels contained in the original story: first, the predicament of isolation on an abandoned, desert (that is, unaccommodated) island; and second, his settling down, out of necessity, to the task of building a world. The latter affirms that principle of sheer inventiveness of which Crusoe is an archetype, and is the final basis of the timeless appeal of this classic adventure. In "The Figure of Crusoe" (1965), where Walcott explains the significance of the Crusoe theme in his writing of the period, he underlines his positive identification with the original Crusoe's isolation and survival.[6] As this essay shows quite clearly, the emphases in his response to Crusoe's effort eschew the ideological shortcomings of Crusoe's expansionist enterprise. For example, he bypasses the Puritan capitalistic ethos inherent in that effort. Accordingly, he underplays the extension of this ethos in the imperial will to own and civilize other, "savage" races. We will return to this highly significant approach to the Friday context later. Walcott's emphases in the essay, however, all point to the core, positive appeal that Crusoe holds for him as a symbol of the exercise of an autonomous intelligence engaged in constructing a world from undeveloped, virgin territory.

Walcott lights on one other component in the portraiture of this hero. It is the introspective concern with the man–God relationship, as a principle inherent in Crusoe's internal processes as an autonomous intelligence in solitude. This refers not so much to Crusoe's loud meditations on the doctrines of divine Providence and penitence, as to a "spiritualizing presence" in his deeper psyche (operating at a subliminal level), in which Michael McKeon perceptively detects an internalization of divinity attendant on his achievement of mastery of his world.[7] It is from empathy with that process that Walcott extends his own aspiration for autonomous creation. It becomes in his case the consciousness of the godlike capacity to break and refashion worlds expressed in "The Castaway": from "God-like, annihilating godhead, art / And self" to "abandon dead metaphors". The contemplative activity becomes internalized to serve in his own confrontation with the exhausted concepts of God and Man, which, as we have seen, is an important part of his effort in "The Castaway".

A most instructive aspect of this identification with Crusoe is the extent to which it subordinates, at this stage, the question of Friday. This implies that Walcott, setting out with the sense of a creative commitment from the outset, sees himself less as a Friday than as a Crusoe, and the cause of his region more in terms of the responsibility of self-determination than in terms of the legacy of servitude and dispossession. This is not to say that he shows no concern with this legacy of servitude, which obviously remains a major preoccupation in his work, receiving full, intensive treatment in *Dream*. In the poems of *The Castaway* and in "The Figure of Crusoe", he identifies primarily with the issue of Friday's conversion to the Word/God of the master. The Crusoe–Friday and Prospero–Caliban contexts are now well established in both West Indian literature and postcolonial criticism as classic paradigms of the colonial encounter. Walcott's perspective decidedly shifts away from the Friday/Caliban aspect, contrasting with Lamming, for example, whose approach through Caliban gives primacy to the issues of dispossession and resistance. In choosing to arrogate a position usually identified with the master, Walcott engages in something of a subversive act: he tacitly refuses the condition of servitude and inferiority as the primary term of his identity. Properly focused, and seen in the historical context of a literature in its younger, pioneering phase, it represents a fully revolutionary act, and signs his particular orientation towards independence.

Thus internalized and adapted, the Crusoe/castaway context borrowed from Defoe becomes a truly indigenized fable in its representation of the condition and needs of the region as Walcott sees it. As such – and dramatically projected as his poet's mask – it becomes the node of a core of seminal ideas explored and formulated during this phase, ideas which underlie his thought and outlook on the destiny of the region. The exploration originates in the sense of void reflected by the landscape, so powerfully condensed in "The Castaway". In essence, it was that sense of a common background of a cultural void from which the first generation of West Indian writers, all colonials, began the search for something to affirm. In his concern with the various manifestations of this condition of void in the setting, Walcott zeroes in on the issue of history, which becomes his main "madness", as he puts it (*AL*). The image of amnesia, of a void in memory, emerges during this period as the true starting point of his response to the history of the region. But the very earnestness of his mission and aspiration compels him to take a dual approach to the crisis of historylessness. This dual approach is an original source of the creative tension in his work. The other face of that void, its dialectical counterpart, is, for Walcott, the condition of virgin territory, which issues the challenge to search out a fresh order of intelligence. This is the very essence of his pledge to "abandon dead metaphors". This particular apprehension turns on an early insight which is to direct the course of his thought. It is his perception that the root of the failures of the region's history, and the wider failure of world history (the whole of which it is a part), lies in the failures of the older, Western dispensation and its "concept man" ("Guyana I"). This perception becomes the basis of his ultimate faith in the New World concept and possibility (to be developed later into his particular vision of renewal).

What should also be quite clear at this stage is that the essentials of the experience of his place and its people are encompassed in the Crusoe/castaway metaphor. His people were, in Walcott's terms, genuine castaways of history – a people exiled from their ancestral roots and heritage by slavery and colonialism, and abandoned to the chaos of a landscape despoiled by these experiences. One needs to go back beyond the last three or four decades (the bid for national identity began in the 1950s), and the region's advance in cultural confidence, to appreciate the reality of that outlook. It is of utmost importance to grasp how vitally that reality is embraced in the "castaway" theme, in order to understand the relationship between Walcott as individual poet and his engagement with the cause of the region as an original point of departure in his quest for identity during this phase. The "castaway" mask includes a strictly private level which has to do with his isolation as questing consciousness. This private isolation, as we shall see, compounds the core negations of the castaway condition which he shares with his people. All West

Indian writers of Walcott's generation show this substantive regional engagement, from Lamming to Naipaul; it is an inbuilt factor of a literature with a pioneering, revolutionary goal. As sensitive a critic as Denis Donoghue, however, misses this altogether in his comment on Walcott's poetry of the period: "It is enough for any poet that he is responsible for his own feeling: he answers to his scruple, his conscience, hard master. But Mr Walcott's poems try to serve a second master, the predicament of his people."[8] The point is, though, that Walcott's own feelings, given his aims and ambitions, emerge from the predicament and sensibility he shares with his people.

Finally, the several strands and implications of the thought content we have been considering are brought together in another major statement of the *Castaway* volume, "Crusoe's Journal". The poem, working as a review of his purposes and efforts in *The Castaway,* is a clear articulation of the structure of ideas and the associated group of images embraced in the Crusoe/castaway theme. Dramatizing his role/situation as Crusoe/castaway persona, Walcott begins by placing himself in the physical configuration of his setting – "perched between ocean and green, churning forest". (This physical configuration provides the characteristic imagery of the majority of the poems from *The Castaway* to *The Gulf.*) Defining his own representative roots and process as artist within that territory and its symbolic meanings, the poem articulates his conception of that role in terms of the metaphor of a New World Adam engaged in a fresh act of genesis. This early Adamic concept expresses a core belief in the primal act of naming. The belief in naming will mature into a seminal article of his New World faith, as witnessed by this central epigraph in *Another Life*: "the only task appropriate to the milieu that was slowly revealing to me the nature of its values: Adam's task of giving things their names".[9] The relevant passage in the poem gives insight into the essentially mythic character of naming in Walcott's thinking, a feature vital to an understanding of his work:

> came our first book, our profane Genesis
> > whose Adam speaks that prose
> which, blessing some sea-rock, startles itself
> > with poetry's surprise,
> in a green world, one without metaphors;

> > > (*CP,* 92–93)

This conception of naming extends into his affirmation of the messianic purpose inherent in his task as a poet who must bear the Word to his people.

The interesting conflation of Christ (Word-bearing/making) and Columbus (New World discoverer) underlines his identification of this messianic purpose with a New World covenant:

> like Christofer he bears
>> in speech mnemonic as a missionary's
>>> the Word to savages

(CP, 93)

The messianic focus is consistent with his early orientation to accord primacy to an order of belief by which humankind can live. The poem explores these ideas with an intellectual concentration and consistency that is most remarkable. The messianic, Word-bearing mission comes burdened with the problematic issue of the relationship of the colonized to the Word/language of the former colonizer. The poem proceeds to confront that contradictory, ironic involvement of the native in the inherited Word, and specifically recognizes the relationships with the older Word that must be part of the process of a newer discovery. It is in this context that the Friday factor becomes most pertinent: it is cited with reference to the fact of his conversion to the Word/language of the master. At this juncture, Walcott articulates an important aspect of his position on the fundamental question of the relationship of the ex-colonized to the heritage of the colonizer's language. His firm belief is that the route for the native effort lies through an imitation whose dialectical process must end in a true possession, an indigenization of the language. (He gives a profound exposition of this theme in a major essay, "The Caribbean: Culture or Mimicry?".)[10] In this lies the original possibility of Friday's freedom: "parroting our master's / style and voice, we make his language ours" (*CP*, 93).

The final movement of "Crusoe's Journal" reflects on a feature which represents his individual sense of what it means to engage this task as a Caribbean artist. Walcott sees that calling as inescapably hermetic in nature. The poet is consigned to pursue that mission in an isolation which, given the acute void of opportunity the West Indies presented to its pioneering artists at that time, deepened into a chronic sense of exile and estrangement. The latter is pervasive in *The Castaway* and *The Gulf*. "The Figure of Crusoe" is in fact subtitled "On the Theme of Isolation in West Indian Writing", and it explains his employment of the Crusoe/castaway mask with close reference to this hermetic necessity. (Furthermore, he projects this self-image of the poet-hermit in his characterization of Makak, the hero of *Dream on Monkey Mountain*, as the lone dreamer figure of Monkey Mountain.) "Crusoe's

Journal" ends by associating this "hermetic skill" with the search for God: "God's loneliness moves in His smallest creatures" (*CP*, 94). It is a conclusion which underlines the essential unity of his concept of naming, the quest for faith, and a messianic New World purpose – all vital to his peculiar appropriation of the Crusoe metaphor.

The Poetics of Abandoning Dead Metaphors

There is one definitive feature characterizing Walcott's indigenization of the Crusoe metaphor, which marks the significant change of purpose from what obtained in his apprenticeship. The search for fresh, indigenous metaphors begins in, and evolves through, a dialectical relationship to the older metaphors of the western European tradition. It is a relationship which, serving as a functional principle, determines the peculiar poetics of the effort to abandon dead metaphors. Generally, the older metaphors stand, implicitly and explicitly, as counters against which alternatives, and different terms and values, are defined. This turns on a dialogic relationship with the colonizer's tradition – a relationship characterized by argument and debate, and which is finally subversive in spirit. The effort seeks to overcome at first hand the problem of indentureship to the Western Word and cultural heritage, so specifically acute in Walcott's case.

This dialogic relationship lies at the heart of his first and most seminal apprehensions and conception of the crises of identity. It is precisely against the measure of the tiered, cumulative history and tradition of the colonizer's world that the void and historylessness of his own landscape defines itself. For Walcott, the substance of that history is enshrined primarily in a heritage of mainstream Western metaphors, representative of the values and faiths that have determined the course of its civilization. This perspective lies behind the line, as earlier noted (chapter 1), that sums up a fundamental aspect of his outlook on landscape at this stage: "in a green world, one without metaphors". This image of "a green world" affirms positive notes of promise and possibility, as in its immediate context in "Crusoe's Journal"; but it is, at the same time, the greenness of a world devoid of history and metaphor. Walcott uses the image of amnesia to explore this condition of a world devoid of history or metaphors. An almost neurotic preoccupation, it is one of the root factors compounding the pervasive sense of negation earlier noted; and an original spur to the creative struggle embarked on during this period. Walcott himself harks back to these sources in this retrospective comment on the earlier phases of his struggle as a colonial artist: "naturally I arrived at the heresy that history and landscape had failed me" ("Twilight", 28).

"Goats and Monkeys" (*The Castaway*) highlights some of the original facets of this dynamic function of the older metaphors in Walcott's effort during this phase. The predicament of Othello and Desdemona in Shakespeare's play is used as a metaphor to comment on the cause of black resistance during the rise of racial violence in the United States during the Civil Rights era (the mid-1960s). The metaphor is, like that of Crusoe, directly borrowed; but this borrowing presents a polemical departure, by contrast with those of his apprenticeship. Othello's tragedy is invoked as the tragedy of the betrayal of an ultimate faith, the absolute embodied in Desdemona. The focus completely subordinates the matter of Othello's tragic error, given Desdemona's fidelity and innocence. Empathizing with Othello's sense of betrayal, Walcott defends the cause of the black man in revolt. It is not racial revenge that motivates this revolt, but rather the collapse of the belief system purveyed and corrupted by the white world itself. This betrayal leaves the black man in the Western world without a humanity to believe in:

> was not his racial, panther-black revenge
> pulsing her chamber with raw musk, its sweat,
> but horror of the moon's change,
> of the corruption of an absolute
>
> (*CP*, 84)

Keeping close to Shakespeare's terms of reference, Walcott turns these, in effect, into a polemical statement on the failure of the Western order, and, more specifically, the American dream of a better order. What is most crucial about his treatment at this stage is that it enters into a dialogue with the Western world, a questioning which bears directly, and characteristically for Walcott, on its tradition of belief. "Goats and Monkeys" prefigures quite clearly the nature of the struggle which he has termed "one race's quarrel with another's god",[11] where the effort to abandon dead metaphors begins. This peculiar angle of approach to the racial crisis is that of the colonial nurtured on the colonizer's tradition and straining against its contradictory ties.

For the classic model of this dialogic mode we need to borrow from a much later phase of Walcott's career the major poem, "The Sea Is History" (*SAK*). Coming from the mature Walcott, it testifies to the seminal and generic role of this principle in the thinking that has shaped his aesthetic. More immediately, it also gives the clearest illustration of the modality of the poetics we are considering, its final aims and implications, and achievements.

"The Sea Is History" sets out to refute the charge of the historylessness of the region, the bogey surviving from Walcott's earliest period. To do so, it takes the form of a head-on argument with the Western notion of a history of achievement, and is a sustained rebuttal of the premises of epic-heroic achievement by which the Caribbean is deemed historyless (a people "without a character and purpose of their own"). Thus it starts out with the motion to be contested: "Where are your monuments, your battles, martyrs? / Where is your tribal memory?" (*CP*, 364).

The strategy of this argument is the substance of its discourse. For each stage in the progress of Western civilization, it identifies an equivalent in the untoward, contrary experience of the Caribbean past. It retraces the records of the Judaeo-Christian narrative – the record of its spiritual history – from its mythology right through its major historic epochs: from the Old Testament, through the Renaissance, through the colonizing/Christianizing era, which trails into the Caribbean's own emergence into nationhood. In each case, however, the Caribbean past yields, from the crucible of its abnegations and sufferings, a parallel, equal in depth, of self-achievement. Thus "the lantern of a caravel" was the light of the dread Genesis of the Caribbean people, signalling their beginnings in the journey into bondage; they had their Exodus in the brute horrors suffered in the holds of the slave ships; produced their own songs of Babylonian bondage, epitomized in the tradition of black American spirituals (Walcott's native theme is typically inclusive of the entire black diaspora).

The Caribbean equivalent of the "Songs of Babylonian bondage" is especially striking, and will offer a closer view of what is happening in this effort:

> Then came from the plucked wires
> of sunlight on the sea floor
>
> the plangent harps of Babylonian bondage,
>
> (CP, 364–65)

This is a powerfully graphic figuration of the piercings of desire and hope stirring the soul at the most naked reaches of its despair – an original metaphor of the soul awakening into song out of pain and yearning. Ingeniously, Walcott uses the model of the biblical harp to craft this metaphor, so that the Caribbean version appears at first as a virtual reprint of the harp, stressing the factor of equivalence. But the iconography of this Caribbean equivalent, and the distinct values inscribed in that iconography, are quite different from the Western original. The natural, elemental icons – "sunlight on the sea-floor" – reflect the bare, elemental sources from which the sorrow songs of the black tradition came; affirming, therefore, the inner levels at which the human soul is engaged in its self-achieving odyssey. True achievement, the poem says, is to be found at these "invisible" levels, and it is at that level that Walcott claims a history for his people. Thus the naturalistic icons of the native setting prove truer than and displace the epic-heroic embellishments and trappings prized in the older tradition.

Closely observed, however, the argument is not that Old World, Western civilization has no true history of achievement: rather, Walcott's affirmation reflects the core of real, invisible history in the older metaphors, what subsists beneath their traditionally more privileged, epic, visible moulds. It amounts to a rediscovery of the root, human levels at which history is made. "The Sea Is History" thus highlights this essential achievement: fresh metaphors are generated, countering and refuting the values of the older ones, and answering to indigenous needs and realities. An integral facet of this process, however, is the reflexive action of renewing the primal principles hidden in the older tradition. This achievement points to certain key ideas in Walcott's credo, which begin to emerge in this early bid to "abandon dead metaphors". It is a credo which centres, as earlier mentioned, on his concept of a New World purpose of Adamic naming, culminating in the realization of a faith in renewal. This particular import of naming is classically defined in the integrated achievement just examined in "The Sea Is History".

We need to return to the connections between the concept of Adamic naming and the metaphorical enterprise considered earlier in the introductory chapter. What are the particular imperatives of Walcott's route through metaphor (by contrast with, for example, Harris's approach through "variables of myth" in the region)? As we saw in that chapter, when he speaks of "borrowed metaphors", he is referring to the constructs of imagery (in art, literature, religion) which encode a civilization's or culture's vision of a higher order of truth, its spiritual tradition. Underlying this, moreover, there is a definitive concept of metaphor in its distinct role and function as an element of language which is seminal to Walcott's thought. Metaphor in Walcott does not merely serve the function of rhetorical substitution, as held by the

Aristotelian school. It is metaphor in its original, generative and cognitive function, the level to which Ernst Cassirer returns in his *Language and Myth*: a linguistic element which, through the principle of correspondences, serves the primordial act of naming, that first act of "recognizing things humanly". In Walcott's thinking, as we also saw, the act of "recognizing things humanly", at its most original, engages the inwardness of the human and its related anthropomorphic principle. As Cassirer stresses, metaphor is, at this level, essentially spiritual in motive, and mythico-religious in origin.[12] Walcott's perception of the historyless condition and virgin needs of his region is congruent with this belief in metaphorical naming. He makes an early state- ment of his commitment to this level of engagement in "Origins", a poem which, though often passed over by his editors, he considers important enough to include in his *Collected Poems 1948–1984*:

> The mind, among sea-wrack, sees its mythopoeic coast,
> Seeks, like the polyp, to take root in itself.
> Here, in the rattle of receding shoal,
> Among these shallows I seek my own name and a man.
>
> (*CP*, 14)

But, as our focus on the dialectical relationship to the colonizer's tradition has shown, it is naming of a complex, novel kind. It first comprises the purpose of discovering fresh metaphors. But this takes place within the context of a questioning, quarrelling engagement with the colonizer's tradition of meta- phors, prompted by a deeply revolutionary cause. The engagement also entails a fresh recovery of archetypes. The recovery of root meaning earlier consid- ered in "The Sea Is History" thus amounts to a virtual "renaming", repre- sentative of a kind of revisionism most typical of his later achievement. The fresh naming and this "renaming" are integral, interactive facets of what Adamic naming means in Walcott, within the necessary context of the relationship to the older tradition left by history.

We return to Cassirer here. The metaphorical function operative in the act of naming is the very process of generating language: the creation of the verbal world begins in the act of identification that is itself based on the principle of correspondences. The poetics of Walcott's peculiar route through metaphor is thus an authentic route to the wider, overarching goal of indigenizing, naturalizing the given language in his art. He sees this from quite early as the ultimate terms of the revolutionary challenge, and articulates this imperative with the force of a manifesto in "Crusoe's Journal": to "make his language ours" (*CP*, 93). In his view it is a *given* language which he, even more urgently than an Achebe, cannot refuse.[13] The process of indigenizing the language is initiated during this phase, comprising the generation of fresh metaphors from his own cultural ground; and, along with this, the recovery of primal meanings that lie buried beneath the extrinsic accretions of older, given ones.

At this first stage, however, what he faces in the prospect of abandoning dead metaphors is a complex, arduous, exploratory process, fraught with an inevitable burden of pain and possibility, as well as residual ambivalence. The abandoning of dead metaphors and the generation of new ones is, to all intents and purposes, a veritable battleground, an arena of struggle in which he is divided between pain and possibility. The urgencies of this struggle engage him throughout *The Castaway* and *The Gulf.* Notably, the poems concerned with this effort are mainly interiorized and reflective. The latter exist side by side, however, with a number of "public" poems dealing directly with race, politics and society. In terms of concerns and modes, interiorized and public pieces do overlap, as always in Walcott. It has been convenient, however, given our focus in this chapter, to group the interiorized poems together here, and to leave the more public poems to chapter 4, which attempts to focus on Walcott's outlook on revolutionary possibility.

The poems we proceed to examine here are concerned with the two related facets of the effort identified in "The Castaway": the crisis of an oppressive nothingness, and the counteractive purpose of genesis in reading "nature's plan". Fresh indigenous metaphors are generated and shaped to explore both these strains. The burden of negation is represented in major pieces such as "The Swamp", "Missing the Sea", "Laventille" (*The Castaway*); "Air", "Homecoming: Anse La Raye" (*The Gulf*). The effort towards genesis finds expression in attempts at a fresh order of spiritual intelligence, and is concentrated in "Guyana", a sequence of six poems (*The Gulf*). Inextricable from this central effort is another major related preoccupation of this phase: the hermetic nature of this task, and its acute pressures for the Caribbean poet of that time, as in "Crusoe's Island", and "Love in the Valley".

Landscape as Negation

> [N]aturally I arrived at the heresy that landscape and history had failed me.
> ("Twilight", 28)

The many, complex sources of the negation that troubles Walcott during this phase come together in what he experiences primarily as the desolation of the native landscape. Behind the peculiar destitution it presents is the ever-imminent spectre of the region's past. Slavery, the true beginning of its history, left only a legacy of degradation and inferiority; to be followed by the experience of colonialism – Walcott's immediate background – which entrenched a virtual tradition of dependence upon and subservience to an alien "mother" culture. For Walcott, as pioneering native artist facing the bleakness of this situation – imprinted, as it were, in the disfigurements of the human and physical environment ("Tales of the Islands") – the most painful aspect of the total crisis was the loss of any real claim to an ancestral memory, in this case, of the other parent tradition of Africa. It is the crisis of an amnesiac history to which he gives classic expression in the poem "Laventille" (*The Castaway*):

> some deep, amnesiac blow. We left
> somewhere a life we never found,
>
> customs and gods that are not born again,
> some crib, some grille of light
> clanged shut on us in bondage . . .

(CP, 88)

Walcott's sense of negation also concerns the difficulty of engaging his creative mission in such a landscape. The latter intensifies his early anxieties about the futility and impotence of his art in that environment, presaging the crises of acute alienation which surface every so often during the phase.

"The Swamp", placed right after the title poem in *The Castaway,* gives concentrated expression to the desolation that is the experience of landscape. Walcott finds in that physical feature, its peculiar aspects and physiognomy in the tropical setting, an image to embody the characteristic condition of oppressive negation. "The Swamp" is a poem of great artistic intensity and concentration. A powerful, metaphoric technique traces the human, psychic equivalent of the condition featured in the swamp. It works through a principle of metaphoric play and correspondence to effect the merging of the physical image of the swamp, the human presence and, subsumed in the latter, the persona of the poet as representative of the effort at creative being. The human figuration is meticulously traced in the processes and features of the swamp: thus its "black mouth", breath, black mood, blood, sexual organs (vulva and phalli). Within this predominant context, there is scope for dramatic treatment. Thus the persona of the poet, functioning as the medium of the experience, registers as the original consciousness being subjected to the live ills of the swamp: "Its black mood / Each sunset takes a smear of your life's blood". In the concluding movement, the metaphor expands the correspondence between the elemental and the human landscape in this picture of the progressive engulfment of all forms of organic life in the swamp habitat – bird, sapling and human figure:

> In the fast-filling night, note
> How the last bird drinks darkness with its throat,
> How the wild saplings slip
>
> Backward to darkness, go black
>
>   . . . merge
>
> Limb, tongue and sinew into a knot

(CP, 60)

Manifesting the chaos of the aboriginal life-force, the swamp presents the scene of a proliferation of life-forms (plant, reptile, amphibian) in a habitat that reeks of degenerative rot. The rank growth of its flora and fauna seems to mirror all kinds of deformities: "outlandish phalloi", mangrove "roots obscene / As a six-fingered hand":

> Each mangrove sapling
> Serpentlike, its roots obscene
> As a six-fingered hand,
> Conceals within its clutch the mossbacked toad,
> Toadstools, the potent ginger-lily
> Petals of blood,

(CP, 59)

For the sensibility alert to its intimations, the swamp exerts a dread fascination and menace. Its "rich decrescence", the dynamic of its active chaos, is a pull into regression, away from all evolutionary, civilizing process, from wholeness and creative being. Thus the forceful conceit: "It begins nothing". The fear and threat of this pull backward is the central emotional experience of the poem. It is the pull backward into the dissolution, the extinction of consciousness itself, rendered in the final oblivion of the overwhelming darkness/blackness of the concluding movement. That backward pull is like no "gentle going", though; its strains are enervating, visceral, and its final darkness a kind of constricting paralysis.

> How the wild saplings slip
> Backward to darkness, go black

> With widening amnesia, take the edge
> Of nothing to them slowly, merge
>
> Limb, tongue, and sinew into a knot
> Like chaos, like the road
> Ahead.

(CP, 60)

This is a poem, ultimately, about a condition inimical to creative being, and about the trauma of trying to engage the creative process in that setting – the bird "drinking darkness with its throat" being an emblem of the poet as would-be singer.

While the poem relies closely on the metaphorical development of the swamp image to realize this crisis, there are signals, explicit and implicit, which invoke the historico-cultural context of that sensibility. The perceptions and responses which go into "naming" that particular desolation hark back to the realities of a slave and colonial past. There is the reference to the condition of blacks in North America in the allusion to the hard-labour prison camps of the Everglades swamplands in Florida, occupied by black prisoners, along with white "cracker" convicts deemed the scum of the earth. The "Negroes" predominate in this habitat – a limbo whose impassable terrain and inhuman conditions represent a live example of the dehumanizing, regressive state the poem has been considering. In the perception of this threat of regression lies, subliminally, the deeper burden of a history which reversed the course of a civilizing process to leave only a sense of amnesia, absence.

What gives authority and validity, finally, to his definition of landscape and history as negation at this stage is his honest exploration of the pain of an absurd past, and the "naming" of its unique mental and emotional climate and milieu. The motif of blackness/darkness, pervasive in the poem, is a significant element of this "naming". Blackness/darkness here is, first, the true colour of the desolation being described; it defines the state itself. It is, at the same time, influenced by and inseparable from the historical stigma and shadow of race itself.

One other aspect of the poem further distinguishes the singular accent of the experience being explored. The tone and spirit of the lines are in striking contradiction to the theme of negation and dissolution. There is a combative energy and power in the lines which runs counter to despair; an energy of resistance in the purposive forward thrust of the rhythms of the underlying iambic pentameter, and in its forceful diction. It expresses the positive spirit of exploratory struggle with which the poet confronts the pain, effectively captured in the concluding lines of the poem: "Like chaos, like the road / Ahead". The spirit of resistance comes through in the double impact of the simultaneous recognition of "chaos" and "the road / Ahead". This remains a salient aspect of Walcott's expressions of negation during this period.

Finally, we need to note that the swamp image comes from a naturalistic, elemental configuration specifically introduced in the title poem, "The Castaway". He searches out and shapes most of his native metaphors, as the rest of this chapter will show, from this naturalistic configuration. Emerging during this phase, it remains the source of the body of imagery most seminal to the Walcott universe and its iconography (from the omnipresent sea, to the mountain forest setting of Makak in *Dream on Monkey Mountain*). There are, for sure, other areas of and courses to indigenous metaphors. But this naturalistic sphere, authentic to the physiognomy of the landscape, takes its special value from the recognition of the revolutionary opportunity of "a green world" to unburden itself of the dead weight of imperial metaphors. How liberating and productive a route this proves is the testimony of Walcott's total achievement. But it is already there in the native content of a poem like "The Swamp".

The poem which shows, above all, how deeply this sense of negation has implanted itself on Walcott's consciousness is "Air", a major poem appearing in the later volume *The Gulf* (1969). In this poem he reflects discursively on the region's history to give his most thorough explanation of the idea of the absence of ancestral memory in the void of that landscape. He takes his cue from Froude's notorious assessment of the West Indies, which serves as the epigraph to the poem: "The natural graces of life do not show themselves under such conditions. There are no people there in the true sense of the word, with a character and purpose of their own."[14] Froude's ethnocentric verdict – that the region was therefore a place which would never amount to anything – has been treated with the opprobrium it deserves.[15] This verdict, however, incites Walcott to probe the deeper, human dimensions of this nothingness in the denials and pain of a people.

We move from the swamp into the rainforest setting in this poem. Walcott encounters the representative image of his "green, churning forest" in the rainforest of the Guyanese interior. The Guyanese rainforest – where his own island's rainforest seems repeated on a phenomenal scale – had a tremendous impact on his imagination, producing the sequence of poems "Guyana", a major definitional sequence of the period. "Air" stands at the head of this sequence. The rainforest presents, to the senses of the poet, the organic process of an elemental force drawing in and consuming all forms of life energy to emit only an ill, vaporous air, as if this were its sole aim and *raison-d'être*. That vaporous air visibly overhanging the forest becomes the emblem of this primordial annihilative process.

The rainforest/air configuration represents, therefore, the spectacle of nature untamed, unreclaimed, with its characteristic ethos of nothingness in the landscape. The poem engages from the outset with the human import of this phenomenon, with what it intimates about the possibility of a human accommodation in that setting. The remorseless "grinding" of the forest impinges on the consciousness as an indifference, imperviousness to the human, which presages a sense of disavowal of all meaning:

> The unheard, omnivorous
> jaws of this rain forest
> not merely devour all
> but allow nothing vain;
> they never rest,
> grinding their disavowal
> of human pain.

(CP, 113)

Later in the poem it becomes, in Walcott's deepening imaginative apprehension, a manifestation of the pre- and ahuman.

The encounter with an untamed setting estranging and unaccommodating to the human takes Walcott straight back to a past which confirms the failure of the human experiment in this setting. This speculation on the region's past is the main focus of Walcott's response and thought in the poem. From the aboriginal peoples to the slave ancestors of the more recent past, it has been a pattern of successive defeat:

> Long, long before us
> those hot jaws, like an oven
> steaming, were open
> to genocide; they devoured
> two minor yellow races, and
> half of a black; . . .

(CP, 113)

The Caribs and Arawaks, and the African Maroons who repaired to the Guyanese forest in their refusal to succumb to white oppression, were all consumed in "the hot jaws" and "undiscriminating stomach" of savage, unreclaimed nature – a fate that conversion to Christianity was powerless to avert. Walcott gives a generalized account of the total effacement of the two Amerindian tribes, his viewpoint no doubt influenced by his sense of loss and amnesia as the prevailing climate of the setting. (He must have been aware, however, of the existence of several other Amerindian tribes scattered in the interior of Harris's Guyana.)[16] The poem's imagery suggests that these aboriginal cultures (significantly the two main ones associated with the Caribbean islands) were already foredoomed in a setting so inimical to the human:

> which devoured
> the god-refusing Carib, petal
> by golden petal, then forgot,
> and the Arawak
> who leaves not the lightest fern-trace
> of his fossil to be cultured
> by black rock,

> (*CP*, 114)

The Caribs are identified in the flower motif, alluding to the myth of El Dorado, "the gilded one": their legendary aesthetic proved powerless against that fate, disintegrating "petal / by golden petal". The Arawaks, whose culture is generally considered to have been less resilient, were totally effaced, leaving not even such legendary fragments. In the concrete images registering the fate of the Arawaks, the primary reference is metaphorical: "not even the lightest fern-trace / . . . to be cultured by black rock". The implication is that they left no traces which the succeeding race of black people might benefit from in their attempt to cultivate a native world on that bare, naked ground. Alluding to the phenomenal historical movements of the Amerindian peoples through the seas and lands of the Americas, the poem concludes with the reflection that the "vague sea", no less than unreclaimed forest, seems to have given no acquiescence to their early efforts at survival:

> and the vague sea
> where the lost exodus
> of corials sunk without trace –

> (*CP*, 114)

(By the time of *Another Life,* however, Walcott has made a significant shift from this despairing view of the total effacement of an Amerindian legacy, and is intent on identifying and claiming the primal traces of the Amerindian past as components of an indigenous, ancestral legacy.) But, in these reflections on the fate of the aboriginal peoples of the region, Walcott intends no distortion of history. He places the brutal reality of genocide early in his account: "these hot jaws . . . / were open to genocide". It is important to pay close attention to his subtle placement of genocide in relation to his idea of a setting hostile to human culture and survival, expressed in the carefully chosen phrase: "open to genocide". It suggests, first of all, that these aboriginal tribes, unaccommodated in that setting, fell easy victims to the fate of genocide at the hands of the white man. But the further, more significant idea is that this proved a fitting milieu for the unleashing of the old human savagery that fuelled the act of genocide. Here Walcott, on South American soil, is very much focused on the fate of the Amerindians at the hands of the conquistadors.

The poem confronts the present with an argument that develops conclusively out of this line of thought. It aims that argument directly at white colonizing civilization to deliver its central, categorical message: "The forest is unconverted." It zeroes in on the failure of Christianity, the main instrument of their more recent, civilizing experiment. It too, like the other faiths before it, failed to tame the forest, and was totally ineffectual in this setting. It is the characteristic angle of his protest in this first phase of the quest for identity – the quarrel with the white man's God; and here, it becomes the crux of his response to Froude. Walcott does something very interesting at this point: he draws the imagery of the Christian church, its rituals and symbolism, into the forest to develop his argument about the nonconversion of the forest:

> the forest is unconverted,
> because that shell-like noise
> which roars like silence, or
> ocean's surpliced choirs
> entering its nave, to a censer
> of swung mist, is not
> the rustling of prayer
> but nothing; milling air,

> (*CP*, 114)

There are multiple facets and effects to the deployment of this imagery, which provide a strong illustration of the aesthetic being developed during this phase. It is used, first of all, to show the ironic gaps between Christianity's features and those of the forest. But, at a vital level, it is "borrowed" imagery being exploited to craft the reverse face of the unholy, godless, unchurched forest. This is a kind of reflexive enhancement: behind it lies the dialectical relationship to the Western tradition earlier discussed and indeed this poem serves to highlight its functional aspects. The reflexive effect is more than a matter of visual enhancement: it is a device which works to give presence to absence, to invest absence/nothingness with substance. Walcott achieved a similar effect in describing the swamp: "It begins nothing." Here the effects and details of Christian religious and ceremonial ritual are transposed to the bare elementals of the forest – so that the ahuman influences of its nothingness assume an autonomous, godlike power of their own: "a faith, infested, cannibal, / which eats gods". The symbols themselves have a spiritualizing presence, so that despite the irony, the rhythms retain a sense of the solemn and religious. Out of this dialectical process Walcott has virtually brought into existence an alternative myth, one of whose primary purposes is to counter the Christian one.

But the core significance behind this investiture of the "infested, cannibal faith" of the forest is that it comes close to a discovery of the mythic, aboriginal void on native ground. Here it is pertinent to note that while he quarrels with the formal religion, his imagination is steeped in the Judaeo-Christian archetype, and in effect, he has come to the forest with a mythic intention. This aboriginal void, however, is of a distinct variety. It is not merely the condition of unknowing and formlessness before creation. It is loaded with a sense of defilement, corruption and active animadversion – precisely because human history of a kind has happened here, one that, absurdly, amounted to nothing. The crux of the "nothingness" that Walcott confronts here is that it is loaded with history: "There is too much nothing here." In emotional and psychic terms, what this poem expresses is his apprehension of the deep alienation and confounding effects of the void of landscape. It is an apprehension charged, as already seen, with spiritual urgency – which is precisely where his response to negation differs from Naipaul's – pointing to the imperative of human reclamation, which will be undertaken in the "Guyana" sequence.

It is, finally, by virtue of the metaphor into which he transmutes the forest setting that he has been able to identify and explore these singular aspects of the native condition. A look at the conception of this metaphor, the sense impressions from which it begins, gives insight into its freshness and expressive power. Walcott begins with an intuitional, sensory response to the forest. Its combination of stillness and endless grinding sounds reaches him as a heard, voluble emptiness, the tangible equivalent of which is there in the mist, the air overhanging the forest. Thus air becomes the "incarnation" of the ill spirit of nothingness emanating from the landscape, essentialized concretely and figuratively in the forest setting. The metaphor is born out of the interchange between this lyrical/intuitional response on the one hand, and emotions and sentiments of sociocultural reference, articulated in the discourse on history. As in "Swamp", he draws on the elementals characteristic of his milieu for the substance of this metaphor. "Air" also illustrates another striking feature of this developing aesthetic: sea and forest/native vegetation are one continuous space and share intimations of the characteristic genius of that space. Thus the incidence of "shell-like noise" and "ocean's surpliced choirs" in the forest.

There are allusions, in both of the poems seen so far, to the adverse effect of this experience of void on the artistic effort itself (signified in the motif of the straining, disabled bird); and indeed it is the experience of negation for Walcott as private artist that takes prominence during this phase. In "The Figure of Crusoe", subtitled "On the Theme of Isolation in West Indian Writing", he dwells on the acute crisis of isolation for West Indian artists, especially those who chose to remain in the environment. He quotes Naipaul and Lamming on the conditions which forced them to opt for the pleasures of exile in England.[17] For Naipaul, the incapacity of a society still trapped in a legacy of self-contempt was dearth to the spirit of the artist; for Lamming, it was a society equally unsupportive because it was not yet ready for its artists. The pressures of this kind of isolation lie behind a number of poems in *The Castaway* and *The Gulf*: they tell of the extreme difficulty of sustaining Walcott's artistic endeavour, of spells of paralysis, of crises of confidence in his art, presaging the crisis of alienation at its most acute and traumatic in *The Gulf*.

"Missing the Sea" (*The Castaway*) extends an early moment of the crisis of void for Walcott the artist – a moment of stasis, a suspension of the creative urge. It is one of those early poems which, for perfect coordination of theme and execution, will continue to hold its own among the most fully realized works in the entire Walcott corpus. The poem is outstanding for the sheer power with which it captures the emotion of that stasis and its impact on Walcott's sensibility – a staggering sense of estrangement and displacement. Most remarkably, the creative energy which goes into the apprehension of that moment becomes itself an overture of resistance, moving towards a resolution of the crisis, as we also noted in "Swamp". It is a feature which makes "Missing the Sea" the consummate example of the counteractive movement so characteristic of this phase of Walcott's effort:

> Something removed roars in the ears of this house,
> Hangs its drapes windless, stuns mirrors
> Till reflections lack substance.
>
> Some sound like the gnashing of windmills ground
> to a dead halt;
> A deafening absence, a blow.

(CP, 63)

Walcott instinctively associates this sensation of a sudden stasis or suspension of energies with missing the familiar sounds of his native island sea (here the rough Atlantic coast rather than the Caribbean), with missing the vital energies and life-force of its sounds and rhythms. It is like being cut off from the very rhythm of his creative energies which are at one with those of that sea, energies which fuel his own poetic being and inspiration. Thus he feels the first impact of absence as an inability to hear the sounds from which his verse takes its rhythms. The poem probably comes out of a genuine occasion of being away from his island home, and is a powerful instance of how deeply Walcott has internalized its sea setting. It is an early instance of a focal idea in Walcott, of the organic bond between the self and the landscape which it inhabits. The total experience of "deafening absence" in the poem is, on an important level, the objective correlative for this core, literal sensation of missing the sea, itself synonymous with the suspension of vital energies.

Out of this core experience issues a metaphor which enables him to realize and probe its effects on his psyche. His own consciousness as poet is cast as the house on the sea coast (the essentials of his Crusoe/castaway habitat) suddenly and strangely left vacant of all sounds, motions and signs of life. The poem enacts, in the aspects and effects of this house as poet's persona, the psychological impact of this stasis on Walcott's consciousness. The impact resounds in the bombardment of its images and rhythms. They convey, beginning with the "roars in the ears of this house", the loudness of the silence, the visceral strain of the emptiness and, at the same time, the echo of violent energies clamouring to break through to some release. But the reality of this absence remains most imminent, and its final quality is of the uncanny, unnatural sense of estrangement evoked in this original image (which surfaces out of Walcott's early personal background):

> Like the clothes of the dead left exactly
> As the dead behaved by the beloved,
>
> Incredulous, expecting occupancy.

(CP, 63)

Characteristically, the vacancy looks not to extinction, but occupancy.

"Missing the Sea" attains power as a metaphor fully original to the particular angst and temperament of this poet in his engagement with the particular conditions of his environment. The temperament is in tune with the raw, elemental energies of the Atlantic, which gives his frustration its characteristic temper – a frustration impelled towards an equally forceful resistance, rather than weariness and despondence. The frustration of that combative purpose echoed in "Missing the Sea", at its most extreme, keels over into the need for "a fist to smash the glare of skylight open" ("The White Town", *The Gulf*). There are schizophrenic tensions on the other side of that combative purpose. The schizophrenia comes to the fore and is much more strident in *The Gulf.* In "Moon" ("Metamorphoses"), for example, artistic paralysis feels like "being gripped by demons of inaction? / Whose silence shrieks so soon". When Walcott's lines "howl and overwhelm" it is no mere rhetoric, but the reality of that sensibility, a sensibility fully reflected in his own self-image in Makak (*Dream*).

It is clear when we come to *The Gulf* that the crisis of exile at home which Walcott described in "The Figure of Crusoe" has remained unabated, and indeed has deepened into the chronic strains of estrangement contained in the gulf motif. It presages the bouts of acute alienation alternating with attempts at creative possibility in this volume, as throughout this phase of his endeavour. Compounded with doubts about the efficacy or meaningfulness of his role as artist, this alienation induces its own paralysis. It is the inroads of paralysis from this artistic isolation, the fear of that paralysis, that Walcott suffers most acutely. "Moon" gives stark expression to the pain and desolation of that experience. In "Missing the Sea" the impact of silence stunned the poet; in "Moon" it shrieks (the shriek of silence survives to become the key motif in a major poem, "The Star-Apple Kingdom", fifteen years later). "Moon" is a poem about what the artistic self, trapped in isolation, is forced to become: it is essentially, the poem says, reduced to the primate's howl: "O lolling Orphic head silently howling, / my own head rises from its surf of cloud" (*The Gulf*, 12).[18] In effect, Walcott himself becomes a disembodied howl, which is the quality of his terrible anguish – with shades of the regressive process enacted in "The Swamp". The repetition of the "O" in the first of the lines cited virtually enacts a return to the prearticulate "O", sound-symbol of that howl. As disembodied "O"/howl, the poet's identity merges into that of a number of objects and features which echo, phonetically or visually, the same "O" sound – owl, bell, aureole, and the moon itself, beguiling symbol of the creative imagination. From (howling) owl, to bell (sounding), through aureole, to moon, it is a progressive essentialization into the pure self-consuming force of that condition, of which the "white light" of the moon becomes the ill genius. Walcott effects here an authentic conceit, for the process of the creative imagination forced in isolation into a manic activity of feeding on itself: "I watch the moonstruck image of the moon burn / A candle mesmerized by its own aura" (*The Gulf*, 12).

In addition to his internalization of the negations of the environment, the hermetic skill itself compounds the problem of isolation as an occupational hazard. The nature of this experience for Walcott as victim is contained in the "howl" of the poem, its desolating effects reflected in this traumatic image: "O lolling Orphic head silently howling, / my own head rises from its surf of cloud". Resurfacing from an earlier poem ("Crusoe's Island"), this image of his own severed head is expressive of the inroads of self-alienation during this phase, representative of spells when he stumbles in the intense test of faith and courage called for in this beginning.

If we reduce "Moon" to its central image, it is one of the bleakest, most forbidding statements in Walcott's work. The creative imagination, under duress, becomes a "howling head" (one of his series of bitterly ironic "meta-morphoses").[19] It is redeemed, though, by the strong passion which reverber-ates in its intense recovery of the primitive sound-sense equivalent of that pain. In this respect the poem gives yet another effective illustration of the pattern of dynamic counteraction in Walcott: thus the opening line, "Resisting poetry I am becoming a poem" (*The Gulf*, 12). A poem is indeed forced out of the live pressures of poetic inaction, and in a very real sense the "I"/Walcott as essence of that crisis does organically, internally realize that becoming. What "becomes", though, consists of the howl, "O", of that state. It is in this very area that it achieves its most significant action: as a poem about the realization of sound, the prearticulate "O", it returns to the primal sources of the making of poetry, language. Thus: "Slowly my body grows a single sound."

So far, we have been examining Walcott's interiorized apprehensions of negation in his environment, where he culls his imagery from the natural setting (sea, swamp, forest). It is the mode that predominates during this phase, especially in *The Castaway*. This internalization of void closely informs some of his responses to and commentary on society in important poems of the period – for example, "Laventille" (*The Castaway*), "Mass Man" and "Homecoming: Anse La Raye" (*The Gulf*). These poems do, of course, serve the important function of spelling out the social and communal conditions of the crisis. However, the thematic focus in these encounters with society is unquestionably on the spectre of history behind the void of landscape. We also get direct insight into the sources of the frustration which causes Walcott, every so often, to turn in "hopelessness and rage" against the very community for which he suffers, driving him back into the traumatic exile of the sense of a futile effort. We turn to "Laventille" and "Homecoming: Anse La Raye" to examine these features.

Walcott makes in Laventille, the Port of Spain slum from which the poem takes its name, a concrete encounter with the scars and abrasions of the human landscape, and he sees in them the legacy of a past that began with the middle passage. Laventille stands out as a landmark over the city: curiously sited on a hill overlooking the privileged suburbs, it is the home of Port of Spain's most depressed segment of urban blacks. As one of the extreme examples of the culture of poverty in the region, the slum has its distinct personality, celebrated by Earl Lovelace in his famous novel *The Dragon Can't Dance* (1979). It is the birthplace of the steelband, with whose "metallic" notes the poem opens. Walcott is in Laventille to serve as godfather to a friend's child in a christening ceremony – a role which becomes emblematic, as the poem unfolds, of his poet's mission to explore and name an identity on behalf of his people. Travelling up "the hill", as Laventille is called, he gives a graphic portrait of its physical appearance and the living conditions of its residents – narrow, steep streets winding uphill, crowded hovels with their characteristic ills of overbreeding, delinquency and violence. The poem sums up the condition of Laventille as "the height of poverty / for the desperate and black" (*CP*, 86). "Height" (of poverty) is loaded with a focal irony: the curious siting of Laventille makes it a paradigm of the upside-downness of the West Indian condition – "To go downhill / from here was to ascend" (*CP*, 86).

As the full scene of its human destitution unfolds, Laventille becomes in Walcott's eyes the live embodiment of the surviving ills of the middle passage. It is the veritable extension of the soul-bruising horrors of that journey of dispossession which, at the deepest level, links his friends in Laventille, himself

as suffering poet, the equally naked, privileged classes below, and the African
ancestors so vividly recalled in that setting. Thus:

> The salt blood knew it well,
> you, me, Samuel's daughter, Samuel
> and those ancestors clamped below its grate
>
> *(CP, 86)*

The imprint of the ancestors in the holds of the slave ships reappears, with
Walcott's characteristic visual crafting, in the overcrowded hovels "where the
inheritors of the Middle Passage stewed, / five to a room, still clamped below
their hatch" (*CP*, 86).

His mind thus comes to bear on the historical middle passage, drawing his
gaze to the sea, the original site of that journey. An inescapable presence from
his position on the hill, the open, empty expanse of the sea is the concrete,
tangible image of the severance of the descendants of the slave ancestors from
their ancestral worlds, and the consequent toll on them as a people. It
represents the hiatus in memory which is, for Walcott, the most critical
damage of the middle passage.

Looking out to that sea becomes a vicarious experience of "widening
memory". It leads Walcott to the classic, definitive articulation of his early
view of the region's history in this poem:

> Something inside is laid wide like a wound,
>
> some open passage that has cleft the brain,
> some deep, amnesiac blow. We left
> somewhere a life we never found
>
> customs and gods that are not born again
> some crib, some grille of light
> clanged shut on us in bondage, . . .
>
> . . . .
>
> and in its swaddling cerements we're still bound.
>
> *(CP, 88)*

Walcott speaks through a resourceful play on the graphic image of "passage",
whose interlocking meanings tell the full story of the damage of that historic
journey from Africa to the Caribbean. The passage represents, first, the brutal
severance, rupture of the descendants of Africa from their ancestral land,
which left the passage as the empty space, the gap between them. This is
repeated in the open gap, the void in memory – now being suffered by the

poet – that separates uprooted descendant from ancestral Africa. That gap is like a gaping wound, lesion to the mind and sensibility, its violence and abrasions still being suffered by the descendants of the middle passage. In the focus on "passage" as severance from ancestral traditions, Walcott articulates his early idea of the limbo condition of a people born to no spiritual heritage, still bound "in swaddling cerements" (see image of the Bolom in *Ti Jean*).[20] Both in theme and rhythm his lines deliberately echo Claude McKay's "Outcast", which bemoans the plight of the black man as an alien in the Western world, condemned to the permanent loss of Africa: "something in me is lost, forever lost, / some vital thing has gone out of my heart".[21]

Behind this expressive sequence of images – open passage, wound, limbo condition – it is the sea itself which remains the primary, generative symbol in this definition of history as soul-bruising amnesia. The sea, a vast and multifaceted symbol in Walcott, represents here the space/time vacuum between the Caribbean and the ancestral world from which it was separated; it is, as Walcott once indicated to this writer, the visible image of the hiatus between Africa and the Caribbean.[22] This is a face which contrasts with the more familiar one of the sea as source of living, generative energies ("Missing the Sea"). We are, in both of these, a far cry from the calm, paradisal sea of "A Sea Chantey". His association of the sea with the pain of dispossession is, however, very real. Ultimately, healed of history, it becomes in the mature Walcott the custodian of both regional and world memory.[23] In this poem, it remains the very element of the harsh, abrasive quality of the wound reopened by the visit to Laventille, as expressed in "salt blood" and "retching waters".

Another specific aspect of Laventille's plight causes Walcott just as much distress as the spectacle of "lives fixed in the unalterable groove / of grinding poverty" (*CP*, 88). What rubs the wound raw are the attitudes and values displayed by the people in the christening ceremony – their concern to observe the manners and customs of a Christian bourgeois culture at variance with the harsh realities of their lives:

> The black, fawning verger
> his bow tie akimbo, grinning, the clown-gloved
> fashionable wear of those I deeply loved
>
> (*CP*, 87)

Walcott responds to the mimicry with "hopelessness and rage". It becomes the occasion for a scathing, inevitable attack on the church, the Catholic "hill-top shrine" which continues to preside over their degradation and servitude, like the vultures which patrol Port of Spain's Labasse (dumping ground) nearby. But the real struggle is against hopelessness, disgust for a people who seem incapable of and beyond upliftment. Out of this tug-of-war comes a line most expressive of what the pain of landscape means for him at this stage: "twisting my love within me like a knife" (*CP*, 87). The poem is dedicated to Naipaul, with whose hopelessness he expresses some empathy here. His message to Naipaul, though, signalled in the epigraph taken from Blake, is to find a way out of fatalistic contempt through a holy rage. He himself goes beyond contempt in this poem in his perception of the burden of a past which he, and the entire society, shares with Laventille.

We come, finally, to "Homecoming: Anse La Raye", the poem which brings together the two interrelated aspects of the negation we have been examining so far – the void of the surrounding landscape, and the crisis of artistic isolation precipitated by the sense of a frustrated and futile effort. He arrives in this poem at the nadir of the sense of disconnectedness between the West Indian artist and an environment trapped in an intransigent, impenetrable plight. A poem from the darker mood of alienation in *The Gulf,* it is one of the few places where his pessimism about his mission is unrelieved by the strains of resistance. Its sombre despairing mood is conveyed in heavy, trochaic rhythms quite uncommon in the voice we have heard so far.

"Homecoming: Anse La Raye" captures a most authentic, immediate emotional experience of the pain of landscape, because the situation here involves personal nostalgia for Walcott: he is returning to his native St Lucian soil after a number of years. The occasion of the poem is a visit to Anse La Raye, a tiny, ramshackle fishing village on the northwestern side of the island, where conditions of stark poverty and backwardness remain unchanged – a place which, like D'Ennery, seems "born for being buried there". His immediate reaction is to the peculiar discrepancy in his own situation as a returning native son in that setting: he receives no welcome or recognition as a St Lucian poet, and remains totally anonymous. He feels keenly the absence of honours and graces commonly associated with such occasions, especially in the classical education of his boyhood. The poem opens with this reaction and train of thought, to face the reality that his is, virtually, no homecoming, as is emphasized in the bitterly ironic phrasing of "homecomings without home".

There is sincere and honest disappointment for Walcott in this nonrecognition, as expressed in this later admission of the failure of his early ambition: "but hoped it would mean something to declare / today, I am your poet, yours".

Walcott is not, however, decrying and deploring in "Anse La Raye" the familiar neglect and rejection of the artist in an uncultured, insensitive community. Rather, the underlying and more painful concern is that his own effort and contribution have proved incapable of enabling the change and upliftment that would have allowed for such a welcome. It has been without influence in a setting where conditions remain too unfavourable and intransigent to foster the growth of such values and cherished sanctities. The lack of a true homecoming, then, alerts him to the core grievance that "he gives them nothing", and resolves into the key realization of the visit – that his contribution as a poet amounts to nothing:[24]

> a drifting petal fallen in a cup,
> with nothing but its image,
> you sway, reflecting nothing.

> (*CP*, 128)

This is the burden of artistic exile to which he returns in Anse La Raye, to find "no home" on native soil. The crisis confronts him again with the blight of an irremediable past. The actual experience of this poem also illuminates the strains and stresses of the paralysis we met in poems such as "Swamp", "Air" and "Moon". It is with precisely this crisis of artistic exile that he identifies in Garth St Omer, the St Lucian novelist to whom the poem is dedicated. St Omer's protagonist is the educated native son, whose hopes of making a contribution are balked by the persistent dearth, poverty and backwardness to which he returns. The home to which he returns frustrates his purpose and induces psychic paralysis.[25]

The poem begins by invoking the classical model of the Homeric return to bemoan the absence of welcoming rites for the hero. It employs the same style of dialectical transference of borrowed metaphors we met in "Air", and the parallelling technique of "The Sea Is History". It traces the local counterparts of the classical rituals and symbols in the features and details of the narrow fishing beach scene around which the village huddles. The honour guard of hoisted swords for the returning warrior hero finds its mocking, parodic counterpart in the dry fronds of the coconut palms and the brown leaves of the sea grape trees native to the setting; helmets are mimicked in the shells of the sea crabs; the sacrificial oxen of the festive ceremony in the dried branches of the coconut palms; and the sea itself echoes not the soothing, healing love-weave of Penelope's loom but the lingering nighttime notes of doom:

only, when her looms fade,
drilled in our skulls, the doom-
surge-haunted nights,
only this well-known passage

under the coconuts' salt-rusted
swords, those rotted
leathery sea-grape leaves,
the seacrabs' brittle helmets, and
this barbecue of branches, like the ribs
of sacrificial oxen on scorched sand;

(CP, 127)

The technique gives graphic presence to the physiognomy of that beach in its stark contrast to the classical original – a scene of barrenness, rot and "fish-gut-reeking" squalor, as offensive and punishing to the spirit as to the senses. This dialectical model carries a good deal of the meaning of the poem. It serves, as we have just seen, to carve out the contrasting face of the native landscape. It also carries a polemical bias which makes a central point about the absence of gods, of rites conferring human dignity and honour, in a place where "borrowed ancestors" will not take root. The reference to Helen, after whom St Lucia was named "the Helen of the West", underlines the irony. An implicit reproach is aimed at the anomalies of colonial education which left, in the classical vocabulary "drilled into [the] skulls" of Walcott's generation, such a legacy of mockery.

Most distressing of all is the spectacle of the "spindly, sugar-headed children" ("sugar-headed" from being sunbleached), disfigured by malnutrition, who "pelt up from the shallows", as if the characteristic progeny of that beach. The condition of the children is what deals the most painful blow in this return to his native land, giving rise to the profoundly disturbing image of a wound rubbed raw in a traumatic mixture of pain and recoil: "They swarm like flies / round your heart's sore". The lives of the children of Anse La Raye seem fixed between frolicking in the water and waiting to fleece tourists; oblivious of and, to all intents and purposes, cut off from any prospects or future beyond this. It is their plight, especially, which brings home to him the sense of the failure and powerlessness of his mission as poet, after nearly a decade. His effort has not succeeded in making any difference to their plight; it has failed to contribute, as he would have hoped, to some upliftment in the consciousness as well as the material conditions of the setting. So that the sharpest sting of the unwelcome – and the sticking-place of Walcott's pain –

is the brash indifference of these children when they discover that he is no tourist and has nothing material to give. The native poet must thus admonish himself not to shirk engagement with of the grievous, despairing image they present, and he does so in a reflective moment deep with the echoes of two of Christ's sayings in the New Testament: "Suffer them to come, / entering your needle's eye". Suffering them to enter his "needle's eye", his clairvoyance and sensitivity to their foredoomed fates – a grim prognosis of the society's – is also a realization that his own exile carries a reflection of their own. (This is the quality of the sensitivity he sees underlying Naipaul's detached, strenuous ease in exile, as he recreates this writer's case in "Exile" [*The Gulf*].) Thus the poem's theme includes an anthem for the doomed children of that setting.[26] Appropriately, then, it is the seascape (of Anse La Raye) itself which takes on the inhospitable aspect of oppressive nothingness, the ill-favoured contempt that allows no homecoming, to leave him with the final sense of the futility of his mission:

> You give them nothing.
> Their curses melt in air.
> The black cliffs scowl,
> the ocean sucks its teeth,
> like that dugout canoe
> a drifting petal fallen in a cup,
> with nothing but its image,
>
> you sway, reflecting nothing.

(CP, 128)

A metaphor has been sketched out of the bleak temper, human and physical, of that village. There is, however, some ambiguity in Walcott's concluding observations in the poem, as he shifts to the portrait of the fishermen playing draughts in the shade, "crossing, eating their islands". The fishermen seem well accommodated to their setting; they show a native confidence and authority, which suggests that the bitter pain of alienation and futility remains Walcott's own problem, the curse of the poet's sensibility. (He made a similar comment in "Return to D'Ennery".) The parting shot, though, seems to undercut this advantage of the fisherman's:

> and one, with a politician's
> ignorant sweet smile, nods,
> as if all fate
> swayed in his lifted hand

(CP, 129)

In the end, despite the pessimism, "Homecoming: Anse La Raye" bears witness to the deep love in the anguish of exile which makes it impossible for him to abandon the effort.

Landscape as Possibility

> He was a flower,
> weightless. He would float down.
>
> (*CP*, 117)

Throughout the period represented by the two volumes, efforts towards the search for creative release and possibility occur side by side with the expressions of negation examined above. The incidence of the two next to each other reflects the interactive dynamic of Walcott's struggle, as identified in "The Castaway". The privations and isolation of the castaway condition presage the corresponding necessity of an experiment in invention, signalled, as we saw, in the peculiar spirit and passion of the poems of negation. Taken as a whole, the following pattern emerges from Walcott's effort during this seminal phase of his career: the expression of negation is a necessary part of the struggle, impelling him towards an equally intense search for possibility. A sequence in each volume is devoted to this search for possibility – in *The Castaway*, "A Tropical Bestiary"; in *The Gulf*, the outstanding "Guyana".

Essentially, Walcott is striving to look past the amnesia and isolation reflected in the emptiness of the landscape to see, on the other side of that emptiness, the features and signals of a natural, "virginal" setting, and to try to respond to its potentialities. It offers him an opportunity, to cite the symbolic language of his castaway mask, to observe "nature's plan" ("The Castaway"), "To be like beast or natural object, pure" ("Crusoe's Island"). This means the ideal of a fresh experiment to relate humanly to the natural world. The search for possibility thus engages him in a creative interaction with the elemental landscape which, closely observed, is an attempt to find an alternative order of spiritual intelligence grounded in the natural. It is the quest for an alternative which will directly answer to the need to overcome the amnesia and the void of landscape, and the legacy of dead metaphors compounded in that crisis. The thrust of this purpose emerges most clearly in the "Guyana" sequence, which represents the culmination of this phase of the search for possibility. Its orientation is a movement away from the Western Platonist tradition of transcendence, towards a revisioned adjustment in an earthly, immanent order.

Fresh metaphors are being generated in this interaction with landscape, which pivots on the original principle of correspondences between human and natural worlds. The poems of landscape as possibility present a fund of indigenous metaphors shaped out of the forest/ocean configuration we met in the expressions of negation. Here they stand out all the more clearly, by virtue of serving the purpose of ontological and spiritual perception. By contrast, the metaphors of negation are more consistently engaged in the quarrel with the colonizer's tradition (as in "Air" and "Laventille").

The two sequences, as well as a number of other poems, show, in their themes and concerns, this preoccupation with a fresh order of intelligence. Walcott's sequences are always an indication of his focal areas of preoccupation in any period. In "A Tropical Bestiary" we find such existential themes as the levelling of desire to its earthly mean ("Octopus", "Ibis"); the question of humankind's unstable and multiple interpretations of the cosmos vis-à-vis an underlying, unchanging order ("Man O' War Bird"); the artistic process as a paradigm of the relationship between humankind and its universe ("Tarpon"). The latter, strongly focused in "The Bush" ("Guyana" sequence), is a major feature which serves as a central, functional context: the poetic self becomes the medium of these explorations in a self-consciously hermetic effort. The Guyana sequence presents a synthesis of these themes in the spiritual odyssey of its journey into the interior.

Walcott has selected only "Tarpon" from "A Tropical Bestiary" for inclusion in his 1948–84 collection. But it is useful to look at other areas of the sequence for what these show of the early preoccupations of this search for possibility in engagement with the landscape. He has obviously been influenced by Ted Hughes to turn to the fauna of his native sea setting, comprising such creatures as the octopus, frigate bird, tarpon and sea crab. Like Hughes, he observes principles in the behaviour of these creatures which point to a corresponding natural truth or necessity in the human habitat. Factual and objective observation of the animal world is claimed as the criterion for arrival at these "truths"; but the particular choice of truths is never quite disengaged. In Hughes it is the wholeness of instinct in the animal world which reflects negatively on an emasculated culture. In Walcott the "truths" are no less predisposed by his prevailing angst of the period. "Man O' War Bird" is interesting in this respect. It is a poem which gives cogent expression to an idea indicative of his earliest philosophical orientation. It is the idea, recurring in *The Castaway,* of a universe that retains an underlying, inviolate order, independent of humankind's various and subjective constructions. The poem makes this statement through a quite resourceful take-off of Hughes's "Hawk Roosting",[27] which is a good illustration of the freedom and independence with which he has begun to treat his borrowings. Hughes's bird assumes the vantage point of the supreme Eye, to assert his authority in a world to which he is perfectly accommodated. Walcott's frigate bird hovers above in shifting and changing relationship to the seeing human eye below, and reflects different worlds, depending on the varying angles from which it is viewed: now a peaceable world from its calm poise in seeking out its prey (by contrast to Hughes's hawk); or, from "its piercing height", the sense of human insignificance against the span of the limitless and infinite. Beyond the final subjectivity and partiality of these readings, the poem suggests, there is an impersonal Eye which "weighs this world exactly as it pleases" – representative of an immutable, if elusive, order of things. This is really an expression of Walcott's desire to be free of inherited creeds and philosophies; and if it is no less illusory than the inherited creeds, it shows his early leaning towards faith in a universe finally greater than humankind's constructions of "truth".

"The Flock" approaches this same concern from a much richer, more complex angle. One of the stronger poems of this group, it explores this philosophical concern within the framework of historico-cultural reference. The poem begins in a significant experience. Walcott, situated in a winter landscape (possibly in the United States) is watching a flock of birds migrating south in search of tropical warmth – a scene which echoes his own yearnings for his "different sky". The sight of the birds in seasonal flight triggers off a number of analogues and answering metaphors, some in dialogic play with each other. First, like dark figures of augury against the vacant whiteness of the winter landscape, they represent the graphic equivalent of his own quest as artist engaged in making symbols on the blank, white page, in the magical effort to divine meaning. This resemblance will anchor a deeper aspiration, in the poem, to keep in tune with the changing intimations of these symbols, their comings and goings, with an openness and freedom similar to the seasonal rhythm of the birds. But, at a more immediate level, the sight of the migrating birds takes him back to another set of images first evoked by that winter landscape:

while I

awoke this sunrise to a violence
of images migrating from the mind.
Skeletal forest, a sepulchral knight
riding in silence at a black tarn's edge,
hooves cannonading snow
in the white funeral of the year,
ant-like across the forehead of an alp
in iron contradiction crouched
against those gusts that urge the mallards south.
Vizor'd with blind defiance of his quest,

(*CP*, 77)

This iconography of the medieval knight on his winter quest is a representative facet of the mythology of the North, and the characteristic ethos of that mythology. It confronts the frozen wasteland of the season with an "iron contradiction", in radical contrast to the natural response of the birds to the changing needs of the season, their quest in tune with the "gusts that urge [them] south". The poem engages in a close deconstruction of the mindset of that mythology: it shows a human will pitted against the inimical forces of winter death ("skeletal forest", "sepulchral knight", "white funeral of the year" reiterate the death motif). The knight's "iron contradiction" signifies a draconian resistance against adversity of cosmic proportions; and it is also described, significantly, as "blind defiance". Implicitly wary of the inflexible, iron postures of the ethos represented by the knight, the poem seeks to embrace instead the alternative intimated by the flock of birds in seasonal flight. Walcott, in fact, makes in this poem one of his sustained critical deconstructions of the traditional metaphors of Western culture. Here the metaphors are related to the particular geography and landscape of that culture (as is also the case in "Love in the Valley"). Thus the criticism continues in this reference to the monolithic thought systems and ideologies bred out of this "Arctic" landscape:

The dark impartial Arctic,

whose glaciers encased the mastodon,
froze giant minds in marble attitudes,

(*CP*, 78)

The giant minds of the European past are virtually being identified with the formidable dimensions of the oversized mastodon; the frozen "marble attitudes" of these minds suggest an unbreachable fixity, hinting at the superhuman. A later poem, "Forest of Europe" (*SAK*), makes the same point in identical imagery: "mastodons force their systems through the snow" (*CP*, 378).

Beginning from this functional contrast between birds in seasonal migration and the iron contradiction of the knight facing the wasteland of winter, the poem's discourse turns on a number of parallel, paired opposites: temperate and tropical climes, dark and light, white and black, north and south, Arctic pole and equinox, history and cosmos. The deeper aim, however, is not to separate or see these constituent elements in opposition to each other, but to embrace the changes and differences between them – from winter dark to tropical light – as part of one cohesive, cyclic process. It is from this perspective that Walcott proceeds to reflect on a cosmos whose process persists through time with "determined grace", independent of ("impartial") the phenomenal changes in human civilization and its unceasing quests – recognizing a divine, if still unfathomable ("dark"), order:

> The style, tension of motion and the dark,
> inflexible direction of the world
> as it revolves upon its centuries
> with change of language, climate, customs, light,
> with our own prepossession day by day
> year after year with images of flight,
> survive our condemnation and the sun's
> exultant larks.

(CP, 78)

Seeking to relate positively to this complex tension between changelessness and change, Walcott's final aspiration is for the ability to combine inward stability and integratedness with openness, flexibility, suppleness. This aspiration looks forward to some of the key ideas of his thought. It is a prayer for balance in acceptance of the changing seasons of existence, from winter dark through tropic light, right on to that ripeness when the "black wings"/shadows of mortality can cross "the equinox of the clear eye" (where night and day, light and dark are of equal duration) "like a blessing".

"Tarpon"[28] is another significant poem in Walcott's attempt to observe "nature's plan". Responding to the picture presented by a tarpon, a fish remarkable in size (approximately six feet long), he perceives a pattern which seems a true paradigm of the relation between the nature of the universe and the human imagination. The poem records an actual, close-up view of a tarpon on a beach at Cedros, a small fishing district in Trinidad. Arrested by the spectacle it presents, first in its dying throes, and then of its dead bulk, Walcott is struck by the rich variety of the visual aspects and effects of that bulk in its silvery, streamlined form. As his imagination plays with the range of resemblances and correspondences they suggest, he marvels at the fact that such complexity of design can be contained within the simple, generic form of the fish – a shape "simple, like a cross". The final discovery in the poem turns on this observation.

The poem captures the full wonder and adventure of this experience for Walcott. We see the actual play of colours, lines and details on the tarpon's surface, and the pictorial images they define. His artistic eye traces the contours of these images, as they manifest resemblances to our wider world, human and natural. There is, first of all, the reality of a world of terror in the impact of the "brute pain" of the huge fish in its dying throes. At the other pole, a world of beauty lies revealed in its dead bulk, "examined in detail". This beauty is especially rich in its effects and its implications:

> Bronze, with a brass-green mould, the scales
> age like a corselet of coins,
> a net of tarnished silver joins
> the back's deep-sea blue to the tail's
> wedged, tapering Y.
> Set in a stone, triangular skull,
> ringing with gold, the open eye
> is simply, tiringly there.

(CP, 61–62)

This rich coordination of pictorial design and colours, recalling traditional ornaments in human culture, reveals a nature which is fully provident of its own aesthetic; and which, simultaneously, serves to foster the aesthetic faculty in humankind. Accordingly, a diamond reflects itself, or a ship takes shape out of the scale held up against the light. There are also, finally, images which answer to the needs of our inner world, such as the heraldic symbol of the cross, and of the ship itself.

Thus, as Walcott's eye seeks out these images, a replica of the universe, phenomenal and experiential, appears configured in the tarpon. As an analogue of the universe, however, it is its overall pattern that is most significant, the pattern of a basically simple and innocent form capable of holding a complexity representative of a world of such variety, ambiguity and contradiction:

> Can such complexity of shape,
> such bulk, terror and fury fit
> in a design so innocent,

(CP, 62)

It is in the original intimation of this unity between the One and the Many, and its mystery, that the tarpon – as apprehended by Walcott – serves as a cosmic fable. The imagination, playing a participatory role in bringing this to light, is an integral component of the whole. For a proper appreciation of this role, we need first to focus on what is being revealed about the nature of the universe in this fable. The moment of genuine epiphany for Walcott lies in the recognition of the basic *innocence* of that pattern – and understandably so, since the complexity and ambiguity are already given. It is the Blakean innocence of an order for good, of wholeness and unity. (The presence of Walcott's son at the scene provides the child motif which underlines the significance of this innocence.) The recognition also focuses the integral balance, "tension of motion" ("The Flock"), between this innocence and the complexity: "moving, but motionlessly". The imagination, without which this reality remains unseen and unrealized, is also, paradoxically, its offspring: it receives its stimulus from the rich and complex facets waiting to be explored. The imagination retains here its seminal role of questing for knowledge, prospecting for truth through the "opaque phantasmal mist", the ambiguity of the protean world it descries. Thus, in the end, Walcott's implicit ideal is for an imagination in tune with the overall pattern manifested in the tarpon: one that will maintain the same balance between innocence and complexity, remaining in touch with basic, naked reality in its questing role.

"Tarpon" is a moment of epiphany which confirms the integrity and innocence of Walcott's inclination to this faith in the wholeness and inner cohesion of the universe, and the sense of the mystery it holds for him. Importantly, in this faith, the imagination, if it is a world-making faculty, also appears as a child of nature. These are early accesses of perception that will come to fruition in the mature Walcott; and they are consistent with what it means to begin from "nature's plan". They have, moreover, significant implications in the general orientation of his search for possibility.

The search for possibility finds its fullest expression in "Guyana", as already mentioned. In this sequence of six poems, Walcott enacts the search in a metaphoric journey through the interior, taking his cue from Wilson Harris's fictional journeys through his native Guyanese landscape.[29] His explicit aim in this journey is a quest for "the lost concept, 'man' " ("Guyana I"). It is the place where he makes his first concerted effort to apprehend an order of human destiny in keeping with the goal of a fresh humanist intelligence. As such, "Guyana" is a synthesis of his various readings and perceptions of nature so far.

From the 1950s through the 1960s, a number of significant works dealing with this theme of journey through interior landscape had emerged from the Caribbean area. In addition to Harris's, there was William Hudson's *Green Mansions,* which, published as early as 1904, was reissued no less than sixteen times in the 1960s; there were also Denis Williams's *Other Leopards* (1963) and Alejo Carpentier's *Lost Steps* (1953)[30] – a work to which Walcott returns again and again for its articulation of the concept of naming. Walcott is conscious of community with these writers. Harris remains, however, the most immediate and substantial influence in his Guyana sequence, serving as an implicit guide through the Guyanese setting. The sequence closely adapts and reconstructs the essential, interlinked contexts of the novels comprising Harris's Guyana Quartet – *Palace of the Peacock* (1960), *The Far Journey of Oudin* (1961), *The Whole Armour* (1962), *The Secret Ladder* (1963) – and of *Heartland* (1964).[31] The journey into the Guyanese interior is, first of all, the opportunity to continue the mythic encounter with the natural phenomenal world of "green churning forest" on a full scale, the reverse side of which we have already seen in "Air". Walcott already shares a strong affinity with Harris in the engagement with landscape. On the stylistic level, he is also drawn to the advantages of the narrative-dramatic structure as a means of breaking out of the residual isolation of the lyric/hermetic mode which has dominated in *The Castaway.* Moreover, he has always been alert to the advantages of marrying the two (see "Tales of the Islands"). It allows him, most importantly, to extend into human society and community – a need which has become more immediate with the greater urgency of public and social issues in *The Gulf* (see chapter 4). Thus the journey involves continuous traffic between the Guyanese interior and the capital city of Georgetown.

It is useful, given Walcott's close adaptation of Harris in the sequence, to begin with a brief examination of the theme of the journey inwards in the two writers. There are basic affinities as well as important differences between them, both of which help to put Walcott's effort in the sequence into perspective. In both writers the geography of a natural, virgin landscape is a ground of primal and mythic possibility. Indeed, while many of this first generation of writers accord an important place to geography in their definitions of the region, it is in Harris and Walcott that it gains special prominence as an integral component of culture. In Harris's world, this natural phenomenal landscape constitutes the effective primordial ground for the broken and vestigial traces of the numerous traditions history has left in the region. Harris conceives of this as a returning to "the flora and fauna of legend".[32] His goal is to seek out the gateway through these vestiges to the single unifying principle between these traditions, and to arrive thereby at the ultimate ideal of the renascence of the imagination at its most original. Walcott shows a close affinity to Harris in this view. To him (especially by the time of *Another Life* and *Omeros*) the incidence of the fragments of Old World epic traditions on virgin, unexplored ground hold the potential for a primal and mythic renewal – a renewal which, returning to human interaction with the natural world, must be the roots of a fresh experiment in humanity. These ideals commit Harris and Walcott to the idea of a New World possibility; and, in both, this New World possibility has to do with the reawakened creative imagination reclaiming a primary spiritual kinship with the wider universe.

In terms of their visionary routes and modes of apprehension, there are obvious differences between the two writers. A comparison between the resolution of the Harrisian journey in *Palace of the Peacock* and Walcott's in the "Guyana" sequence highlights a significant difference. The difference will help to put certain aspects of Walcott's own orientation into perspective. In *Palace of the Peacock*, Donne and his crew, after their climactic glimpse into the miracle of creation through the waterfall, arrive at this visionary realization: "buoyed up and supported above dreams by the undivided soul and anima of the universe" (*Palace*, 152). It is a way of mystical transcendence and of apotheosis.[33] By contrast, the climactic experience of Walcott's protagonist at the waterfall ("The Falls") actively rejects the way of transcendence and apotheosis. Standing at the waterfall, his is a hubristic desire for a spiritual power capable of transcending the dangers of his mortal condition, a spiritual power that can measure up to the totality represented by the waterfall as symbol of cosmos. He comes instead to the realization that his humanity, always less than totality or cosmos, is creatively accommodated within the great flux. (The passage of the flower down the waterfall is emblematic of this.) He thus finds deliverance in acceptance of this humanity, its terrestrial condition.

This refusal of apotheosis, clearly expressed in *Dream on Monkey Mountain,* is of far-reaching revolutionary import in Walcott.[34] It comes from an instinctive sense and deeply pondered distrust of the link between the peculiar presumption of transcendence, the hierarchical principle, and the imperial ethos in the Western order. It is directly informed by his concern with the muse of man in history contained in the western European tradition of metaphors, a concern which begins to develop during this widely exploratory phase of his career. The movement towards an alternative order in abandoning dead, borrowed metaphors will come to bear especially on the challenge of an alternative to the Western muse of history. The latter appears in *Another Life* as an integral dimension of the vision of possibility which finds its true genesis here.

The journey inward is generic as an odyssey of self-discovery, but it takes quite a distinct course, and defines its own modes of struggle and apprehension in the unreclaimed territory represented by the forest of this particular landscape. The spiritual dynamic turns primarily on an inner, human nature in correspondence with an immediately experienced, natural elemental world. There are fundamental affinities between Walcott and Harris at this level, as will emerge from his adaptation of Harris's contexts. Walcott's version of the journey in "Guyana", though, is finally his own – Harris, in fact, provides a springboard for an independent logic closely determined by his earliest responses to and perceptions of the "unreclaimed" condition of the landscape. It takes the following course in this sequence of six poems: in "Guyana I" the mythic necessity of a quest is presaged by an encounter with the annihilative chaos of the untamed forest of "Air". The questing persona proceeds in "The Bush" to make, out of that very chaos, a condition of primordial unknowing – a condition which serves as access to at-onement with the natural elemental flow; from there to arrive, in "The Falls" (IV), at a discovery of self in relation to cosmos and totality. The journey concludes with the attempt at an integrative naming of that order in "A Map of the Continent" (V) and "A Georgetown Journal" (VI).

Walcott combines the experiences of the Dreamer in *Palace of the Peacock,* and the surveyor Fenwick in *The Secret Ladder* – a later incarnation associated with technology and development – for the dream journey of his own composite protagonist. In "Guyana I" he specifically adapts the context of Harris's *Secret Ladder* to present the questing persona in the guise of a surveyor engaged in exploring the interior. In that novel, the surveyor Fenwick is on a hydrographic mission aimed at reclamation of the interior, when he comes into confrontation with Poseidon, the primitive proprietor of the forest descended from a runaway African slave. The confrontation changes the nature of the task for Fenwick: the image of this ancestral figure as "a wild cannibal man of the swamps" awakens his conscience to the awesome necessity of our humanness to meet the responsibility of a secret ladder of ascent. Walcott's narrative takes off from precisely the critical turning point where Harris's surveyor finds his scientific, conventional perspectives displaced, and must begin to find new bearings. In Fenwick's case this occurs when he "beholds instead the accusing image of Poseidon" through his inverted telescope. For the surveyor of "Guyana I", "straighten[ing] from his theodolite", it is an experience of extreme psychological disorientation, brought on not by a Poseidon/god-figure but by the overpowering impact of the features and properties of the forest setting on his senses. It is the same experience of an active inner dissolution presaged by the forest in "Air". Like Lestrade hunting Makak in the bush (*Dream*), he loses his sense of his own solidity, and is undermined by fears of alien, mysterious forces which threaten his very being. "His vision whirls with dervishes, he is dust" (*CP*, 115). He experiences, in effect, the inner vortex which Walcott most fears in the state he defines as amnesia.

The task to which the surveyor returns from this kind of disorientation assumes altogether different, more complex proportions. The necessity he now faces as he "screw[s] a continent to his eyes" is to recover, with the lost sense of self, nothing less than the "lost concept, 'man' ".[35] The narrative shifts immediately onto a mythic, symbolic plane, as signified in descriptive motifs seminal to Walcott's concept of genesis out of chaos ("The Castaway"). Like "an archaic photographer, hooded in shade", he is engaged in a magical hermetic act of descrying an image; and for this, he reverts to the "crouching" animal posture, symbolic of the primordial state before human reclamation. Here the telescope, combining practical and allegorical functions, enables Walcott to re-engage, as he did in "Tarpon", the pristine mode of proceeding from the physical to the metaphysical. What appears through the telescope are dualistic and polarized perspectives: "The vault that balances on a grass blade, / the nerve-cracked ground too close for the word 'measureless' " (*CP*,

115). In the image of "the vault that balances on a grass blade", a tiny particle among the natural forms of the cosmos appears in contiguous relation to the wider cosmic span – showing, that is, the infinitesimal as an integral part of immensity/infinity. Pulling against this is the immediacy of the friable, fissured, physical earth, which features in the "too-close" exposure of the "nerve-cracked ground". The grass blade in its tussock of earth traces the figuration of man himself, consistent with the prevailing idea of man in nature central to Walcott's effort during this phase. This twofold reading thus represents a metaphysical reflection of the human scale of reality in the wider scheme of the cosmos: it focuses the dual allegiance of the human condition between the limitless and infinite on the one hand, and on the other, the bondage to finite matter, reiterated in the conceit "Ant-sized to God, god to an ant's eyes". Remarkably, time and space are grasped as one indivisible continuum (the two fuse in the aspect of a limitless vault) – an effect which gains its authority from the original power of natural observation. Walcott's surveyor persona finally confronts here the existential challenge of a humanity strung between the antinomies of infinity/essence and the finite/earthly, which represent root principles from which he must begin.

If he entered the forest/interior with the conventional, materialist preconceptions of the task, confident of his own authority and identity in relation to the territory, it is his very self that comes under siege as the territory to be explored. He must now "tread himself" – that is, search out a viable measure of wholeness through trial and struggle. The arduous, testing nature of that struggle is conveyed in the condensed power of that phrase "tread / himself". He takes up the burden of a necessarily purgatorial quest: "shouldering science he begins to tread / himself, a world that must be measured in three days" (*CP*, 115). This new goal of measuring the outer in relation to his own inner world entails, as the mythical allusion to "three days" indicates, an archetypally ritual passage – the suffering/Gethsemane of the first unreal world, death to that world, and rebirth into another. Significantly, the threefold archetype invokes the figure of Christ, deftly suggested in the icon of the cross described in the shouldering of the theodolite (the cause being that of science/progress itself). Walcott's three-day archetype contrasts with the seven-day counterpart in Harris's novel, pinpointing the differences earlier noted between the two writers. The way for Walcott lies through Gethsemane to rebirth into a pre-existent order, by contrast with the emphasis in Harris on the transformative, re-creational route of the alchemical imagination. The perils and trials of that passage, however, are peculiarly those of Walcott's world:

> The frothing shallows of the river,
> the forest so distant that it tires of blue,
> the merciless idiocy of green, green . . .

> (*CP*, 115)

These repeat the strains and stresses of his suffering of landscape as negation – the struggle against futility in the face of the endless monotony of a greenness never seeming to arrive at fruition; the desolating effects on the sensibility of what he sensed as the uncreating principle in the relentless nothingness of that same condition in "Air" and "The Swamp". Under the pressure of these agonies, the "shape [which] dilates towards him through the haze" may be, as for Makak in *Dream on Monkey Mountain,* as much hallucination as vision. It awaits discovery in the further stages of the journey.

This first poem exploits a focal metaphor which provides the operative framework for the entire sequence. It moves between the image of the bush/forest/tree of man, and that of man in the *territory* of bush/forest/tree. The narrative, playing between these related levels, extends further correspondences which form one essential network. The actual forest, embracing the entire South American landscape in which Guyana is situated, represents undeveloped New World territory; so that the persona charting this environment is exploring his own possibility as New World man. This purpose, implied in the search for the "lost concept, 'man' " ("Guyana I"), will be explicitly spelt out in "A Map of the Continent". It is important to note, however, that the New World configuration – at once man and setting – comprises not only the condition of unreclaimed nature, but also the historico-cultural setting that carries referential relationships to the Old World, as is also highlighted in "A Map of the Continent". The historico-cultural setting accounts, of necessity, for Walcott's dialectical engagement with the Old World, discussed above. The seminal principle upholding this construct of meanings remains, however, the metaphoric correspondence between man and bush/forest/tree. Branching out of this is the associated imagery of leaves, birds, flowers which, already present in the poems seen so far, will take on, in this sequence, hieroglyphic and iconographic significance.

The most concentrated deployment of this central metaphor occurs in the next poem of the sequence, "The Bush", a short poem outstanding for its compact realization of the deeper ideas contained in that metaphor. It begins the process of creative advance in the quest: the persona seeks to embrace the very state of unknowing (overcoming the threat of an annihilative chaos) as a means of purging an unregenerate consciousness, leaving himself open, in the process, to an organic at-onement with the natural, elemental flow. The central experience is a surrender to a cleansing darkness identified with a primordial return to the bush:

> Together they walked through a thickness pinned with birds
>
> . . . .
>
> Dark climbed their knees until their heads were dark.

> (*CP*, 116)

The poem dramatizes this process through a graphic delineation of the repetition of the tree form in the human, an ingeniously crafted conceit which has the appeal of an authentic visual resemblance. The thickness being trekked is the bush of his own head of hair, burdened by rank images/thoughts and their sterile strivings, the latter symbolized by the fake, artificial birds (grackles and flycatchers) "pinned" to its foliage/hair. The climbing elemental power travels upwards from the knee/trunk/body, where the organic bond with earth and the natural and elemental begins. The "darkness" is that of this elemental power in its primordial state of unknowing, and it climbs from here to effect its purgatorial purpose: to rid the consciousness of the oppressive weight of unregenerate thoughts, concepts and values. They are mowed down like so many dead leaves: "Thoughts fell from him like leaves" (*CP*, 116). (The reference to the castaway's goal of abandoning dead metaphors is implicit.) A subtle assimilation of the medusa motif from *The Secret Ladder* underlines the point: the crew who accompany Fenwick represent false selves/heads (especially Jordan, his Gorgon-headed storekeeper) that must be overcome. Walcott picks up this allusion in the "they" who walk together at the beginning of the poem, representative of corruptive selves/thoughts/words. At the end of that cleansing experience, the pronoun changes from the plural "they" to the singular "he"/"him", marking the emergence of a single cohesive self.

This reference to "he" is directly associated with the presence of Walcott's persona as poet in the poem. The presence of his poetic persona, subsumed in a composite explorer figure comprising surveyor, artist and anthropologist, is an important and distinctive feature. With it, the act of artistic creation, the making of the poem, comes into the foreground of the poem's meaning. Thus the experience progresses from the initial gesture of "shaking words from their heads" to the completion of "pacing the poem". Essentially, the act of artistic creation is projected as a paradigm of the consciousness in the process of becoming, its movement identical with what we have just seen happening in this phase of the quest. As such, it expresses, first, the significance of the personal odyssey of Walcott the poet as the basis of these perceptions and insights.[36] More crucially, it serves as the focus for identifying an ideal of artistic discovery:

> He followed, that was all,
> his mind, one step behind,
> pacing the poem, going where it was going.
>
> (*CP*, 116)

The act of poetry as defined here consists in a process of self-discovery in which one is guided by the natural, organic principles of one's being, as against being mind-directed. This does not mean, however, a jettisoning of the mind: the latter is still in responsive attendance, taking direction from the organic rhythms and flow of the natural, elemental body/earth. The poem conveys this complex of ideas with an impressive succinctness and a colloquial ease which has come into its own strength by the time of *The Gulf.*

This emphasis on a consciousness directed from "nature" rather than "mind" bears a polemical thrust. It is informed by what we have identified as Walcott's growing disaffection with the premises of the Old World, Western tradition. One can see in this emphasis – probably unconscious and therefore all the more effective – a virtual reversal of the Cartesian premise *Cogito, ergo sum*, representative of the primacy of the mind factor in the Western metaphysical tradition. One notable image focuses the particular terms of this reversal for Walcott – the image of "the clotting sun" towards which mock birds strain unnaturally. This image cluster expresses the idea of an unnatural, forced striving upward, out of the darkness of the native bush towards the sun as pre-eminent, transcendent symbol of light and life. The self-immolating, corruptive effects of the unnatural striving towards this "one target" are reflected in a baleful, apocalyptic clotting sun. The sun, traditionally mythologized as cosmic Eye/Light, stands as an archetypal emblem of faith in the god/essence/supremacy factor: it carries the associations of the hierarchical, imperial principle which, as we have seen, Walcott is moving to resist during this phase. Interestingly, the poem virtually turns the sun's symbolic position upside down for an "ascent" relocated in the lower sphere of the natural.

The next poem in the sequence presents a significant development. So far, it is predominantly the inner self that has been engaged in Walcott's reading of "nature's plan"; here he moves out of the residual apartness of that hermetic, reflective mode (a source of painful misgivings in poems like "Crusoe's Island") to take account of the equally vital element of living community. This dimension is integral to the culminating discovery of "The Falls". "The White Town" achieves this through a dramatic shift in the journey: an outreach from the Guyanese interior, a vast hinterland, into Georgetown, the capital. Georgetown presents the image of a community in the grip of some dumb force and ill genius, as if waiting for an explosive release. The disturbing vacancy of that condition seems to stare back from the striking whiteness of the town in physical appearance. (Until the 1960s, Georgetown was still a city of white wooden buildings.) That whiteness strikes Walcott as the signal of a deep disturbance, and continues to haunt him throughout the journey in the recurrent phrase "the white town". The Georgetown which Walcott was visiting during this period of the mid-1960s was just recovering from a quite severe spell of riots, strikes and burnings, the result of racial and political crises. The physical whiteness of the town, as if belying the horrors and squalor of this aftermath, appears as a strange pall of abnormality hanging over the society. The impact of this is captured most forcefully in the following image: "the burghers glare of whitewashed houses / outstaring guilt" (*CP*, 116). It is as if that whiteness, characteristic especially of the homes of the bourgeoisie, is proffered in bold, unashamed denial of the transgressions of that class. But the poem is most concerned with the plight of Guyana's artists, the native sons who are most sensitive to and have internalized its problems. They all manifest some form or other of a deep derangement:

> "Man, all the men in that damned country mad!"
> There was the joke on W. and Mayakovsky.
> There was the charred bush of a man found in the morning,
>
> . . . .
>
>   there was the anthropologist
> dropping on soft pads from the thorn branches
> to the first stance hearing the vowels
> fur in his throat the hoarse
> pebbles of consonants rattling his parched gullet,
> there was the poet howling in vines of syntax
>
>   (*CP*, 116)

Several outstanding case histories of Guyana's artists are cited in this testimony. There is the case of Wilson Harris himself, who, lost on a surveying expedition for some time, sent the authorities to Mayakovsky, the Russian revolutionary writer, for an answer on his return; of Mittelholzer, who burnt himself to death in an English field. It also invokes the case of Denis Williams, as reflected in his novel *Other Leopards*. In that novel the protagonist Lionel Froad, an archaeological draughtsman, after stabbing his paternalistic English boss, goes mad in the desert, strips himself naked and climbs a thorn tree. The madness of that brotherhood seems to suggest some encounter with "the bush within" – the bush that looms behind the crisis of the beleaguered society. By the same token, the case histories extend to include those of other Caribbean artists like Walcott himself, who lies at the centre of "Guyana's" protagonist: "there was the poet howling in vines of syntax". The crisis of the white town, like the journey, is of course that of Caribbean society as a whole.

"The Falls" marks the climax of the journey. We arrive here at the fulfilment of the specific goal undertaken in "Guyana I" – the quester's realization of self in relation to world/cosmos, which means the rediscovery of a human order. In terms of actual, narrative progress, he is now at the waterfall (the famous Kaieteur Falls of Guyana), and is contemplating a fearless leap down the waterfall to a transcendent death.[37] Thus:

> Their barrelling roar would open like a white oven
> for him,
> who was a spirit now, who could not burn or drown.

(CP, 117)

The waterfall has served, archetypally, as a powerful symbol encoding complex metaphysical and mythic ideas. It is the natural, elemental form which most strikingly manifests the principle of cosmic motion known as the Heraclitean flux – the cyclic transmutation of the four elements (fire, air, water, earth) into one, indivisible cosmic energy.[38] Its graphic image as "the smoke that thundered" is emblematic of the core metaphysical idea in the Heraclitean concept: the reconciliation of conflicting elements (fire and water as the most polarized) into one harmonized continuum. Thus the quester, in seeking a door through the waterfall, aspires to a transcendent state beyond his earthly and mortal sphere, where he remains a creature susceptible to separate, conflicting properties (burning or drowning). As with Harris's crew "hammering in blindness and frustration with the fist of the waterfall" (*Palace,*

141), he has arrived here at the final limits of imaginative risk. It is a point at which he must either perish, or find regeneration through a radical transformation in consciousness.

At this point of extremity, the distant sounds of the human traffic of the white town overtake him at the waterfall. The spiritual transcendence he yearns for at this stage is very much a yearning for a higher deliverance from the characteristic afflictions of "white" Georgetown, the pressures of which have proved inescapable, as seen in the preceding stage of the journey. Now the sounds of its familiar, daily human traffic, their force and volume indistinguishable from that of the waterfall, come with the impact of a sudden realization:

> but the noise boiled to the traffic of a white town
> of bicycles, pigeons, bells, smoke, trains at the rush hour
>
> revolving to this roar.

(*CP*, 117)

This striking coincidence leads to a profound recognition, and marks the visionary climax of the journey. In effect, the ordinary, lesser currents of everyday living gather to a totality answering to that of the cosmic flux, a totality which, similarly, constitutes the cyclic continuum of life in the human counterpart. This recognition is what will reorient him towards a creative adjustment to the element of his own humanity, by which he is virtually being reclaimed at this point. We need to look closely, however, at the depth of suggestion contained in the particles of experience Walcott brings together in "bicycles, pigeons, bells, smoke, trains at the rush hour". They comprise domestic, routine objects and features, all associated with familiar motions and activities of the daily round. They are objects associated with the "ambush of little infinities" which Walcott affirms as the familiar substance that upholds our humanity ("Guyana VI"). They betoken, as he puts it elsewhere, "terror enough in the habitual, / miracle enough in the familiar" ("Ebb", *The Gulf*). It is as if the hearing is burrowing beneath "the tumult and the shouting" of the larger social crises that besiege the white town, to what subsists in this tenacious content. Thus there are bicycles riding to the fulfilment of some purpose; trains at the rush hour signifying acceleration in times of urgency; bells which echo both annunciation/joy and tolling rhythms; signals of aspiration in the flight of the pigeon and rising smoke. In effect, together they represent a plenitude "containing" the rising and falling rhythms, the conflicting currents of the flux of humanity – as in the Heraclitean reconciliation of elements in the cosmic flux.

This coincidence of town and waterfall is not a matter of the human traffic aspiring to a power equal to that of the cosmic. It is rather, on Walcott's part, the intuitional grasp of one indivisible life principle extending through external nature and nature in the human, and its essential wholeness. Thus it is the graphic picture of the flower above the waterfall (an original feature at Kaieteur Falls) which, with sudden revelatory impact, crystallizes the pattern of the human relation to the totality of its world. Poised above the waterfall, the flower, as a lesser form, is not threatened by its tremendous force: instead it is creatively accommodated by its very frailty, its "weightlessness", to be borne along by the greater flow, and sustained within it. Thus creatively adjusted, it remains less than essence/totality, but attains its own wholeness and completeness as efflorescence, flowering out of essence. The course of its passage/destiny along the great flux, therefore, even as it moves towards finitude, constitutes its own fulfilment and completion. It is in the light of this deeply perceived design that Walcott's questing persona renounces the desire to attain essence and, instead, orients himself as "a flower" within the totality of the wider flux:

> He was a flower,
> weightless. He would float down.

(CP, 117)

(This parallels Makak's renunciation of "essence" in the white goddess.) In moral and spiritual terms, it means the acceptance of his own element in a humanity complete in its condition of frailty and conflicting currents; and, importantly, with a strong faith in the greater wholeness behind it all. This is the belief that Walcott terms the finding of "earth". It represents the foundations of his vision as a "metaphysical realist", as Brodsky rightly defines it.[39] An especially remarkable feature is the authority of the speaking voice in this poem – the earthiness of idiom, directness and economy with which it delivers these visionary ideas.

The rejection of the fearless, mystical leap of transcendence for this creative adjustment represents the beginnings of a break with the dominant mode of the metaphysics of the Western tradition in this exploratory phase of Walcott's career. The "Guyana" sequence thus represents a milestone in the process of abandoning dead metaphors, an effort that culminates in *Another Life*. The effort pivots, as noted earlier, on the rejection of what he detects as the inherent error of the way of transcendence: the seeds of the principle of godlike triumph, of hubris, and the will to dominion as the origin of the imperial ideal.

The poem is also demonstrative of the dynamic of renewal in Walcott's emerging aesthetic. The latter is the other, related facet of the dialectical engagement with the Old World tradition, as identified in our analysis of "The Sea Is History". The dynamic pivots on his recovery of archetypal, human principles as they begin in the natural and elemental. We have a classic example of this in the fresh apprehension of the principles underlying the concept of Heraclitean flux, as it is manifested in the waterfall. We witness an almost miraculous return to the process of natural observation from which ontological meaning and mythologies derive. Here we can return to Harris's apt description of the phenomenon as the "revitalization of the fauna and flora of legend".[40] It is a feature that testifies to the mythic and spiritual value of Walcott's route through "nature's plan". It is fascinating to note, in the context of this renewal, how Walcott's flower echoes the biblical flower in its theme of frailty (Psalm 103); echoes too, its resurgence in Joyce's Bloom as "the flower that bloometh"; carrying forward the seminal faiths in both, and, at the same time, extending and enriching their meanings with the particular philosophical emphases of what is a truly novel, indigenous variant of the image: "the waterfall reciting its single flower" ("Guyana V").

The next poem is virtually a review of the journey through the interior, placing it in the context of the wider significance of its peculiar setting. Walcott devises an original and yet strikingly accurate conceit to engage this discourse. Seeing the representative Guyanese landscape as one with the wider South American configuration, he charts in "a map of the continent" the boundaries within which the unique resources, purpose and possibilities of the area define themselves. It is bordered at one end by the legacy of past civilization and its traditions, as featured in the achievement of Jorge Luis Borges, the Argentinian writer; and, at the other end, by the unreclaimed world of the buck in the Rupununi. Within this essential complex of history, tradition and landscape the map unfolds to show the features which make for a unique New World promise, the first formal definition of which occurs here.

The informing idea in the conception of the map is that Borges, as lexicographer and artist, represents "shelves forested with titles", by contrast with "trunks that wait for names" at the naked edge of the world inhabited by the Amazonian Indian. "A Map of the Continent" employs, as earlier observed, the focal metaphor of the tree/bush of man to explore its meanings. Borges is identified with books recording civilizations, which equals territories and worlds already explored. In the case of the Amazonian Indian, the "trunks that wait for names" stand for unreclaimed territory, hence, by contrast with the former, unrecorded and untitled. Walcott's terms of reference hark back to the engagement with landscape as negation – the explored and historied versus the unexplored and unhistoried. Here the explored is further equated with the "named", spelling out this important concept. More immediately, these two references bring into the foreground the remarkable coincidence of seeming opposites which give the region its distinct novelty; and which are, indeed, the very poles within which Walcott's own imagination works, as we have tried to show in this chapter. The territory of Borges seems worlds apart from that of the Amazonian Indian; but the argument works to uncover the essential interchangeability and sameness of the two, to the point where they cohere into one continuous reality.

It is necessary to attempt a review of Borges's achievement and its special significance for Walcott, in order to properly enter the context of the argument. Both as the well-known librarian of Buenos Aires, and in his peculiar achievement as an artist, Borges is aptly described as the custodian of letters and tradition. His works range over civilizations and traditions through the ages and climes, and the essential focus is on the various metaphysical efforts they present. Borges reconstructs them in ingeniously disguised fictions to project a sceptical perspective: he sees a nightmarish proliferation of labyrinthine explanations "devised by men, . . . destined to be deciphered by men", while a perennial, inscrutable order of the universe persists intact (*Labyrinths*).[41] Given this kind of engagement, Borges is steeped in an archaism to which Walcott responds most deeply. This archaism distils, for him, a quality of timelessness and instantaneity which are associated with a singular concept of time. It is there that he locates the true genius of Borges. He explains it in the following way. Seasonal, temperate nature fostered the concept of cyclic time and its successive rhythms of change. In Borges's world, by contrast, that of seasonless, equatorial nature, what seemed manifestations of change were heraldic of an instantaneity, an incidence of simultaneity, consistent with the deepest rhythms of the earth.[42] Walcott is factually incorrect in placing Borges in seasonless equatorial nature, since Argentina is in the temperate zone. But he slips into this oversight from a perspective that is fundamental to his outlook on the region. He sees the entire South American configuration as one, vis-à-vis the North; and he is clearly thinking in broad, generic terms of the temperate North versus the nontemperate South. Borges, as one of the main voices of the South American setting, is representative of what Walcott perceives as the characteristic genius of the ex-colonized New World territory of the South; and of the particular epistemological difference between North and South articulated in his comment cited abocve. The oversight about Argentina's climate notwithstanding, therefore, it is important to cite his profound reflection on the recognition of instantaneity and simultaneity versus the concept of cyclic time and its successive rhythms. In his reading of Borges, it is by virtue of this very grasp on instantaneity and simultaneity that the latter, as arch-traditionalist, becomes paradoxically expressive of the profoundly primal genius of his landscape.

This seminal meaning is carried within the interplay of the metaphor of the tree of man between the world of Borges and that of the Amerindian. Essential correspondences between civilized and primal spheres emerge from this metaphoric play, powerful in imaginative and intellectual concentration. It fuses two of the major facets of the dynamic of metaphor in Walcott: the more seminal one of discovery of the principle of correspondences that run from nature to culture; and the development of argument through the exercise of wit, in the manner of the metaphysical conceit. In the opening comparison, for example, the image makes us see the leaves and tree trunks of the Amerindian's forest repeated in the books and bookshelves of Borges's realm, comprised of the same basic material; it goes right back, in fact, to the organic roots of this correspondence, expressed in the semantic transfer from leaves of trees to leaves of books. (This organic link between metaphor and linguistic process is integral to Walcott's aesthetic.) The focus is, however, on the actions and purposes associated with these respective forests of man, as indicated in the antithesis between "with titles" (of Borges's forest) and "wait for names"/untitled (in the Amerindian's). The "titled" [book-] shelves of Borges signify territories already explored, by contrast with the Amerindian's territory which, awaiting exploration, remains unnamed. The vital factor being focused in this dialectic is the act of discovery, and the task of naming (extended in the motif of titling books), that sacred article in Walcott's credo, consists in this act of discovery. It is this primal necessity of discovery/naming, the central purpose of the journey through the interior, that is the crucial link between them.

The poem goes on to stress this point in the pairing of the motifs of pen and spear: "One hefts a pen, the other a bone spear" (*CP*, 118). The pen is "heft" in the acts of imaginative exploration recorded in the books (the artistic persona continues to serve as generic quester), just as the spear is "heft" by the Amerindian to explore and exploit his untamed world. The next line captures the shared posture of the effort in a most significant aspect: "the fish thrashing green air / on a pen's hook" (*CP*, 118). Conflating the "fishing" in metaphysical and physical spheres, the image is rich in philosophical implications. It shows the act of exploration as a struggle with green air, a Walcottian motif which here combines the notions of the immature and the risk of the unknown, in the face of the mystery of the universe. Man in this effort is always something of a fish out of its element: "the fish thrashing green air / on a pen's hook". Significantly, it is the primal feature, the spear-flash, which takes the lead in illuminating this truth. The perception stresses the sameness of the enterprise, despite the vast records of knowledge that separate the world of the buck from that of Borges. Borges's ironic eye sees this repetition as a perpetuation of labyrinths. In Walcott's version, though, the greater truth of an affirmative order prevails "above" in the reality of the "falls reciting its single flower" (*CP*, 118).

This pattern of equivalence refers to the reality of one shared territory between the two extremities of the continent, and the incidence of the "vigorous, rotting leaves" (*CP*, 118) stretching continuous between them underlines this in a dramatic way. A very literal image, it also carries intimations of the numinous. Vigorous and rotting, the rhythms of living and dying, of origins and detritus, are incident and simultaneous in the shared, continuous territory between Borges and the Amerindian – invoking the "instantaneity" of Borges's apprehension of time, signalling the crossing of past civilization and precivilized, primal zones in his vision. It is, in fact, in Borges's eyes that the map of the continent "uncurls" to reveal its final pattern of reality. This is effectively dramatized. Borges becomes the medium of the meeting of the primal world with that of the past, in what is a veritable transfusion between them. Returning through aeons of time, he takes on the aspect of the motionless, the "sleep" of the timeless. It is the very point at which he recaptures the primal reality of the Amerindian's sphere: "The lexicographer's lizard eyes are curled / in sleep. The Amazonian Indian enters them" (*CP*, 118). We see the penetration of the Amazonian Indian's sphere into Borges's "needle's eyes"; that is, Borges's interiorization of that sphere. Walcott identifies Borges with the prehistoric lizard – an image which recurs when, some years later, he experiences an epiphany in the presence of the repose of the aging writer.[43] The "heraldic lizard" retains a permanent place in Walcott's mythic vocabulary as a symbol of the prehistoric surviving across historic time. It becomes a fitting emblem for the Borges who radiates the primal through his very immersion in time and traditions.

It is important to note, however, that the emphasis falls on the synthesis between old and new territory involved in the crossing of the two worlds. It is not the recovery of the purely primal (as Walcott's naming is not that of the first Adam) but a hold on the primal, deepened and enriched by the knowledge and cumulative experience of the past. Thus: "thunders, thickens and shimmers the one age of the world". It is this synthesis which carries its peculiar possibility of renewal. "A Map of the Continent" thus confirms and deepens our insight into the vision of renewal in Walcott. The New World is finally, uniquely placed for the long view across history to prehistory, and to revitalize, thereby, the original human covenant of naming/discovery in which the spiritual bond begins.

"Guyana V" marks the end of the engagement with the interior. "Guyana VI: A Georgetown Journal", moving back into Georgetown, is the effort at a new orientation to the actual setting of the white town. The poem becomes a meditative response to the conditions and prospects of the country. Walcott, as poet/observer, returns to the disheartening conditions of the white town, which become a test of the faiths realized in the interior. Thus the poem begins in elegiac strains in tune with the despairing mood and torpor of the town's sluggish canals (another distinctive feature of Georgetown). This should be a young country poised for emergence and self-discovery. Instead, overtures of aspiration (signalled in the actor "ris[ing] to the roar of the playhouse") seem sadly thwarted, destined to yield to the dampening effects of unchanging emptiness and neglect in the setting (like its "rust[ing]" train, "travelling to a few sad sparks"). Walcott responds with an elegy for this unfulfilled condition; but he extends an expression of prayerful and prophetic faith in the future of the country, in the light of the truths discovered in "The Falls":

> The age will know its own name when it comes,
>
> . . . .
>
> with the same care, the precise exhilaration
> with which the heron's foot pronounces "earth".

(CP, 122)

There is, in this poem, a tug of war between the strains of pessimism in keeping with the plight of the country, and this will to faith: it smacks, possibly, of the kind of resignation which led Gordon Rohlehr to see *The Gulf* as expressive of Walcott's early "withering into truth".[44] Despite the strains of pessimism, however, the elation and faith of a fresh order of intelligence win through in the end. We have an earnest of this in Walcott's identification of his own inner process, as poet in quest of Imagination, with that of the country, which also signals the effort to integrate the poetic self into its living community:

> What if, impulsive, delicate bird,
> one instinct made you rise,
> out of this life, into another's,
> then from another's, circling to your own?

(CP, 122)

Postscript – "Love in the Valley"

We conclude with "Love in the Valley", a poem which serves as a fitting postscript to what this chapter has identified as the informing purpose of this exploratory phase of Walcott's career: the abandoning of dead metaphors. In this powerfully allusive poem, he gives expression to an anguished need to resist the residual pull of Western metaphors, of certain particular aspects of their metaphysics. He wants, specifically, to resist the kind of love epitomized in the towering stature of the tragic heroines of Hardy and Pasternak:

> I feared the depth of whiteness,
>
> I feared the numbing kiss
> of those women of winter,
> Bathsheba, Lara, Tess
>
> whose tragedy made less
> of life, whose love was more
> than love or literature.[45]

(The Gulf, 64)

The sentiments expressed in these lines penetrate to an original analysis of the Western imagination. Love of that order is the product of a winter landscape, conceived in the shadow of its seasonal death. That is, as love conceived in answer to internalization of that death, it is larger than life, and ends up vitiating the reality of life itself. It is, therefore, the way of the truly pernicious death of paralysis and alienation. The biblical reverberations of the "valley of the shadow of death" permeate the poem, deepening these intimations. Walcott wants to resist its seductions, and fears the kiss of death he climactically identifies with its whiteness. This whiteness is, as the poem states, extremely deep: it is the whiteness of winter snow seen as inseparable from the whiteness of colour/race and culture. It makes this poem an original perception of the organic connection between climate, ethnicity and cosmology.[46]

"Love in the Valley" is a deeply personal and confessional statement about Walcott's struggle to overcome artistic aspiration (love as ideal of creativity) of the transcendent scale analysed here. He is well aware of the lingering effects of this tradition of "whiteness" in aggravating the soul-searing isolation of his different landscape, and its tests of faith. Thus the surreal play of images from Hardy and Pasternak that continue to haunt him. But he has also come to know of an alternative possibility that begins in that very landscape.

CHAPTER FOUR

Revolutionary Creed, Race, Politics and Society

Towards the Definition of a Revolutionary Creed: "What the Twilight Says" and "The Muse of History"

Chapter 3 presented a Walcott fully engaged in the internalized explorations of *The Castaway* and *The Gulf*. From the mid-1960s, however, the period of composition of the poems of *The Gulf* and the beginning of *Another Life*, dramatic developments on the public scene are engaging his attention equally strongly, as is reflected in a number of important poems in *The Gulf*. This period sees the peak of revolutionary activity in the United States (the transition from the era of Martin Luther King to that of Malcolm X); it also sees the intensification of Third World anti-imperialist struggle, under the impetus of leftist ideology, spearheaded in the region by the example of Cuba. In Trinidad, these influences lie behind an upsurge in militant anti-establishment activity which rallied and gained momentum under the banner of black nationalism. It was to climax in the historic Black Power uprising of

February 1970,[1] a mass protest against local white and foreign monopoly of the economy, which nearly toppled the Eric Williams government that had brought the island to national independence in 1962.

The closing years of the 1960s, building up to this explosion, is a scene rife with the espousal and active expression of black nationalist doctrine, especially visible in the cultivation of Africa and its symbols. Marrying black nationalist with socialist faiths, the revolutionary movement draws its exponents from diverse segments of the society: trade union leaders, intellectuals, academics and university students, and the grassroots. Walcott, the poet/hermit was never anything but a public figure – necessarily so as resident artist, as director of the Theatre Workshop, and from his stint in local journalism (1962–66). He is a directly concerned party in this climate of revolutionary definition and expression. He becomes acutely sensitive to its polemics of political and cultural definition, and is prompted to make a definitive statement, especially since his own effort comes implicitly under siege for its clear links with the Western tradition. He makes his statement in two important essays written during the period, "What the Twilight Says" (1970), and "The Muse of History".[2]

These two essays stand as important testimonies in Walcott's oeuvre for the following reason: he undertakes in them a sustained, systematic reflection on the core ideas and values underlying his artistic directions, with a view to articulating his position on revolutionary possibility and regional identity. They are all the more clearly focused and definitive in this aim because written under the pressure and urgency of polemical defence. Composition of "Twilight" began in 1968, while the Black Power movement was gaining momentum; and "The Muse of History" was written in the aftermath of the Black Power revolution, when the new "black aesthetic" was well on its way to consolidating itself. Walcott turns appropriately to the essay form as the ideal medium for his expository and polemical purpose. (West Indian artists, incidentally, have made extensive use of the essay form for exposition of their views on the issue of identity, preceding the critics in their sense of the urgency of revolutionary definition.) An examination of his views and definitions in these pieces will help towards an appreciation of the revolutionary creed which developed from these earlier phases of his career. The essentials of this creed underlie his entire achievement.

"What the Twilight Says" takes its place in Walcott's creative oeuvre as a classic in its own right. On the formal level, it takes the essay mode to fresh levels of accomplishment. As a document containing much of the essential Walcott, it will remain vital to the study of his work. Its distinction derives from a singular combination of stylistic and thematic strengths. It presents a prose deeply inspired by the lyrical voice of Walcott, and, side by side with this, the blistering polemical tone no less inspired – bringing two prominent voices of the Walcott sensibility together in one place. He writes this essay as an overture to *Dream on Monkey Mountain and Other Plays* (1970), the first international publication of his plays. For this overture, he takes the approach of an autobiographical record, tracing the stages of his creative struggle towards a native discovery, as carried in the development of his work in drama and theatre, and reflected in the developing style of his plays. The overture retraces this progress from his early classical apprenticeship (*Henri Christophe*), through his growing penetration into the cultural and social environment (*The Sea at Dauphin* and *Ti-Jean and His Brothers*), to the discovery of a native aesthetic culminating in *Dream*, a seminal statement on identity. The "twilight" symbol which provides his title is typically multiple in metaphorical significance. On the primary level, however, it focuses the importance and integrity of this autobiographical testimony. Featuring almost as a personal coat of arms for Walcott, it signals his beginnings (and those of his generation) in the period of "the withdrawal of empire and the beginning of our doubt".[3] It claims and establishes his colonial origins; and, evoking the dividedness and marginality of these origins, its symbolism also heralds the mission of searching out a clear light and truth. As in *Another Life,* the levels of his personal, artistic growth and his growth in social and cultural awareness are integrated in this autobiographical context. "What the Twilight Says" thus includes a very strong confessional, self-diagnostic strain, reflecting on his own "wrestling contradiction of being white in mind and black in body", and the crucial struggle to come to terms with this core conflict.[4]

This autobiographical record, however, serves mainly to contextualize his substantive theme and objective: the exposition and defence of the core principles and beliefs underlying his directions, and his quarrel with the tenets of a contemporary revolutionary doctrine radically opposed to his own. His most immediate quarrel is with black nationalist doctrine and its ideology of African revival as the basis of revolutionary possibility. This doctrine is at root, in Walcott's view, a vision of liberation based on race, which he is strictly concerned to denounce. The rebuttal of its values engages him in the most strident and thoroughgoing polemics of his career so far, carrying over into

"The Muse of History" and the salvos of chapters 19 and 22 in *Another Life*. He defends this essential position again in an interview entitled "Any Revolution Based on Race Is Suicidal" (1973), an important piece to which we will return.[5]

But what is most pressing for Walcott from the outset is the issue of the black aesthetic advocated by this doctrine. The racial premise of this aesthetic strikes at the core question of the heritage of the colonizer's language and tradition, and their place in the struggle for independent expression. It is here that we come to the "sticking place" of Walcott's polemical cause in these essays: his own definitive acceptance of the legacy of the English tongue in an aesthetic aimed at self-definition. He is intent, in "Twilight", on affirming the acceptance of and commitment to that legacy, and the terms on which he does so. He resumes this purpose in "The Muse of History". The latter, an essay of much wider scope, undertakes a sustained analysis of the indigenization of the diasporan legacies of the Old World in a New World setting. In his discourse on this theme, Walcott's defence of the assimilation/appropriation of the colonizer's language remains a major emphasis, aimed at refuting the claims of a black aesthetic.

Certain key points emerge from his defence of his position in the two essays. Made with the force of declarative statements, they come together, in review, as the core articles of one cohesive faith. One of the earliest of these statements occurs in "Twilight": "Pastoralists of the African revival should know that what is needed is not new names for old things, or old names for old things, but the faith of using the old names anew . . .".[6] Given Walcott's perspective on the middle passage experience as the amnesiac loss of the names and gods of ancestral Africa (see "Laventille"), it is consistent that he should regard the effort at an African revival as "new names for old things, or old names for old things". Accordingly, the old names to be renewed by faith are, primarily, the "given" ones of the Western colonial heritage. We need to put aside for the time being this "placing" of the two ancestries in the dialectic, to note that Walcott's argument is privileging a faith which has the power to renew as a distinct possibility for the region. The recognition bears the seeds of a key article of the Walcott credo, the concept of a New World renewal which is developed during this exploratory phase of his career. Renewal in Walcott, though, is a process of far more complex and far-reaching aspects than is encompassed in the statement cited above. It has a twofold, related movement in his work. First, his engagement with the given names/metaphors of the

Western tradition is primarily a dialectical one, which seeks to subvert the constructs of its history, and to recover timeless, primal values from the reaches of prehistory. Renewal also finds its vital element in a faith – the faith invoked in the statement being considered – generated in the task of naming/discovery which is a prime necessity of the region as new territory. Both of these distinct routes to renewal are already manifest in the aesthetic emerging from his work so far.

The idea of renewal of the old names, however, links in with another major statement on the significance of his particular approach. Speaking of his personal experience of adapting the given language to his environment, the "torture of articulation" this involves, he describes the originality of endeavour and peculiar challenge which the effort represents: "the only way to re-create this language was to share in the torture of its articulation. This did not mean the jettisoning of 'culture' but, by the writer's making creative use of his schizophrenia, *an electric fusion of the old and the new*" (my italics).[7] "An electric fusion of the old and the new" is one of the most comprehensive and inclusive definitions of Walcott's effort and its dynamic. To understand where he locates revolutionary possibility, we need to identify the nature of this fusion, and the constituents of its end product in his work. It is a matter which calls for careful analysis, to be attempted in the ensuing pages of this section. One initial, fundamental import of the process signified in this "electric fusion", however, is the assimilation of the old to the purposes of the new – in which the principle of renewal is being reiterated.

It is "The Muse of History", as already observed, that gives prominence to the question of the nature of the relationship and the achievement involved in this engagement with the Old World legacy of the colonizer, which Walcott sees as part of historical necessity in the ex-colonized, New World setting. He goes to a number of writers in the same zone who share this ex-colonial environment – from the French-speaking Antilles, St John Perse and Aimé Césaire; and from the Hispanic South American setting, Borges and Neruda. The list extends also to Whitman, the poet of the early New World landscape of North America. In their diverse concerns, he contends – and his appreciation of their works is informed by strong poetic empathy – these writers show fundamental community and fellowship in one salient particular: an inherited language is infused with the ethos and spirit of elemental discovery. Responding to Neruda and these "great poets of the New World", he expresses it thus: "this awe of the numinous, this elemental privilege of naming the New World which annihilates history in our great poets, an elation common to all of them, whether they are aligned by heritage to Crusoe and Prospero or to Friday and Caliban".[8] Alejo Carpentier, though not mentioned here, is firmly established in this community as the writer who crystallizes the central meaning of this new spirit for Walcott, providing an important epigraph to *Another Life*: "the milieu which was slowly revealing to me the nature of its values: Adam's task of giving things their names".[9] It is this act of naming, served in the ethos of elemental discovery, that finally distinguishes a New World community of purpose. Giving primacy to this concept of naming, "Muse" foregrounds an important element in the process of recreating the inherited legacy/language – the incidence of this legacy in a "new" landscape. The "virginal" landscape itself makes a difference and is the very agent of this act of naming/discovery. Walcott cites examples of the spirit of elemental discovery that infuses the lyricism of poets like Neruda and Césaire. In this example from Césaire, a celebratory lyricism of awakening to landscape is shot through with the rhythms of an embattled self-assertion:

> I want to hear a song in which the rainbow breaks
> and the curlew alights among forgotten shores
> I want the liana creeping on the palm-tree
> (on the trunk of the present 'tis our stubborn future)
> I want the conquistador with unsealed armour
> lying down in death of perfumed flowers,[10]

The same dynamic of elemental discovery accounts for the strong presence of landscape and the profound lyricism it generates in Walcott's work.[11]

Walcott's route to renewal is, as we have seen, mainly through a dialectical relationship to the Western Old World tradition, and bears a strong revolutionary purpose in seeking to break with the established myths and premises of its older heritage of metaphors, in order to seek out a fresh order of humanist intelligence. (The effort to "abandon dead metaphors", begun in *The Castaway* and *The Gulf*, will come to culmination in *Another Life*.) The key question, though, is this: in what way does this path to renewal answer to a revolutionary alternative that establishes the ethnic and cultural particulars of a Caribbean, New World identity? Put another way: does Walcott offer, in place of the African ethnicity invoked by black nationalist doctrine, an alternative concept of Caribbean identity that has its own ethnic and cultural definition; or does what he offers remain filial, tributary, and finally in dependent relationship to the colonizer's tradition? This is the deeper, inclusive level at which the question of revolutionary possibility must be answered.

The notion of fusion, one context of which we have already met, is often cited in Walcott's comments on West Indianness. It is repeated, especially in "Twilight", in terms like "hybrid", "mongrel", "mulatto of culture" (that double-faced coinage). Is he then claiming both European and African ancestries as constitutive of a new mixed entity in which West Indianness consists – expressing a belief, therefore, in a syncretic model (which would also apply to the other "disadvantaged" ancestries that have undergone the colonial experience)? In Walcott's case there would be immediately problematic aspects to this definition, since it is clear that the Western legacy dominates in his work. Where are the traces of the African legacy in the poetry? (The situation in the drama is different, for reasons to be dealt with later.) We need to proceed carefully here. Walcott has always expressed a sincere atavistic bond, an instinctual gut loyalty to his African roots;[12] but it is not the same thing as going the route of African ancestral tradition in a "hybrid" aesthetic. The following is the kind of affirmation from Walcott which makes it important to answer this question of the incidence of the African legacy in his work: "so that mongrel as I am, something prickles in me when I see the word 'Ashanti' as with the word 'Warwickshire', both separately intimating my grandfathers' roots, both baptising this neither proud nor ashamed bastard, this hybrid, this West Indian".[13]

For a final understanding of Walcott's idea of a hybrid identity – and, indeed, where and how European and African components come into play – we need to return to and examine closely his claim of an "electric fusion of the old and the new". He himself finds the classic elucidation of this fusion in the Afro-Christian tradition of black America, and cites it as an integral part of his argument in "Muse". He is looking at the way in which the Africans, displaced into the exile of that slave setting, underwent conversion to the white man's religion to virtually make it into a culture of their own. He explains it thus: "but the phenomenon is the zeal with which the slave accepted both the Christian and the Hebraic, resigned his gaze to the death of his pantheon, and yet deliberately began to invest a decaying faith with a political belief".[14] Conversion then became a matter of the appropriation of that alien religion; which, transfused with the faith of their own cause of deliverance, became their own cultural possession. It is a consummate paradigm of the process of indigenization which lies at the heart of Walcott's concept of a regional identity. In this process, as he carefully notes in his explication, the African comes to an authentic assimilation of the old Hebraic archetype of deliverance from bondage, the two ancestors meeting at this original level of primal necessity. (In his idea of "electric fusion", Walcott identifies the *old* with this input of ancestral memory.) The meeting between them, however, turns on the axis of a new purpose in a new historical environment – the purpose of liberation and discovery, which is the sociohistorical destiny of that environment. This latter indigenous quantity – the *new* – is the determining one; and what is produced out of the process of appropriation/adaptation is, accordingly, a third, other thing, distinctly of the new environment. For Walcott, it is in this other, third entity, and the process of indigenization from which it is produced, that a native identity consists. As such, it is an identity which, carrying the traces of earlier ancestries, is complete with its own ethnic and cultural integrity. As a clear illustration of that achievement, Walcott gives a fine appreciation of the black American tradition of spiritual music as the unique cultural expression of black America, coming out of that conversion.

Walcott's concept of an identity founded on indigenization is consistent with his wider faith in a New World destiny that begins at the level of an elemental discovery/naming. This elemental naming – it is a special recognition he brings to the concept of indigenization – accounts for a vital quotient of the new entity created out of that process. The new purpose of that environment is reinforced with an energy, a fresh lease of life, reflected in the zeal and potency of Afro-Christianity, for example. The renewed energy and fresh lease of life come from the recovered contact with nature in the body, a recovery itself enabled by the elemental reaches of discovery necessitated by that environment. The significance of Walcott's elemental discoveries in the journey through the interior ("Guyana" sequence), as well as the castaway's effort of "reading nature's plan", falls into place here. This takes us back to the meeting of the ancestors at these primal levels of renewal. In Walcott's view, the African component was already strongly placed for this access to the primal – the Africa which, dispossessed of its language and tradition of symbols in the New World, survives mainly "in the body's memory", that is, a semiotics of the body and its peculiar sensibility.[15] (Thus the retentions of Africa occur mainly in the region's ritual expressions and culture of performance, featuring originally in his drama.) Continuing to draw upon the Afro-American example, he puts it this way: "for the subject African had come to the New World in an elemental intimacy with nature, with a profounder terror of blasphemy than the exhausted, hypocritical Christian".[16] Walcott is intuitively sensitive to the informing spirit of African belief in this observation. But here one might pause to note that what is missing from his affirmation is a specific naming of the elements of African belief and culture that define this "profounder intimacy with nature". It perhaps remains an area of inadequacy in his effort that he does not seek to properly identify or research the New World survivals of Africa, to make good the historical vagueness of the colonial about this ancestor. In the context of our theme, however, the substantive point is that both ancestors feature in the process of indigenization; but they are both virtually subsumed in the end product of that process.[17] Thus Walcott himself finally sums up his concept of identity in these terms: "I give the strange and bitter and yet ennobling thanks for the monumental groaning and soldering of two great worlds . . . that exiled from your own Edens you have placed me in the wonder of another."[18] It is in this light that we come to understand the integrity of that strange coinage of Walcott's, *Afro-Greek*, which stresses the uniqueness of that identity.[19]

In this grasp of the process from assimilation of the Old World heritage to indigenous possession and creation, Walcott bears a strong resemblance to C.L.R. James (1901–89), a man who distilled the true genius of the West Indian intelligence. It seems an unlikely comparison at first glance. James was a pan-Africanist, a frontline campaigner and activist for black nationalism, and a Marxist committed to ideology and active struggle – a revolutionary career which puts him in an altogether different category from Walcott. James combined this political passion, however, with strong aesthetic and cultural ones, among these the love of West Indian cricket, with which his name is linked forever. The essential and total James is expressed in his classic *Beyond a Boundary* (1963). In this book he shows how cricket, brought in from England to the West Indian colonial setting, took root to become a uniquely West Indian achievement, the sport synonymous with West Indian culture. He gives a thorough sociological analysis of the way in which cricket met the several spheres of the region's needs: as an instrument of its social and political cause, its self-development, as well as its cultural fulfilment. Most pertinently, James is not afraid to make links with the classical legacy of Greek intelligence, or the Victorian model of conduct with which the game was associated in England to understand why cricket, going beyond racial and cultural boundaries, should have so taken root and attained this wholeness on new soil. In this presentation of cricket as an indigenized product, claiming and subsuming traces of its sources, James coincides totally with Walcott's position on origins and identity. He himself represents a true incarnation of that concept of identity, as a man who, while he knew and remained committed to the value of liberation on the racial and proletarian fronts, was totally eclectic in his syntheses and applications of world intelligence. That strength came from the unique reality of his mixed origins as a West Indian.[20]

Walcott believes in a new, autonomous regional identity founded on a concept of indigenization. It is a concept of indigenization which returns to the purer, stricter logic of "creolization" as naturalization. Firmly rooted in the principle of renewal, the identity he affirms represents the possibility of an alternative dispensation, and has distinct revolutionary values. To begin with, while remaining linked to its origins in the Old World, it has the potential to generate a New World structure of ancestry of its own – one that, like all truly new phenomena, departs so radically from the traditional idea that it remains virtually unrecognizable, even unacceptable. The very nature of this ancestry, however, its mixed sources, means the capacity to go "beyond the boundary" of racial absolutes. In terms of a practicable, livable reality, it manifests itself in the virtue of "openness" with which Walcott identifies so strongly in the social milieu of multiracial Trinidad.[21] On a profound ideological level, it is the revolutionary capacity so prophetically envisioned by Harris: the power of the "headless", vestigial traditions, coming together in the postcolonial New World setting, to break with the monolithic structures of the older ancestries. Harris's model has the distinct advantage of encompassing all the ancestries incident in the region – inclusive of African, European, East Indian and Amerindian, all coming from the same ex-colonized or disadvantaged background. Walcott shares a basic area of affinity with him in this respect. While Europe and Africa naturally predominate, given his personal background, the Amerindian legacy gains increasing significance in his work from *Another Life* onwards; and his grounding in indigenization does extend to embrace the East Indian presence in the region. He is deeply responsive to the latter in poems like "The Saddhu of Couva" (*SAK*) and "Exile" (*The Gulf*), as also, climactically, in his Nobel Lecture "The Antilles: Fragments of Epic Memory" (*Twilight*).

This capacity to break with the monolithic moulds of the older ancestries remains the salient promise of this indigenous identity: it has tremendous political and social potential for continuing to herald, if not actualize, the ideal of a cross-cultural and more egalitarian order, and for manifesting the possibility of Harris's "community of man". It also means, as Walcott emphasizes in "Muse", the liberating power of going beyond the awe of historical time, and the nostalgia for the ancestral order associated with it, which is peculiarly Naipaul's angst. It is an emphasis of particular urgency to Walcott, who knows the intensity of the struggle to overcome the sense of history and landscape as negation (chapter 3).

There remains, though, the question of the connection between creolization/indigenization in Walcott, given its terms and expressions in his work, and creolization in the grassroots and popular tradition – where not only is fusion more evident, but the African legacy also has a substantial presence. This is a question that applies to the poetry rather than the drama, which, as already noted, directly connects with and exploits the popular tradition. Walcott's own definition of his role as a filter "purifying the language of the tribe" provides some answer to this question.[22] He is echoing Mallarmé's classic definition, which refers to the heightened, interpretive role of the artist in drawing out the essence of the communal experience and its lingua franca. "Purifying the dialect of the tribe" is, in effect, finding its integrative order of meaning, its deep structure. Walcott fulfils this purpose in the following essential: he distils and extends – that is, gives further depth and significance to – the primal values in the folk tradition and its sensibility, which is organically of the body. He does so by virtue of his inner hold on the natural, elemental, which comprises the original iconography and true alphabet of his world (chapter 3). This hold on the natural, elemental signifies the recovery of the first principles of the human as inscribed in nature, the phenomenon which Harris, with his visionary acumen, has described as "the revitalization of the fauna and flora of legend".[23] Such a consciousness of the primal as noted earlier in this chapter, also means being especially finely tuned to the sense of the old, of archetypes. The feature is highlighted in the notable achievement of "The Sea Is History" (*SAK*) where, breaking through the ornamental, architectural encrustations of the older metaphors, he returns to their core human principles.

The play *Ti-Jean and His Brothers* provides an especially appropriate example of this feature because in it, Walcott is recreating what is in the first instance a product of creolization on the part of the folk. The Ti-Jean cycle of tales[24] represents an adaptation of the French folk hero Ti-Jean by the New World African slaves; so that the Western content is, pertinently, quite strong. Approaching the tale from the more familiar Judaeo-Christian tradition, Walcott works through the David/Goliath theme to the portrayal of Ti-Jean as a trickster figure: it meets authentically with the Anancy-trickster motif of African memory at the core of the tale. Indeed, what he thus serves to uncover is a coincidence implicit in the folk's recreation of the original. (Harris is concerned with this very coincidence in his "gateway complex". See chapter 3.) Furthermore, in *Ti-Jean* he adds a substantive, highly significant factor. Decoding the sociohistorical context and cause submerged in the tale, he amplifies it to make *Ti-Jean* a narrative of liberation on the most inclusive level, spiritual as well as political. Maya Deren's classic exposition of the indigenized dynamic of Haitian Vodun, and its function as a ritual of liberation, is congruent with this paradigm represented in *Ti-Jean*.[25] The *Ti-Jean* paradigm also shows, at the same time, how the wider informing purpose of liberation, fusing spiritual and political, relates to the renewal of a primal, mythic level of consciousness. Walcott thus serves to filter the essence and deeper significance of the indigenous folk imagination.

It has been necessary to spend some time on the question of Walcott's relationship to the oral tradition because the question of what goes into a Caribbean aesthetic is not straightforward, hinging, as it does, on the larger issue of identifying the constituent sources of an indigenized Caribbean culture. Rohlehr comes close to the answer in his idea of a Caribbean aesthetic based on a sophisticated use of popular forms by the artist: "an alternative and complex tradition does exist, both in primary folk forms and in what a more sophisticated art has shaped and can shape from these basic forms".[26] The only problem is that this definition does not indicate what constitutes this sophistication on the part of the artist. The case of the early Lamming in *Season of Adventure* (1960), analysed perceptively by Rohlehr himself, focuses the problematic of locating a creative meeting point between what Brathwaite has separated out as the great and little traditions in the region.[27] In *Season of Adventure* Lamming makes one of the earliest affirmative recognitions of the folk tradition (from a peasant culture rooted in the African legacy) as bearer of the potential for a native empowerment. But Lamming, Rohlehr maintains, shows a residual ambiguity at the end of the novel. After these grassroots resources have served their liberating purposes, they are found to be incompatible with the engines of progress and must be, to cite Rohlehr's words, "replaced by the dry panacea of Baako's scientific politics, technology and liberal minded agnosticism".[28] Commenting on Lamming's dilemma, Rohlehr himself focuses on the gap between educated intellectual and grassroots figure as the final explanation of the ambiguity with which the novel ends.

Walcott goes a long way towards bridging this (finally factitious) gap by his belief in an indigenization which runs the continuum from educated medium through the dialects of the region. It is a concept of indigenization which enables him to enter into and "purify the dialect of the tribe", which, in all cultures, requires an epiphany. In the end, there is a complementarity between Walcott's more standard medium as poet (it acquires great range and flexibility in the later volumes) and the "voice" of the oral tradition, a complementarity that reflects the possibility of one integrative principle, a wholeness, behind the diverse and seemingly disparate admixtures that feed into Caribbean culture. There is, moreover, another related dimension to Walcott's contribution in bridging the gap between educated intellectual and the grassroots. The truth is that he is the artist who *includes* the intellectual, who often remains unsure about his link with the Western intellect, and tends to profess the cause of the grassroots, while living somewhere else. Walcott is the West Indian writer who lives inwardly the relationships and tensions between the educated and the grassroots, and attempts to create out of it.

Given this conception of a native identity and revolutionary possibility, and its constituent characteristics and definitions, we are better able to put into perspective his attack on the new revolutionary doctrine – the other part of his twofold mission in "Twilight" and "Muse". His attack on its advocacy of Africanness, which he rejects outright as a race-based ideology, is of particular vehemence, as earlier noted. His case against this ideology of African revival begins from his perception that its racial vision is anchored in a belief in ancestral history and a commitment to redeeming it. It is a perception which derives from a profound philosophical preoccupation with what he calls "the muse of history", the title of one of the two major essays under review, and a prominent theme in this phase of his career (see chapter 1). The preoccupation, which begins to develop during this period, is the final context of his polemic and strictures against the doctrines of black nationalism. The commitment to redeeming race in ancestral history falls into the endemic error of giving primacy to successive, cumulative history as the ultimate measure of human achievement. This represents, for Walcott, the epic fallacy of the muse of history which has dominated the course of Old World civilization(s). It is this epic conception which underlies the established view of history as cycles of despair and cycles of achievement;[29] and the Manichaean division that approaches history in terms of the viewpoint of hero or of victim. In the Caribbean context, the glorification of ancestral Africa thus resolves into romantic nostalgia, or more critically and precipitately, into the obsession with ancestral victimhood – "the masochistic veneration of / chains" (*AL, CP*, 287).

These are, for Walcott, the predominant directions of the black radicalism of the 1970s, and it is for the latter – the cult of victimhood – that he reserves his most virulent attack, concentrated in "Muse" and a companion piece, chapter 19 of *Another Life*. The intensity of his attack on this cult of victimhood comes to bear directly on the aesthetic that it propagates. That aesthetic must remain of necessity, in Walcott's terms, confined to the nostalgia mentioned above; or, more perniciously, must fall into the twin binds of a literature of shame or a literature of revenge. Thus his opening argument in "Muse":

> In the New World servitude to the muse of history has produced a literature of recrimination and despair, a literature of revenge written by the descendants of slaves or a literature of remorse written by the descendants of master. . . . The truly tough aesthetic of the New World neither explains nor forgives. It refuses to recognise it [history] as a creative or culpable force.[30]

From these grounds he goes on to denounce the aesthetic of shame and revenge as totally reactionary and degenerative. In levelling this criticism at black nationalism Walcott seems totally insensitive to the positive impetus of the movement to rehabilitate the civilization of a race from a prolonged phase of denial and abnegation. But if such omissions make for certain imbalances in his viewpoint, his deeply philosophical approach does succeed in highlighting the excesses and pitfalls of making absolutes of the twin gods of ancestry and history in serving the cause of race. It is also fair to observe that the tendencies he criticizes were among the mixed aspects of the movement. What finally confirms the integrity of his position in this matter is the fact that his biggest quarrel with the epic muse of history is levelled at historically privileged, imperial Europe. He makes his most searching exploration of the errors of that muse in respect of Old World Western civilization. Concentrated in *Another Life,* the major work well in progress during this period, that exploration is undertaken as an integral part of his effort as the ex-colonial seeking to break with an older, oppressive order of thought.

In this focus on the deification of history as the underlying muse of the reclamation of Africa, Walcott also aims at Edward Brathwaite, the West Indian poet and historian, who had emerged by this time as the culture hero of the black nationalist movement. He is in the vanguard of the "epic-minded poets" ("Muse", *Twilight*, 43–45) who come under scrutiny in "Muse". As the exponent of diasporan Africa in *The Arrivants* (1978)[31] and proponent of

African-rooted culture, he is the main purveyor of a black aesthetic. There are several sides to Brathwaite's achievements and intentions in the trilogy, and it may well be that Walcott, in accusing him of the vindication of epic Africa, is uncovering an indirect effect outside Brathwaite's conscious intention. There are, however, more direct, palpable intentions which he targets in Brathwaite. Setting out to recover the continuities of Afro-America and the Afro-Caribbean with the motherland, his purpose is also to rehabilitate their spiritual wholeness in relation to the cosmic intelligence and religion of Africa. This latter is a substantive issue in his quarrel with Brathwaite, whose mythic journey through Africa in *The Arrivants* is the counterpart and, in principle, the opposite of Walcott's own journey through the interior in "Guyana". In his eyes – and he accepts with Eliot that religion is the basis of culture[32] – Brathwaite's tacit identification with the African religious mind undersigns his commitment to an African-rooted culture and indeed, the concomitant purpose of establishing a black aesthetic.[33] On this score, his refutation of Brathwaite as a founding father of the black revolutionary ideology is consistent with his strongest convictions about the route of renewal through assimilation and indigenization: and they stand.

But it must be admitted that Walcott is less than fair to Brathwaite when he lumps him in with the mediocre talents on the bandwagon of the movement, limiting him to their characteristic lack of originality and deficiencies in creativity. His definitive statements should, at this juncture, be more responsible. In actual fact, the lack of discrimination shown in his blanket attack on the "epic-minded poet" contradicts his position elsewhere. Reviewing *The Arrivants*, he hailed *Rights of Passage* in glowing terms as an affirmation of the oral tradition ("drama in itself"), and proceeded to produce it in the Theatre Workshop.[34] Such lapses and contradictions do occur in Walcott, often associated with the heat of polemics.

Ultimately, Walcott is up in arms against what appears a concerted effort to establish an alternative, black tradition, a "New Vision". His attack on the "New Vision" is thoroughgoing, careful to include its exponents and disseminators from all spheres – radicals, politicians, intellectuals, as well as metropolitan liberal champions of a black aesthetic, and of course, its new poets, the "brood of thin querulous fledglings".[35] The attack is carried over from "Twilight" and "Muse" into *Another Life,* and its characteristic tone and style is captured in this passage from the latter, where he heaps scorn and contumely on the "magicians of the New Vision":

> Those who peel, from their own leprous flesh, their names,
> who chafe and nurture the scars of rusted chains,
> like primates favouring scabs, those who charge tickets
> for another free ride on the middle passage,
> those who explain to the peasant why he is African,
> their catamites and eunuchs banging tambourines,
> whores with slave bangles banging tambourines,
> and the academics crouched like rats
> listening to tambourines
> jackals and rodents feathering their holes
> hoarding the sea-glass of their ancestors' eyes,
> sea-lice, sea-parasites on the ancestral sea-wrack,
> whose god is history . . .

(CP, 269)

For sheer power of fury and artistic intensity Walcott comes close to Dante's mastery of invective in the *Inferno,* and indeed it is during this phase of confrontation that he perfects the art of vituperation, or "cussing". The blanket charges are of the "masochistic veneration of chains", careerist opportunism, fraudulence and prostitution in the cultivation and parade of an Africa not genuinely possessed. They sum up some of the worst features of the band-wagon culture that developed during the period. Similarly, he rightly criticizes the "New Poetry" serving the movement as propagandistic, audio-programmed for the public ear, and poor in artistic merit (see "Any Revolution Based on Race"). What is tendentious and excessive is the discrediting of all efforts identified with black or folk definition as devoid of integrity or merit. Thus the anthropologists are about romanticizing the folk; and the academics, the "syntactical apologists of dialect", with whom he has a special grouse, are limited to feathering their own holes.

In fact, this kind of extremism runs into his all-out offensive on the "apotheosis of the folk" and the oral tradition in the two essays concerned. There is the same blanket rejection, and the spirit of the attack borders on a contempt and arrogance towards the folk tradition as incapable of "high art". This is, of course, contrary to what we have seen to be an organic and active connection between Walcott and the grassroots tradition. Walcott is on the defensive, and there are, in these excesses, strains of the paranoia he describes in "Twilight": "He alone would roll the Sisyphean boulder uphill, even if it cracked his backbone. . . . But who would help should he let go the stone, or, when he rested, help prop it with scotching heels and groaning back?"[36] From the paranoia of this kind of effort one tends to leave very jealous of his monopoly on the truth. He reacts, though, to a very real threat to the strongly held beliefs of his own aesthetic; and on its terms, his fundamental objection to the danger of exclusivity in black revolutionary directions is sound. The final truth lies between the two sides of this polemic about alternative revolutionary routes. The advocacy and pursuit of black culture unearthed and liberated a hitherto submerged and neglected area of creativity; the resistance of the exclusivity of its claims on the part of a Walcott spoke for a selfhood that must begin from native ground, with all its complex sources and allegiances. The prejudices and excesses we have been considering are localized to the heat of polemics on a vital issue, but his underlying strictures against a revolution based on race, and the philosophical underpinnings of its errors, were timely and remain valid.

Finally, Walcott's New World concept stands for a vision of liberation whose primary front is the imagination: it makes its first appeal to the inner spirit as the true basis of power. As such, its terms are uncompromisingly those of the artist, enhanced and commissioned by the purpose of New World vision. Thus he announces this article of faith with utmost and prophetic conviction: "The future of West Indian militancy lies in art." [37] On these terms his revolutionary vision is free and steers clear of the rigidities of political ideologies and their systems. Thus he remains essentially nonaligned with respect to the experiments at a socialist alternative in the region. Recognizing and identifying in principle with efforts to redress the injustices and inequities of society, he is sympathetic to Michael Manley's experiment in democratic socialism, disastrous though it proved (*SAK*);[38] but he is wary of Castro's hard-line model of state control as a threat to the life of the individual spirit (*Midsummer*).[39] In addition to the urgency and immediacy of the anticolonial cause, Walcott's political faiths were nurtured in the expansive reaches of the ideal of a New World republican order – anti-imperialist, antihierarchical and antipaternalistic in principle and purpose. From the early Walcott right into the period under consideration, the main expressions of these political faiths are made with reference to Whitman's "democratic vistas".[40] The commitment is emphasized explicitly and implicitly in his preoccupation with North America's betrayal of that democratic ideal. His political outlook retains the widest spirit of that ideal.

But Walcott also started with an early idea of the progressive model viable for his own emergent West Indian nation, one suited to its needs and commensurate with its prospects. It was the impossible dream of an archipel-ago devoted to culture, a "new Aegean", for which the Greek city states provided a first and lasting inspiration. It was a dream which his master and mentor, Harold Simmons, also shared. Thus: "When twenty years ago we imagined cities devoted neither to power nor to money but to art, one had the true vision."[41] It also means that Walcott was, and remains, a staunch regionalist, and like all the pioneering revolutionaries of his generation, was strongly committed to the West Indian Federation (1958–62). He still laments its failure some twenty years later in "The Sea Is History": "and then each rock broke into its own nation" (*CP*, 367). Yet, if that dream remains perpetually deferred by *realpolitik*, it has proved essentially true in that the only real power of the Caribbean is its culture.

Despite these idealisms, however, Walcott remains very much alive to the pragmatic realities of both politics and race. The full picture emerges from his keen and direct engagement with these realities in the poetry of the period, to which we now turn.

Race, Politics and Society in the Poetry of the Period

As compared to *The Castaway,* there is a marked increase in commentary on racial and political issues in *The Gulf,* the volume coming out of the second half of the 1960s, which saw the acceleration of revolutionary and militant activity in several parts of the world, including the Caribbean. The title poem of the volume is directly concerned with the explosion of racial violence in the United States during that period, and other major public poems, such as "Elegy", "Blues" and "Negatives", show alertness and sensitivity to events and crises on the worldwide scene – quite apart from developments on the local scene, which found urgent, concentrated expression in the essays examined above. The public poems are engaged in direct, full responses to the social and political actualities of these issues, showing, for example, the depth of Walcott's empathy with the despair of racial oppression. Set beside the faiths and principles examined in the first part of this chapter, the poetry of the period both affirms and gives further dimension to his position, extending our understanding of his concerns with and views on these issues.

The major responses to and statements on race are all associated with the United States, his most important poem on race during this period being "The Gulf". This aspect of his engagement with race – the concentration on the

United States – presents an interesting and significant feature. It is in that setting that he, as a West Indian, first becomes truly sensitive to the ills of racism in their extremity, and begins to internalize them. "The Glory Trumpeter", an outstanding poem from *The Castaway,* virtually testifies to the experience of growing wise in that environment to the reality of racism as exile and defeat – an experience which occurred during his first visit to the United States on a theatre scholarship, at about the age of twenty-nine.

Walcott comes to this recognition of the reality of racial oppression, significantly, on experiencing a performance of black spiritual music by a glory trumpeter, the old Eddie of the poem. The poem recaptures the deeply moving impression of Eddie's performance on Walcott, its value as a learning experience for him. He is arrested first by the sheer power of the turbulent, visceral emotions ("propelled . . . frenzy") which infuse blues and spiritual alike in the old trumpeter's performance. His ears and eyes are opened to the plight and ethos of black America in the sensibility and statement of that music: the tragic reaches of despair sounded in its controlled, soul-searing frenzy, and the powerful will to resistance and deliverance which reaches consummation in the artistic intensity of Eddie's "fury of indifference":

> The bony, idle fingers on the valves
> Of his knee-cradled horn could tear
> Through "Georgia on My Mind" or "Jesus Saves"
> With the same fury of indifference
> If what propelled such frenzy was despair.

(CP, 64)

He comes to recognize, in that performance, the role and value of this unique musical tradition as the essential weapon and vehicle of black America. So that, with sudden revelatory impact, a figure like Eddie assumes full stature and significance as the equivalent of the Old Testament Joshua leading his people's struggle against bondage; his trumpet, like Joshua's ram's horn – its primitive precursor – the medium of the clarion call of "patient bitterness or bitter siege" to an oppressed people. The experience seems to have been one of the major influences in his early recognition of this music as the most expressive instrument of the spiritual militancy of black America, and as the reservoir of its soul as a people. He often draws on this tradition of black American music in his exposition of the poetics of an appropriated faith in "Muse".

One of the major factors contributing to the impact of this recognition is the difference between the relative inexperience of Walcott as a young West Indian black, and the figure of the black American older in the knowledge of that pain. This difference represents an important context within which the poem arrives at its central meanings. On a primary, personal level, the encounter is one of self-confrontation for Walcott, as he comes to face the limitations in his understanding of the tragedy of race and his attitudes to it so far. He does so with misgivings, feelings of guilt about the relative security and complacency with which he comes to Eddie's performance from his own background. Thus, as Eddie's eyes "fix" him in their intensity they are both avuncular, those of the caring older kin, and derisive, bearing a measure of reproachful mockery. The line "Secure in childhood I did not know then" (*CP*, 64) is loaded with these implications of a "guilty" and innocence. The poem underscores this in concluding with his personal confession about an uncle living in America whom he never had the courage to visit. It is as if an initial disinclination was aggravated by the experience of Eddie's music. The confession is as much an expression of his own guilt as a comment on the unbearable extremes of racism in that setting. The encounter is, fully, an awakening both of consciousness and conscience to the reality of racism as exile and defeat.

Walcott's sense of relative "security" and immaturity about racial despair, while personally acknowledged, is also that of his Caribbean background. Behind it lies the basic difference in the experience of race in Caribbean society as compared to that of America. Institutionalized racism in white-supremacist America relegates the black American to the status of a second-class citizen, with all the peculiar severities that attach to the privations of that condition. The Caribbean person finds himself at a more "benign" distance from the extremes of racism, coming from circumstances of dependence on the white absentee system of the colonial past and its surviving strictures and influences. Thus Walcott's first experience of oppression and denial is associated with the colonial dependence syndrome, and its related *angst* of history and landscape as negation. The burden of conscience which he personally assumes as an artist listening to the glory trumpeter is also that of his society. The allusive terms and motifs in the poem also establish this important context. His is the carefree complacency of the "young crowd out fêting, swilling liquor" (*CP*, 65) – implicitly from the fête-loving Caribbean; and equally, the "security" of childhood is that of his Caribbean nation vis-à-vis black America, represented by Eddie, aged and seasoned in the knowledge of race as exile.

Walcott proceeds from this recognition to make a signal act in this poem, of [re]claiming the bond of a common, ancestral "racial" pain, and embracing the extremity of the black American cause as one with his own. For this reason the glory trumpeter assumes emblematic significance as a family relation from the outset. As embodiment of the soul of black America, older in tragic wisdom, he bears an avuncular relationship and is a guardian/teacher figure, to a younger West Indian kin. Ultimately, the poet discovers in Eddie an ancestral figure. Thus, a crowning moment in the poem is the moment when Walcott arrives at full realization of that ancestral bond, in a flash of illumination linking Eddie with the memory of his grandmother in her barracks on the wharves of Castries, St Lucia:

> Now, as the eyes sealed in the ashen flesh,
> And Eddie, like a deacon at his prayer,
> Rose, tilting the bright horn, I saw a flash
> Of gulls and pigeons from the dunes of coal
> Near my grandmother's barracks on the wharves,
>
> (*CP*, 64)

It is a moment of epiphany. The movement from the image of the bright tilted horn to that of the "flash / of gulls and pigeons from the dunes of coal" is one of spontaneous, involuntary memory. As the bright flashes of the tilted horn and of the rising gulls and pigeons connect, they mutually illuminate the intimations of these images as overtures of upliftment from the reduced, extreme reaches of black despair. There is an essential oneness connecting Eddie's to his grandmother's world. That flash of illumination also opens a window into a childhood of strange, uncertain images about life in America, from migrant West Indians returning home from there:

> I saw the sallow faces of those men
> Who sighed as if they spoke into their graves
> About the Negro in America . . .
> . . . .
> To the bowed heads of lean, compliant men
> Back from the States in their funereal serge,
> Black rusty homburgs and limp waiters' ties,
> Slow, honey accents and lard-coloured eyes,
>
> (*CP*, 64–65)

These postures and the demeanour of alienation and defeat now fall into place, as Walcott understands the full meaning of Eddie's medium to the black race in America.

Walcott stresses the ancestral significance of this folk artist in a highly emblematic portrait. Every detail and effect in the portrait gives definition to his meaning as a figure whose "features held our fate" (*CP*, 64). Armed with his horn he bears, like the Old Testament Joshua, an archetypal mission in the forefront of the struggle. As a medium who bears the suffering of a people and seeks spiritual release on their behalf, his is, "like a deacon at his prayer", a sacred, priestly role. The wrinkles of his aging face take on the depth and timeless aspect of the Mississippi, that ancestral heartland of the Deep South. Reiterating this timeless, ancestral aspect, his "eyes sealed in the ashen flesh", hint at a visage already preserved among the immortals. The glory trumpeter thus, in his representative role, also assumes heraldic significance in the critical cause of race shared by the diasporan peoples of the New World. It is, especially, race as the archetype of their common roots in oppression.

"The Gulf", as already indicated, is the poem which contains Walcott's fullest response and most representative statement on race during this phase of his career. It is now some six years after the initiation recorded in "The Glory Trumpeter", and the very peak of active black militancy in the United States. We see a Walcott in full-bore engagement with racial strife in one of its most intense spells, as he brings the full force of his moral imagination to bear on the crisis. The poem is one of the most outstanding pieces in the Walcott corpus: it is an achievement which comes out of and demonstrates the deep spirituality which informs his engagement with the issues of race and politics. Its public theme is steeped in biblical and religious idiom. It opens with the mystical idea of the "divine union" from St John of the Cross, and closes with the Old Testament's invocation of the vengeance of the Lord in "coals of fire . . . heaped upon the head / of all whose gospel is the whip and flame" (*CP*, 108). Much of this Old Testament and religious content is echoed from the religious tradition and idiom of black America itself.

The poem is responding to the explosion of racial violence, starting in 1965, in the "long hot summers" of looting and burning,[42] the period when black militancy rallied under the influence of Malcolm X and the Black Panther movement. On a flight out of Texas, Walcott takes an aerial view of the smoke of "bursting ghettoes" across the United States, and reflects on the spectacle of a country consumed in the near holocaust of racial violence, a country which presents the image of the universe as "a cauldron boiling with its wars". His gaze is trained on the tragedy of the racial gulf that divides the "United" States. He had had a lucid perception of that gulf image from the time of "The Glory Trumpeter", where the geographical Gulf of Mexico had appeared as a physical extension of the gulf of race, as he watched Eddie aim his horn at Mobile and Galveston, "those cities of the Gulf" (*CP*, 65). Virtually hanging in air above these "divided states", he now has a full view of this inevitable gulf in a society structured on an ethic of force. The poem makes its statement in the rejection of that ethic. It formally denounces "in the Lord God's name" the gospel of "the whip and flame" inbuilt into such a racist system, condemning its deep travesty of humanity.

Targeting the entire system, this rejection of the gospel of the "whip and flame" is implicitly aimed at both white violence and the black reprisal it provokes. To appreciate the integrity of this final judgement, we need to follow the subtle process of his thinking in a metaphysical argument carefully developed in the structuring of the poem. He begins in part 1 with a meditation on the mystical idea of the divine union – its message of the need for the soul's detachment from the love of created things. He gets his poetic cue for this speculation from being "in the air" (the situation which generates the "gulf of air" motif, one of the many evoked in the play on the gulf image in the poem).[43] The immediate experience of leaving the attachments he had made during his stay in Texas becomes the occasion of his personal penetration of this mystical idea, and a recovery of its meaning. Its truth is that no love has any final, proprietal claim to the object(s) loved, or to the goal(s) envisioned; and the final surrender of all love's claims is the higher, divine order of necessity to which our humanity is called. To arrive at harmony with this higher purpose is to be possessed of the divine union. The "skeletal candour" of this truth strikes with revelatory impact:

> scenes where we learn,
> exchanging the least gifts, this rose, this napkin,
> that those we love are objects we return,
>
> that this lens on the desert's wrinkled skin
> has priced our flesh, all that we love in pawn
> to that brass ball, that the gifts, multiplying,
>
> clutter and choke the heart, and that I shall

> watch love reclaim its things as I lie dying.
> My very flesh and blood! . . .

(CP, 105)

Walcott is engaged here in a profound visionary apprehension of the para-doxical bond between love and mortality that ultimately humanizes us; and it is this order of perception that will inform his resolutions on the racial crisis he surveys.

It is a measure of his understanding of the extreme difficulty of fulfilling the imperatives of the divine union that he first meditates on the tragic anguish of this paradox in the sphere of artistic endeavour. His preoccupation with what it means to the artist in this first section of the poem represents an effort to further internalize its meaning. He comes face to face with the reality that art, the most selfless and unconditional of loves, must surrender to this necessity in the sense that there is no reward, no ultimate fulfilment of its purpose; it too is a gift returned. All that remains are the books/records of the exercise of these loves. What the efforts of the great artists and minds of the past amount to is revealed in an image which strikes with the same visionary force as the "skeletal candour" of the surrendering flesh and blood: the "detached radiance" of the "gilded gravestone spines" of their works. Both these images extend a powerfully original perception of love irradiated by death. Their radiance is that of the numinous, and, as such, is affirmative of that reality; but it is a reality pregnant with painful contradictions, to be accepted in a spirit of humility and tragic wisdom. Walcott's meditation in this theme of the divine union is on love, mortality and the limits of love's power; and the real threnody sounded in the elegiac strains of this first movement is not on account of death, but for love that must so surrender to limits. Thus, contemplating the artist's love, he comments thus on the "gilded gravestone spines" of the generations of artists that went before: "Circling like us; no comfort for their loves!" (*CP*, 106). It remains a source of the deepest anguish that the artist's love does not succeed in changing the basic condition of things; it never, like the "uninstructing dead" of the concluding line of the poem, fulfils its final mission.

Walcott's faith in the truth of the divine union as a higher necessity is, however, equally strong. Looking down at "our old earth" below, he perceives this truth as continuous with the principle of renewal at work in elemental nature:

> some cratered valley heals itself with sage,
> through that grey, fading massacre a blue
>
> lighthearted creek flutes of some siege
> to the amnesia of drumming water.
>
> *(CP, 106)*

But it is from the inwardness of his sense of love's inescapable surrender, and the tragic wisdom it imparts, that he enters into his diagnosis of the racial tragedy below, to penetrate its inherent ills and errors. Its sources lie in the existential delusion that we have a proprietary claim on the world – on the objects/achievements of our loves/desires. This is what fuels the muse of dominion and possession that at core informs a misguided system such as racism. It is this which he finally recognizes as self-defeating and self-destructive, calling down, in its own doom, the Lord's vengeance.

The gulf image itself encompasses the full span of Walcott's moral and visionary perspectives in responding to the crisis, and is most effective in ultimately fixing these meanings. Including the several related facets of his perception, it is an outstanding example of his genius for completeness of statement through metaphor. The image acquires multiple associated layers of meaning, generated out of the instinct for correspondences so seminal to his aesthetic. The central reference is to the racial gulf itself, linked by association, as already observed, to the geographical Gulf of Mexico (a correspondence surfacing from his deeply imbedded sense of the sea as amnesiac divide).[44] The other major gulf reference comes, fortuitously, from the "Gulf" chain of filling stations prominent throughout the length and breadth of the United States (signalling the Middle Eastern sources of the oil supply). Walcott lights on the wry irony of this filling station sign as the fitting emblem of the racial gulf, capturing the true quality of its desolation both on the graphic/physical and moral levels. The gaseous emissions of "the smoke of bursting ghettoes" are fed by the poison of the racial hatred which contaminates the entire landscape from the northern to the southern states:

> down every coast where filling station signs
> proclaim the Gulf, an air, heavy with gas,
> sickens the state, from Newark to New Orleans.
>
> *(CP, 107)*

Another linked image expressive of that explosive racial strife is the "gulf of air" earlier noted. Humankind is forced to occupy a "gulf of air" (Walcott's own location in the poem), given the reality of an uninhabitable earth exploding with fire and smoke – which reflects the theme of homelessness and exile with which the poem ends:

> I have no home
> as long as summer bubbling to its head
> boils for that day when in the Lord God's name . . .
>
> *(CP,* 107–8)

Finally, the gulf image bears an underlying, existential meaning inclusive of all the rest: it is the gulf of humankind's estrangement from the truths of his own humanity, as contained in the burden of the divine union. In fact, the poem places the burden of the divine union versus this final meaning of the gulf motif as the opposite terms of its discourse. Thus, after the contemplation of the divine union in part 1, it turns to face, at the end of part 2, the disastrous consequences of this gulf in the threat of racial apocalypse that lies below:

> the divine union
> of these detached, divided states, whose slaughter
> darkens each summer now, as one by one,
> the smoke of bursting ghettoes clouds the glass
>
> *(CP,* 106)

Part 3 moves straight from this image of the bursting ghettoes to a close-up view of black America and its cause in this crisis. Sensitive to the realities of oppression and resistance, Walcott's judgement is informed, as this section establishes, by a concern with the pragmatic issues. He is engaged in an act of sympathetic identification with the cause of the black man in that society; and testifies, characteristically, from his own personal experience of being black in the United States. It was in the South, at once familiar and alien soil, that he had known the keenest sting of racial disorientation – the disorientation and alienation of suddenly taking on the status of "a secondary soul" (so truly foreign to his sensibility as a West Indian):[45]

> But fear
> thickened my voice, that strange, familiar soil
>
> prickled and barbed the texture of my hair,
> my status as a secondary soul
>
> *(CP,* 107)

He has known something of the soul-destroying edge of that state. Thus he is in full empathy with the desperation that fuels the "black might" of the retaliatory violence led by the Black Panthers of the time. In the spirit of this empathy the poem squarely, and climactically, points the finger of blame at white America. The message of nemesis, albeit a mutual tragedy, is specifically aimed at a white system, the violence of which now erupts in these extremes of black retaliation. The scourge of this black retaliation is here identified with that of the Jewish Passover (when God's angel passed over and killed the firstborn of every Egyptian household), "when the black X's / mark their passover with slain seraphim". The allusion is suggestive of a divine agency in the nemesis overtaking a white guilt which has brought down this doom upon its own head. Walcott echoes the voice and language of the black spirituals to deliver this message of apocalypse:

> The Gulf, your gulf, is daily widening,
>
> each blood-red rose warns of that coming night
> when there's no rock cleft to go hidin' in
> and all the rocks catch fire, when that black might,
>
> . . . .
> mark their passover with slain seraphim.

(CP, 107)

This is an appropriate point at which to review Walcott's position on the role of militant activism in the cause of resistance. From the corpus so far, as well as this poem, it is clear that he is fully committed to the cause of resistance against racial and political oppression. It is equally clear, from his views in the essays examined above, that he rejects militant activism as it serves an ideology of revenge, or as the main instrument of revolutionary change. From what we have seen up to this point, there appears to be some area of indeterminacy and contradiction in his position on the place of militant activism in resistance. In the present poem, for example, the extremist militancy of the Black Panthers – with whose cause he empathizes – is defined as "moonless", signifying the extinction of a guiding light of belief (as in "Goats and Monkeys"). The exposure to racism in the United States, though, does help to open his consciousness to the value of militant action in the cause of resistance. He is, no doubt, influenced in this direction by his keen penetration of the extremity of racial despair in that environment. Ultimately, "The Gulf" comes out of the same depth of concern with the extremes of black victimization at the core of the tragedy as we saw in "The Glory Trumpeter"; and throughout the period he is responsive to the various ways in which the travesties of being "a secondary soul" manifest themselves in the condition of black America. In "Blues", for example, he goes out to meet the bitter, brutal end of these travesties on the pavements of the ghettoes of New York. There he comes into stark confrontation with the harsh reality of love turned inside out, as young coloured Americans beat each other "black and blue". A "yellow nigger", he bears witness as a personal victim as they fight out this lack of love among themselves.

It is from the background of such knowledge that Walcott makes this very significant appreciation of the contribution of Malcolm X in "Any Revolution Based on Race Is Suicidal" (1973), the very interview in which he is concerned to reject race as an ultimate creed: "Why is it that a politician cannot get up and say, so and so is the situation? . . . When Malcolm X got up and spoke and said it, he said it. He gets killed. All right, but look at what he's done for the whole movement in America."[46] Significantly, it is not Martin Luther King but Malcolm X whom he sees as the true catalyst of change in the racial struggle of black America. The fact is that Walcott identifies closely with all Third World revolutionaries inspired by the widest humanist vision: this is his first loyalty. It is the basis of the appeal of the figure whom he hails as the revolutionary of the decade – Ernesto "Che" Guevara, revolutionary and activist in his holistic anti-imperialist cause.[47] The depth of Walcott's commitment to the humanist cause leads him to embrace, in a Guevara, the activist committed to the guerrilla method as an integral means to a wider end – just as he is able to appreciate the crisis point in America's racial history which calls for the radicalism of a Malcolm X. This helps to put Walcott's overall position into proper perspective. What he rejects is an ideology of militancy, in which armed struggle tends to come with an inbuilt principle of self-perpetuating violence. He is, moreover, most perceptive about how quickly and inexorably what begins as a strategy of militancy generates and perpetuates itself to die hard as an ideology.[48] But, for him, there is a vast difference between this and militant action as part of an integrated humanist vision – with which he does identify. It also means that Walcott, well aware of the fact that race is politics, recognizes the value of racial militancy as a means to an end. This position remains consistent with his fundamental, larger belief that race can never be the end and absolute basis of a social order. The America of the "long hot summers" is consummate proof of the self-destructive, suicidal route of a racist system. It is for this reason that, along with the deeply spiritual condemnation of the "gospel of the whip and flame", "The Gulf" carries a strong angle of protest aimed at a white supremacist America responsible for institutionalizing a racist system.

This represents the characteristic angle of protest in Walcott's concern with race and politics in the poetry of the period. When we put "The Gulf" together with other significant public poems such as "Elegy" and "Negatives" (*The Gulf*), Walcott's is primarily the voice of the disadvantaged, emergent Third World – embracing the ex-colonized and racially oppressed – aiming its protest at the metropolitan developed world of imperialist power. The main quarrel is with the nearby United States as the contemporary stronghold of neo-imperialism. The preoccupation with the United States also comes from his early consciousness of how closely the destiny of the Caribbean region is bound up with that of the Americas. One effective image from "Elegy" extends his view of this relationship: "Our hammock swung between Americas" (*CP*, 109). The Caribbean archipelago is bounded at one end by the hegemonic presence of North America; at the other end it is linked to the South American continent by virtue of a shared purpose of New World liberation and discovery ("A Map of the Continent"). Walcott also conveys his sense of the precariousness of his small, impoverished archipelago hanging "in air" between the two (a motif which, as we saw, was prominent in "The Gulf"). On the positive side, the hammock image is emblematically associated with Che Guevara who, in his revolutionary commitment and career, embodied the unity of the Caribbean and South American region. Guevara also had a clear commitment to proletarian internationalism, with which Walcott's essentially Third World perspective closely identifies. The concern with issues of race and politics in this volume, for example, ranges over the revolutionary movements at home; the "long hot summers" of the United States; and the Biafran war in "Negatives", where, in a profoundly turned conceit on the reversed black and white graphics of the film negative, he aims this message at the white metropolitan world:

> The soldiers' helmeted shadows
> could have been white, and yours
> one of those sun-wrapped bodies on the white road

(CP, 124)

Walcott makes one of his most searching comments on the political culture that the United States stands for in "Elegy". It is a comment that zeroes in on that country's betrayal of the New World democratic ideal, of its promise as the land of the future, as Whitman believed.[49] The poem surveys the face of its crisis-ridden society in the turbulent decade of the 1960s – the era of the assassination of John Kennedy, of the Vietnam War, of racial uprising, and of the disaffection of the youth, which found expression in the alternative culture of the hippie movement. They are all symptoms of a deep distemper in the society – a distemper presaged by the original, endemic ill of North American civilization: the violation of the principle of freedom. The poem, dated June 1968, seems to have been directly triggered by the death of Che Guevara (1967),[50] and the considerable power of its statement on the corruption of the American dream is a measure of Walcott's sense of the tragedy of the loss of Guevara to this part of the world. He makes his special act of homage to Guevara in "Che" (*The Gulf*) where, rescuing him from his unceremonious death "in [the] brown trash" (of the Bolivian Indian village), he consecrates and commits him to the enduring properties of the "veined, white Andean iron" of his native landscape. In "Elegy", which opens with the falling of his bullet-riddled body, he is the latest of those who fought for the recovery of the original New World dream of freedom, and joins the company of "those who cried, the Republic must first die / to be reborn" (*CP*, 109). Thus, there is reference to North American precursors in that struggle, such as Lincoln – and, by extension, Kennedy. Both were victims of assassination, which is important to Walcott's focus, as is intimated in his deliberate echo of Whitman's "When Lilacs Last in the Dooryard Bloom'd".[51] Both were also, significantly, sympathetic to the cause of racial liberation. The elegy is therefore for all who have so engaged and died in this struggle for change, reflecting on the bleak realization that none of these survive the chronic and intransigent conditions of the established order. Guevera's death is like the last nail in the coffin, sounding the death of liberty itself:

> Che's
> bullet-riddled body falls,
> And those who cried, the Republic must first die
> to be reborn, are dead,
> the freeborn citizen's ballot in the head.
>
> (*CP*, 109)

Ultimately, the elegy is for the death of the spirit of liberty, incapable of thriving in the North American environment.

The diagnostic portrait of the next few stanzas brings the contemporary scenario and the early history of the country into one span, in an attempt to account for the society in its state of crisis. Essentially a foreshortened view of North American civilization, it is a remarkable feat of compression. The portrait concentrates on the interweaving of present and past from the outset. Surveying the strains and stresses in the characteristic expressions of various segments of the society, it zeroes in on the original sin/wound of racial genocide as source and surviving scourge of its civilization. In his savage encounter with the native American, the white settler's relentless, brutal extermination of the Other has left a legacy of human violation buried deep in the North American psyche – a legacy of human violation which persists in the underlying system of race as shaping force in the society. Thus the ravages of this violation are painfully evident in the voice of its most chronic victim, black America, howling out in song like a bear trapped in the cage of white civilization. The search for release from the pervasive pressures and tensions of this unwholesome climate drives the youth in their delirious pursuit of an anti-establishment millennium:

> Some splintered arrowhead lodged in her brain
> sets the black singer howling in his bear trap,
> shines young eyes with the brightness of the mad,
> tires the old with her residual sadness;

(*CP*, 109)

The context of that original encounter with the American Indians has already been invoked in the echo of Norman Mailer with which the portrait opens: "But the old choice of running, howling, wounded / wolf-deep in her woods" (*CP*, 109). The reference notes the contrast between the fate of the American Indians, hunted back into the woods, and the now open manifestations of a pain so pervasive that its public and private sources are one. But a core statement in this poem is that there is as yet no release for a society still entrapped in the persistent violations of that original sin/wound.

The reference to the assassination of political figures with which the poem begins is also an important aspect of the diagnosis. Evoking the fate of Lincoln, the line from Whitman cited earlier sounds this theme of the recurrence of presidential assassinations. As suggested earlier, Lincoln's, as well as Kennedy's,[52] sympathy with the cause of black freedom does linger in this allusion, and bears its ironic reflection in Walcott's comment on the fate of the few who have been committed to the republican ideal. But the emphasis is on the deliberately ironic twist he gives to Whitman's line: his *"yearly* lilacs in her dooryard bloom" is intended primarily to cast the shadow of this grim fate which haunts the country's political establishment. The figure of the assassin thus appears in the last stanza, stalking Washington as its veritable nemesis. Walcott's critical gaze is trained on a Washington that continues to bear the major share of the responsibility for the iniquity that so afflicts the society, as it persists in the role it first played in administering the crime against the American Indians. He gives an incisive summation of that role in the lines: "while the white papers snow on / genocide" (*CP*, 109). The lines allude to the breach of promises in treaties made with the American Indians – an official policy of masking over deception on the part of the early white settlers. The poem projects the image of the Washington of the present, secure and isolated in the illusions of the power and greatness of an idyllic system. Walcott's evocation of that idyll is subtle and felicitous: the pastoral effects of the cherry orchard which enhance the setting of the Washington Monument recall and merge with the echoes of Chekhov's *The Cherry Orchard* (1904), intimating the sense of an illusion fatally out of touch with reality. The figure of the assassin which stalks that idyll represents the ironic backlash of the corruptions of the system.

"Elegy" is a poem of remarkable intellectual concentration in its attempt to put contemporary American society into historical perspective, the approach through history being typical of Walcott. It is also a poem which illustrates a major aspect of the function and value of assimilation and allusiveness in his work. He enters and recovers the course of this history mainly through the literature of the country, which for him always means the substance and genius of a place essentialized in its classics. Thus he reenters through Mailer the encounter with the native Americans. Against the background of Whitman's idealization of the new republican order and its heroes, he goes to his critical focus on the performance of the government of the United States and its legacy. The seminal significance of the Puritan ethos in the process and production of American civilization is also recognized. Walcott concludes his poem with a definitive reflection on this feature, behind which echoes of Lowell can be heard. The poem also encompasses "live" contemporary history in picking up the popular tropes and icons of the cultural milieu. Thus, "Still, everybody wants to go to bed / with Miss America" (*CP*, 109) chronicles the sensational cult of Marilyn Monroe, prime sex-glamour symbol and popular American (tragic) muse of the period. The feature provides, in turn, the symbol of the irresistible seductions and glamour of materialism with which

America, despite its ills, remains synonymous. In this same context, the historic unconscious irony of Marie Antoinette's comment on the hunger of the masses in revolutionary France finds its way into the poem: "if there's no bread, / let them eat cherry pie" (*CP*, 109).

The concluding images of the poem round off this diagnosis in foregrounding the root sources of the hereditary violation and self-violation which still afflicts the society:

> and the cherry orchard's surf
> blinds Washington and whispers
> to the assassin in his furnished room
> of an ideal America, whose flickering screens
> show, in slow herds, the ghosts of the Cheyennes
> scuffling across the staked and wired plains
> with whispering, rag-bound feet,

(CP, 109–10)

The assassin's dream of an ideal America (purged of the iniquities of Washington) is mocked by the scenes which flash across the screen of historical memory. Their images tell the story of an "ideal America" perverted from the outset. The shadow of its genocidal origins returns in the image of the American Indians herded along the infamous Trail of Tears (late 1830s). Travelled by the American Indians in their enforced displacement from southeastern homelands westward to "Indian territory", this Trail of Tears has gone down in history as one of the worst experiences in protracted, unspeakable human misery and devastation.[53] The image which follows is a psychic projection of the ethos that fuelled the white settlers in this destructive course. Its waspish farm couple, driven by the fanaticism of their grassroots Puritanism, are turned infernal in their fixation with an ideal America rooted free of evil:

> while the farm couple framed in their Gothic door
> like Calvin's saints, waspish, pragmatic, poor,
> gripping the devil's pitchfork
> stare rigidly towards the immortal wheat.

(CP, 110)

The rigidity of their stare defines a dream transmogrified. This concluding image of the atavistic Puritan-driven ethos to root out evil/the Other – in witch-hunt or race-hunt – appropriately undersigns it all. Walcott holds out to North America in this poem a very bleak and despairing self-image – a measure of his profound disenchantment with it and concern for its iniquities.[54]

Informed by the commitment to the struggle of the emergent postcolonial world on the whole, this critical engagement with the issues of race and politics in North America carries the cause of his society as well. But, outside the wider context of revolutionary creed (part 1), the issues of race and politics immediate to his environment are, at this stage, more pressing and substantive in the crisis of history and landscape as negation (chapter 3), and are engaged primarily at this level. The emphasis in Walcott's internal criticism of Caribbean society falls, rather, on the moral shortcomings of the peculiar mores and character of its people. It finds expression in social disgust with what he sees as the spiritual prostitution and self-debasement betrayed in some of these mores and attitudes. He responds, for example, with "hopelessness and rage" at the apish habits of bourgeois Christian culture practised by the depressed people of Laventille ("Laventille"); and he berates the mindless gaiety of the carnival celebration in "Mass Man". But there are two sides to this quite complex disgust of Walcott's. Some of these failings are the effects of the bitter disfigurements of the landscape and its past, as in the case of the apish habits of Laventille. These are the habits that provoke the kind of anger that "twist[s] [his] love within him like a knife". The other side is an unadulterated disgust provoked by the moral shortcomings for which Caribbean people must assume native responsibility. Walcott's anger at Caribbean society remains strung between the two in the poems of these middle volumes.

One of the most critical failings, in his view, is the propensity to this moral irresponsibility ingrained in the fête-loving, virtually hedonist culture of the society. A most characteristic and full comment on this feature occurs in "Mass Man" (*The Gulf*), a poem which dramatizes his response to a carnival celebration in Trinidad – carnival being, among other things, the quintessential expression of the fête-loving personality of that island. The axis of the poem turns on the gap between the total, gay abandon of the mass-men (masqueraders) engaged in the revelry, and the figure of an unwilling participant, Walcott himself, incapable of joining in the unbridled gaiety, and suffering, instead, a "terrible calm". Walcott the poet is there in his own person; and the real trauma and desperation of this experience for him is conveyed in the disguise of the bat-figure which he plays. Its sinister, dark silence is remote from the gaiety and glitter of the general revelry: "But somewhere in that whirlwind's radiance / a child, rigged like a bat, collapses, sobbing" (*CP*, 99). The bat is a traditional feature surviving from the earlier, more ritual forms of the Trinidad carnival, popularly known as ole mas.[55] It harks back to the origins of West Indian carnival in the resistance efforts as well as the terrors of the slave past. These terrors are deftly evoked in the allusion to the silk-cotton tree and the "bull-whipped body". (Slaves were hung from the silk-cotton tree, which thus became associated with supernatural lore and customs.)[56] Against the echoes of these earlier terrors, he hears and feels, as the child "rigged like a bat", the emptiness and void of the mindless abandon of the revellers, a great distance away from the consciousness and cause that marked the beginnings of carnival in the region.

Walcott totally recoils from this void, although he is quite capable of responding appreciatively to the singular richness of the "coruscating fantasies" of the roles portrayed by the masqueraders. Marvelling in the opening lines at their wit and resourcefulness, he captures their spirit and rhythm in the idiolect which is their very element:

> Hector Mannix, waterworks clerk, San Juan, has entered a lion,
> Boysie, two golden mangoes bobbing for breastplates, barges
> like Cleopatra down her river, making style.
> "Join us," they shout. "Oh God, child, you can't dance?"
>
> (*CP*, 99)

But in his view the humour and whirlwind energy remain more truly escapist in their extravagance than cathartic. As he subtly implies in the play on "withholds the man", the performance amounts to an evasion of self and of consciousness.

"Mass Man" was received by local critics as a problematic, controversial statement on carnival. Appearing in the period of the rallying call for cultural nationalism, it seemed a curious attack on one of the major cultural expressions of West Indian society. Its unduly morbid reaction was, moreover, a misrepresentation of carnival.[57] Gordon Rohlehr succinctly sums up the case against Walcott's position in the poem: "The Dionysiac masquerader knows, perhaps better than the Apollonian poet, that Carnival is a dance of death."[58] Rohlehr hits upon important areas of the truth, both in terms of insight into the hedonism of carnival, and some of the reasons behind the particular bias of Walcott's response. The truth is that Walcott seems by temperament, at least at this stage, incapable of fully giving himself to the mass and heedless exuberance of carnival. It is, perhaps, the temperament of the small-islander who can never quite enter a peculiar style of carnival fever and "possession" that is exclusively Trinidadian, and who remains something of an outsider. In his case this outsiderness is particularly acute. In "On Choosing Port of Spain", an important essay on Trinidad as his country by adoption, his comments on carnival give insight into these sources:

> its truth being that Trinidadian, or Creole gaiety at its most exuberant can be the most depressing experience in the world. How so when its wildest display is at Carnival, "a Creole bacchanal"?
>
> Carnival is all that is claimed for it. It is exultation of the mass will, its hedonism is so sacred that to withdraw from it, not to jump up, to be a contemplative outside of its frenzy is a heresy.[59]

Incidentally, he does acknowledge here the intrinsic powers of its hedonism. In this entry from "American without America" (University of the West Indies Collection), his desperation as an outsider is expressed in an image which conveys the sense of a true phobia: "If you didn't jump up, something was wrong with you. Refusal could produce a nightmarish inferiority in a contemptuous crowd of fêting Trinidadians. It could produce on your cold-sweating face the desperate grin of a man bitten by a tarantula who dances in the sun."[60]

But this negative reaction of "Mass Man" and the comments cited above are far from being Walcott's only or last word on carnival. He tells the truth about carnival when he goes on in "On Choosing Port of Spain" to describe it as a "myriad-faceted spectacle", which also means that it presents contradictory features: "There is always one aspect at least that the heretic enjoys."[61] If he is unable to identify with its particular variety of exuberance, he has been very affirmative of the creative values and resources of some of its other, fundamental aspects. The evidence is there in his drama and in statements made in essays and occasional pieces. In this context, it is important to observe that it is Walcott who sees in the creativity of carnival this classic paradigm of a vital aspect of Caribbean culture: a process which, starting in imitation, ends in invention. He argues this in another major essay, "The Caribbean: Culture or Mimicry?", where he defends the integrity of West Indian culture:

> The ceremony which best exemplifies this attitude to history is the ritual of carnival. . . . The impromptu elements of the calypso, like the improvisation and invention of steelband music supersedes its traditional origins, that is the

steeldrum supersedes the attempt to copy melody from the xylophone and the drum, the calypso supersedes its ancient ritual forms in group chanting. From the viewpoint of history, these forms originated in imitation if you want, and ended in invention, and the same is true of the Carnival costume, its intricate, massive and delicate sculpture improvised without self-conscious awe of reality, for the simple duplication of ancient sculptures is not enough to make a true Carnival costume. Here are three forms, originating from the mass, which are original and temporarily as inimitable as what they first attempted to copy. [62]

One of the strongest endorsements of the Trinidadian and West Indian carnival to date occurs in this essay. [63]

Ultimately, the core concern in "Mass Man" remains the fête mentality itself, which has been a recurrent source of misgiving from as far back as the well-known "Poopa, da' was a fête!" ("Tales, Chapter VI", *Green Night*) where the thematic context is very much the same: a scene of "jump and jive", a far cry from the earlier awe and spiritual engagement of the practices of folk religion enacted in the area. It reappears in the reflection of West Indian immaturity in the "young crowd out fêting, swilling liquor" in "The Glory Trumpeter". In his eyes the exuberance is primarily a manifestation of this habitual escapism. It is this which, beyond the personal phobia, provokes his moral repugnance in "Mass Man". Thus, in the end, he is the sacrificial poet assuming the purgatorial rites of conscience for a spiritually bankrupt and wasted community, but in a spirit of recrimination expressed in raw and caustic terms: "some mind must squat down howling in your dust, / some hand must crawl and recollect your rubbish" (*CP*, 99). It is a mood which echoes the despairing attitude towards the negations of landscape against which he struggles from *The Castaway* through *The Gulf*, and there are strains of the desolating stasis of "Anse La Raye" and "Moon" in the terrible calm of "Mass Man". But typically, there is the equally strong purposive side to this quarrel with West Indian hedonism. Walcott's final impatience and exasperation is with the society's delinquency in assuming the self-responsibility that must go towards the urgent necessity of decolonizing the mind, and towards the attainment of true self-determination. It is, for him, the first necessity of revolutionary possibility, given the peculiar past of Caribbean society.

Another Life
Alter/Native Metaphors in Fulfilment

Another Life (1973), Walcott's long autobiographical poem, is wellestablished as a watershed in his poetic achievement. This was the work which brought him recognition as one of the foremost poets writing in English and secured his international reputation. For William Plomer the work placed Walcott among the first four poets writing in English; and Robert Lowell was exultant in a letter to Walcott: "O let me congratulate you again on your tremendous book!"[1] Its impact has been rivalled only by *Omeros* (1990).

Walcott returns in this work to his artistic beginnings in his native St Lucia, recapturing an experience shared with certain individuals who feature prominently in the poem – two fellow St Lucian artists, Dunstan St Omer and Harold Simmons, and his first love, a St Lucian girl called Andreuille Alcée. It is useful to begin with a look at the genesis of the poem and its period of composition, as these help to put into perspective its aims and achievements. As E. Baugh notes in his pioneering monograph on *Another Life*,[2] it was inspired by "Leaving School" (1965), the autobiographical essay which contains the essential biographical context of the poem. Prompted by the flood of memories released in this essay, Walcott began, in April 1965, to write the prose version from which the completed poem emerged in 1972.[3] The process of development from prose narrative to poem makes, in itself, a fascinating study. The period of composition, though, is of immediate significance here. During this period Walcott is engaged in writing, along with *Another Life*, a number of the major definitional pieces of his middle career. These include the poems of *The Gulf* (1969), with the outstanding "Guyana" sequence and the title poem; *Dream on Monkey Mountain* (begun in 1959); the important statement essays, "What the Twilight Says" (begun in 1968) and "The Muse of History", as well as "The Figure of Crusoe". This is also the period of keen engagement with the public and social scene we examined in the last chapter.

A number of key themes and ideas cut across all the works of this period in what emerges as one single, exploratory and definitional phase. The interior quest for a fresh discovery of self, beginning in an elemental naming, is central in the "Guyana" sequence and in *Dream on Monkey Mountain*; and the dialectical inquiry into the Old World, Western tradition and its muse of history is a prominent link between the two essays discussed above (chapter 4) and *Another Life. Another Life*, spanning the period, represents the veritable confluence of these concerns, and is the place where they find their deepest resolutions and definitions. It marks a culmination of his thought and ideas as a Caribbean poet, and the arrival, at this midpoint of his career, at a consciousness which remains seminal to his total achievement.

Deep Narrative, Structure and Thematic Unity in Another Life

Within the autobiographical framework of Walcott's return to his artistic beginnings, *Another Life* presents his own story, along with those of the two compatriots earlier mentioned, closely engaged, like him, in the pioneering endeavour of the late 1940s. Dunstan St Omer (b. 1927), now a painter of Caribbean repute, was a fellow apprentice in painting and a close friend. Harold Simmons (1915–66), a professional painter himself and the oldest of the trio, served as art tutor and mentor to the younger two. Retracing their life stories as artists some twenty years later, *Another Life* is, at the most immediate level, the biography of a brotherhood of artists. As such, it is a narrative directly concerned with the pattern of their spiritual growth; and its essential resemblance to Wordsworth's *The Prelude* (1805) in this respect has been noted by Baugh and others.[4]

The poem presents a form, however, which differs significantly from Wordsworth's epical progress in the *Prelude*. Beginning with a prelude of his own artistic boyhood ("The Divided Child", book 1), Walcott structures the work around the three figures who dominate this combined biography: that of St Omer, called Gregorias in the poem (book 2); that of Anna, the name he gives to Andreuille Alcée, the first love whose story stands for his own (book 3); and that of Simmons, the "master" of Gregorias and himself (book 4). Around these lives he orchestrates a number of interrelated themes, some already familiar from other works of the period, as indicated above. To enter into an appreciation of the complex of meanings explored in *Another Life*, it is necessary from the outset to identify the deepest, root level of the creative purpose unifying the entire work – that is, the deep narrative carried within the primary narrative of the three lives, which the latter, in fact, subserves. Walcott himself gives the cue into this deep narrative in this summation at the end of "A Simple Flame" (book 3), originally intended as the conclusion of the work:

> No metaphor, no metamorphosis,
> as the charcoal-burner turns
> into his door of smoke,
> three lives dissolve in the imagination,
> three loves, art, love, and death . . .[5]

(CP, 257)

These lines identify the essentially philosophical purpose of the work: it is an exploration, anchored in the lived experience, of the relationship between art, the human urge for fulfilment in creativity; love, its motive force and very element; and death/mortality, which sets their limits at every turn. Walcott embarks on an age-old theme in this preoccupation with art, love and death, significantly designated the "three loves". They are humanity's three fundamental preoccupations with the problem of destiny, and together constitute its single, threefold existential angst; composing, in Yeats's words, "man's image and his cry". We should not miss, though, the especially fresh focus in the identification of death as one of the loves. It is, effectively, a placing of death within the overarching embrace of love, telling us that the existential angst over death, as with art/creativity, is a function of the love factor. (This particular focus will profoundly influence the kind of revaluations and meanings that distinguish Walcott's search for a revisioned humanity.) Altogether, however, this trinity of lives/loves which gives the poem its structure stands for the life narrative itself: the deep narrative of *Another Life,* searching out a fresh intelligence of art, love and death, is working towards a philosophy of humankind. In so doing, it continues Walcott's underlying quest for a fresh "other" order of humanist intelligence – which is the final significance of the title *Another Life.*

The "three loves" remain firmly anchored, however, in the biographies of the three individuals concerned. The spirit of art is identified in the personal story and characteristic achievement of St Omer. His was the kind of soul so wholly possessed of that spirit of creativity that it found its own original paths of discovery, to break revolutionary ground. The Anna experience, representative of Walcott's own story as artist/lover, carries the narrative of love – whose original light/flame is reflected in the idealism, with all the attendant contradictions and ambiguities, embodied in the image of Andreuille Alcée as first love. The burden of death manifests itself in the uncannily emblematic fate of Harold Simmons, who, succumbing to despair and failure, committed suicide during the period of the poem's composition. The shadow of death, made so palpable in the "master's" tragedy, permeates all flames to haunt "that mortal glow" in which the poem comes to discover the final light of existence.[6] This light/flame motif, and the imagery it generates, is integral to the deep narrative of the work.

A vital and functional principle of *Another Life* is Walcott's artistic treatment of the biographical material which yields these meanings. He is concerned, strictly, to distil in re-creation the inner essence of these lived experiences, and it is an aesthetic which directly serves the deep narrative we have identified. This aesthetic presents a significant affinity with Nabokov's *The Gift* (1963), a work which Walcott was reading at the time, and which he has acknowledged as a liberating influence in his approach to this work.[7] *The Gift* is likewise the autobiography of a young artist reviewing the experiences that went into his making. Nabokov exploits one informing idea in creating this work: the integrity and authority of the inner truth of the lived experience, over and above strict historical accuracy, even to the extent of radical departure from and editing of the actual experience.[8] *The Gift* is thus a powerful paradigm of the fictive process searching out meaning and reality in the substance of experience; and, therefore, also a search for the truth of the imagination. From the very beginnings of this work, Walcott shows a strong preoccupation with the relationship between fiction and autobiography. One of his entries on the subject describes autobiography as the "supreme fiction", requiring, therefore, third person narration.[9] Robert Lowell, seizing upon the modality of this supreme fiction in *Another Life,* makes important observations about its dynamic: "I'm sure autobiographical works such as we write are fiction, are selective (if honest) an assemblage and invention out of what we lived, as real as that."[10] Following Lowell's formulation, if autobiography is the authoritative testimony of experience and its meanings, it is in the fictive factor – that is, art itself – that it finds its final access of reality. Walcott's quest for reality in these biographies is also, implicitly and explicitly, an exploration of the relationship between art/Imagination and life. His reflection on the meanings of the three lives/loves in the passage earlier cited extends into his paradoxical affirmation of their reality as immanent in, yet other than, the actual:

> not one is real, they cannot live or die,
> they all exist, they never have existed:

> (*CP*, 257)

The truths which these lives manifest belong not in the realm of the empirical, but of the imagination, which alone can confer infinity on things. This opens out into another primary, related aspect of the fictive treatment of these biographies in the poem. Just as the concerns of art, love and death are mutually inclusive and interinvolved, so each individual narrative comprehends and compounds related elements and features of the other lives. Thus the narrative of Simmons's tragic defeat incorporates the story of St Omer's near-suicide in failure and despair, and of Walcott's own experience of bitter struggle in a climate of close, reactionary hostility to his artistic efforts (book 4). Similarly, the burden of "the estranging sea", of mortal limitations as divine necessity, repeats itself from the "goodbyes" of first love ("A Simple Flame") to the deeper tragedy of Simmons's despairing end ("The Estranging Sea"). Merging into each other in this way, it is out of the synthesis of their combined meanings that the poem arrives at its single vision of "another life"/possibility. The stories of St Omer, Walcott/Anna, and Simmons, in fact, as explored in *Another Life,* constitute one artistic odyssey, and together define one single, poetic fiction of life.

In thus filtering out the inner meanings of these lives, the biographical aesthetic of *Another Life* invests them with metaphoric and mythic value. Their metaphoric and mythic aspects are an integral part of a larger, inclusive achievement. Out of the figures of St Omer, Simmons, Anna, Walcott raises up native archetypes who embody the particular order of meanings/values through which the deep narrative of the "three loves" comes to realization and fulfilment. In the portraits of these figures, and in the presentation of their experience, he employs figural and iconographic techniques which throw this aspect of their significance into relief. This discovery and shaping out of archetypes from life experiences original to the environment – and it extends, as we shall see, to the generation of definitive metaphors out of the constituent matrix of its experience – is a fundamental part of the revolutionary achievement of this work. The response of an American critic, Paul Breslin, to the pervasiveness of Walcott's metaphoric treatment of biographical material obliquely reflects on its singular import in the poem. Breslin, in whose view *Another Life* is generally a failure, states one of his main objections as follows: "In *Another Life,* everything seems to be ready to turn into myth or metaphor before it is first solidly there."[11] He is especially unhappy with Walcott's precipitate treatment of the familiar and quotidian in this metaphoric/mythic style, and speaks about its failure to observe a "hierarchy of intensity" such as Wordsworth does in *The Prelude.* Breslin's comments in the piece suggest that he is missing what Bakhtin speaks of as the "epic distance" associated with the privileged absoluteness of the epic mode, and its related hierarchical values.[12] Walcott's concentrated selection of the familiar, quotidian and immediate for visionary treatment is, in fact, a purposive, subversive break with that tradition. Thus, from the earliest efforts in the prose version, he is very sensitive to the value of the obscurity and modesty of his biographical raw material: he notes in one entry that he has chosen in St Omer, then identified as the central protagonist of the work, an artist undistinguished by fame or outstanding achievement.[13] Breslin points, by default, to what is one of the most inventive aspects of Walcott's unorthodox style: aiming to recover the immanence of the metaphoric/mythic in the ordinary, it is reaching for an alternative order of values which runs directly counter to the traditional "hierarchy of intensity" and its epic construct.

This brings us to the crux of Walcott's discourse in the poem. At all major points of definition, the order of values being mediated through these lives is explored in dialectical/dialogic relation to the earlier order of the Old World Western tradition. This discourse hinges, definitively, on an inquiry into the Old World European muse of history, to aim, virtually, at deconstruction of the muse of humanity that has been its moving spirit – which ultimately means its informing vision of the trinity of art, love and death. It is this which constitutes the substantive, unifying argument through the main sections of the poem. Each of the three main narratives climaxes in this dialectically angled theme: a questioning of the older muse of humanity, and, answering this, the apprehension of an alternative, truer possibility. Characteristically for Walcott, the muse of a civilization or culture is crystallized and essentialized in its metaphors and images. (See chapter 1.) The dialectic is thus conducted through metaphors. Fresh metaphors are generated out of the matrix of a native experience whose root differences are dictated by history and setting, and set counter to earlier Western counterparts – the erstwhile "borrowed metaphors" of the colonizer's tradition – to effectively refute and displace the latter. In book 2 (Gregorias) the alter/native metaphor is drawn from the story of the leaping Caribs of Grenada, who, during the early attempts at European settlement of the region, jumped off of cliffs to their deaths rather than surrender to the French.[14] Theirs is a truer image of the combative engagement of human destiny than the ideal of heroic virtue enshrined in the legend of the Fighting Fifth "who wore the feather without stain"[15] – a metaphor of the Western martial imagination. In book 3 (Anna) the Anna of first love is a metaphor inspired by the Western other-worldly Platonist ideal of fulfilment. That metaphor gives way to Anna as the embodiment of the "simple flame" of love/creative being naturally immanent through existence. This is an order of apprehension accessible especially to the imagination of a newer, "virginal" world. The concluding effort in book 4 deciphers in the features of Rampanalgas, a small obscure village on the northeast coast of Trinidad, an alternative muse of history, timeless and mythic in its more real dimension. This is undertaken in refutation of the Old World epic muse, represented in such foundational examples as the Pharaonic monuments. Rampanalgas is thus invested with metaphoric/mythic value. The quest for a more meaningful order of humanist intelligence, firmly anchored in the region's past and its cause, finds these resolutions in terms of the threefold theme of art, love and death.

In this presentation of the biography of three native artists, Walcott is also doing something quite innovative and modernistic. The Greeks found the paradigm for their collective odyssey as a people in the epic adventure of heroic battles against foes, and its mythical extension in their sea voyages; in Dante's time, the Christian sojourn provided the paradigm. Here, by comparison, it is the artistic quest itself that is being proffered as the indigenous paradigm of a people's bid for creativity and identity in emergence from an oppressive past. In this context, Walcott achieves what he first conceived in this autobiography: to write "the spiritual history of a people".[16]

The Three Loves

Prelude: "The Divided Child"

Book 1, "The Divided Child", serves as a prelude to the exploration of the "three loves" defined in the artistic odyssey of this brotherhood of pioneers. As prelude, it comprises an introductory account of Walcott's own beginnings as an artist, and, extending out of this, an interpretive, reflective review of the motive causes and characteristic aspects of that beginning. In terms of the narrative structure of the work, to begin with the story of his own birth as an artist is particularly apposite, since he is to serve as witness and protagonist in the narrative of the three lives.

The opening sequences cite the very first influences behind his awakening to painting, his earliest formal apprenticeship, followed by his first interest in the possibility of a native poetry. Painting began with his passion for the world of the masters, which he first encountered in Thomas Craven's *Treasury of Art Masterpieces* (1939).[17] The latter was to prove a dominant influence, serving as a veritable museum (*CP*, 220) throughout the period. The inspiration to the goal of a native, revolutionary poetry found one of its earliest stimuli in the work of the Jamaican poet, George Campbell, whose lines were among the first to celebrate humanity and dignity in the black man's features. Campbell's lines are cited in the poem:

> Holy be
> the white head of a Negro
> sacred be
> the black flax of a black child . . .[18]

> (*CP*, 149)

Chapter 1 (book 1) also introduces the figure at the centre of both these apprenticeships – Harold Simmons, the "master", who, as art tutor and mentor, was responsible for Walcott's discovery of both Craven and Campbell. This was the man who imparted to both Walcott and St Omer his own strong commitment to a mission of native discovery. We see Simmons, an all too human figure, straining beyond the physical myopia from which he suffered – here made emblematic of the generic shortsightedness of humankind, as he shares in this endeavour: "Let us see" (*CP*, 147).

Two culminating moments, presented in the final chapter, recall Walcott's particular experience of awakening to the artistic calling, and specifically mark his birth as an artist. They were both moments of utmost sacredness and intensity. The first was the experience of opening and consecrating himself to the call of vision; the second an answering dedication of life and self to art as vocation. In the first, which occurred when he was fourteen years old, he "lost [him]self somewhere above a valley" (*CP*, 184) during a visit to the country.[19] Walcott describes a moment of near-mystical visitation, when he opened to the sense of creation in the universe, the condition of humanity, and, touched by the scene of the small labourer's houses in the valley below him, was overcome by the call to compassion. The other, the moment of decisive commitment to art, is recalled as a veritable experience of conversion. Recaptured in strains of religious exaltation, it is identified with the "unhorsing of Saul", an image which was to exert a lasting hold on his imagination.[20] It came, like Saul's, with the overpowering, revelatory impact of a total sundering from the old life, and surrender to another life/light:

> Our father,
> > who floated in the vaults of Michelangelo,
> St Raphael,
> > of sienna and gold leaf,
> it was then . . .
> > that he fell in love, having no care
> for truth,
> . . . .
> > that the lances of Uccello shivered him,
> > like Saul, unhorsed,
> that he fell in love with art,
> > and life began.

(CP, 186)

As is highlighted in this passage, the ideal of art to which Walcott makes this early commitment as the highest truth takes its image from the world of the Renaissance masters. The "amber glow" of their style was the light which suffused this period of his awakening, as now his memory of it. It represented a predominant influence. The realities of his native setting and society are an equally strong area of engagement in this beginning. A snapshot of one of his earliest efforts as an art student, appearing early in the sequence, virtually "places" Walcott between these two dominant attachments. He is endeavouring, in this early sketch, to transpose the amber light of the masters onto the shacks of the Morne overlooking his native town of Castries:

> and for the tidal amber glare to glaze
> the last shacks of the Morne till they became
> transfigured sheerly by the student's will,
>
> (*CP*, 146)

This effort encapsulates the core realities of his artistic beginnings. It shows, first, Walcott's original purpose, apprenticed to the Western tradition, to enhance the local landscape with its "borrowed" light. (See chapter 2.) At the same time, it focuses the disparity between that transfiguring amber light and the stark reality of the poor shacks, to zero in on the critical issue of dividedness in Walcott's simultaneous allegiance to Western art and to his native land-scape. Stemming from this original source, this dividedness remains the single most important factor accounting for the peculiar course of his development. It represents, in this book, the informing perspective in Walcott's testimony about his artistic childhood and its decidedly colonial background. The perspective remains inherent in the discourse of the other three books. In a fundamental sense, his quest for "another life" begins from the need to resolve the contradictions of this dividedness. The theme cuts through the heart of his discourse in *Another Life,* setting the terms of his concern with Old World values vis-à-vis those generated from his New World, native setting.

The depth of his engagement with landscape and its focal presence are registered in the special prominence of the St Lucian setting and society in this introduction. Five of the seven chapters of book 1 (chapters 2–6) are devoted to the biography of the island, as the necessary context of this artistic childhood. Certain key features recreate the St Lucia of that time. There is, first, the portrait gallery of a host of derelicts and eccentrics, who, all living legends in his native town of Castries, were representative of the extreme ends of the destitution of the "barefoot town". They assumed truly tragic propor-tions in his imagination (book 1, chapter 3). Next, and by far the most prominent, is the focus on the dominant presence of religion in the culture of the island. The scenes move from one to the other of its several facets and features, reflecting its complex clashes and contradictions in the lives of the people. "The Pact" (chapter 4), for example, highlights the practice of obeah in the tale of Auguste Manoir, whose strange death is believed to be the result of his pact with the devil. A trip down the coast recovers the stark, destitute conditions of life in the villages, dominated throughout by the overwhelming presence of Roman Catholicism, which played a key role in keeping that life entrapped in mental servitude. The grim picture of that St Lucia merits the heavy irony of this pun on "Virgil's tag": "A safe anchorage for sheeps".[21] Dramatizing this trip as a veritable odyssey of betrayal, Walcott comes to this final summation of the plight of the island: "Lost, lost, rain-hidden, precipitous, debased" (*CP*, 182). That image, behind which lies the spectre of a history of void and neglect, contains the full weight of the pain of landscape that burdened the earliest strivings of his native commitment. It was a primary source of the angst that motivated his revolutionary purpose.

Walcott's purpose in this return is reflective and interpretive, and while his focus is very much on the clashes and incongruities of dividedness, he is also concerned to recognize the positive elements and aspects of the total experience of that beginning. Thus, the return to his childhood environment begins with an acknowledgement of the lasting virtues and blessings of the home in which he grew up. He pays tribute to a mother who, in her own dutiful caring, created an atmosphere of familial piety, alive with the memory of his father and the bequest of his artistic gifts, fostering a sense of reverence for the things of the spirit. The latter was rendered even more tenacious by a strong religious upbringing in the Methodist faith to which the family adhered – itself quite intense amidst the island's prevailing climate of religiosity, albeit predominantly Catholic. Of the influences coming from the surrounding environment, some were even then beginning to enter into significant kinds of interaction with the borrowed world of Western art which shared his commitment. He is engaged in a sustained retrospective exploration of this feature in the aforementioned portrait gallery of chapter 3, a moving tableau of the town's derelicts and eccentrics, presented in alphabetical sequence. He claims them as his "alphabet of the emaciated". Reliving the early fascination which inspired him to find their counterparts among the Greek heroes of Homer,[22] he penetrates to the essential value of what he learnt from them. They represent, ultimately, his first real-life glimpse of human extremity and the tragic; and it was out of an intuition of the classic depth of their condition that he sought to uplift their statures to the enhanced levels of the world of the Greek heroes.

There is, however, a very important dimension to this linking of the two worlds of native setting and artistic model. During that early phase of apprenticeship, the stronger pull was to the heightened truth of the imagined world of such classical models; and it was that very pull that enkindled his sensitivity to the deeper reaches of the plight of the town's destitutes. Art itself, that is, provided the impetus. In retracing the complex, varied strands of his divided childhood, Walcott is very much concerned to probe and claim a dynamic point of departure in this primary allegiance to art, albeit that of the borrowed, Western tradition. Thus he takes this epigraph to book 1 from Malraux's *The Psychology of Art*: "[W]hat makes the artist is the circumstance that in his youth he was more deeply moved by the sight of works of art than by that of the things which they portray." In that psychology lay the genesis of his commitment to the principle of Imagination itself. This commitment remains seminal to his main orientation and purpose in the work, which embarks on the search for "another life / light" of the imagination.

In chapter 3 Walcott, looking back, culls a rich variety of effects from the matching of the disparate worlds of native setting and classical metaphor. The ironic discrepancies between them are a source of a great deal of playful and deflationary humour that sometimes cuts both ways. Homer's Ajax, for example, epitomizing the heroism of brawn, finds his local likeness in the carthorse from a nearby stable – "debased, bored animal". In the more serious portraits, however, something highly significant happens: the parallels mutually illuminate each other to reveal, on the one side, the classic condition of native desolation and, on the other, the naked extremes at the core of Greek mythology. We get a striking example of this in the portrait of Berthilia, the local counterpart of Cassandra. The horribly crippled Berthilia, carried on her son's back, occupies her daily perch on the city's sidewalk, where she maintains her unending flow of mutterings: "Cassandra, with her drone unheeded" (*CP*, 159). What sounds again in Walcott's memory of these mutterings are the intimations of an inner self ravaged in her wretched deformity; which echoes, in turn, the strains of the nakedness of the distress that must have possessed Cassandra, the raw desolation that fuelled her own drone of prophetic utterance. Above all, however, it is the plight of the inner Berthilia, penetrated in depth by this double focus, that comes to the fore. Along with hers comes the plight of her dutiful son, who wrests this desperate virtue from a wretched lot:

> a hump on her son's back, is carried
> to her straw mat, her day-long perch,
> . . . .
> horsey back, horsey-back;
> when he describes his cross he sounds content,
>
> (*CP*, 159)

In a book which gives us many examples of the differences and clashes of dividedness between the native world and that of the Western heritage, the

Greek parallels in this "alphabet of the emaciated" stand out as a singular area of affinity. This is a reflection of Walcott's early instinct for the primal power of the Hellenic imagination, which finds its fullest expression in the later *Omeros* (1990). The portrait of Janie, another outstanding one in the sequence, bears a similarly penetrating resemblance to her Greek counterpart. Janie, the town's top prostitute, is the local equivalent of Helen as the woman who, from the modernistic viewpoint, pursues an illusive, elusive fulfilment in her many relationships. The portrait probes through this resemblance to the inward Janie. That inward Janie represents a facet of dividedness crucial to Walcott's overall testimony on the theme. Hers is a condition which cuts through the entire society "christened, married, and buried in borrowed white" (*CP*, 152), one which Walcott himself knows only too well. As "the town's one clear-complexioned whore" she will sleep with sailors – meaning white customers – only. From his own deep empathy with that susceptibility, Walcott penetrates to the psychology of that choice, zeroing in on her dream/illusion of whiteness as the never-never paradisal beyond:

> Janie, the town's one clear-complexioned whore,
> with two tow-headed children in her tow,
>
> . . . .
> rolling broad-beamed she leaves
> a plump and pumping vacancy,
> "O promise me" . . .

(CP, 161)

In the end the lasting import of these figures, sharpened by memory, consists in this: sensitized by art, Walcott responded early to the imaginative and spiritual charges trapped within their cramped lives, fraught with such desperate disadvantages and deformities.

In his recollections of the pervasive influence of religion in the island, the focus falls on the curious admixture that gave the island its peculiar religious environment. The admixture comprised Roman Catholicism, then over 95 percent strong; the quite small Protestant contingents including his own "pragmatic Methodism"; as well as the practice of obeah, a folk religion harking back to the memory of ancestral Africa. A most remarkable phenomenon was the meeting of the formal with this folk religion. Suffusing the atmosphere of religiosity in the island, that doubleness seemed etched in the very physiognomy of the landscape: "One step beyond the city was the bush. / One step behind the churchdoor stood the devil" (*CP*, 167). It was, however, the power of obeah which proved the most remarkable, exerting its irresistible pull even on the middle-class community of devout Christians. Walcott recalls its impact on his own consciousness: "stronger than their Mass / stronger than chapel", its root sources in the body's atavistic memory of Africa (*CP*, 166–67). He recovers its power in "The Pact", which stands out as a special testimony in his narrative of the island. "The Pact" tells the tale of Auguste Manoir, "pillar of business and the Church", who lies dying in bed the morning after a strange dog, found nosing Manoir's business premises, is struck a blow. The only trace left by the ill-fated dog is a stain of "rich red" blood quite uncharacteristic of mongrels. In obeah, persons make a pact with the Devil – virtually sell their souls to him – for their own infernal ends, usually for lucre, or to do harm to their enemies. (Manoir, "the first black merchant", would have sold his soul to the Devil in exchange for prosperity in business.) The pact empowers them to take unnatural "animal" forms in order to do the Devil's work, so to speak. The person can be divested of his infernal powers, or "disengaged" – the term in St Lucian French patois is *dégagé* – while in this unnatural form, with the kind of sinister manifestations and disastrous or fatal consequences presented in the case of Manoir. He lies dying from the blow he suffered while in the form of a dog. Walcott renders in the scene the interchange between dog and human taking place in his person:

> Monsieur Manoir
> urged his ringed, hairy hand to climb his stomach
> to nuzzle at his heart.
> Its crabbed jaw clenched the crucifix;
> he heaved there, wheezing,
> in the pose of one swearing eternal fealty,

(CP, 168)

The description bears witness to the intrinsic logic of the structure of this belief. Manoir's death struggle is a manifestation of the deep sin of his abdication of the human, its perversion into the unhuman. From the power of such manifestations and their atavistic lore came Walcott's first sensings of the reality of good and evil in the human soul. As this tale shows, they left an imprint on his consciousness as strong as his pull, at the other pole, to the transcendent soul of the Western tradition in Craven's book. Both of these are sources which underlie the strong sense of the mythic and spiritual in Walcott.

The crowning testimony of that early biography is, however, the life that began with "falling in love with art". An integral and vital part of his return is the concern with the visionary perspectives, the ways of seeing of that first "life", penetrating straight to the existential questions of art, love and death. The concern turns on a revaluation of earlier meanings of these life issues in the altered light of experience. The life/light motif of *Another Life* is focused from here. Images of art, love and death, recaptured in the earlier light of that awakening, are now being reappraised and displaced by another light of Imagination, anchored in the knowledge of lived experience. Book 1 thus gives us a preview of the deep narrative identified above, prefiguring the essential perspectives on the three loves to be explored in the next three books. It functions as a veritable "Prelude" in this respect, focusing the core retrospective purpose of altered perspectives on the three loves.

The light of that first life was that of the European tradition, especially as epitomized by the works of the Renaissance masters in Craven's book, where, as Walcott puts it in MS One, he found his soul.[23] It is, to all intents and purposes, with reference to the metaphysics of the Western tradition that images of art, love and death are being revisioned. "Whiteness", extending from the problem of dividedness, thus becomes the key referential image in this introductory discourse on changing, altered lights. Walcott begins here to ring several changes on, and virtually invent a new semantics, of whiteness. This is a feature which will be resumed in the main sections of the book.

The moments of meditation on art, love and death occur as culminating points in the narrative of book 1. Snapshots from memory recapture the earlier outlook on each of these three loves. Against each, the countering image of an altered perspective now defines itself. The pattern of imagery generated from this and its dialectic will be carried over into the main narrative represented by the three subsequent books. The earlier ideal of art, for example, is epitomized in this scenic view of the Vigie promontory of his native Castries:

> Begin with twilight, when a glare
> which held a cry of bugles
>
> . . . .
>
> It mesmerized like fire without wind,
> and as its amber climbed
> the beer-stein ovals of the British fort
> above the promontory, the sky
> grew drunk with light.
>
> (CP, 145)

The amber glaze of the masters was Renaissance art's emblematic colour of a heightened, transcendent world. It found its corresponding, cosmic symbol in the moon, traditional genius of the visionary otherness of the Western imagination. The image of twilight repeated the hues and significations of amber and moon. As such, moon, amber and twilight constitute an image cluster which becomes representative of the erstwhile depth of Walcott's attachment to the metaphysical absolutes of the Western tradition. To the yearning eyes of the colonial, whiteness, as the signal of that tradition, was "the colour of wisdom and higher things".[24] It was the mirror in which he sought an ultimate measure of truth/candour, inspiring his yearning for a higher transformation. This earlier faith virtually amounted to a semantic valuation of (Western) whiteness as wisdom. It is precisely this semantic valuation of whiteness as wisdom that is being turned on its head as Walcott moves to apprehend a quality of whiteness quite other and more meaningful than that of the transcendent, deifying perfections of the Western ideal. In this altered vision it becomes the whiteness/transparency of "skeletal candour" as the final and humanizing truth of finitude/mortality. The dialectic is stated in a subtle, antithetical play of images. The older moon, as symbol of the Western visionary ideal, is now replaced by a "younger" one whose light resembles that of the electric bulb – as agency of an illumination mediated through, and functional of, the vital energies of the sublunary earth. The bulb image is thus associated with the living light of day versus the other-worldly, mystical light of moon/amber/twilight. The significance of this change from the first to the "other" light is compressed in one powerful image:

> while the tired filaments of another moon,
> one that was younger,
> fade, with the elate extinction of a bulb?

(CP, 151)

Death, likewise, took its first reflection from Western metaphysics. This reflection is preserved in the memory of what must have been one of his earliest, most affecting encounters with death – significantly, the death of a child. He recalls his response to the death of a ten-year-old niece of Simmons, named Pinkie, and his idea of her destination in death. Pinkie was passing on to a paradisal, celestial sphere. Her fair-skinned features merged in his subconscious, as Walcott now recalls, with those of the dead child in a painting by Thomas Alva Lawrence (1769–1830): "another Pinkie, in her rose-gown floating?" (*CP*, 151). The highest light of the West was here again mediated through its art: "Gone to her harvest of flax-headed angels, / of seraphs blowing pink-palated conchs" (*CP*, 151). For the countering "light" to this one of seraphic transfiguration, Walcott envisions a photographic still of the characters of the town in that time:

> all that town's characters, its casts of thousands
> arrested in one still!
> As if a sudden flashbulb showed their deaths.
>
> (*CP*, 151)

It is an interesting variant of a futuristic image, projected, as it is, from a retrospective viewpoint. The focus is especially on the destiny of the children of that past, captured in a film negative. In the film negative, their white shadow – a graphic inversion of traditionally privileged whiteness – is the clairvoyant equivalent of their existential "negative": the shadow of death as immanent destiny.[25] This elegiac consciousness of their "white shadows" denies and replaces the faith in the transfiguring reaches of Pinkie's celestial destination. Walcott's dialectical concern with the traditional meaning of whiteness is most strongly condensed in this line: "Well, everything whitens" (*CP*, 151). It is a forceful, polemical puncturing of his former faith in the Western complexion of wisdom. Its final import, though, is that the whiteness of transcendent other-worldliness is virtually reversed to the whiteness of "skeletal candour" ("The Gulf"), the translucent no-thingness of death perceived and embraced as numinous truth.

Book 1 concludes with the meditation on love, the all-embracing muse of the trinity of loves – art, love and death. The experience of first love was deeply rooted in the experience of "falling in love with art" and its influences. Walcott cites his eighteenth year as his golden year, "annus mirabilis" of art and love.[26] The creative structuring of his biographical material is most pertinent at this point. Falling in love with Andreuille/Anna directly follows the crowning experience of "falling in love with art". The two, flowing into each other in an organic, psychic fusion, are also one in their "light"/metaphysic. To Walcott as artist and lover, Anna's beauty took its reflection from the spiritualized, transfigured madonnas of a Fra Angelico:

> A schoolgirl in blue and white uniform,
> her golden plaits a simple coronet
> out of Angelico, . . .
>
> (*CP*, 187)

Contradicting the perfections of love thus idealized and consecrated in Anna is the reality – from his vantage point some twenty years later – of a relationship whose promise remained unfulfilled, and which had its actual, swift outcome in separation. The biographical facts penetrate, definitively, to the existential reality of severance and separation. In the earliest version of the work Walcott's first musings on that experience of first love had brought back echoes of Arnold's "Letter to Marguerite", with its thematic image of "the estranging sea": "a god their severance ruled". He registers here the sense of a divinely ordained estrangement/severance in a sequence of impressionistic images, his verse moving, at this point, into choric recitative strains:

> that rigid iron lines were drawn between
> > him and that garden chair
>
> . . . .
>
> > that watching her rise
> from that bright boathouse door was like some station
> > where either stood, transfixed
> by the rattling telegraph of carriage windows
> > flashing goodbyes,
>
> > > > > (*CP*, 187)

The images fuse motifs from his own experience and that of Pasternak's *Doctor Zhivago,* investing with archetypal echoes the memories of the sights and scenes of his own loss in love, like those of the separation between Lara and Zhivago in Pasternak's novel. Love, in the face of this necessity of loss and separation, will find its true image in the pattern of resolutions embracing art and death. All three must ultimately have their single truth in the "mortal glow" of existence.

Gregorias: Art ("Homage to Gregorias")

Both in terms of Walcott's recollection of that period of artistic awakening, and of his concept of the original spirit of art, Dunstan St Omer's is the "life" identified with art. This close companion of his boyhood apprenticeship is christened Gregorias in the poem. St Omer, who has spent most of his lifetime's career as a painter in the island, is now the resident father-figure of painting in St Lucia, and a painter of regional stature, in the Caribbean as well as Latin America.[27] His work is fully representative of his life's ambition and early commitment to his native setting. The paintings include a large number of landscapes, seascapes and religious paintings in his own distinctive style, aimed at indigenizing the face of Christianity – the colonizer's religion creolized and naturalized in the native setting. His religious paintings adorn the walls of village and country churches in the island.[28] St Omer also stands out as an unusual and remarkable personality. Although now mellowed with age, he is very much the man captured in Walcott's portrait of Gregorias – a free spirit of "self-combustible energies",[29] an individual for whom, in earlier times, pious Catholic faith and this free-spiritedness were not incompatible. The self-combustible energies, the free-spiritedness, are qualities that stand at the centre of his significance in Walcott's testimony. In the spirit of his "self-combustible energies", he lit quite early on an original mode and style of painting which captured the character and sensibility of the landscape. In so doing, he became the pacesetter in a primary and most sacred function of art – that of naming its world. For Walcott, the true genius of St Omer's spirit and what it achieved consists in this naming, as pristine act of the imagination. What also comes back, with even more immediacy, is the impact of St Omer's personality in giving that beginning its exhilaration, fervour, sense of infinite possibility. Looking back at his friend's singular gifts of personality and talent Walcott is inspired to see him as the local equivalent of Mayakovsky, the poet genius of revolutionary Russia. He was rereading, at the time of writing the poem, Pasternak's *Safe Conduct* (*CP*, 273). This passage from Pasternak's tribute to Mayakovsky in that work seems to capture the essence of the comparison:

> He was the one who had the newness of the times climactically in his blood. He was strange through and through with the strangenesses of the age which were as yet half-realised. I began to call to mind the traits of his character, his independence, that in many ways was utterly peculiar to him. They could all be explained by his being accustomed to conditions which, although they were implicit in time, had not yet come into their everyday strength.[30]

Gregorias becomes, for these and the reasons cited above, the personification of seminal values and principles that will inform Walcott's revisioning of the ideal of art/imagination. Walcott goes instinctively to his story and portrait to begin MS One.

The essential focus of the narrative, however, is on their joint effort as pioneers, and their pursuit of a venture that made one of that effort. Walcott's own part in that story is thus carried alongside St Omer's. They were one in their commitment to the discovery "in paint, in words", of a hitherto unpainted, unwritten landscape. Between them, that commitment was something of a sacred vow, as Walcott recalls:

> But drunkenly, or secretly, we swore,
> disciples of that astigmatic saint,
> that we would never leave the island
> until we had put down, in paint, in words,
> as palmists learn the network of a hand,
> all of its sunken, leaf-choked ravines,

(CP, 194)

Their bond in that cause was strengthened by another actual, shared condition. They were, in significant ways, starting off as a pair of orphaned figures. Both were fatherless, not only in the literal sense, but also culturally, in terms of being traditionless. The following line sums up the essential condition in which they set out on their pioneering mission: "painter and poet walked / the hot road, history-less" (*CP*, 218). This is a strong emblematic coding of Walcott's thematic focus in dealing with their joint effort. United at these fundamental levels, their two stories define one indivisible biography, anchored in the meaning of Gregorias's genius. The narrative content and structuring of "Homage to Gregorias" must be seen in this context. Encompassed within the narrative, their individual stories as pioneering artists meet in correspondences, comparison and complementariness, to culminate in a synthesis which resolves into one single intelligence of art/imagination, an intelligence that will prove pivotal in Walcott's revisioning of human destiny.

Book 2 begins with a portrait which, paying full tribute to St Omer, establishes his central role as the pacesetter in their endeavour. Drawing on images, anecdotes and scenes from St Omer's family background and their days as apprentice painters, the portrait presents St Omer as an individual entirely of himself, remarkable in the strengths as well as the idiosyncrasies of his personality. Recovering these memories, Walcott comes to the awesome recognition, in this friend who could "ignite his imagination at will", of a real-life embodiment of "aboriginal force". He sees in the St Omer of those times an incarnation of the Dionysiac spirit in its original, native quality. Thus, he dubs him a "black Greek", which signifies, according to the Walcott credo, the meeting of Greek and African ancestries at these levels of primal power. It was that very "aboriginal force" which directed St Omer straight to his distinctly subjective style in painting. That style came from an approach at opposite poles, Walcott observes, from his own careful adherence to the disciplines of traditional painting: "Gregorias abandoned apprenticeship / to the errors of his own soul" (*CP*, 201). The soul it expressed, in its native, instinctual drives, was in tune with, inhabited by, the temper, character and physiognomy of its elemental environment. Walcott insets a composite sample of the characteristic motifs of St Omer's paintings to highlight this imprint of landscape in his style. The sample is also representative of his prevailing ambition to indigenize the face and sensibility of the Christian faith in his native setting:

> as Gregorias
> bent to his handful of earth,
> his black nudes gleaming sweat,
> in the tiger shade of the fronds.
>
> . . . .
>
> brown-bottomed tumbling cherubim,
> broad-bladed breadfruit leaves
> surround his oval virgin
> under her ringing sky,
> the primal vegetation
> the mute clangour of lilies,
>
> (*CP*, 203)

The imprint of landscape expressed in this sample of St Omer's style points to his core significance as the pacesetter. He was the first to realize and give expression to the genius of their elemental setting; the first to seize on the most seminal task of naming which, as underlined in the epigraph to this book, was the unique promise and gift of their virginal, unpainted world. Thus "every landscape we entered / was already signed with his name" (*CP*, 201). An earlier passage of homage to Gregorias, recalling the sheer exhilaration and headiness of those first days of painting, explores more fully the significance of this naming and "signing" of landscape. It comprises a sequence of impressionistic images of Gregorias in the characteristic overflow of his energies, totally possessing and possessed of the landscape. The images suggest, ultimately, a personality subtly merging into the spirit and properties of the landscape. We get this snapshot of Gregorias literally immersing himself in the elements of his natural setting:

> Days welded by the sun's torch into days!
> Gregorias plunging whole-suit in the shallows,
> painting under water, roaring, and spewing spray,
>
> (*CP*, 193)

As memory pans the setting of these exploits, it produces this finely crafted seascape, which seems a substantiation of the very spirit of Gregorias:

> a stinging haze
> of thorn trees bent like green flames by the Trades,
> under a sky tacked to the horizon, drumskin tight,
> as shaggy combers leisurely beard the rocks,
> while the asphalt sweats its mirages and the beaks
> of fledgling ginger lilies
> gasped for rain.
>
> (*CP*, 194)

The characteristic aspect and temper of their naked island setting are captured in this seascape – the resilient energies and pressures of its "hot road, history-less", dominated by the bare elements of relentless sun, winds, sea and sky. At the inner, expressive level, the piece is tracing the process of nature in creative struggle in this setting. The end product or "flowering" of that struggle is represented by the drought-resistant "fledgling ginger-lilies, gasp[ing] for rain". The human figuration is simultaneously being etched in this process, signified in the motifs of sweating, of strenuous energies/labour ("drumskin tight"), of the "stinging haze" charged with its own elation: so that the whole becomes, finally, a natural analogue of the artistic process itself. Gregorias remains present as the artistic persona/muse in this process, the seascape being "framed", significantly, between two snapshots of his exploits. His spirit spills over to impart its elation, its radiance in creative resilience: "thorn trees bent like green flames by the Trades". Walcott recalls the sheer power and joy of this elation in a passage which follows another of Gregorias's characteristic exploits. The music and thunder of the earth surges forth in the wake of this exuberance inspired by his passion and faith in a New World possibility:

> And it all sang,
> surpliced, processional,
> the waves clapped their hands, hallelujah!
> . . . .
> swift notes, and under earth
> the stifled overtures of cannon thunder.
>
> (*CP*, 207)

Walcott presents no paragon or superhuman figure in his portrait of St Omer/Gregorias. The ecstasies and virtues of Gregorias remain authentic, true to the bare necessities and modest means of his environment. His paradise of "sea-salt, rum and paint" nurtures a homegrown Dionysiac spirit, which, if fuelled mainly by liquor, manifests this archetypal truth: "all / drunkenness is Dionysiac, divine" (*CP*, 219). A very significant pattern thus emerges in Walcott's discovery of archetypes in these native lives: human elementals, extending to the domestic milieu, answer to the elementals of nature and landscape. This represents a vital aspect of the aesthetic of naming and renewal at the core of the alter/native truth being explored in *Another Life*.

Walcott goes on, in chapter 9 (section 1), to give testimony of his own experience of initiation into the bond with landscape during that apprentice-ship in painting. This is one of the most outstanding sections in *Another Life*. It recreates the act of painting,[31] exploring its psychic process as this extends, in the full light of memory, to frontiers of self- and existential discovery. In the developing thematic context of this book, chapter 9 (section 1) is also an affirmation of the singular virtues of painting as access to discovery: its efficacy, as a more directly physical and sensuous medium, in penetrating the relationship between inner and outer spheres of the artist's world. It is, by extension, a further affirmation of the power of Gregorias's medium in leading the way. Walcott will go on to compare and relate this particular efficacy of painting to his own different accesses and leanings as an artist whose element is in a different medium, poetry/metaphor. The sensuous (painting) and reflective (metaphor) will meet in complementariness, for a synthesis which is his final goal in presenting their stories alongside each other.

Walcott, present in his own person as protagonist in this act, is the total artist here, fusing painterly, poetic and dramatic skills to render this experi-ence. It is a dramatic reenactment of what takes place between the eye of the painter and the external forms of the scene being painted – to all intents and purposes a landscape – to issue in its finished form on canvas. The sensibility of the artist, fully engaged and activated in this complex process, comes into the foreground. We get an inside view of the interaction between the external world/nature and the interior world/nature of the artist. The style takes on an experimental complexity here, but the process and chemistry of this psychic interplay is discernible. Constituent principles, forces latent in his own im-pulses, sensations, moods, are finding co-responsive echoes and intimations in the aspects and properties of external forms and features. Feelings and sentiments that previously lay inert, amorphous in his own temperament, are now deepened, rendered more lucid. The artist moves to recast, remould external features in tune with his own subjective being: what appears on canvas is infused with, and expressive of, his own extended sensibility. The end product is thus not a representation of the external, but bears the inscape of his soul:

> From the reeds of your lashes, the wild commas
> of crows are beginning to rise.
> At your feet
> the dead cricket grows into a dragon,
> the razor grass bristles resentment,
> gnats are sawing the air,

(CP, 198)

For a further and climactic exploration of this process, Walcott extends from his own personal testimony into the world of the post-Impressionist masters, Van Gogh and Gauguin, as arch-exemplars of the very dynamic of this act of painting. The principle at the core of the revolutionary breakthrough to the post-Impressionist mode held that the work of art is, above all, the expression of the personality of the artist, his distinctive apprehension of the object. Walcott comes to the post-Impressionist aesthetic, though, through a genuine empathy with these masters that begins from his own fresh ground. To the master Simmons and his students alike, the post-Impressionists were among the foremost models of that apprenticeship; and were to remain a lasting influence, as *Another Life* records. Importantly, these models represented, in Walcott's case, a significance quite different from that of the Renaissance masters who had claimed his earliest childhood loyalties. They were not, like the latter, the exponents of the soul and order of the mainstream European tradition (which would later come into question). Rather, they were fellow artists who had engaged in a revolutionary effort to break with that tradition – an exploratory effort which was, in many ways, as naked as the St Lucians' own. Certain specific areas of affinity and resemblance, in fact, helped to foster a sense of kinship with the masters. Both Van Gogh and Gauguin were virtually outcasts, breaking with metropolitan society to embrace provincial landscapes (Van Gogh's Brittany and Provence; Gauguin's Polynesian Islands). They drew their inspiration from settings in which, like that of the native group, the natural and elemental predominated. Thus the focal presence of the sun in Van Gogh's works (as Walcott's portrait underlines). Their preference for such outdoor settings also helps to account for their use of primary colours (yellows, blues), and the striking role of this element of colour in their works. To the St Lucian pioneering trio, though, the strongest pull probably lay in Van Gogh and Gauguin's personal stories. They were revolutionary spirits who, breaking free of tradition, staked their lives wholly on their art; who, even with its cost in sacrificial and tragic extremes, achieved the consummation of their calling. Gauguin's *Noa Noa* was to remain with Simmons as a last(ing) solace when all else failed.[32] Walcott reclaims Van Gogh and Gauguin here as progenitors of the modern artist, pointing the way and risks of "the hot, history-less road" of discovery through art.

To enter the inner drama of Van Gogh's world in the act of painting, Walcott insets a collage of some of the major motifs of this painter's work (the method also employed in the case of St Omer):

> The sun explodes into irises,
> the shadows are crossing like crows,
> they settle, clawing the hair,
> yellow is screaming.
> Dear Theo, I shall go mad.

(CP, 199)

This is a powerful rediffusion of the emotional intensities and psychic turbulence that possessed this painter, as they find expression in such masterpieces as his *Crows over the Wheatfield, Irises,* and *Sunflowers.*[33] The terrors and exaltations of that experience are visually transfused into the external forms and features that comprise the paintings, to bear the impact of that temperament. Van Gogh's bold use of the primary yellow reflects a blinding glare which resounds with the potency of the pre-articulate scream. The corrosive strains of his pathological despair gather into a sense of doom, featured in the crows crowding in on him (over the wheatfield), harrowing his sensibility.[34] Walcott takes us back, through the very process of these images, to the furthest reaches of the inordinate passions that presaged the madness, the self-violence (the cutting of his ear) that consumed his life (suicide), echoed in that haunting outcry to his brother: "Dear Theo, I shall go mad" (*CP*, 199). He focuses on the sun, its permeating presence in Van Gogh's works, as the original element of that sensibility: the organic intensity of such consuming passions answer to that of the sun, in its primacy as pure cosmic force, energy. Thus sunstroke, often associated with Van Gogh's states of delirium, becomes the veritable emblem of the peculiar consummation attained by the Van Gogh sensibility in this experience of art. The sunstroke emblem encodes the revelatory pattern of that consummation. From the death-dealing blow of his consuming passions comes the creative outburst into birth. The sun whose "yellow screams" is the same sun which "explodes into irises". The tones of terror, despair, and jubilation alternating in this painter's style pass through the consuming fire (sunstroke) to be transformed into one indivisible whole. The process of the creative act thus penetrates, in the culminating example of this master, to the deeper reaches of human discovery. These reaches of human discovery represent a further dimension of naming whose route lies, particularly, through such direct intercourse with landscape. The artist gains entry into the fire of nature, within and without, through the door of landscape:

> Nature is a fire,
> through the door of this landscape
> I have entered a furnace.
>
> I rise, ringing with sunstroke!
>
> (*CP*, 199)

That entry into the organic fire of nature/creation is, in its transformative power, of the divine. Van Gogh, as well as Gauguin, thus attains sainthood in Walcott's book: both are formally consecrated here as "saints of all sunstroke". The sun itself, as arch-emblem of the capacity for such reaches of elemental energy, passion, fire, is the bond between the post-Impressionist experience of landscape and the efforts of the St Lucian trio at this native route to discovery. In the final process of this consummation symbolized by sunstroke (as explored in Van Gogh's case), the artist attains, through an inner recovery of these primal dimensions of self, a consciousness of the oneness of his human powers and limits. This order of perception, firmly rooted in his testimony of the creative act, provides one of the strongest groundings in Walcott's development towards a metaphysics of immanence.

The second part of this chapter proceeds from this full incursion into the sphere of painting to a consideration of the art which is his own truer, native medium – poetry. This means turning to the narrative of his own areas of strongest engagement and approaches as a pioneering artist. The effort begins in a comparative appraisal of the two arts – St Omer's gift of painting and his own gift of poetry. Recalling his actual failure to make it as a painter, Walcott reflects on the differences between the two gifts as different accesses of creative discovery, serving different artistic temperaments. The more direct and sensuous medium of painting was ideally suited to a faith like Gregorias's and its characteristic temper, rooted in instinct, giving primacy to the individual self in relation with one's world. He himself lived more truly in the poet's reflective concern with the order of the universe; seeking to apprehend, through metaphor, its totality as a "crystal of ambiguities" (*CP*, 200). Of the two, as already seen, it was Gregorias's route that led most directly to naming and to making the bond with landscape. This is the point at which Walcott pays him explicit tribute as the pacesetter, acknowledging his own position as the runner who, in the more classic orientation of his search, lagged behind in apprenticeship to the traditions of the colonizer. But Walcott is moving through the considerations of these differences to the more integral recognition of their essential complementariness, a complementariness generic to the interactive connection between paired opposites: Romantic and Classic; fire and water; passion and thought; painter and poet. His own act of imagination will effect the necessary integration of St Omer's Dionysiac passion and his own metaphysical bent into a new wholeness. It is the synthesis of these two representative components that underlies his advance towards a fresh truth, another light of the imagination in this and subsequent sections of the book.

Turning to focus on his own medium and effort, Walcott returns straight to preoccupation with the question of history, which, as he puts it, was his main "madness"/obsession from his earliest awakening. It was the issue which most dominated his own dream and ambition. This is all of a piece with what we have seen of his development so far. Fuelled by the angst of historylessness and the crisis of identity, history became the main area of inquiry engaging his speculative, classic bent. The question of history, extending to the existential issues of time and human destiny, comes into the foreground in the concluding discourse of the poem (book 4). The exploration begins here; and it is precisely in terms of this theme of history that the climactic resolutions of "Homage to Gregorias" will define themselves. This is concentrated in the outstanding chapter 11, where Walcott undertakes a revisitation of the lore of imperial, martial history that held him captive during his colonial boyhood. The revisitation becomes a critical revaluation of that lore. The dialectical, counterdiscursive pattern characteristic of this work comes into play. The codes of western European martial history and its representative metaphors are deconstructed, to be countered and refuted by an alternative paradigm of human struggle. Walcott finds this paradigm in an outstanding event in the early encounter between the native Amerindians of the region and the European settlers: the historic action of a group of Caribs in Grenada, who, in 1642, leapt off the cliffs of Sauteurs to their deaths rather than surrender to the invading French.[35]

Chapter 11 begins with his boyhood memory of a tapestry of a battle epic – "possibly Waterloo" – expressive of the glory and chivalry of imperial warfare, and the impact it had made on his imagination. This recollection appropriately heads the chapter, as it sets the terms of the discourse on history. He remembers it as a classically chaotic canvas, which depicted a legion of dragoons on "snorting, dappled chargers", making a veritable idyll of the scene of battle. The postures and attitudes of its heroes, their feats in the fray, all conveyed the sense of a chivalric paradise. A sensuously celestial mystique gave the scene its mood and temper. Against the background of a "tainted, cry-haunted fog", that mystique transfigured the wounds and carnage of the scene of battle, investing all with "sweetness and light":

> the whole charge like a pukkha, without blood;
> in the tainted, cry-haunted fog,
> in the grey, flickering mist,
> no mouth of pain,
> every chivalric wound
> rose-lipped, dandiacal, sweet,
> every self-sacrifice perfumed;

(CP, 210)

Walcott is making here a full confession of the ecstatic faith which such expressions of chivalry aroused in him. But another, fundamental purpose informs this confession. He is decoding the aesthetic of the Western martial imagination – of which the tapestry is a veritable metaphor – to penetrate to the very metaphysic informing that imagination. In essence, the spirit of conquest is affirmed in a paradisal aesthetic which, in thus transfiguring the wounds, sacrifices and pain of battle, virtually vindicates and triumphs over these and their burden of mortality. Thus: "their arms crooked in a scything sweep, / vaulting a heap of dying" (*CP*, 210). The root faith inspiring the metaphorical statement of the tapestry is in heroic transcendence as the absolute of combat. This represents, as Walcott penetrates it, the muse of the martial imagination that has, itself, been a main engine of Western civilization. In its final import, this martial muse reflects that civilization's vision of existential combat. Walcott, as we have seen, is very alert to that final dimension of meaning. It is important to observe here that he is not, moreover, being anachronistic in going back, in the age of modern warfare, to descry that Western muse in a long dead chivalric ideal. For he is zeroing in on this muse in full consciousness of the reality that tradition perpetuates itself and dies hard in the continuum from metaphysical to ideological constructs: in full consciousness, therefore, that the ideal of heroic conquest and its peculiar conception of power continues to live in the Western imperialist ethos. This perception, as we shall see, underlies his purposive deconstruction of the Western metaphors of his earlier faiths. It is against a metaphor such as the tapestry of Waterloo that the example of the leaping Caribs will define a different image of human struggle.

These are intimations whose full meanings will be crystallized in the concluding movements of this chapter. The story of his boyhood romance with the lore of imperial combat, beginning with the memory of the tapestry, is an important biographical context for the meditation on history. The depth of his faith in the older muse of history and its order of values goes back to these impressionable roots: "I bled for all. I thought it full of glory" (*CP*, 211). To a great extent, this faith accounted for the measure of the angst of historylessness that set in with "the twilight of Empire, and the beginning of our doubt".[36] Recollecting that experience is thus a meditative act which begins an examination of the delusions and errors of imperial lore. A number of significant factors had served to nourish the young colonial's adulation of the martial exploits of the mother country. There were, first, the historic sites of the Morne (Fortune)[37] and the Vigie promontory, dominating and virtually enclosing the small capital town of Castries on two sides. They were the sites of the ruins of old barracks and memorials of eighteenth-century battles between the French and the English.[38] Colonial education had also, of course, played its key role, inculcating its roll-call of historic dates of conquest learnt by rote. His generation had grown up on a culture of "hymns of battles not our own", celebrating such British imperial victories as Lucknow and Cawn-pore. One of his teachers had also exerted an especially strong influence. Walcott includes a portrait of that mentor, who had imparted his own patriot's fervour, intensified in exile, for the glory of empire: "a lonely Englishman who loved parades, / sailing, and Conrad's prose" (*CP*, 212).

It was the visible remains of history on "the plumed imperial hillsides" (the Morne and Vigie) that most excited his imagination, inspiring fantasies in which he relived the heroic exploits of the British redcoats. As he revisits those former haunts of his imagination, the image of the redcoats in that landscape, their exploits and fate, takes on a quite different light – quietly, peaceably, exploding the deeper myths of chivalry. For one thing, he comes with the knowledge (from a historiography wider than Williamson's *History of the*

British Empire)[39] of the grim reality of those battles: "A history of ennui, defence, disease" (*CP*, 212).[40] But it is a change in vision that begins, more profoundly, in the poet's responsiveness to the pre-eminent presence of elemental nature in that landscape. Sensitive to the superior force of its organic action, what the poet intuits – instead of the impress of the past – is a curious sense of absence, which gives testimony of a virtual effacement and disavowal of the historic action of the regiments:

> This forest keeps no wounds, this nature heals
> the newest scar, each cloud wraps like a bandage
> whatever we enact. What? Chivalry. The fiction
> of rusted soldiers fallen on a schoolboy's page.
>
> (*CP*, 212)

This is not solely a reflection of finitude. The recognition here is of a nature which, in its ceaseless cycle of generation and decay (of origins and detritus), renews and recreates even as it consumes and effaces; its cycle balances the negation of decay and loss with the gift of renewal and healing. The corollary is equally important: "keeping no wounds", this order also preserves no honours of "whatever we enact". As part of this order of nature, humankind and its enactments are both reduced/humbled and celebrated/praised, within the wholeness of its twofold dynamic and its necessary complicity with time. Walcott is virtually reinscribing the narrative of the earlier martial history in the light of the natural history of his own elemental setting. "Whatever we enact" is subordinated to and neutralized by its superior order; so that neither the praise nor the humbling is privileged. Both are, to cite Eliot's phrase, of "equal duration". This is the fresh wisdom that informs the new seeing of past heroic action in that setting:

> tumuli of red soldier crabs
> that calcified in heaps, their carapaces
> freckled with yellow fever,
> until the Morne hummed like a hospital,
> the gold helmets of dragoons like flowers
> tumbling down blue crevasses
> in this "Gibraltar of the Gulf of Mexico,"
> and on the slate-grey graves more
> flowers, medalling their breasts, too late,
>
> (*CP*, 213)

The redcoats find their reduced double in the red soldier crabs of the forest setting; the emblematic gold of their helmets, their medals, is replaced by the more real honours and celebration of the flowers. The ghosts of chivalry are being laid in an affirmation which bears a true spirit of reverence towards these deeper existential realities. Thus it also bears a spirit of compassion, and a will to pronounce peace on the delusions and errors of that older faith. It is an order of apprehension, moreover, that comes out of what Walcott has been recovering as the seminal strengths of the pioneering endeavour of a pair of artists "walking the hot road, history-less" – the deepening communion with earth and its concomitant bond of naming.

It is at this point, with the fading of the muse of martial history, that the image of an other, more real, muse of human struggle comes to the poet in a sudden, revelatory flash. It is the muse of the Caribs of Grenada in their historic leap from the cliffs of Sauteurs named after them. That leap is at once, for the poet, a lightning flash/leap of Imagination into existential truth. This occurs at a climactic juncture. Laying the last ghosts of chivalry, Walcott has just moved to make peace with the memory of the Fighting Fifth, "who wore the feather without stain". This legend of the famous British legion epitomized pure, untainted heroism, making them a veritable icon of the chivalric lore depicted in the tapestry:

> fade, "like the white plumes of the Fighting Fifth
> who wore the feather without stain."
>
> The leaping Caribs whiten,
> in one flash, . . .

(CP, 213)

The image of the leaping Caribs arises in direct answer to the Fighting Fifth, to supersede their faded myth. The "whitening" of their leap displaces and refutes the whiteness of the feathers of the Fighting Fifth as the more real thing. It is whiteness redefined as the translucence of existential truth, the whiteness of "skeletal candour" cited in "The Gulf". (This dialectic harks back to his earlier, revisionary soundings of whiteness in book 1.) This antithesis of the Caribs vis-à-vis the Fighting Fifth, along with its pictorial equivalent in the tapestry, is subtly etched in the imagery of that revelatory moment. The leap of the Caribs creates the visual effect of a waterfall's "bounding lace"; and here Walcott has fused in the memory of the visual splendour of Guyana's Kaieteur Falls, which does have the effect of a sheer fall of richly textured white lace, into this epiphanic moment of the leap of the Caribs. (The two remain associated in his mind, probably from the time of "Guyana V: The

Falls".) The "bounding lace" is the counterpart to the emblematic decor of the feathers of the Fighting Fifth (as it is to the embellishments imbuing the tapestry with "sweetness and light"). The image also captures, along with the visual, the sound impact of the waterfall, its simultaneous qualities of awesome thunder and radiance – "one scream of bounding lace". The reverberations of that "scream" underscore another distinctive aspect of that leap. Simultaneously a fall into mortality, it defines a significant contrast to the triumphant/transcendent posture of the dragoons in the tapestry: "vaulting a heap of dying". The whiteness of their leap, as a lightning flash, comprises all these truths.

The image of the "leaping Caribs", extending from here through the concluding movements of this chapter, represents one of the major visionary climaxes in *Another Life*. Their story needs to be placed in its full historical context at this stage. It is one of the more remarkable events in the history of the early encounters between European settlers and the native Amerindian inhabitants of the region. It stands out as an extraordinary act of resistance on the part of the Caribs of Grenada, refusing to surrender to the French settlers, who, in the middle years of the seventeenth century, set out to dispossess them of the island. Baugh quotes this account of their historic action in the final encounter of 1651, as they faced defeat at the hands of the French:

> A heroic stand was made by a band of them who, driven to the north of the island, took refuge on a promontory surrounded by beetling precipices, and inaccessible except by a narrow and difficult secret path. But their persecutors succeeded in reaching them, and they were completely defeated, notwithstanding a most vigorous defence. About forty who escaped the weapons of the French precipitated themselves over the cliffs to the rocks below, from which their bruised corpses were floated over the surges of the Atlantic.[41]

This final act of resistance, as the responses of both Walcott and Lamming[42] highlight, was a profoundly self- and life-affirming one, for it was prompted by a refusal to submit to the abnegation of self and spirit that surrender to the French would mean. Walcott reaches into the final philosophical import of this paradoxical affirmation: it signified, in essence, an engagement of life even unto the tragic necessity of embracing death. It is in the light of that meaning that he celebrates that historic leap as "a leap into light" – that is, truth. It presents to his imagination a pattern of the existential truth of the challenge of life, creative being, as indivisible from the challenge of mortality; of their paradoxical oneness. It is on this, rather than on their heroism, that his meaning turns.[43] In that brighter light, the historic action of the leaping Caribs/Sauteurs presents a truer paradigm of human struggle than that of the Fighting Fifth.

This visionary moment of the leaping Caribs thus comprehends a climax at once profoundly philosophical and revolutionary, and is, in fact, the most important of the climaxes in this work. The order of meanings contained in that paradoxical "leap into light" amounts to a virtual revolution in consciousness, necessitating, at this juncture, an act of conversion on the part of the poet. Walcott consciously embraces this moment of consciousness as his own moment of being "like Saul, unhorsed". He has revisited the older martial imagination of the colonizer's world as much for confessional reasons as to deconstruct its myths. The act of conversion is of utmost importance, first, as a personal need to free himself of the colonial's deep bondage to the borrowed faiths of the colonizer's world. It is also representative as a larger tribal, messianic act on the part of the poet. This act of conversion follows on compellingly in the deeply ritual and symbolic movement of section 4 of this outstanding chapter:

> I am pounding the faces of gods back into the red clay they
> leapt from with the mattock of heel after heel, as if heel
> after heel were my thumbs that once gouged out as sacred
> vessels for women the sockets of eyes, the deaf howl
> of their mouths, and I have wept less for them dead than I did
> when they leapt from my thumbs into birth, than my
> heels which have never hurt horses that now pound them
> back into what they should never have sprung from,
> staying un-named and un-praised where I found them –
> in the god-breeding, god-devouring earth!
>
> (*CP*, 213)

This passage stands out in *Another Life* for its extraordinary density and intensity; its language and rhythms enact an experience of ecstatic, ritualistic transport, strongly shamanistic in its intimations. Its meanings, subtly coded, are correspondingly complex. But there is an identifiable rationale to this act of conversion from the outset. It renounces the older faith in raising up gods, that is, faith in the absolutes through which humankind seeks transcendence or apotheosis; doing so, it reorients consciousness in the knowledge that what are cherished as absolutes are subject to the superior, immutable order of an earth which gives and reclaims, produces and consumes ("god-breeding" and "god-devouring"). That reality calls for the conscious will to embrace – like the leaping Caribs – our mortal condition with its frailties, wounds and afflictions, immanent as these are in the wholeness of earth/existence.

Walcott's discourse, articulated in imagery rich in associations and implications, combines visionary depth with a remarkable breadth across history. The imagery is strictly coded to focus a dialectic. Antithetically structured, it develops the opposition between the former custom of raising up gods (naming and praising them) and the returning of gods back to the earth, "un-named and un-praised". The functional images here are the thumbs and the heels, in their opposite roles. The thumbs are identified with the former making of gods, which, deftly evoked in the allusion to the custom of making sacred and religious objects in earlier cultures, is an activity suggestive of artifice, fabrication; it signifies an unnatural, factitious making. Thus: "my thumbs that once gouged out as sacred / vessels for women the sockets of eyes". That action of the thumbs is invoked as the inverse of the present substantive task being done by the heels – "pounding . . . back . . . as if heel / after heel were my thumbs that once gouged out as sacred vessels". This has the effect of suggesting that the authentic and rightful action of the heel was "usurped" by that of the thumb. The heel, reversing that usurped function to reinstate its own, now works like a mattock, pounding and grinding these thumb-moulded artefacts back into red clay (earth) – which constitutes a virtual process of unmaking these artefacts/gods. Remarkably, Walcott remains in the world of the Caribs for these motifs – the red clay and pounding mattock used in their craft of pottery; the making of sacred and religious objects. Here one needs to note that while these aboriginal peoples carved the faces of gods, the ethos of these gods remained at one with the twofold rhythm of the earth. That consciousness is manifested in their embracing of the awesome paradox of the "god-breeding, god-devouring earth". In their aboriginal tradition, the faces of gods were still integrated into nature: thus, the burden of their fall, its legacy, is honoured by the wind-god, Hourucan, combing the hair of Walcott as descendant in his own leap into their "light" (*CP*, 214).[44] Walcott's two main icons are firmly localized in their cultural milieu and the original context of a major episode in their history: the thumbs used in their craft of pottery; the image of heels featuring prominently in the leaping and falling at Grenada's Morne des Sauteurs.

The central act of conversion, then, consists in this ritual pounding of the faces of gods back into the earth. It is affirmed as the true moment of consecration (versus the "goug[ing] out as sacred/vessels for women the sockets of eyes"), gathering strains of the numinous as ritualistic repetition invokes the transformative power of the pounding heels: "with the mattock of heel after heel, as if heel / after heel". The process of grinding involved in this pounding (fully highlighted in the ensuing passage) carries a most significant play on meanings. It refers, first, to the literal process of grinding these thumb-moulded gods back into the red clay of earth, with the symbolic implications of "grinding" as the arduous effort of human travail. Second, it is the heel in the act of finding ground. Together the two, effecting the returning of gods back to the earth, amount to the act of becoming grounded in the reality of earth.

The critical question is this: What does the dialectic of this imagery say about the full implications of the error involved in the former dispensation, that is, the making/raising of gods, the error that is being renounced? In this matter of the making of gods, Walcott is speaking of the functional principle informing the (essentially Platonist) belief system of Old World Western civilization – the erection of virtues into absolutes. Naming and praising these absolutes/gods, which is the process of constructing them, means investing them with attributes of totality and infinity; making them, thereby, the measure and earnest of an envisioned apotheosis, a superhuman transcendence. (In *Dream on Monkey Mountain* it is Makak's desire to "leave the earth"; in the case of the Fighting Fifth, it is the heroic ideal of pure, untainted courage represented by "the feather without stain".) These attributes they do not possess: in this lies the fundamental error blinding humankind to the reality that the very earth which generates these desires and virtues just as organically consumes and reclaims the fruits of desires and virtues. Walcott's point is that this error withholds humankind from the realization of the other, more real access of power as one that is equal to the inherent tensions of this indivisible, twofold dynamic of the "god-breeding, god-devouring earth". As we have seen, the paradoxical truth of Sauteurs aims directly at a categorical refutation of this error. It is this focus which gives the revelatory moment its polemical and profoundly revolutionary purpose. For Walcott's heels versus thumbs antinomy is closely concerned with denouncing and deconstructing this fatal flaw of the epic-heroic muse of transcendence in the Old World Western imagination and the perpetuation of that muse in the imperialistic legacy. He anchors this entire act of transvaluation, as we have seen, in his own personal renunciation of that muse, whose irresistible spell had claimed the allegiance of his colonial boyhood. Ultimately, the personal testimony is carried within this larger, comprehensive purpose of denouncing this fatal flaw of the Western muse of apotheosis/transcendence.

Crucially, these perceptions and resolutions are the product of the act/leap of Imagination through which Walcott the artist enters into the meaning of the act of the leaping Caribs – as is signified in the flash of illumination: "the leaping Caribs whiten, / in one flash . . ." (*CP*, 213). What comes to climax here is the act of creative imagination as the ultimate act of self and existential discovery (as in the preceding "act of painting"). This latter – art as the ultimate act of self and existential discovery – is Walcott's major definitional focus on art in "Homage to Gregorias". Thus he proceeds, in the concluding passage of chapter 11, to enact the fusion of his own leap into meaning with the moment of the Caribs' "leap into light". The enactment also recovers and equates his first leap in answer to the artistic calling. Internalizing this fusion, it is for the artist as it was for the Caribs – who emerge as truly ancestral – a moment *in extremis*. Walcott re-enters the thunder of that moment in a powerfully kinetic experience. Each physical sense is keenly fused and inter-active with the other, as he relives its simultaneous dread and exaltation. An impressionistic rush of images recreates the experience, in strains of ecstatic transport similar to those of the ritual of pounding the faces of gods back into the earth:

> and the horns of green branches come
> lowering past me and the sea's crazed horses the foam
> of their whinnying mouths and white mane and the pelting red
> pepper of flowers that make my eyes water, . . .
>
> (*CP*, 213–14)

There is a remarkable double reference featured in this complex of images. They represent the graphic details and phenomena of the scene at the cliffs of Sauteurs. They are, at the same time, the iconography of sea and seascape recurrent in Walcott as primal configuration of the elemental energies and currents of life/cosmos – the motion of the waves as sea-horses, the visual effect of its foam as their "white manes". The combination functions as a powerful metaphor for the race of destiny, the extremity of its creative struggle, represented by the leap of the artist conjoined with that of Sauteurs. It is, however, a struggle transfused by a tragic elation whose reality consists in the very interpenetration of the dread and exaltation of the moment, which realizes, therefore, its own catharsis. Its essential quality is compressed in the image "red / pepper of flowers", which echoes the strains of Van Gogh's screaming yellow sun "exploding into irises".

Walcott is here virtually naming the spiritual dynamic of a destiny in which generative, life-bearing currents are permeated through and through with the currents of mortality. The section appropriately begins with a meditation on the fall to earth, as twin necessity of the leap – which is the condition of becoming grounded in the reality of our terrestrial life. The latter carries, as already seen, the specific implication of being "ground / grinded back" into the travail of its wounds and afflictions: "We are ground as the hooves of their horses open the wound / of those widening cliffs" (*CP*, 213). This necessity of becoming grounded, then, is being claimed as an integral part of the wholeness of the act of life described in the leap. It means a "hardening of the tendons", the process of becoming rooted. Its philosophical import is in direct contrast to that of the tapestry's dragoons "vaulting a heap of dying". It is important, though, to get the right accent of the tragic elation which affirms the leap. The meaning of "falling to earth" takes into account the tragic toll in suffering and death – the grim reality of the fate of the Caribs, and what he calls, invoking the similar fate of the Greeks at Thermopylae, the "break[ing] on loud sand". But it is on the dynamic of the leap/fall as an act of life, in all its paradox, that ultimate value is placed. The Caribs found and earned their name "Sauteurs" from leaping to their deaths; but the true significance of the event, reread and renamed, rests, finally, on the leap itself as an act of life.

A spirit of elation in creative resistance, principles of risk and sacrifice are among the necessary strengths of the more real muse of humanity being mediated in this leap of Imagination. The elemental energies and passions it engages recover the Dionysiac at primal root sources, here on Walcott's native ground (a Dionysiac spirit heralded in the person of Gregorias/St Omer). But this is far removed from the heroic/hubristic ethos of the Nietzschean ideal. For Walcott, caught up in the thunder of these elemental passions, is yet sensitive to the equally real pull of his human frailty and smallness (intimations of the god-devouring earth), urging him towards the image of the child (his son), representative of the recurrent motif of human childlikeness in his thought. With this image he acknowledges the counterbalancing pole of human vulnerability, which opens us towards compassion and tenderness, where the heart, and not the will, is the true engine of creative purpose. At these frontiers of self-knowledge, he comes to this perception of a truer posture of humankind in meeting the tremendous challenge of destiny: "I am no more / than that lithe dreaming runner . . ." (*CP*, 214). This original image captures the essentials of Walcott's belief in "the finding of earth", stressing the value of the suppleness of the human spirit as the necessary adjustment of our frailty in keeping rhythm with the tremendous challenge of destiny.

An integral and vital part of the complex of meanings explored in this vision of the leaping Caribs, as already indicated, is the act of naming realized in their (pre)historic leap, as also in Walcott's apprehension of its meaning. The Caribs of Grenada acquired and earned their name as "leapers" (into light). Firmly grounded in this actual and symbolic truth, Walcott is also performing here the signal act of claiming and proclaiming them as his true indigenous Caribbean ancestor. Their bequest as ancestor is the naming of the Caribbean people as a "race" whose purpose and destiny compels them into that order of consciousness, the roots of an identity presaged out of the necessity of their past and setting. In thus formally claiming this ancestry, Walcott redeems the aboriginal peoples of the region from the ignominy of their traditional image as an obliterated race. This reverses, moreover, his own earlier views on an amnesiac past that includes the Carib, as in the poem "Air". Definitively, as already indicated, the leap of Sauteurs and the act of Imagination which recovers its full meanings are one in the achievement of this naming. Walcott's final testimony here as artist includes this important emphasis: that naming is, in essence, an act of Imagination, engaging the deepest urges and resources of the human spirit. In the wider context of "Homage to Gregorias", naming as act of Imagination also represents the fulfilment of the presiding genius of Gregorias/St Omer.

A number of additional, related values are enunciated in Walcott's redeployment of this act of naming. Firstly and focally, he conceives of the possibilities and realizations of this "other light" wholly in terms of a shared destiny, and focuses especially the inseparable bond between artist and community. Insisting on that bond, he sees himself as one who, in his peculiar quest as artist, is like a cresting wave "bear[ing] / down the torch of this race" (*CP*, 214). But at the same time, as an individual, he can find realization only in solidarity with his community: "who feels as he falls with the thousand now his tendons harden" (*CP*, 214). This very hold on community is all of a piece with another, critical value affirmed in these concluding movements of chapter 11. It takes Walcott beyond the boundary of the Caribbean race, to the wider brotherhood and universal kinship of a shared humanity. Thus he reaches back through history and across cultures to find, and claim, in the legendary Greeks at Thermopylae, a veritable analogue and mythic equivalent of the leaping Caribs. Their self-sacrificing act at Thermopylae is loaded, for him, with the same meaning as that of Sauteurs, and is as primal and ancestral. They number, therefore, among the mythic "thousand" with whom he looks to share the truth of that destiny. What Walcott effects here is remarkable. It is nothing less than a renaming of the Thermopylae story – a fresh naming in terms of the elegiac leap/fall into destiny, as against the heroic name of the older Western dispensation. For the naming of the Caribbean race, following from the legacy of Sauteurs, is conceived in these existential terms; and, even as it comprises a transvaluation of the older name, it gains its validity as a universal, world-embracing possibility. This very coincidence of naming and renaming anchors the meaning of Walcott's belief in a New World purpose and destiny. The equating of the significance of Thermopylae with that of the leaping Caribs is the fundamental and crowning aspect of his total achievement in book 2. The story of the leaping Caribs has been uplifted, established in its true mythic, historic significance. Their image rises out of its former obscurity as a veritable metaphor, encoding this other/alternative muse of humanity – displacing and replacing such metaphors as the Fighting Fifth of the older muse.

Anna: Love ("A Simple Flame")

Book 3, "A Simple Flame", deals with Walcott's experience of first love with Andreuille Alcée, the St Lucian girl whom he has named Anna in the poem. Second of the three lives being told in *Another Life,* Anna's is the narrative of love. As such it represents Walcott's personal story. It is a story of the typical idylls of first love, compounded by the reflections of the love/metaphors of the western European tradition. Memory becomes an act of identifying the overreachings and misdirections of that first way of love; and, accordingly, a search for another way, light of love. The deep narrative of Anna/Walcott's story traces the change from the transcendent absolutes of that way to the realization of an alternative truth expressed in the image of "a simple flame".

Walcott sets out to tell the full story of this important experience in his personal life. In fact, where the preceeding books present a more fragmentary and composite structure, here the biographical context is in the foreground and the narrative continuous. The relationship with Andreuille Alcée began when he was eighteen years old, and Andreuille was in the final years of secondary school at the St Joseph's Convent. It lasted some three years, ending with his departure for university. Andreuille Alcée was very fair in complexion – Walcott describes her as "golden" – and attractive. She came from a middle-class family quite light in complexion, well known and popular for their club-restaurant, Luna Park, which was at one time the hub of social life in Castries.[45] Both here and in "Leaving School", the autobiographical essay which chronicles the events of the poem, Walcott recalls 1948 as a landmark in his beginnings, his "annus mirabilis". It was the year that saw the special coincidence of this love, the publication of *Green Night,* and with the latter, his commitment to poetry as vocation. Another major event that signed the significance of that year was the Great Castries Fire, which practically destroyed the town.[46] Historic in necessitating a fresh start in the society, the fire took on a special significance for him, as recorded in the widely anthologized "A City's Death by Fire" (*Green Night*) and in "Leaving School". Nothing shows the earnestness of his early poetic mission more than his response to that fire, immortalized in the poem. It held the promise of his young poet's dream of another, transformed life for his native setting. The coincidence of that event with the ardours of first love made Anna the very embodiment of that hope. "She arose out of the flame", he writes in MS One. The beloved becomes inseparable from the phoenix-like, miraculous possibility which was, for Walcott, the positive side to the fire's destruction. Dante is also an important influence, but this real-life experience was the main source of the theme and image of the flame/light of love embodied in Anna. The latter is felicitously fixed in the following lines:

> while Anna slept,
> her golden body like a lamp blown out
> that holds, just blown, the image of the flame.

(CP, 228)

This original and remarkable image anticipates the central theme to be explored in book 3.

Infused with such metaphoric intimations from the outset, the earlier sections of the narrative relive the felicities and bounties of first love and the perfections of the "first loved", to tell of the idealization of Anna. The narrative is also concerned to tell of the fate of the relationship, foredoomed to end with his departure for university. Recalling the spirit of this departure, his deep response to the call of the wider world beyond the narrow confines of his small island, he regards that choice as something of a betrayal of the relationship (as also of his island). There is thus, on the autobiographical level, a strong confessional strain; and with it, a desire to make his peace with that past. But this recollection of the experience of first love has its singular and most substantive significance on this level: it is the story of the artist/lover, and his creation of the loved one into a visionary ideal.

Walcott's autobiographical effort becomes an act of retrospective meditation on the gains and losses of this congenital susceptibility on the part of the artist. One of the things that makes the strongest, most original impact in *Another Life* is the psychological realism of the portrait of the artist as young lover. We are given insight into an organic fusion between passional love and the love of art in the psyche of the artist. Its essential dynamic had already been recaptured in "Leaving School": "It is so self-content, so assured of immortality, that it irradiates not only the first-loved but her landscape with a profound benediction."[47] Love/Anna becomes the meeting place of all the fantasies of innocence and the poetic aspirations of the period; and, especially for a young poet committed to the discovery of landscape, of a soul's desire inseparable from his yearnings for landscape – as with his hope of the fire's renewal. The woman became indeed both a stimulus and confluence of all the images that harboured his young ideals. She became, that is, a veritable muse.

Moments and snapshots from memory recapture the enriching experience and manifold bounties of this first flush of romantic love. Especially keen is the singular wonder of waking to the creative harmonies of a universe shared with the beloved, and the beloved herself as the generative source of its bounties. Metaphors of morning and waking, featuring prominently in this book, answer with equal freshness to these feelings and sentiments; and Walcott has given these metaphors original and lasting resonance as the very element of first love. Some of these moments relive the quickening of energies, the experience of awakening to keener sensations of the natural world. These are among the sources of a lyrical freshness especially rich in "A Simple Flame". Walcott recalls, for example, the spirit and atmosphere of a Christmas of that first love, when he and Anna went carolling among the refugees of the fire at Vigie. It returns with the lifting spirits of the cooler Christmas season, the memory of the wind freshening and polishing everything in the glow of her presence; even while, we note, her "profile of hammered gold", shining out amidst the mainly black carollers, evokes a "head by Angelico":

> A fresh wind, irrepressibly elate,
> lifted the leaves' skirts, romped
> down the Roman balconies,
> polishing all that was already polished,
> the sky, leaves, metal, and her face.
>
> *(CP, 231)*

One of the strongest memories of early courtship was the daily experience of rowing across the Castries harbour to visit Anna.[48] That trip returns as a magical journey to the paradisal, enabling a full attunement to the natural harmonies of the sounds and motions of rowing. Here Walcott, as conscious returning artist, plumbs deep into these love-inspired harmonies to sound the nature and harmonies of poetry itself:

> the pause upheld after each finished stroke,
> unstudied, easy, pentametrical,
> one action, and one thought. Halfway across
> the chord between the downstroke of the oar
> and its uplifted sigh . . .
>
> *(CP, 227)*

The poetry which defines itself here is initiated by and has its roots in love itself. This is one of the many glimpses we will get into the poetry of loving in these recollections of first love.

Deeply remembered too are the moments of total fulfilment known to love in its season of plenty – those times when love comes close to beatitude in the realization of a plenitude folding peace and contentment into one. A most miraculous conceit recreates this experience. It is one of the many things which proclaim the new, original reaches of Walcott's artistic mastery in this work. Sunday – a day which becomes synonymous with plenitude and benediction in his work – is personified as bearer of the good life, overflowing with bounties which blend both spiritual and sensuous, earthly satisfactions. This is the Walcott in whom the joy of language and metaphor is one with the joy of life itself. Sunday as persona merges felicitously into the figure of a woman, who is, of course, Anna – the beloved as abounding source of the good life. Anna/Sunday radiant, full-bodied and sensuous, comes to an epiphany that is very much of and within a familiar, domestic setting:

> Then Sundays, smiling, carried in both hands
> a towelled dish bubbling with the good life

> whose fervour, steaming, beaded her clear brow,
> from which damp skeins were brushed,
> and ladled out her fullness to the brim.
>
> . . . .
>
> hours that ripened till the fullest hour
> could burst with peace.

(CP, 235)

Walcott has probably been influenced here by the female figures of Bonnard, the post-Impressionist painter in whom he expressed keen interest during this period.[49] He may also be drawing on impressions from "house-warm" married life long after Anna. He is, moreover, moving in this work towards an aesthetic of the sensuous and earthly versus the seraphic. This too comes into play here, and it is, happily, consistent with his description of the real Anna – "firm of sinew and purpose", with "nothing frail" about her.[50] Nonetheless, while this full-bodied, sensuous Anna is very tangible in these recollections, such trans-figurations as the "profile of hammered gold" from Angelico, as we will see, are also pervasive.

There is also an intensive exploration of a seminal aspect of love in this first flush, as a quickening, enabling experience awaking our every sense to the qualities and properties of the physical world, and to our organic bond with it. The beloved is the exquisite source of all stimuli, and medium of every separate sensation and response:

> the chill of water entered
> the shell of her palm,
> in membranous twilight
> the match of the first star
>
> through the door of a sunset always left ajar.
> And all bread savoured
> of her sunburnt nape,

(CP, 229–30)

The sense of waking wonder is pristine and elemental. We are witnessing here another manifestation of Walcott's own incipient bonding with the elementals of his landscape, stimulated by this intimate experience of first love. Meta-phors of awaking, morning and birth spring naturally out of the memories of that experience, merging Anna and landscape into one. Along with these primary metaphors comes a surge of fresh, original imagery all generated from naturalistic, domestic and familiar spheres. This surge of fresh imagery, especially prominent here but extending throughout *Another Life,* is one of the definitive achievements of this work. In the throes of this experience of "waking wonder" the pair of lovers have this Edenic vision of their surrounding universe: "And now we were the first guests of the earth / and everything stood still for us to name" (*CP,* 231). This is a striking example of the original sources of the principle of naming/renewal seminal to Walcott's credo. The idyllic sense of himself and Anna as the new Adam and Eve is a natural climax to the felicities of "waking wonder" being celebrated; simultaneously, its mythic and archetypal echoes are intrinsic. The peculiar quality and ambiance of this Eden remains, however, wholly that of their green world, calling them to the necessity of naming as the basis of a true claim and inheritance. Remarkably, Walcott has brought us to this fundamental value through sentiments and feelings that strike deep and responsive chords. As earlier noted, this context of psychological realism is one of the most important features in "A Simple Flame". We gain, through empathy, genuine insight into the poetry of loving; and are made to see the authentic oneness of the woman loved, her landscape, and the spirit of poetry. For this achievement, "A Simple Flame" must rank among the greatest love poetry ever written.

It is in the recovery of such natural layers of that experience that Walcott will find the roots and very element of love, as is climactically expressed in "Anna Awaking". But other important factors play a vital part in what was, in the event, the actual process and character of that love – the creation of Anna into a visionary ideal, a muse for the poet/lover. The sublimities and intensities of the pristine moments examined above pass easily enough into that process; but an equally strong and most palpable influence comes from the imagination of the eager young poet steeped in artistic tradition. In addition to the wealth of spontaneously generated images from the native experience (for example, the fire/flame image), there is a vast store of "borrowed" images from the Western tradition for which Anna becomes the magnetic centre. Even the boyhood romance of chivalry and redcoats casts its glow round her: "It was their lost blood that rose in her cheek, / their broken buckles which flashed in her hair" (*CP,* 215). Featuring most prominently, though, are images of idealized womanhood from the Western tradition – literature, painting and myth. Some of these have surfaced in the preceding books, but they all converge here. The earliest are the celestial, seraphic transfigurations of woman from the Renaissance masters in "Craven's book":

> A schoolgirl in blue and white uniform,
> her golden plaits a simple coronet
> out of Angelico, . . .
>
> (*CP*, 187)

There are also Old Testament models of transcendent virtue, whose beauty shines out in sterling qualities of character, such as the fidelity of Ruth or the patriotic truth of Judith. For Walcott returning in memory to that love, however, it is as if Pasternak's Lara in *Doctor Zhivago* (1958) provides the total model for all the virtues and strengths he envisioned in that Anna. The figure of Lara dominates these metaphors in "A Simple Flame". Lara, with a few others such as Anna Karenina, represents something of a phenomenon in early modernist literature as the last ideal of womanly completeness (Molly Bloom being an altogether different incarnation). She combined a solid, flesh-and-blood presence with depth and strength of character. She was Zhivago's total woman for all seasons – passionate lover; the woman who could make a haven of home; the friend who shared his dreams and beliefs; his companion at arms in active struggle (the nurse who shared in his medical work in the war); the healer of his wounds. (Coincidentally, Andreuille Alcée went on to make nursing her life's career.) In the portrait Walcott creates, almost every attribute of this deeply internalized heroine is repeated in this first-loved woman. They answer to his most cherished aspirations:

> Who were you, then?
> The golden partisan of my young Revolution,
> my braided, practical, seasoned commissar,
>
> (*CP*, 239)

For Walcott the resemblance extended to the physical. Even Julie Christie's portrayal of Lara in David Lean's film (1965) becomes absorbed into the magic of the Lara/Anna likeness: "Christie, Karenina, big-boned and passive" (*CP*, 238). Christie, "big-boned and passive", has the sensuous, earthy, golden appeal of Andreuille/Anna and her imagined double, Lara.

Not only Pasternak's heroine, but the very landscape she inhabited became part of the climate of that romance for the young poet/lover. Walcott has always looked instinctively for the reality of any country in its great writers. (See chapter 4.) The Russia of Pasternak and other major voices of the nineteenth and twentieth centuries was for him a strong presence. Thus reflections of Lara also echo and evoke other heroines of that landscape, such as Anna Karenina, and Anna Akhmatova, the woman beloved of Russia as much for her beauty as her poetic genius.[51] (Interestingly, Walcott makes no distinction between real and fictional heroines, embracing film stars as well.) Theirs was a landscape of vast, open spaces, inviting metaphysical speculation; it seemed to him an other, ideal country of the imagination. Thus, years later, as he puts it, Anna is suddenly the word "wheat" (*CP*, 239) – a word/world redolent of hints and hues of the "orient and immortal", harking back to the early period of his immersion in the Metaphysical poets. He was, however, sensitive to the darker side of that Russia of the imagination, as a country of "metaphysical sadness", "so desolate it mocked destinations" ("Forest of Europe", *CP*, 376). Just as keenly absorbed, therefore, was Pasternak's haunting sense in *Doctor Zhivago,* of inescapable separation, of the cruel necessity of things – in the upheavals of revolutionary Russia – that prevented a potentially complete love from finding fulfilment. The very first memories of Anna in book 1 are poignantly reminiscent of a hapless Zhivago, haunted by mirage-like, illusory glimpses of Lara flashing past on trains:

> that watching her rise
> from the bright boathouse door was like some station
> where either stood, transfixed
> by the rattling telegraph of carriage windows
> flashing goodbyes,
>
> (*CP*, 187)

As Walcott contemplates the parallel in the fate of his own relationship with Anna, these echoes of Pasternak and their existential soundings deepen into a central theme in "A Simple Flame" – the larger truth of an Anna "enduring all goodbyes".[52] Empathizing with the poet's soul in that novel (and for him Pasternak was always the quintessential poet) his own imagination of love found there perhaps its strongest impetus towards existential frontiers. Walcott's first love was thus hedged round with images that came laden with visionary significations – from the other-worldly transfigurations of the Renaissance masters, to the terrestrial completeness of Lara. The woman thus imbued became of necessity, and above all else, the muse of his poet's soul. It is one of Walcott's key concerns in this book to recognize this truth of the experience, and to acknowledge in it the reason for the failure of the relationship with the real Andreuille. Seeking to make amends in the acknowledgement, he tells the plain truth now in his own voice, now in Anna's: "that I found life within some novel's leaves / more real than you, already chosen /

as his doomed heroine" (*CP*, 238–39); and "but you brought the tears / of too many contradictions, / I became a metaphor . . ." (*CP*, 243).

Anna as metaphor, then, dominated the Anna who remained its earthly inspiration. This means that the real Andreuille was somewhat eclipsed in what was the larger, impersonal love of the artist. Thus Anna's retrospective comment: "It was your selflessness which loved me as the world, / I was a child, as much / as you" (*CP*, 243). It is in this very factor of a double-edged betrayal that Walcott will recover ultimate value. Within it lies the kernel which, amplified and explored by the revisiting imagination, becomes a genuine, lived paradigm of the artist's quest for the existential truth of love. Walcott, strongly grounded in the psychological reality of that past, makes the following analysis of the subtle contradiction involved. He is recalling a moment of total harmony between himself and the beloved:

> And which of them in time would be betrayed
> was never questioned by that poetry
> which breathed within the evening naturally,
> but by the noble treachery of art
> that looks for fear when it is least afraid,
> that coldly takes the pulse-beat of the heart
> in happiness; . . .

(CP, 236)

In its restless pull towards concern with the permanence of that love and its perfections, the artistic sensibility did betray, rendering him incapable of seeing and accepting then the wholeness immanent in the natural, simple truth of love.[53] (Walcott's aphoristic comment in this book is especially profound here: "A man lives half of life / the second half is memory".) But that very failure was the sacrificial necessity of the much larger cause of the Imagination's search for answers to the inescapable questions of finitude and change, without which there is no peace in love's happiness. Genuinely regretting the loss, the mature Walcott now accepts it as the cost of this nobler, sacred purpose. His analysis also gives, moreover, another insight into the organic absorption of the actual and visionary experiences of this love one into the other, and its psychological truth. Indeed, as already observed, we never lose sight of the autobiographical content in this narrative. Here one might usefully compare it with the Beatrice experience in Dante's *Divine Comedy*. Where Dante's childhood infatuation with the twelve-year-old original of Beatrice receives allegorical treatment, in "A Simple Flame" the actual experience remains solidly there, the visionary drawing its full life from the passional, flesh and blood reality. It is precisely because of this fusion that Walcott's story of personal love gains its value as the "supreme fiction" of himself as artist/lover.

Ideals of transcendent virtue in woman, the sublimities of first love, come to a natural confluence in the desire for love's absolute. This is, archetypally, the yearning for completion in union with the ideal other, where the imagination expands towards the larger, existential questions of love. The moment of such access to completion came, for Walcott in love, in the arrival at Anna's side of the harbour – the culmination of the canoe trip across the Castries harbour to this "paradisal" destination. Enacted in chapter 13 (section 4), it is a moment of enraptured entry into the joy of the beloved's presence – the source of a beatitude whose light is radiant in her every feature. The peculiar richness of that light is that of the real Anna, reflected from the native, sensuous burnish of her own complexion (Walcott savours again the "freckled forearm") – whose tints, at the same time, evoke the "other country" of "borrowed" autumn. The moment of beatitude is at once the desire for eternal possession, for permanence and perpetuity:

> Reader,
>
> imagine the boat stayed,
> the harbour stayed, the oar's
> uplifted wand,
>
> hold the light's changes to
> a single light, repeat
> the voyage, delay the arrival,
> in that bright air,
>
> he wished himself moving
> yet forever there.
>
> (*CP*, 229)

The imagination arrives at a true point of consummation in this desire to arrest the moment of happiness, all its finite particulars, in living continuity. Immediate and personal in content, it is a moment which also reverberates on classic and timeless levels. Walcott's lines are pregnant with the echoes of numerous others – especially of Keats in "Ode on a Grecian Urn" and Yeats in the Byzantium poems – who have arrived at this last post, where Imagination is most keenly pierced by the angst of mortality. Here is the desire for a state above the barriers that separate finite from infinite, for the resolution of all inherent conflicts, to attain the ineffable, mystical "stillness in motion". Walcott's own intimate experience of this yearning for the eternal is simple and direct in utterance: "he wished himself moving / yet forever there".

That testimony renews our insight into a seminal and profound truth of love. Love is what brings us, most truly, to consciousness of the eternal in us, urging our desire for final possession; it is what presages, by the same token, the painful, contradictory awareness of mortality as love's necessary burden. Here the inextricable bond of love and death as twin necessities defines itself to the imagination: it is because of love that we care about death. The depth of Walcott's perception into "the noble treachery of art" also reveals its full significance at this point:

> but by the noble treachery of art
> that looks for fear when it is least afraid,
> that coldly takes the pulse-beat of the heart
> in happiness; that praised its need to die
> to the bright candour of the evening sky,
> that preferred love to immortality;

(CP, 236)

For the imagination coming to this recognition in first love, the first cry, primal and archetypal, is for transcendence; for a supernal, other-worldly plane of wisdom. Walcott's visionary moments, essentially epiphanic and revelatory in character, find manifestation in images of light (as in the Caribs' leap into the light) – which, increasingly since *Another Life*, acquires the potency of a private symbol in his work. The aspiration of this first way is for the one higher, transcendent light that will rise clear of the contradictions of the many changing faces of light: "hold the light's changes to / a single light" (*CP*, 229). It is this aspiration that has evolved into the more mature, grounded one captured in the original image of a "crystal of ambiguities", which expresses the desire for a clarity which can comprehend and hold together the multiple, changing faces of reality.

The climactic passage examined above underlines important aspects of the aesthetic that is coming to maturity in *Another Life*. We see, first, a remarkable coincidence of the familiar and ordinary with the mythic/archetypal in the images that describe this experience. The coincidence is wholly natural, easy, unobtrusive. Memory recaptures the concrete, naturalistic details of the experience: rowing across the water to the other side of the harbour, the boat, the oar. At the same time, these elementals together inscribe the mythic narrative of a sea voyage to the paradisal. The harbour image represents an especially rich culmination in this combination. It quietly yields its full metaphoric significance in this passage from actual incident to myth-making remembrance, to become the final haven, home, place of love's anchorage after journey. Along with the light/fire/flame cluster of images, this harbour motif is focal to the meanings of "A Simple Flame", and from here on will take its place as an integral part of Walcott's iconography.[54] The organic coincidence of naturalistic and mythic provides another illustration of a fundamental principle in Walcott's credo: the persistence of the classical/timeless in the elemental; which is also the fact that metaphor and myth have their substance in these origins. Thus, the same principle accounts for the numerous echoes of other poets who have dreamed of love freed of mortality and time. He meets them on archetypal ground, and their voices are intrinsic in what yet remains a fully realized, personal moment.

This very incidence of an intrinsic affinity with other traditional voices takes us back to the important question of the "borrowed metaphors" of the Western tradition, which, as we have seen, are a powerful source of inspiration in Walcott's idealization of first love on this higher, transcendent plane. The affinity has a significant import. From his own passage through this experience as artist/lover, Walcott has come to know love's yearning for transcendent, supernal otherness as an innate, human susceptibility. It has brought him, in effect, to inward knowledge of and sympathy with the genesis of the Platonist ideal that has, to all intents and purposes, shaped this construction of love in the Western imagination. But the retrospective and reappraising consciousness is now undeceived: it is now wise to the errors and fatal lures of this absolute of transcendence. The idealized images of Anna are often countered with ironic observations on the taints of the carnal, and the human contradictions that mock their purities and perfections. The memory of Anna as his ideal Judith, a heroine who seemed to hold a powerful fascination for him, prompts this kind of searing self-irony:

> I see her stride
> as ruthless as that flax-bright harvester
> Judith, with Holofernes' lantern in her hand.

(CP, 231)

The viewpoint here, it should be noted, is not of woman as the eternal confounder/beheader of man. It is, rather, Walcott's projection of himself as a victim brutally foredoomed by his own "flax-bright" idealization. (This is an echo of the white goddess theme in *Dream on Monkey Mountain,* a work of the same period.) There are similar ironic intimations interwoven into the recollection of some of the "perfect" moments of the love trip across the harbour. Thus an image of love fully absorbed in the charmed circle of its own bliss carries hints of inherent, self-seducing narcissistic dangers:

> Magical lagoon, stunned
> by its own reflection!
> The boat, the stone
> pier, the water-odorous
> boathouse, the trees
> so quiet they were always
> far. I could drown there, . .

(CP, 228)

Another such moment is described: "the self-delighting, self-transfiguring stone / stare of the demi-god" (*CP*, 236). Here there is even more telling recognition of signal dangers: self-transfiguration, which equals self-apotheosis, is the risk of transmogrification. Walcott shows here a Yeatsian ambiguity in his fascination with the stone image. The "stone stare" combines the symbolic implications of permanence/endurance with the idea of a nonhuman fixity.

"Love in the Valley" (*The Gulf*), as we saw in chapter 3, is a poem of far-reaching insight into Walcott's concern with the question of the muse of love as enshrined in the Western imagination. It gives anguished expression to his fear of the overreachings of the loves of three major heroines of European literature: "Bathsheba, Lara, Tess". This line in the poem bears the full import of his intensive preoccupation with and purpose in dealing with these characteristic aspects of the Western mind: "I knew the depth of whiteness". This is the period of his preoccupation with the theme of the white goddess in *Dream on Monkey Mountain,* where Makak is caught in the grip of "the white light that paralysed [his] mind" as a black man (*Dream,* 319). For the black, ex-colonized man the lure of that envisioned white/"pure" transfiguration is deeply chronic and seductive. Shedding the metaphysic of the older Western world thus has additional urgency for him. It means shedding the self-alienating lures of the cultural and racial complexion of "borrowed whiteness" (*CP,* 152). This compels Walcott, as we have seen elsewhere, into an alternative semantics of "whiteness". It is such intensive probing of the dangers and contradictions that informs his renunciation of this ideal of love enshrined *par excellence* in the Western mind. It compels, accordingly, the central purpose informing his retrospective effort in this narrative of the experience of first love: in what consists another, truer light of love? Thus, as in the case of his preoccupation with the martial muse of transcendence in virtuous/heroic death, the counteractive purpose continues to underpin his discourse.

The retrospective consciousness answers the fundamental question of an alternative truth of love's fulfilment in the section immediately following, chapter 14, entitled "Anna Awaking". In this section Anna, awaking, comes to apprehension of the immanence of the simple flame of creative being in the world about her, and its perfect attunement to the world within. This is an experience of illumination equivalent to the "whitening flash" of the leaping Caribs (book 2). The illumination is realized and delivered by Anna herself, enacted in her own person and voice. This dramatic manoeuvre is a very effective and significant one. There is, first, authority in the directness and simplicity of Anna's own voice in this experience, unencumbered by the complexities and ambiguities of the "noble treachery of art" affecting the poet. Anna also recovers in this role the archetypal function of the beloved woman as the intelligence of love, invoking the parallel of Dante's Beatrice, who represents an important prototype behind "A Simple Flame".

Walcott's skills as a dramatist come to the fore in this presentation of Anna's awakening, which, remaining fully naturalistic, is at the same time deeply lyrical and mythic. Anna experiences a familiar morning scene, whose original setting is that of Andreuille Alcée's home on the northern side of the Castries harbour. She is responding, in the early hours of the morning, to the sights and scenes of her immediate domestic setting and its beach environs. She opens in sensitivity to the exhilaration of the breeze; the glow of the water; the quietude and stillness that still envelops the first stirrings of the early canoes. Herself enkindled by love, Anna comes alive to and within these natural stimuli as within her own element. She comes to know and internalize, in her own attunement to them, an innate felicity, peace and harmony in the morning world about her:

> When the oil green water glows but doesn't catch,
> only its burnish, something wakes me early,
> draws me out breezily to the pebbly shelf
> of shallows where the water chuckles
> and the ribbed boats sleep like children,

> buoyed on their creases. I have nothing to do,
> the burnished kettle is already polished,
> to see my own blush burn,
> and the last thing the breeze needs is my exhilaration.
>
> (*CP*, 233)

In the natural speech of a natural situation, Anna's experience realizes its own natural lyricism. It mediates, equally naturally, an epiphany that marks a veritable birth of consciousness. The consciousness awakens to the creative principle alive throughout the physical and human universe, upholding and binding all together; and comes to recognition, thereby, of the immanence of that principle of creative being and its wholeness as existential truth. It is this essential reality that is captured in the image of "a simple flame". Harking back to its original in Dante's *Divine Comedy* (*Paradiso*), the image is reminiscent of this epiphany of love as the living, organic principle of creation, unifying all:

> O grace abounding, whereby I presumed
> To fix upon the eternal light my gaze
> So deep, that in it I my sight consumed!
> I beheld leaves within the unfathomable blaze
> Into one volume bound by love, the same
> That the universe holds scattered through its maze.
> Substance and accidents, and their modes, became
> As if together fused, all in such wise
> That what I speak of is one simple flame.
>
> (*Paradise*, XXXIII, 82–90)[55]

The manifestations of the "simple flame" in Walcott, however – countering the representative "amber glow" of the world and woman-muses of the Renaissance masters – answer to the necessities of his own world in its place and time. Anna, the strongly personalized presence in whom this consciousness is being realized, perceives the wider, existential meanings of this native epiphany. She opens to the understanding that, pristine and pre-existent like the wind, that vital creative principle is independent of human or other agency: "and the last thing the breeze needs is my exhilaration". She intuits the ministrations of this pre-existent, creative principle, for example, in the "unconscious" rhythmic waddling of the ducks on the water; in a nature ever provident of its own aesthetic endowments, coming equipped, for example, with its own insignia of the ceremonious: "The pleats of the shallows are neatly creased / and decorous and processional" (*CP*, 233). The order which reveals itself through it all, in its essential innocence and nakedness, is one that naturally, simply exists. The recognition is generative of faith. But the enlightenment of the "simple flame" also embraces the other, darker side of existence, presaging concern with the contradictions of a changeful, mortal condition. Anna, reflecting forward – which is, from the vantage point of the returning Walcott, the retroactive role of memory – knows the inescapable necessity of the unhappier lights that time and experience must bring: from the quiet radiance of this morning of her girlhood, to the fierceness of life's noontime; the lengthening shadows of its evening, to the terrrors of its night. The awakened faith of that consciousness, however, is strengthened in the understanding that the indwelling truth of the simple flame persists coexistent with the equally natural shadows and their pain; that the truth of love infolds the shadows into its totality:

> Mother, I am in love.
> Harbour, I am waking.
> I know the pain in your budding, nippled limes,
> I know why your limbs shake, windless, pliant trees.
> I shall grow grey as this light.
> The first flush will pass.
> But there will always be morning,
> and I shall have this fever waken me,
> whoever I lie to, lying close to, sleeping
> like a ribbed boat in the last shallows of night.

(CP, 234)

The strains of this elegiac wisdom, then, permeate and temper the lyric joy of Anna's awakening. It is a wisdom which distils, in the more serene key of this epiphany, the final temper of the Walcott faith (which will find its most sustained expression in "The Estranging Sea"). That faith lives in an elation generated in the creative tension between the indivisible power of love, and the contending currents of mortal pain – in the very angst that binds them. It calls for the virtues of openness, of the spirit's strength and grace in adaptability – qualities which Walcott tries to convey in his ideal of "litheness".[56] It is Brodsky who, sensitive to the essential Walcott, finds the apt definition for this faith in immanence when he calls Walcott a "metaphysical realist".[57] The wisdom embodied in the awakened Anna represents, in fact, a genuine alternative to the Platonist pursuit of changeless, mystical, immortal light. Its spiritual imperatives echo those of "the pounding of the faces of gods back into the red clay". As in the climactic resolutions of "Homage to Gregorias", they represent a purposive denial and refutation of the egotistic and superhuman thrust of the older way.

In chapter 14, then, the actual love experience deepens, compellingly, into a metaphysical fable. This chapter is indeed a cameo of the dynamic movement from biographical content to philosophical text operative throughout "A Simple Flame". In the course of the narrative, mythic content surges upward into the flow of Anna's sentiments and feelings. Anna speaks, for example, of emergence from the darkness of sleep, nonbeing, into light/existence; from the cave of unknowing in the womb of Mother Earth, to life in consciousness. What remains in the foreground, however, is the familiar, everyday substance of the experience; and it is in this, as already observed, that the sense of the miraculous primarily resides. This familiar, everyday content, moreover, is all the more natural and authentic for being wholly of the immediate, native setting. The latter is of particular significance. Walcott's morning scene comes to epiphany in and through Anna; it is also, indivisibly, the epiphany of her native landscape. Anna awakens to the elementals of her native setting: the island breeze, the morning glow of sunlight on water; to the "prime simplicities" of characteristic activities and sights such as the waking ritual of making coffee, the early canoes setting out. The external stimuli and processes to which she comes alive represent, simultaneously, the awakening of the native landscape in its essentially virginal quality and ambiance. In this unison between Anna and landscape we see the true fruition of the early, instinctual identification of the beloved with landscape by Walcott as young poet/lover. Landscape thus remains focal in the alternative order of possibilities being affirmed here, as is the case with the other two loves. So that, of the many diverse elements that come together in the idealization of Anna, it is this native, spontaneous lyricism that remains the most organic, to come to fruition in the realizations of the "simple flame".

This focuses and affirms a fundamental aspect of the whole: the unique access of this landscape to the fresh manifestation, bodying forth this vision of immanence. Walcott returns again and again to the special, enabling strengths of his native landscape: its virginal, primal, that is, largely "unhistoried" condition; its unhistoried "newness" nonetheless necessarily conditioned by its particular conjuncture with world history and in constant intercourse with it. These properties lie behind the order of Imagination that comes to birth with the true Anna. Here, as in the resolutions of each of the three loves in turn, the informing purpose articulated in the epigraph to *Another Life* is fulfilled: "then I shall perceive the unique and essential quality of this place" (Edouard Glissant). Finally, a seminal, integral aspect of the achievement enabled by its unique, essential quality is that of naming (as also in the case of Sauteurs in book 2). The vision of immanence expressed in the image of "a simple flame" turns on a quality of discovery which is the quintessential reality of Walcott's concept of naming. It engages afresh the primal, sacred necessity of discovering the universe we inhabit, establishing our bond with it, and thereby humanizing it. Naming is also, by extension, synonymous with the principle of renewal at root elemental sources. Which means that memory plays a pivotal role, and is always incident in this quality of discovery, on both the biographical and wider historical planes. Thus, on the biographical level, it is only on return to the original experience of innocent love, in the light of subsequent experience, that Walcott can recognize its inherent truth; and enter into possession of the quiet, infinite strength of this native awakening of love. On the further, parallel level, Old World Western memory remains an operative background, whether in dialectical or referential context, against and within which this fresh truth discovers/rediscovers its name.

In the preceding chapter (13), Walcott insets a picture of the local festive Christmas season as fitting background to the sense of new life abounding in the wake of first love. It is one of those pieces which, distilling the true genius of his place, fully reveals and undersigns the originality of his voice. This picture of the native Christmas stands out as a *locus classicus* for another important reason. It strikingly demonstrates and validates his belief in a New World confluence of new life and renewal. The latter, as we have seen, comes to consummation in the order of values affirmed in "Anna Awakening", as also in that of the other climaxes of *Another Life.*

Christmas in the native setting – St Lucian and West Indian – has developed its own variety of customs, and preserves its own spirit. It does retain, along with the traditional Christian religious symbols, sundry traces of the European popular legacy. Walcott's picture decorously acknowledges these traces: the "pretence at cold"; "apples bubbling in barrows". What predominates, though, is the local fare with which the bounty of the season is celebrated. The Caribbean version keeps its indigenous flavour and accent in the preparation and enjoyment of such home brews as sorrel and ginger beer, made from local berries, roots and barks; the indispensable black fruit-cake, made from a rich variety of fruits to a special local recipe:

> And Christmas came with its pretence at cold,
> apples bubbled in barrows, the wind, beggarly
> polished their cheeks;
> along smoked kitchen walls, like a laboratory,
> sweet, devilish concoctions, knuckles, roots,
> blood-jellied jars, pungent and aromatic as the earth
> which kept its secret till this season, were fermenting,
> bark-knuckled ginger, the crimson bulbs
> of sorrel like extinguished lights
> packed up in last year's tinsel, sweated oil,

(CP, 232)

The native celebration captured here is redolent of the glow and brightness, the munificence and sense of the magical associated with Christmas. All its felicities, however, exude a strong flavour of the grassroots, from which they originate. There seems to be, at that grassroots level, a living continuum between the human/domestic preparations and the natural earth as primary producer. The smells of the kitchen remain "pungent and aromatic as the earth"; in concoctions left to brew or ferment overnight (sorrel and ginger beer beverages), the folk seem to have tapped into the mysteries of the organic chemistry of diverse elements in physical nature itself. The Christmas black cake, pièce de résistance, materializes as the special culmination of this communion/continuity between the human and the physical earth. Rich in its variety of fruits and wines, it seems to be the earth itself delivering of its full bounty, being served up as a special culinary delight:

> and the baked earth exuded
> itself, as if, pebbled with clove,
> it could at last be taken from its oven,
> the night smelled like a cake
> seasoned in anise, . . .

(CP, 232)

Traces of the less happy, bitter exertions involved are also subtly blended into these preparations and creations – in references to blood ("blood-jellied jars"); sweat ("sweated oil"); in the processes of fermenting and the seasoning. The rich red which dominates as the colour of the festival is especially significant in this respect. It is the rich red of the sorrel drink and the chapel wine; it is also the rich red of blood, with its sacred connotations. Walcott sounds the mythic significance of this blood motif in the opening lines of this chapter:

"blood for the bloodless birth". In these references to blood, sweat, fermentation there are hints of the principle of the sacrificial, of labour and strife, as organic as the beneficent elements to the total alchemy with which the natural earth produces.

Walcott's faithful rendering of the local Christmas captures its spirit of joy in new life, celebrated in the native bounty of its own soil. In thus honouring and praising life's fertility, it recovers afresh the archetypal, mythic sources of the Christian festival. But in so doing, it defines and maintains its special quality and native difference. That difference hinges on a closer connexion with the natural, root sources of life-properties and processes, from which the mythic and religious expressions/constructions originated. Something of this quality is there in the rich sensuousness of his recreation of the event. The appeal of that sensuousness, in taste, smell, sight, remains earthy, keeps the fragrance of the first take. The indigenized St Lucian/Caribbean Christmas is a grassroots cultural expression that is very much of the people, and, as such, infused with their sensibility and spirit. It also represents a classic illustration of Walcott's concept of creolization. A legacy of the Old World, this indigenized Christmas has found its new name in this local habitation; and it renews, in the process, the significations of the old, making it all of a piece with the key affirmations and aesthetic of this work.

Walcott ends his revisitation of the Anna experience with an overview of its total meaning in his progress towards another light of love. In chapter 15, he moves to define and pay tribute to Anna for her inclusive significance as the first love in whom woman, art and landscape coalesced. His tribute to Anna as the bearer of love is also a meditative tribute to the power of that love. The Anna of chapter 15 is hailed, in a celebratory litany, as "all Annas". What Walcott recognizes and affirms in this acclamation is her larger, inclusive value as the genius of his passage to maturity – the genius of all, in the total experience, that has made possible his (re)discovery of the original truth of "a simple flame". First love, thus fully awakened, proved the true muse and genius of his poetry. Thus in "The Schooner *Flight*" he dedicates his poetry to St Lucia/Anna on another return to his native land:

> I have kept my own
> promise, to leave you the one thing I own,
> you whom I loved first: my poetry.
>
>   (*CP*, 354)

That love was the catalyst, the motive, the enabling principle, opening and sensitizing him to each separate reality in the range and changing process of experience: the times of affirmation and upliftment, of disappointment, pain and loss; to the peculiar savour of the sense impressions associated with the epiphanies of each distinct passing facet of experience. Moments from literature are as real as those of actual experiences in these memories:

> for you became, in fact, another country,
>
> you are Anna of the wheatfield and the weir,
> you are Anna of the solid winter rain,
> Anna of the smoky platform and the cold train,
> in that war of absence, Anna of the steaming stations,
>
> gone from the marsh edge,
> from the drizzled shallows
> puckering with gooseflesh,
> Anna of the first green poems that startingly hardened,
>
> of the mellowing breasts now,
> Anna of the lurching, long flamingoes
> of the harsh salt lingering in the thimble
> of the bather's smile,
>
> Anna of the darkened house, among the reeking shell cases
> lifting my hand and swearing us to her breast,
> unbearably clear-eyed.
>
> (*CP*, 238)

Among the most penetrative blessings of that love was his initiation, in suffering its passage, into knowledge of the humanizing realities of loss and separation. He recognizes his first indelible encounter with this necessity in the failure of the relationship with Andreuille/Anna. Especially under the shadow of Simmons's fate, it deepens into his understanding of absence, separation and loss as inexorable realities estranging humankind from its "deep desire" for infinite possession. That the consciousness of finitude and change should thus hold the foreground in Walcott's concluding affirmations in this book is no contradiction: for, in the order of renewed faith in immanence for which he stands, mortality/death, embraced by love, is itself what enhances the humanity of love and faith.[58] Thus the crowning commendation, seemingly back-handed, of his tribute to Anna: "You are all Annas, enduring all goodbyes, / within the cynical station of your body" (*CP*, 238). Walcott celebrates Anna, ultimately, as the all-embracing genius of his arrival at the intelligence of love. As such, the figure of Anna gains archetypal stature, to find a genuine analogue in Dante's Beatrice – just as emerged in the parallel between Grenada's Sauteurs and the Greeks at Thermopylae. Henceforth, all truth will be defended and affirmed in her name (*CP*, 269).

Simmons: Death ("The Estranging Sea")

The tragedy of Harold Simmons, who committed suicide in despair, brings into focus the theme of death, the last of the trinity of loves. Through the tragic circumstances of Simmons's story, Walcott enters into a meditative reflection on the eternal problems of human suffering, defeat, and the existential realities of change and finitude that lie behind them. The currents of his thought here – and indeed from the preceding books – find confluence in a revisioning of the burden of time itself in human destiny. This finds expression as a climactic act in chapter 22, the outstanding finale to *Another Life*, which first appeared separately as "The Muse of History at Rampanalgas".[59] Resuming in this chapter, the counter-discourse with the Old World Western muse of history, Walcott affirms alternative meanings in definitive answer to the older values. This, as we have seen, is his informing purpose in the work.

Simmons, "the master of Gregorias and [him]self", had been a major influence in Walcott's apprenticeship. His death also had a significant impact on this later stage of the poet's career. For one thing, it stands behind the maturity achieved in this work. News of Simmon's tragic suicide came when Walcott was halfway through the composition of the book. The event is chronicled in these lines, the word play on "stroke" heavy with painful irony: "When I began this work, you were alive, / and with one stroke, you have completed it!" (*CP*, 282). The news of his suicide was the decisive factor in the shaping of this work.[60] (It was also, one senses, to strengthen Walcott's resolve in his commitment to his life's work: "And I only am escaped to tell the tale.")[61] Death, all too close, and compellingly emblematic in the case of this friend, comes replete with answers. It is what helps to crystallize the philosophical intention of the work, and to focus its deep narrative as a meditation on human destiny. Walcott remains sensitive, though, about what he feels is a residually unhappy side of this situation: that his friend's traumatic experiences might thus serve for his own literary achievement:

> And you, master and friend,
> forgive me!

> Forgive me, if this sketch should ever thrive,
> or profit from your gentle, generous spirit.
>
> (*CP*, 282)

Such moments of trying to reach Harry give us Walcott, in his deep bereavement, at his most naked and defenceless: "Never to set eyes on this page, ah Harry, never to read our names" (*CP*, 276).

In terms of structural organization and thematic development, this is perhaps the most accessible of the four books. There is a more lucid connection between the engagement with the personal fate of Simmons, and the larger speculations arising out of it. Walcott begins with a portrait of Simmons in failure and despair; which is followed by a vindication and tribute which represent a fundamental part of the book's purpose. As a visionary who fell victim to his dream, his emblematic story brings into immediate focus the fate of the artist as sacrificial victim and martyr, with Simmons as the native archetype. The focus accommodates an all-out attack on philistine society for its complicity in the tragic destruction of the artist. An integral part of the vindication of Simmons, this attack belongs side by side with his climactic upliftment/sanctification. Book 4 then moves from the biographical to the existential dimension of its elegiac theme, to conclude with the philosophical meditation on time and mortality. It culminates in the revisioning, in chapter 22, of the muse of humanity encoded in the Old World Western muse of history. It is Walcott's persistent focus in this work.

Another Life contains the most significant account of Simmons's life and achievement to date, especially valuable for its appreciation of his contribution and the values for which he stood. A brief introductory profile will provide a supplementary background to Walcott's portrait. Harold Simmons was the first St Lucian to conceive of, and embark on, the task of developing a "native culture" in his island; essentially, he was among the first, along with pioneering counterparts in the other islands during the 1940s, to see the area in terms of a regional culture. Simmons's main gift was in painting; he was, in fact, a fine watercolourist. He cultivated and developed, however, a remarkable range of other interests and talents towards the pursuit of this goal of a native culture. He became a folklorist, the first to investigate the native customs and folklore of the island; an amateur archaeologist,[62] searching out its Amerindian (Carib) remains; a naturalist, interested in identifying its flora and fauna (as a lepidopterist).

Simmons came from one of the better-educated, middle-class families in the island. He held several prominent posts in the civil service, and was also editor of the single national newspaper. These were sinecures that never really claimed him. His marriage to Lister Buch, by which there was one daughter, did not survive long either. Simmons seems to have focused mainly on his artist's commitment to the mission of developing a native culture in his island. Several landscapes and seascapes by him remain in the homes of St Lucians as testimony to this commitment, and he holds the honour of being the first to paint the native black faces and scenes of his island.

It is perhaps in Walcott's own achievement that the essential value of Simmons's contribution survives most strongly. Serving as art tutor and mentor to Walcott and St Omer, "the master" imparted two formative, seminal values. He taught them, first, to see the landscape, and, seeing it, to dedicate their talents to it. The other lesson they learnt from him was the necessity of a selfless surrender to talent, as Walcott records in "Leaving School": "but since our apprentice days on Barnard's Hill, Dunstan and I knew what our professions were. We would be what we could do, what we loved best. Mr Simmons had set up that example."[63] In that article, the present poem, and several other places in the corpus, Walcott pays tribute to Simmons for the vital influences underlying his own achievement. But it would have been a sheer miracle if Simmons himself, given his mission, had survived in the St Lucia of those times. The small, stagnant society of what was still a colonial backwater was simply not yet ready for him, as was observed by one of Walcott's contemporaries. The environment he faced was one of neglect, quite oblivious of and unreceptive to the artist – attitudes that quickly turned to contempt as his personal circumstances deteriorated. After some ten to fifteen years of struggle, both his talent and his will began to fail. By this time, he was suffering from both money and drinking problems, and was selling his paintings for a few shillings to buy the next drink. When he retreated to Garand and Piaille, the remote country districts where he spent the last years of his life, he was a man who had lost his artistic powers and his will to work. At Garand (on the northwestern coast of the island) he lived in conditions of acute poverty, in an earth-floored shack. Walcott, who visited him there once, was of the opinion that he was probably trying to paint again.

Book 4 enters Simmon's story at the point of his retreat to Piaille. A flight from the ills of conventional society to more primitive, spartan country environs, it presents a significant parallel to Paul Gauguin's retreat to the

Polynesian islands. This is underscored by the fact that, as the narrative relates, Simmons seems to have lived that parallel, adopting Gauguin as patron saint, and holding on to *Noa Noa*[64] as a main solace in his exile. Gauguin is to be a presiding genius in this account of Simmons's fateful exile, as the epigraph of this movement shows (chapter 18). Walcott invokes the parallel from the opening lines, with an allusion to Harry's attraction to the young country girls (*jahbals*) just as Gauguin had found his mistresses from among the teenaged girls (*vahines*) of Polynesia. We hear this in the upbeat, relaxed tone of the vernacular, almost as if it were staving off the gloom of what is to come: "You can't beat brushing young things from the country / in the country self . . ." (*CP*, 261). Such country pleasures notwithstanding, the Simmons who goes to Piaille goes in a spirit of purposeful rejection of society, preferring the natural destitutions of rustic Piaille to the synthetic corruptions of the small town. The expletive force of these lines comes from Walcott's own anger:

> Telling himself that although it stank
> this was the vegetable excrement of natural life,
> not their homogenised, chemical-ridden shit,
>
> (*CP*, 261)

But if country districts like Garand and Piaille offered some respite from the frustrations and hardships of trying to live in Castries, it was in such places that he was fated to suffer the inroads of despair to its final extremity. Chapter 18 tries to re-enter his experience in this kind of isolated, sparsely populated setting. He finds himself literally pushed back to the very edge of existence, between ocean and surrounding bush; exposed there – the concrete and metaphorical dovetail into each other – to the threat of a primordial reclamation, a dissolution of self that must have been part of his final trauma. The threat remains palpable in the images of Simmons isolated on his·"leafy ocean", "driving his houseboat deeper in the forest" (*CP*, 261). Thus, as Walcott intuits, the Gauguin whose shadow haunts this exile [65] is the Gauguin of the last, dying spell in the South Seas (1895). Thinking of Simmons's agony, Walcott makes this entry in MS One: "The pain, the pain of Gauguin's *Noa Noa*. Gauguin sick on arsenic, crawling through the bushes back to his hut, unable to die."[66] The focus, in this portrait of Simmons, is on his psychological·deterioration from the despair presaged by the failure of his purpose, talent and will to paint. In a moving, exploratory act of empathy with Simmons, Walcott traces the progressive stages of the decline of the mind and spirit in this crisis. We see Simmons's indifferent efforts against this paralysis; beset by its growing desolation and desperation, as easel is threaded to bedstead. We watch him undergo its unsettling effects, afflicted by increasingly chronic nervous disorders and their physical symptoms ("everything he touches breaks" [*CP*, 263]). At the extreme end of this state comes the breakdown, the dissolution of the self. This is the extremity, at the dread end of despair, where we come to know – and our own empathy has been fully absorbed into Walcott's – the experience of spiritual vacuity: "the worst, the worst, an oceanic nothing" (*CP*, 264). There are strong echoes of Kierkegaard as Walcott sounds the "fear and trembling" of this breakdown. There is the even deeper echo of the Kierkegaard who understood "the living death of nothingness", suffered as the "inability to die":[67]

> it is fear and trembling.
> It is the uncontrollable
> persistence of the heartbeat,
>
> . . . .
>
> to tire of life, and yet not wish to die.

(CP, 264)

Right unto these ontological limits, Simmons's personal crisis retains its immediacy; but Walcott has widened and universalized it to include, and aim it at, "all of us, always, all ways, one after one" (*CP*, 262).

The prevailing, informing purpose of this life story remains elegiac. While the traditional elements of lament, eulogy and philosophical speculation are all present, Walcott has brought a new flexibility to the elegy. He has included a strong current of protest and anger, injecting into the form a spirit of impassioned resistance of what constitutes, finally, a travesty of life itself. Simmons's crisis is the original cause of this anger; but it expands conclusively to embrace an ongoing problem from which other West Indian artists (Walcott included) and the universal brotherhood have suffered and continue to suffer. His emblematic case becomes the axis of a prominent, strident theme in this book: the crucifixion of artists, the visionaries of society, by its perenially reactionary, philistine forces; and the concomitant betrayal of the cause of society itself. Simmons's treatment at the hands of his small, barren community was callous and vicious, and it provides a naked, original example of the kind of crucifixion that helps to destroy the artist. Walcott's bitterness is almost choked with pain, as he makes this very accurate reprise of the attitudes with which Simmons was dismissed:

> they said that, and were already composing,
> . . . .
> like a fistful of dirt
> flung into your grave, from such a man
> what would you expect,
> but a couple of paintings
> and a dog's life?

(CP, 265)

In the shadow of the master's tragedy, Walcott returns to the horrors and frustrations that St Omer and himself had known as victims of similar abuse and rejection. A near-defeated St Omer had once been driven close to suicide. Recalling that story, Walcott confesses to wishing him, at the time, "a spiteful martyrdom". For his own part, Walcott has several lethal axes to grind – with personal enemies, as well as those on the public front. He exposes and vilifies them with savage, unmitigated contempt. It is the characteristic tone of this protest, ultimately cathartic in its power.

Walcott trains the full force of his attack on the purveyors of radical black nationalism, the contemporary revolutionary doctrine of the region in the 1970s. They are the "magicians of the new vision", whom he denounces as enemies of society and of its visionaries, the few who, like Simmons, strive to find a truly creative path. Chapter 19, devoted to this attack, has already received critical scrutiny in our earlier examination of Walcott's revolutionary creed (chapter 4). We must return to it here. From his viewpoint, the core iniquity of that creed is the deification of ancestral history, committing its faithful of the region to an obsession with past victimhood, and its "masochistic veneration of chains" ("Muse"). Incidentally, he completely bypasses their ideology of resistance; the implication being that, for him, the latter remains stillborn, stymied by this cult of victimhood. Surveying the contemporary scene of this new black radicalism, he delivers a blistering salvo on its culture and values. What it offers is no empowerment. The fashionable rituals, symbols and ornamentals which its followers flaunt to proclaim their Africanist faith represent mere vulgarization and prostitution, of self as much as of their borrowings – like "whores with slave bangles banging tambourines" (*CP*, 269). At the vilest level, they amount to nothing more than a brood of parasites feeding off the festering sores and scabs of ancestral pain. The unkindest cut of all, to which Walcott refers more than once, has its source in this very perversion. They virtually prize the catalogue of suicides among their artists, to be sacrificed to this altar of racial pain:

> spitting on their own poets,
> preferring their painters drunkards,
> for their solemn catalogue of suicides,

(CP, 265)

He is also especially vehement about the divisiveness of their inherently racist codes, which commit them to "pronounce their measure / of toms, of traitors, of traditionals and Afro-Saxons" (*CP*, 270). They perpetrate, in this, a travesty no different from the older, white racist practice of measuring the skull with callipers to determine racial superiority. In the name of Simmons, Walcott condemns them and their unregenerate vision, as traitors to the progress of society – the counterparts in contemporary times of the reactionary forces that had earlier thwarted Simmons's effort in his small island. Chapter 19 reeks with images of the rot and putrescence of festering sores, the parasites they breed, expressive of the moral abhorrence and revulsion with which he views this latest phase of society's betrayal. The native, self-created hell, to which he consigns these "magicians of the new vision", finds its local habitation in "the boiling, scabrous, pustular" rocks of the site of St Lucia's extinct volcano. It is another metaphor grounded in landscape, which will become permanently inscribed in his work. The New World Caribbean scene is thus the site of horrors and abominations whose images are a far and mocking cry from St Omer's earlier ideal of "frescoes of the New World" – as the epigraph to this chapter suggests.

The vindication of Simmons is an important climax in the engagement with his story, and the image of the redeemed Simmons which follows in chapter 20 rises as a truly revolutionary answer, refuting the falsehoods denounced in his name. While his untimely death gives sharper definition to the meaning of his brief life, the worth and value of that life itself, its work and achievement make him, in Walcott's words, an archetype of the man who "staggers towards his lineaments" (*CP*, 270). As his eulogist, Walcott chronicles and inscribes its truth, giving utterance to its name, and immortalizing it forever. We experience a remarkable switch from the language of fury and abuse to the tender, compassionate and reverential strains of his appreciation of Simmons. The switch is typical of the rich range and flow of tones in *Another Life*, a feature reflective of the expansiveness and fluidity of the sensibility that finds expression in this book. The image which emerges from Walcott's appreciation is of a man whose deep natural commitment to his native land began at the grassroots level, in all spheres. Simmons, as we have seen, sought to explore several areas of the native setting: its folklore,[68] its natural life, its Amerindian remains. The quality of that commitment was epitomized by his bond with the country people he got to know during the more active period before his troubles. The cultural interests which took him among them were, for him, a way of life rather than an intellectual project; and he was, evidently, the kind of free spirit who found it easy to dispense with middle-class values and conventions. Walcott celebrates a man who was both the champion of the country folk, and a product of his close bond with them. He entered their lives and developed a mutual sympathy with them – sharing in their hardships, as well as the simplicities and graces of their way of life. A full, enhanced portrait of Simmons occurs here.[69] Every peculiar detail of his physical appearance, his very mien, seems moulded out of the basic properties and matter of their lifestyle and its immediate setting. They appear iconic, reflecting an earth-likeness, naturalness and capacity for generous service at one with the qualities of these country folk:

> It was they who had smoothed the wall
> of his clay-coloured forehead,
> who made of his rotundity an earthy
> useful object
> holding the clear water of their simple troubles,

> *(CP*, 276)

The lived elementals of their grassroots life, and its humanity, find a virtual epiphany in the features and personality of Simmons.

Thus, in a crowning tribute to Simmons, Walcott calls on the country folk to join in a solemn ritual of last respects to "Msieu Simmons". He calls on the carpenter, forester, fisherman, a doyenne of the folk dance, to honour him, each in his or her craft and occupation, with appropriate acts of benediction and consecration. He gives this ritual call a greater poignancy and dignity by drawing in their own voice, blending in the idiom and accents of their native French creole. The best of Simmons had been given to the upliftment of these people, to giving them visibility and dignity in their labour, customs, way of life and surroundings. In that call to solemn last respects, Walcott paints a frieze which reflects the summit of Simmons's achievement:

> Leonce, Placide, Alcindor,
> Dominic, from whose plane vowels were shorn
> odorous as forest,
> ask the charcoal-burner to look up

> with his singed eyes,
> ask the lip-cracked fisherman three miles at sea
> with nothing between him and Dahomey's coast
> to dip rainwater over his parched boards
> for Monsieur Simmons, *pour* Msieu Harry Simmons,[70]
>
> (CP, 277)

The genius of Simmons lives on in the spirit of self-discovery and expression he initiated and helped to foster from these roots:

> and he is a man no more
> but the fervour and intelligence
> of a whole country.
>
> (CP, 277)

This spirit reflects the depth of his own bond with landscape. In this important area, we should observe, Simmons proved truly the master. He it was who set in train and tried to live this necessity of developing roots at that primary level. His aspiration and example were to bear fruit in his two pupils – in St Omer's artistic attunement to the aboriginal force of his primal surroundings; and in Walcott's awakening to the immanence of the creative principle alive in its natural, virginal setting.

The prayerlike, sacred strains of this final tribute are in tune with a strong motif of sanctification in the portrait of Simmons, which uplifts his image as the saint "risen" from crucifixion. Walcott makes use of traditional Christian imagery to "hoist him heavenward" into the sainted company of Gauguin, Van Gogh, Orozco, Siquieros – a representative brotherhood, regional and international, of those who have truly served the human spirit and Imagination. Simmons thus evokes a parallel with Christ, like all who have been martyrs to that cause. In keeping with Walcott's aesthetic, however, it is a Christlikeness de-supernaturalized, fully humanized, and incarnate in a man well planted in his natural roots.

This eulogy has affirmed the meaning of Simmons's life vis-à-vis his death. But the shadow of mortality cast by his fate constitutes the centre of speculative concern in this book, which Walcott has significantly entitled "The Estranging Sea". It is consistent with the philosophical dimension of his theme that, considering Simmons, he goes on to seek and extend an image of what it means to meet and accommodate, beyond despair, the necessity of human mortality as a liveable truth. It is this ineluctable necessity that is focused in "the estranging sea", the motif taken from Arnold's "To Marguerite",[71] which serves as the epigraph to this book. The motif alludes to the limitations that, infinite and eternal like the sea, separate and fix the distance between us and the absolutes we yearn for on the other side. The passage from Arnold envisions this as a divine disadvantage, the "happy" existential loss which most deeply humanizes us. Thus: "a God their severance ruled!" In Walcott's faith, it is a message of great revelatory power, embracing the meanings of "enduring all goodbyes", and of the leap of Grenada's Sauteurs. Looking for a way and possibility of survival for ordinary mortals, it is in the example of Gregorias, as survivor, that he finds it. St Omer/Gregorias had been the near-victim of a defeat similar to that of Simmons, as Walcott recalls in chapter 20. He had managed to survive it, to emerge with an extraordinary quality of self-reconciliation. He had come to accept and live within the limitations of his circumstances without ever surrendering his passion, continuing yet to give of his creative flame. Side by side with Simmons, Walcott uplifts his image: "'I see, I see' is what Gregorias cried, / living within that moment where he died" (*CP*, 273).

The philosophical dimension thus comes into the foreground in the ensuing chapters of "The Estranging Sea". Devoted to a meditation on death as last of the three loves, they engage the questions of time, its ever-imminent faces of finitude and change, as these give final meaning and shape to human destiny. Walcott begins in chapter 20 with a speculation on the numerous signals, presentiments and encounters that remind us of the certainty of death, and the precariousness of our lives as mortals. He calls "all of us, all ways" to acknowledgment of such moments and instances when, beneath the veneer and insulations of human culture, we know the reality of that shared nakedness. Such intimations of mortality are themselves the answer to the question "why" – with which the chapter opens – and remind us of the need to internalize and arrive at right consciousness towards our mortal nakedness. Leading this acknowledgment with his personal testimony, he recovers various sources of these signals and presentiments original to the native St Lucian landscape – the landscape which has left its formative and indelible imprints on his sensibility. There are places and features, sounds and sights in that landscape which can emit the climate of a secret primitive fear, to disturb and confront the individual with the sense of his or her radical insecurity. It is there, for example, in the threat of human disintegration staring back from "the shacks . . . / like shattered staves / bound in old wire" (*CP*, 278), a graphic picture of the dread ends of human dereliction and misery. This seems to be a recollection of an earlier shanty district at one end of the wharves of Castries, where the hovels and living conditions must have ranked among those of the world's worst slums.[72] Near bleak coastal villages in their isolated, desolate environs (reminiscent of Dennery with its pigs and poverty), the stark, primitive noises of the sea can sound like the death rattle:

> or follow the path
> of the caked piglet through
> the sea-village's midden,
> past the repeated
> detonations of spray,
> where the death rattle
> gargles in the shale

(CP, 278)

We are in St Lucian territory, where "one step behind the city was the bush" (book 1); and where bush is also, as earlier noted, contiguous with sea, the two sharing the quality of one primal space. The bush thus constitutes a significant presence in this setting, in both its natural/uncultured, as well as its "cultured"/cultivated forms – the latter, for example, in "the frighteningly formal / marches of banana groves" *(CP,* 279).[73] As elsewhere in Walcott it is a major place of this kind of reckoning.[74] Bearing intimations of both the pristine and the primordial, it is a place of close encounter with the threat of oblivion, presaged by the subliminal sense of links with the pre-human, its processes, and the attendant fear of the inchoate. The threat of that chaos and its unnamable void can be far more terrifying than the perils of conscience:

> in the mangroves plunged to wrist, repeating
> the mangroves plunging to the wrist,
> there are spaces
> wider than conscience

(CP, 280)

They are the terrifying spaces Simmons must have known near the bush in Piaille and Garand.

Rampanalgas in Trinidad, to which Walcott repairs for his concluding discourse on the muse of history (chapter 22), bears close resemblances to the St Lucian bush revisited in the chapter just examined. The two bear features characteristic of rustic settings throughout the Caribbean islands. Situated on the northeast coast of Trinidad, Rampanalgas is one of a number of small rustic villages along a main road which connects this remote corner to more developed areas of Trinidad – a highway travelled by town-dwellers in search of the few good, quiet beaches along this rough Atlantic coast of the island's Northern Range of mountains. The residents of Rampanalgas live in some two to three dozen unpainted, wooden houses in a valley that slopes steeply downhill from one side of the high coastal road; and, like the village that time forgot, Rampanalgas might well be completely bypassed but for a bar-cum-general store that serves as a major refreshment stop along the highway. Walcott has also drawn upon the adjoining villages along that coastline for some of the specific features included in his portrait of Rampanalgas. At the entrance to the village are the Rampanalgas river and its bridge; and the coconut and almond trees prominent in the portrait are strewn along a small rocky beach where the river empties into sea. The brackish mangrove swamp with which the chapter opens, however, does not occur in Rampanalgas itself, but is a common feature of these environs where many rivers flow down the mountainous terrain towards the Atlantic. The Chinese grocer's "small red shop", an important icon in the portrait, is taken from the neighbouring village of Cumana.[75] The Rampanalgas of chapter 22, then, is a composite image of the characteristic physiognomy and temper of that rustic coastline, graphically captured in these lines:

> holy the small, almond-leaf-shadowed bridge
> by the small red shop, where everything smells of salt,
> and holiest the break of the blue sea below the trees,
>
> > (*CP*, 289)

Walcott had, moreover, a strong personal attachment to this particular village, to which he and his family retreated when they wished to get away from it all. We should also note its Amerindian name which, outstanding among others such as Matura, Cumana, Balandra and Toco, brings with it the aboriginal reference fundamental, as we shall see, to Walcott's theme. This important-sounding name, moreover, totally belies the reality of a place that remains insignificant and obscure. The insignificance is precisely the starting point of its significance in Walcott's theme. The latter focuses on its characteristic appearance as a place virtually untouched by history, a corner of the hemisphere which has remained effectively outside the "historic" action initiated in the region in Columbian times. Rampanalgas thus presents a concrete manifestation of the historylessness/unhistoried condition so seminal in Walcott's approach to the question of identity. It is for this reason that its remote,

obscure setting captures his imagination as a fitting site for his counter-discourse with the Old World Western muse of history.

Chapter 22 launches into the polemics of this counter-discourse straight
away. It posits the image of the orthodox historian in the bush of the marshy
coastal edges of the environs. It is a setting devoid of all but the most primitive,
minimal signs and processes of physical nature. The historian's purpose is
frustrated, and his presence totally negated in that setting. The opening lines
describe the characteristic features of the scene, its mood and general atmosphere. A sense of torpor hangs over the prevailing conditions of damp, mould
and sluggishness; the smells of the slow underlife of mangrove swamp, the
monotonous repetition of the colours of the foliage, are enervating. The spirit
is repelled and the self almost annulled in such a setting. What the sluggishness
and stasis of this swamp habitat emanates is an intransigent absence, a denial
of human reference: "the cordage of mangrove tightens / bland water to bland
sky"; "water-coloured water" (*CP*, 283). The bird barely visible in the foliage,
the rat scuttling across water are the few signs of the life of its fauna. These
too blend into the general atmosphere of stasis and absence of meaning.
Altogether, this face of Rampanalgas gives the impression of remaining
effectively beyond the pale of the evolutionary, as Walcott suggests in an ironic
parenthesis. The latter makes reference to the presence of a rotting pirogue
from the nearby village, "trying hard to look like / a paleolithic, half-gnawed
memory of pre-history" (*CP*, 283) – but not succeeding.

Walcott manoeuvres deep and subtly devastating levels of satire to drive
home his point about the irrelevance of the purposes and methods of orthodox
history in such a setting:

> let the historian go mad there
> from thirst. Slowly the water rat takes up its reed pen
> and scribbles. . . .

(CP, 283)

The water rat scribbling nothing on water, the egret stamping its footprint on
the mud, are highly charged emblems. The action of the scribbling water rat
is, first, the parodic equivalent of the deciphering, recording historian. There
is a further, more cutting satirical edge to this reductive strategy: here the water
rat has the true authority, displacing that of the historian. This latter also
carries, on the reverse side of the satire, a profoundly positive meaning. From
the alternative, truer perspective also being explored in the muse of history at
Rampanalgas, writing nothing on water signifies the visionary recognition of

no-thingness, its translucence. Similarly, the hieroglyph of the egret's foot on the mud is the profoundly mythic signature of what Walcott envisions as the the finding of earth.[76] At various points in this meditative critique of the muse of history, he plays on either or both sides of the "contra-dicted" (*CP*, 281) meanings of these mythic emblems.

Along with the representative figure of the historian, the related company of functionaries serving the cause of visible history are drawn in to face futility at this site. For Walcott is concerned to dismantle the whole system of values and functions embraced in the ethos of history as achievement. Thus the explorer/anthropologist "stumbles out of the bush crying out for myth" (*CP*, 283); and "The astigmatic geologist / stoops . . . / deciphering – not a sign" (*CP*, 284). Walcott deliberately includes what he has earlier abjured as the cardinal sin of his own region in this regard: "The tired slave vomits his past" (*CP*, 283). This draws attention to a most important aspect of his purpose in the polemic of this chapter. His attack is two-pronged – aimed as much at the Old World European tradition as at his own New World territory for its perpetuation of the old errors. His quarrel with contemporary revolutionary doctrines in the region is repeated in this image of "the tired slave vomit[ing] his past". The diet of victimhood – the wounds and horrors of a brutal past – counts for nothing, proves totally dispensable here, and is disgorged like so much unwholesome excess – the "nothingness" mirrored in Rampanalgas proving, indeed, a kind of purgative.

From this introductory polemic, the chapter moves straight into a system-atic deconstruction of that traditional view of history, to explode its myths. For this climactic act, satire attains fresh and original reaches of power in Walcott's hands: scathing wit combines with the imaginative leap of the conceit to achieve, at climactic points, a remarkable interpenetration of the polemical and the visionary. We shift from the bush to the human face of Rampanalgas, which is represented by the figure of a Chinese grocer in his small shop. The latter will serve as the anchoring point in this act of decon-struction. The act begins with a leap back to the Mediterranean origins of Western civilization to zero in on the Mediterranean accountant "calculating his tables". Juxtaposing this figure and that of the Chinese grocer, Walcott telescopes history to present the two as counterparts of each other, establishing significant links between them. To appreciate the rich implications of this juxtaposition, we need first to pay attention to the Chinese grocer. At first glance seemingly unlikely, this Trinidadian Chinese is in fact a very likely presence in this obscure corner of the island. The Chinese are one of the many races represented in the mixed population of Trinidad.[77] They are traditionally associated with business, and the less privileged are small shopkeepers of the type presented here. Walcott chooses this Trinidadian Chinese to make a special point about the ideal of ancestral greatness cherished in the idea of history as achievement. In this exiled, distant descendant, one of the most ancient and "unbreachable" of ancestries has been reduced, whittled down to a mere relic of its reputed image. It has drifted, in one of the many diasporas of the Old World – the consequence of the waywardness and the ravages of time and history – to what is, on one level, its dead end in this obscure corner of the New World. (As the Walcott of *Omeros* would put it, it is the image of the Old World "reversed" back to an original facelessness and insignificance in the New.)

A single, eloquent snapshot captures the particulars and significations of this distant descendant of China in his daily routine:

> the Chinese grocer's smile is leaden with boredom:
> so many lbs. of cod,
> > so many bales of biscuits,
> on spiked shop paper,

(CP, 283–84)

The Mediterranean accountant, fetched from one of the earliest sources of Western civilization, emerges as an original predecessor of the bored diasporan Chinese grocer engaged in recording his banal, small-time goods. The former – the likeness of Eliot's Mr Eugenides, bringer of trade and commerce (*The Waste Land*) – is historically associated with the rudiments of accountancy. What links the two, the line of succession between them, is this vocation of accountancy. Walcott's argument is that this same activity of accountancy has been the motive force/engine of the history that runs between them, from origins to dead end.[78] Their respective images stress their resemblance to each other in the tedium and drudgery of their tasks, to deftly suggest that no real advance, no meaningful change has occurred in the "history" between them. The surviving principle of accountancy lies behind the ethos of accumulation upon which epic greatness is predicated and constructed: the practice of building up the record of achievements, the measuring of "significant action". It lies at the heart, therefore, of the muse of history as cumulative achievement. Here one should pause to note that Walcott does not deny the creativity of some of these achievements; but he rejects the way that this creativity is expended in being measured and quantified – and thereby travestied – in the prevailing idea of history.

In the light of this quantitative principle at the core of cumulative history, Walcott exposes the glaringly materialist dynamic of epic-monumental greatness, and its final barrenness. Reductive details, echoing each other in the images of Mediterranean accountant and Chinese grocer, are loaded to unmask this reality, and level it down to its essential futility. The Mediterranean accountant at his task, for example, located at the pristine origins of civilization, retains a primal resemblance to "the nose of the water rat, / ideograph of the egret's foot" (*CP*, 283). Like these originals, what he achieves in these exertions amounts to nothing, is devoid of calculable value. The details of the Chinese grocer's bookkeeping are likewise emphatically reductive. It is bookkeeping in its most rudimentary and primitive form, a makeshift filing of credit and sundry business notes by impaling them on a metal spike mounted on a wooden base. The notes are scribbled on equally rudimentary brown shop paper. On the whole, the full force of this reductive act is carried in the picture of the Chinese grocer, fixed in the tedium and dreariness of his small retailer's shop and its banal, unprepossessing surroundings, in which the lowly, workaday saltfish,[79] like his "spiked shop paper", is an especially effective icon. The picture reflects the tedium, dreariness and servitude of that ethos of accumulation and calculation, highlighting its pedestrian and unimaginative spirit.

The dead end of the Chinese grocer's shop remains the site from which Walcott deals the final, crushing blow to the constructs of epic, cumulative history. Continuing with the telescopic span from Mediterranean origins to present-day counterpart, he brings into focus one of the earliest and most outstanding of historic monuments – the pyramids of the Egyptian pharaohs. The latter come, significantly, loaded with associations of death and decay. Another masterly conceit draws their formidable presence into the ambit of the small shop. The sight and smell of a mundane item in the shop provide an associational link with the image of these historic ruins. The result is an ironic juxtaposition in which the historic ruins shrink back to levels equivalent to the insignificance of the characteristic effects of the small shop. Walcott lights on the image of the humble onion to carry out this purpose. It turns on a lucid equation between the structure of the onion – emblematic since Ibsen's *Peer Gynt* – and the mummified pharaohs. The repeated layers of the onion, peeling away to no core, mirror in graphic miniature the "old Pharaohs peeling like onionskin / to the archaeologist's finger" (*CP*, 284). The very smell of the onion evokes the preserving ointment (spikenard) used to embalm the mummies – ineffectual against the process of decay. Walcott's choice of the pharaohs is a strategic and highly significant one, and he makes a definitive philosophical comment on epic-heroic history in that choice. The pyramids are, first, arch-models of monumental history, at once a fountainhead and consummation of its epic-heroic muse. (Egypt is here invoked as one of the sources of the mix of cultures that went into the making of the Mediterranean as cradle of Western civilization.) They were erected as the very apotheosis of the pharaohs, the god-kings of Egypt. As such they were, above all, arch-expressions of the will to triumph over death (the pharaohs were equipped with all requisite creature comforts and material possessions for the next life). As such they represented an investment against the depredations of time, and constituted a phenomenal manifestation of the materialist-cumulative engine pressed into service to that end. The time-hallowed pyramids thus amounted to a virtual bid for proprietorship of eternity on the part of these early progenitors of the Western muse. The ethos survives in the Western "presumption of permanence",[80] as Walcott puts it elsewhere. The spiritual value of this investment is what proves hollow, delusory, as the layers of these historic remains peel away to no core. It is in this image of the mummified pharaohs, then, that Walcott finally punctures the metaphysic and muse of epic, monumental history.

This deconstructive act is another of the major, iconoclastic moments in *Another Life*, infused, like the moment of the leaping Caribs, with revelatory power. The combination has emerged as a singular stylistic strength of Walcott's historical imagination – a historical imagination which, developed from the vantage point of his own regional history, and spanning Old and New Worlds in this way, is one of the distinguishing marks of his genius. What is also remarkable about this iconoclastic and revelatory moment is that it never loses the tone and diction of the speaking voice; so that it can accommodate the plain, raw terms of its reductive purpose. The lines which finally level the monumental legacy of the pharaohs reek of contempt and disgust:

> spikenard, and old Pharaohs peeling like onionskin
> to the archaeologist's finger – all that
> is the Muse of history. . . .

(CP, 284)

The disgust spills over into the reference immediately following, to "Pot-sherds, / and the crusted amphora of cutthroats" (*CP*, 284). "Cutthroats", the parting shot, glances unfavourably at the nearby, focal image of the pharaohs, harking back to the exploitation that went into their colossal structures, and underscoring the cruelty and corruption on which this epic, cumulative purpose depends.

Yet the discourse shifts from this disgust to more tempered, plaintive cadences in the next movement. Walcott's tone becomes compassionate and understanding as he universalizes his theme to comprehend other spheres of human culture that likewise serve this epic muse. He is responding to the human susceptibility involved in very much the same spirit that he pronounced "peace" on the chivalric delusion represented by the Fighting Fifth. Reviewing these other spheres, he cites examples that remain close to home: in literature, "the yellowing poems" – "Like old leather, / . . . peeling in self-contemptuous / curl away from itself" (*CP*, 284); "the myth of the golden Carib" which drew the Europeans into the region in the early centuries of New World exploration. The elegiac consciousness of time and its related burden of "the estranging sea" have remained subsumed within the satirical attacks on the older muse of history; and it is the undercurrents of that consciousness that surface in these compassionate strains. Walcott rounds off his deconstructive act with this elegiac theme, powerfully compressed in these epigrammatic lines:

> All of the epics are blown away with the leaves,
> blown with the careful calculations on brown paper;
> these were the only epics: the leaves.
>
> (*CP*, 284)

Prominent in the rustic, natural setting of Rampanalgas, the leaves are emblematic of the life process at its most reduced, and therefore, in its essential character and value. They are at once rotting ("all of the epics are blown away with the leaves") and vigorous,[81] in the endless continuum of life being generated and life being reclaimed – the dynamic of the "god-breeding, god-devouring earth" (book 2). Our true power and reaches of fulfilment consist in the native properties of the life-force at such root, elemental levels: thus the leaves are the only true "epics".

Walcott proceeds to the second and positive part of his mission at Rampanalgas. He reads and inscribes, in the natural features and properties of this rustic site, an alternative and truer muse of humankind's destiny in time.

Rampanalgas reveals this natural, more simple and deeper truth especially to the eyes of the childlike, innocent of all constructed knowledge and free of the blinders of traditional history. Its bare, humble elementals register the odyssey of the human spirit in its most reduced principles, and the timeless truth of that odyssey. Delineating the pattern of this odyssey, he explores and develops its meanings through the stages of a discourse that traces a remarkable itinerary. It is useful to preview this itinerary since it is within its full context that the alternative muse of Rampanalgas defines itself. The emblematic pattern perceived at Rampanalgas moves backward through history to find its full reflection in the voyages of the many races and ancestries that meet in the Caribbean. From there it reaches outwards to recover the bond of kinship between these diasporan races of the New World Caribbean, and the counterparts who remained on their original shores. This climaxes naturally in an affirmation of the oneness of the human race, arriving at the universal inclusiveness that embraces diversity.

These few, spare details from the naturalistic setting of Rampanalgas describe like hieroglyphs the paradigm of the one timeless voyage of the human spirit: the half-shell of a husked coconut afloat on the brown creek of Rampanalgas river; a twig serving as its mast; a dead almond leaf as its sail. The coconut half-shell with twig for mast and dead almond leaf for sail – a child might put these together as a toy boat – represents the human form fitted out as a vessel for its journey, equipped with its bare instruments. The shrunken creek of a river reflects the course of the individual life, the basic frailty and humbleness of its current. The brown colour of dead leaf, twig, and river bear the traces of desiccation, shading in the tones of detritus and death immanent in the life process. Walcott's discourse traces the passage of that human vessel in its journey of destiny:

> That child who sets his half-shell afloat
> in the brown creek that is Rampanalgas River –
> my son first, then two daughters –
> towards the roar of waters,
> towards the Atlantic with a dead almond leaf for a sail,
> with a twig for a mast,

(CP, 285)

Like "the brown creek that is Rampanalgas River" the naked vessel of the individual life follows its humble, frail course outward to meet the tremendous forces of destiny. The latter are symbolically echoed in the "roar of [the] waters" of the nearby Atlantic, reminiscent of the awesome charges of the leap of Grenada's Sauteurs. The human vessel faces the real challenge of destiny in meeting this "roar of waters". This means the necessity of its striving and travail to undergo the "crossing of water". Through that "crossing of water" and its sea-change is the self, its true power and wholeness, made and found. This deeply significant image of the "crossing of water" surfaces here to take a permanent place in the Walcott credo. It registers, importantly, an altered, positive perspective on the middle passage, which is now virtually mythologized. It is now the historic crossing as perilous journey, and, as such, gathers associations of the Christian cross as sacred, mythic icon of the sacrificial rite of passage. Consistent with the dialectical viewpoint of this work, the implicit emphasis is that the self thus forged in the crucible of that crossing, timeless and mythic in its spiritual imperatives, is the ultimate achievement. In the context of Walcott's wider vision, this is the core reality in which the possibility of self-(re)creation/renewal consists.

As indicated above, the child/childlike motif, which recurs throughout his work, has a seminal significance in this answer to the older muse of history. It represents a state of unknowing, which bears primary reference to the historical reality of the Caribbean people. The state of unknowing is an original, native point of departure from a history that began in the middle passage, as Walcott sees it. An earlier negative has now turned, with maturity, to positive advantage, as seen above in the image of the "crossing of water". Invoked throughout the movement, this childlike state of unknowing and possibility of innocence acquires mythic resonances:

> That child who sets his half-shell afloat
> in the brown creek that is Rampanalgas River –
> my son first, then two daughters –
>
> . . . .
> was, like his father, this child,
> a child without history, without knowledge of its pre-world,
>
> (*CP*, 285)

Characteristically, he stakes his personal biography in this meditative act, placing himself, his son and his two daughters, in generational succession, at its centre. This biographical trope opens outward to give us the universal image of humanity as generations of children.

By virtue of its own beginnings as historyless child, the Caribbean itself has special potential to realize this truer muse of the human voyage; and it is to the unique past and possibility of the region that Walcott moves straight away to explore the order of values contained in its paradigm. This movement constitutes the spiritual climax of book 4, and, like the vision of the leaping Caribs, it coincides with a major definition of native identity. Walcott foregrounds the origins of the Caribbean as a place coming into existence from the diasporas of the older world; it is a place, therefore, where many of the world's ancestries and races meet. At the centre of their common origins in the diasporas of the Old World is the formative experience of the "crossing of water". In this context, the image encodes the total experience of uprootment from and dispossession of original settings, rerooting in and possession of others. It also comprehends the sum total of the pains and gains involved in the process. The "crossing of water" is the collective experience of the many ancestries that come to confluence in the region, generating a vital link between them. The unique virtues of this crossing and confluence are what give the Caribbean people the potential to recover, in the representative "nothing" of Rampanalgas, the timeless odyssey of the human spirit that links and connects all races. The poet becomes the medium of this act of consciousness on behalf of the tribe. A highly effective image combination traces out this possibility and its complex process. Walcott is again the poet as natural scientist:[82] he merges the conch shell and the human ear as authentic replicas in nature, echoing each other – both visually and functionally – in external and human spheres:

> that child who puts the shell's howl to his ear,
> hears nothing, hears everything
> that the historian cannot hear, the howls
> of all the races that crossed the water,
> the howls of grandfathers drowned
> in that intricately swivelled Babel,

(CP, 285)

The physical structure of the ear/conch shell graphically reproduces the complex route and process of that howling cry, the single note echoing from the multiple voices of the many grandfathers/ancestors. The ear/shell comprises an intricate pattern of passages, decorous whorl-like channels, all of which interconnect to issue in one outlet. This structure serves as the graphic equivalent of what Walcott describes as the "intricately swivelled Babel" of the multiple voices of the peoples that meet in these waters. The Babel of their varied tongues and creeds is pictured as so many different channels/passages to the one main, common course of destiny. It is an image which also underlines the inwardness and intensiveness of the act of consciousness required to penetrate this final oneness. The howl resounds as the sound signal of the desolate extremes suffered in the crucible of their crossings, many yet one. It also has resonance as the aboriginal cry echoing across the seas of space and time. Walcott's metaphor remains scientifically accurate, down to the howling sound emitted from the conch shell, especially when blown near the sea. Another fresh metaphor has been generated from the naturalistic setting in a thought process that anticipates the "sea is history" conceit.

Walcott envisions, in this powerful metaphoric conception, the native possibility of renewing this common human bond across races and cultures. The idea has gained this kind of definition and visibility, no doubt, from the immediate example of racially mixed Trinidad. There is thus a ritual recitation of the ethnicities, harking back to ancestral tribes, that meet in this "intricately swivelled Babel" which brings almost all the world's races into the small compass of Caribbean waters. Thus: "hears the fellaheen, the Madrasi, the Mandingo, the Ashanti, / yes, and hears also the echoing green fissures of Canton" (*CP*, 285). This makes the region fertile ground for a promise which is also implicit in Walcott's conception. It is the promise of a unifying, rehumanizing cross-culturalism within the multicultural environment of the region. That New World Caribbean potentiality becomes prophetic of the destiny of the wider globe, in need of just such a possibility in the multicultural map of modern times. The dynamic of the ear/shell metaphor extends in this universal direction. Continuing in his role as representative poet/medium, Walcott enacts the capacity of the region's New World survivors to open in sensitivity to those who have remained on the other side of the globe, "without longing for this other shore" (*CP*, 285). Enabled by the existential imperatives of their own crossing, they (can) open in empathy to the connecting bond with those who remained behind. They respond to the same existential imperatives in the prayers and rituals of worship of these older brotherhoods and sisterhoods, as these carry across from their distant shores:

> and thousands without longing for this other shore
> by the mud tablets of the Indian provinces,
> robed ghostly white and brown, the twigs of uplifted hands,
> of manacles, mantras, of a thousand kaddishes,
> whorled, drilling into the shell,
>
> (*CP*, 285)

Some of the rituals and prayers cited are associated, significantly, with historically oppressed peoples (the manacles of African bondage; the Holocaust overshadowing the Jewish kaddishes); and with the sacred roots of some of the oldest cultures in the Old World, the Hindu and the Hebraic. What echoes from these "manacles, mantras, . . . thousand kaddishes", and strikes a chord across the waters, is the one and same cry for human upliftment and deliverance from bondage. The auditory image generates the visual, conjuring a scene of the Hindu at prayer, enacting an age-old ritual:

> see, in the evening light by the saffron, sacred Benares,
> how they are lifting like herons,
> robed ghostly white and brown,

(CP, 285)

A good deal of the essential meanings of the alternative muse of human destiny revealed at Rampanalgas is compressed in this final image of the movement. Irradiated by the light of evening, the traditional time of prayer, the scene sounds the plaintive, elegiac chord residual in prayer/supplication, and is imbued with its tones and shades. It subtly and carefully repeats the icons and hieroglyphic signals earlier identified at Rampanalgas. Their hands uplifted in ritual attitude of prayer, the Hindu celebrants seek spiritual upliftment, grounded in their "mud tablets of the Indian provinces". Seen from this distance, their silhouette reflects the hieroglyphic lifting of herons from the mud of the Rampanalgas swamp. The ritual white and brown of their robes are also the colours of the herons. Earth colours, they bear associations of death/detritus, as did the "dead almond leaf"; and as is also hinted in their "ghostly" appearance. The frailty of the twig serving as mast for the coconut half-shell (replica of the human form) is repeated in their "twigs of hands". Similarly elemental and reduced, these insignia repeat the truths of the human voyage with the "same skeletal candour".

The repetition of these essentials from older to newer shores confirms the timeless, mythic values of the one human odyssey, and its universal bond. While many critics steer clear of speaking in terms of this inclusiveness/universality in Walcott (Paul Breslin defines and tries to defend it as his essentialism),[83] it is an inclusiveness/universality generated from the cross-culturalism of the multiple worlds encompassed in his work. The cross-culturalism and the universality both turn on the axis of his earliest belief in the New World diasporan destiny, amid all its complexity, as a recovery of the human covenant. He rounds off the movement in this universal vein, affirming the "crossing of water" as a more integral, truly generative muse than that of memory:

> and the crossing of water has erased their memories.
> And the sea, which is always the same,
> accepts them.

(*CP*, 285)

But this is no jettisoning of memory. Coming from his dialectical viewpoint, it is, rather, a contestation of the overdependence on ancestral memory to which our diasporan times are so prone.

But what, above all, underlies and upholds these realizations at Rampanalgas is the multidimensional approach to history engaged in this concern with the muse of history. This multidimensional approach to history finds its crowning expression in the present chapter (22), but is also operative throughout *Another Life*. In the primal environs of Rampanalgas, Walcott situates himself in a consciousness of the aboriginal and pre-Columbian history – one still accessible in his virginal territory – to engage his quarrel with the older muse of established history. That route through prehistory means a grounding in the sense of cosmic and existential realities that prove stronger than the constructed absolutes of the older muse of civilization. So, in earlier examples, the myth of chivalry in combat was disproved by the natural action of the bush on the historic Morne of his native Castries (*AL*, chapter 11, sections 2 and 3); and the aboriginal Caribs of Grenada presented a consciousness closer to existential truth than that of the Fighting Fifth (*AL*, chapter 11, sections 3 and 4). The long view from his New World back to the Mediterranean origins of Western civilization represents another major focus in his approach to history. It enables a philosophical perspective on history-in-time, which means, in Eliot's terms, a sense of the temporal and timeless/mythic together (*Four Quartets*). The perspectives on prehistory and history-in-time converge, their meanings reinforcing each other. The consciousness embracing these dimensions, moreover, remains firmly grounded in the substance and unique character of his region in its own historical-sociological context – as expressed here in the image of the diasporan Caribbean as an "intricately swivelled Babel" through which can be heard the howls of all the grandfathers that "crossed the waters". This multidimensional perspective on history – it is a key statement of the Rampanalgas testament and of *Another Life* on the whole

– is a unique advantage of the New World, and its possibility of an order of consciousness much more complex and expansive than that of the Old World.

Walcott sustains his dialectical viewpoint in chapter 22 to the end. These final affirmations at Rampanalgas (*CP*, 285–86) take him right back to the polemics of his theme. He launches into another searing indictment of current directions in his region, earlier denounced in the name of Simmons. He roundly decries the bogey of history as significant action, heroic achievement, that continues to hold the "magicians of the new vision" in thrall. This glorification of history is morally purblind, and falls into the blunder of idealizing the barbaric exploits of the conquistador, and the equally invidious "greatness" of Aztec religious culture as nearby examples of historic action:

> And those who gild cruelty,
> who read from the entrails of disembowelled Aztecs
> the colors of Hispanic glory
> greater than Greece,
>
> . . . .
> the golden excrement on barbarous altars
> of their beaked and feathered king,
> and the feasts of human flesh,
>
> (*CP*, 286)

This concluding salvo reiterates an important point. Concerned as Walcott has been to aim his rebuttal of the muse of history at the Old World, he is far more preoccupied with the failure of his region to meet the responsibility of real change. What this definitive position also does is draw attention to a critical facet of his own development. He himself has come a long way from the early despair at the condition of historylessness, the sense of history as amnesia. He has undergone an arduous struggle to arrive at this conversion and now, its ghosts fully exorcized, he speaks with authority, secure in this other/fresh faith.

The poem concludes with a benediction of Rampanalgas as the revelatory site and guardian of these truths. It does so in an overture of prayerful thanksgiving:

> but, my son, my sun,
>
> holy is Rampanalgas and its high-circling hawks,
> holy are the rusted, tortured, rust-caked, blind almond trees,
> your great-grandfather's, and your father's torturing limbs,
> holy the small, almond-leaf-shadowed bridge

> by the small red shop, where everything smells of salt,
> and holiest the break of the blue sea below the trees,
>
> *(CP,* 289)

Rampanalgas, outside history, is a place where it is possible to come to the elementals of our condition, and find spiritual value in them. Naming these meanings and values, Walcott uplifts Rampanalgas and makes another metaphor out of its humble setting, as he did in the case of the leaping Caribs. His celebration of it remains elegiac in tone, in the spirit of this meditation on human suffering and mortality, informed by the reflection on Simmons's fate. In keeping with that spirit, the mood and demeanour of Rampanalgas remain sombre throughout – quite different from the radiant glow and vitality of the love-infused landscape of "a simple flame"; or the enraptured, tragic elation of the leap of destiny at the Morne de Sauteurs. But the resolutions of the preceding books of art and love are also interwoven into its muse of humanity – the uplifting elation of creative struggle; the faith in the inextinguishable flame of life/love, brought to light and possessed by the power of the imagination.

Finally, we should not leave *Another Life* without noticing an especially important aspect of its style, which contributes significantly to its total achievement. Especially pronounced in this last book, it is the sheer multiplicity of modes, tones and voices that enrich its texture, and their fluid movements from one to the other. We move with ease through the lyrical and visionary, the meditative, anger and polemics, the elegiac, benediction and consecration. This polyphonic style of *Another Life* is of a specially rich and singular variety, and expressive of the sensibility of the whole: it bears testimony to the dynamic of renewal, its energy and vigour, its native capacity to be in touch with the full range of humanist sentiment and emotion.

CHAPTER SIX

Society and Nationhood in the Caribbean

Towards Another Life

The two works following *Another Life*, *Sea Grapes* (1976) and *The Star-Apple Kingdom* (1979), are closely informed by the mature vision and aesthetic realized in *Another Life*. They show two main areas of concern: in *Sea Grapes*, the poet's private attempt to find anchor in a quality of maturity and serenity consistent with the larger, spiritual truths of *Another Life*; and, in *The Star-Apple Kingdom*, an intensive engagement with the political and public scene of the Caribbean in independence. The latter is the dominant area of concern, accounting for some of the more outstanding poems of these two volumes which, along with *Remembrance and Pantomime* (1980) in the drama, mark the end of Walcott's career as an artist based exclusively in the Caribbean.

The present chapter will deal with this more prominent concern with politics and society in the postindependence Caribbean scene, as represented by the two longer poems in *The Star-Apple Kingdom*, the title poem and "The Schooner *Flight*". The earlier volume, *Sea Grapes*, although it contains a few strident political pieces, is primarily a lyrical, reflective work. It is a work of reconciliation and consecration to the truths arrived at in *Another Life,* as an act of "personal need"[1] for Walcott. *Sea Grapes* was commended as a work of ripeness and serenity, of "grace and luminosity",[2] and comprises some of the finest lyrical pieces in Walcott. Dominating his selection from that volume for *Collected Poems, 1948–1984* (1986), these lyrical pieces give expression to a theme fundamental to the overarching purpose of the work. It is the homing instinct of the mature Walcott, a homing instinct penetrated and deepened by the encroaching intimations of exile and departure. These are closely inter-twined, not unusually, with premonitions of aging and death, as sounded in "Preparing for Exile". Walcott seeks this home and harbour in another quality of love, released from the dream- and guilt-ridden turbulence of an earlier, younger love. It is a love of more resilient strain, tempered and strengthened in the knowledge of pain, loss, and the realities of aging and dying. In "Sunday Lemons" the image of lemons in a bowl on a polished table, and of a ripened woman "remembering / Sundays of other fruit" (*CP*, 298), echo and reflect each other, radiating the still-life/light of that more seasoned love. He seeks the blessing of a love with all the blemishes and faults left in ("Sea Canes"), whose more sober tones and shades are those of "grey water" ("Winding Up"). It is a greyness, though, that radiates its own quality of light, and can "flash silver" ("At Last", *SG*). It finds its epiphanies in the ordinary and familiar. Thus, responding to St Omer's altarpiece at the Roseau Valley Church in St Lucia ("Sainte Lucie"), Walcott stands with religious awe in the presence of "the other life" contained in the "common life outside", as captured in the painting:

> and the massive altarpiece,
> like a dull mirror, life
> repeated there,
> the common life outside
> and the other life it holds;

> (*CP*, 319)

These underlying values and faiths of a ripened, seasoned love are not, however, relegated only to the lyrical pieces; they inform and permeate his public and social preoccupations and perspectives in the work of the period. In fact, one cohesive vision extends from *Another Life* through *Sea Grapes* and *The Star-Apple Kingdom,* interlinking private and public throughout.

Our substantive subject in this chapter, as already indicated, is Walcott's concern with politics and society in the region, fully represented in "The

Schooner *Flight*" and "The Star-Apple Kingdom". Following the long, meditative spell of writing *Another Life* (1965–72), and the "personal need" thus fulfilled in *Sea Grapes,* he turns to give his full attention to this public arena. Notably, a number of vitriolic attacks on the politicians and the Establishment already appear in *Sea Grapes* (all of which, however, are left out of the 1948–84 collection). Social and political comment also engage his creative energies in the drama of the period, and some of his most important statements on contemporary conditions and directions in the Caribbean occur in *Pantomime* and *Remembrance.* Caribbean societies gained independence in the early 1960s, and their performances in meeting the challenges of nationhood are coming under close scrutiny during the decade of the 1970s. The scene which presents itself is a dismal one, of critical failings and misdirections, in some cases, of disastrous proportions. Walcott is generally provoked to anger and social disgust. His first quarrel is with the politicians, as the main offenders in betraying the trust and responsibility of independence. He heaps scorn and contempt on them as venal and self-serving "party hacks", famished of imagination ("Party Nights at the Hilton", *SG*); and guilty of perpetrating all sorts of abuses on the people they were elected to serve ("Parades, Parades", *SG*). He resorts to direct address in these lines from "The Lost Federation", which express his desire for a head-on attack, suggesting that this has become a new mission for him: "turn your head, man, I'm speaking / now, I haven't spoken enough, . . . " (*SG*, 27).

But while the politicians remain the prime target, the wider society is as deeply implicated and also comes under attack. Rendered with his inimitable ironic flourish, this is one of the most definitive comments on the path upon which Caribbean society – leadership and populace alike – is embarked during the period:

> One morning the Caribbean was cut up
> by seven prime ministers who bought the sea in bolts –
> one thousand miles of aquamarine with lace trimmings,
> one million yards of lime-coloured silk,
> one mile of violet, leagues of cerulean satin –
> who sold it at a markup to the conglomerates,
>
> . . . .
>
> who retailed it in turn to the ministers
> with only one bank account, who then resold it
> in ads for the Caribbean Economic Community,
> till everyone owned a little piece of the sea,

> from which some made saris, some made bandannas;
> the rest was offered on trays to white cruise ships
> > ("The Star-Apple Kingdom", *CP*, 390)

Oil-producing Trinidad, his immediate home ground, presented a particularly appropriate example during this period, when it was enjoying an oil boom generated by the international energy crisis of the 1970s. Fuelled by that boom, the country sank rapidly into a runaway culture of materialism, bribery and corruption, extending from the establishment through the ranks of the entire society. He deals with this situation in "The Schooner *Flight*", and these lines capture the tone of his disgust:

> But they had started to poison my soul
> with their big house, big car, big-time bohbohl,[3]
> coolie, nigger, Syrian, and French Creole,
> so I leave it for them and their carnival –
>
> > (*CP*, 346)

The invective, however, is only the more vocal, strident side of his concern. The wider, informing purpose emerges fully when the works of the period, including the plays, are taken together. On the wider level, Walcott is engaged in an appraisal of the progress and prospects of Caribbean self-development in national times. He is keenly aggrieved at the despairing aspects of the scene; but he is equally concerned to weigh and affirm the advances in self-achievement as an earnest of genuine possibility, capable of overcoming the ills and shortcomings – as he does par excellence in *Pantomime*.[4]

"The Schooner *Flight*" and "The Star-Apple Kingdom", however, together comprehend the range and depth of his concerns. They comprise a full statement of Walcott's engagement with the crises of Caribbean self-development, and with the possibilities of a positive social and political direction for the region. The poems document two cases of acute crisis and disorder: "The Schooner *Flight*" deals with the case of Trinidad, whose materialistic spree threatens to destroy the very fabric of the society; "The Star-Apple Kingdom" with the case of Jamaica, where Michael Manley's experiment in democratic socialism (1972–80) has met with total failure, plunging the country into acute economic hardship and political crisis. Walcott's perspectives on these two cases complement each other. "The Schooner *Flight*" gives vent to his anger and disgust with the self-betraying ills of Caribbean society; in "The Star-Apple Kingdom", the Jamaican ordeal, as an example of a failed effort, becomes his point of departure for exploring an alternative ideal of social and political intelligence in the region. In these two long poems which work as companion pieces, then, Walcott responds to representative cases of social and political collapse in the Caribbean of the late 1970s, to extend against these, his definitions of a viable Caribbean selfhood and path towards self-development. The poems bear witness to two related facets of this endeavour: a mission of protest, and equally urgently, that of invoking conscience and consciousness as the means of self-liberation and direction. In both poems, moreover, he develops an aesthetic adequate to deal with these dimensions of his theme, venturing into fresh areas of experimentation in form and language to integrate inner and public perspectives. It is an aesthetic whose modes, values and faiths carry over and develop authentically from *Another Life*. We turn to an examination of the two poems.

"The Schooner Flight*"*

"The Schooner *Flight*" is one of Walcott's best-known poems,[5] outstanding for being his first sustained and accomplished use of the West Indian creole voice, as also for its related, fresh ventures in form. In this long narrative poem, Shabine, the "red nigger" protagonist, flees the Trinidad of the oil boom years "to ship as a seaman on the schooner *Flight*". The form of the poem is fundamental to an understanding of the movement and meaning of Shabine's story. Walcott devises a unique blend of narrative and lyrical modes to present the experience, recounted in the voice of Shabine himself. Within that blend, the figure and role of Shabine – into which Walcott's own poetic persona is fully absorbed – become representative and symbolic. His flight is likewise symbolic: he flees the frustrations and corruptions of Trinidad for a symbolic sea bath, an inner cleansing. Shabine's flight by sea thus serves a twofold purpose: through it, Walcott musters his inner forces to name the apocalypse of political and social degeneracy; and, in the odyssey of self undertaken in that sea journey, he points the way back to a possibility of recovery and wholeness.

The main strengths and achievement of the poem turn on Walcott's inventive experiment in combining a narrative fictional form with lyrical, reflective modes, drawing upon his gifts as both dramatist and poet. The characterization of Shabine is an integral and pivotal feature in this structure, providing a key into many important facets of the poem's theme. A number of important elements of identity are fused in this characterization. Walcott chooses to make his protagonist a "red nigger" named Shabine.[6] The two epithets – "red nigger" and "Shabine" – which are synonymous in the local idiom, describe persons of mixed African and European blood, this being the first point of identification between Walcott and his protagonist. As "red nigger", the lower-class counterpart to the "mulatto", Shabine comes from the ranks of the ordinary man in Caribbean society.[7] Walcott sinks his own poetic persona into this figure of the ordinary Caribbean man, a fusion which represents the first functional aspect of this characterization. It is a dynamic, original and rich fusion, serving many vital purposes in the poem. It serves, first, to integrate the two planes of the poem's discourse: the public, communal one, and the interiorized, reflective process which comes into the foreground in the sea odyssey. Walcott's voice as poetic, visionary faculty merges into that of Shabine: they function as a single entity to give us, effectively, the Shabine/Walcott persona as protagonist.

This bears directly on the other distinctive, integral area of language in the poem. The Trinidadian dialect, which gives the poem its prevailing voice, is the authentic language of Shabine. Walcott is resourceful in his treatment of this medium. He ranges from the straight, vernacular forms of the speaking voice, through various kinds of interaction between the dialect and Standard English. He effects, in the process, what amounts to transfusions of the tone, inflection and idiom of the dialect into Standard English, with consequent modulations of the latter. Mervyn Morris, who writes especially well on the linguistics of Walcott's art, shows how this "modulation between creole and Standard English" works both in the present poem and in "The Spoiler's Return" (*The Fortunate Traveller*), the other major creole poem of the period.[8] Shabine's predominantly creole medium is thus able to serve both dramatic/narrative and lyrical/reflective purposes, giving the poem its prevailing tone and inflection. Seen in its proper, overall perspective, the characterization strategy in this poem identifies and grounds Walcott's own poetic persona with and in that of the ordinary, grassroots figure; and in that strategy, his linguistic experiment plays an integral role. It is, moreover, essentially the same characterization strategy employed in *Dream on Monkey Mountain*. Makak, the charcoal burner, is also the lyrical, visionary faculty, embracing Moustique et al. as natives of his person in the total experience he undergoes. Walcott thus fictionalizes (him)self in the Shabine/Walcott persona, as Baugh maintains;[9] but he does so for the express purpose of bearing the social and communal experience. Seen from another pertinent angle, "The Schooner *Flight*" is an attempt to fictionalize, in the Shabine/Walcott fusion, the biography of a society at a particular phase of its development. A similar fictional treatment will be employed in the case of Manley's Jamaica.

The identification of the protagonist as "red nigger"/"Shabine" carries critical, strategic aspects of the total meaning of his persona in the poem. It is there as a position statement, a declaration of identity. Walcott begins, as earlier observed, with the external signature of his own mixed identity as product of white and black ancestries; but this racial mixture, as always in his work, extends to the far more seminal factor of cultural legacy. In his exposition of the "red nigger" theme, the import of that mixed condition is a position of neutrality between these ancestries. It is from there that he zeroes in on a categorical disavowal of allegiance to either white or black ideologies: the white supremacist imperialist ideology of the past, and the black, race-based radicalism of contemporary times. They are, for him, different complexions of the same thing. Thus:

> After the white man, the niggers didn't want me
> when the power swing to their side.
> The first chain my hands and apologise, "History";
> the next said I wasn't black enough for their pride.
>
> (*CP*, 350)

He goes on to decry the unwholesomeness and futility of each. The still living shadow of that white imperialist past is evoked in one of the most memorable images in the poem – the portrait of a white "parchment Creole" as a personification of history. Based on the image of the earlier creole descendants of the colonists in the region, the figure is a shadowy apparition of anachronistic privilege and sophistication, in a state of desiccation typical of its dying breed. It remains unyielding, though, in its remorseless contempt for a black race it has abused and "bastardized":

> I met History once, but he ain't recognize me,
> a parchment Creole, with warts
> like an old sea-bottle, crawling like a crab
> through the holes of shadow cast by the net
> of a grille balcony; cream linen, cream hat.
> I confront him and shout, "Sir, is Shabine!
> They say I'se your grandson. You remember Grandma,
> your black cook, at all?" The bitch hawk and spat.
> A spit like that worth any number of words.
> But that's all them bastards have left us: words.
>
> (*CP*, 350)

As for the black radicals, with whom Walcott's quarrel remains unsettled, he mocks their own delusions of militant power in the bleak, powerless conditions of their "unknown rocks". It is precisely this rejection of both that becomes the platform for Shabine/Walcott's climactic, polemical statement of identity, which stands as Walcott's virtual manifesto on the issue:

> I'm just a red nigger who love the sea,
> I had a sound colonial education,
> I have Dutch, nigger, and English in me,
> and either I'm nobody, or I'm a nation.

(CP, 346)

Shabine/Walcott begins with a positive claiming and acceptance of his mixed sources, with its implicit disclaimer of belonging to any one ancestry. The import of his "nobody, or a nation" is that this very condition of not belonging to any exclusivist, absolutist ideology may be the basis of a different, other identity with its own accesses of freedom and possibility. The statement is consistent with all that we have seen of Walcott's position in the works considered so far.

Shabine's status and job as an ordinary citizen is another major area of significance in this characterization, pertinent to the subject and setting of the poem. It carries with it the portrait of the society with which Walcott is dealing. An ordinary citizen from the ranks of the lower to lower middle classes, he has been hustling a living by "smuggl[ing] Scotch for O'Hara,[10] big government man" – serving, that is, as middleman in the chain of corruption that is the order of the day. The disruptive effects and pressures of this way of life spill over into his domestic setting: there are frequent fights between himself and his woman, Maria Concepcion. These particulars of Shabine's livelihood and domestic circumstances document the condition and crisis of Trinidadian society during this period. The corruption and its ills spread from the "big boys" at the top, through the ranks of the common men like Shabine, to find the mirror image of its final degradation – and guilt – in the condition of the city's vagrants. The latter were numerous along the pavements of Port of Spain during this period:

> Smuggled Scotch for O'Hara, big government man,
> between Cedros and the Main, so the Coast Guard couldn't
>   touch us,
> and the Spanish pirogues always met us halfway,
>
> . . . .

> What worse, I fighting with Maria Concepcion,
> plates flying and thing, so I swear: "Not again!"
> It was mashing up my house and my family.
> I was so broke all I needed was shades and a cup
> of four shades and four cups in four-cup Port of Spain;
>
> (*CP*, 347–48)

"Shades and a cup" – from which we also get the bonus of the four-letter pun in "four-cup Port of Spain" – specifically evokes the figure of the vagrant. The vagrant was usually equipped with a drinking cup. Shabine observes in this comment that, in addition to the cup, all he needed to join the ranks of the vagrants was a pair of cheap shades for disguise.[11] The image of the vagrant thus evoked serves as a grim reflection of the deeper dereliction pervading the entire society. Shabine's frustrations and ill temper are a manifestation of its psychic toll on the community as a whole. Here Walcott effects an authentic stroke in fusing his own individual circumstances into that of Shabine as "red nigger" Everyman. Shabine's are Walcott's horrors over the break-up of his marriage during this period, torn between his wife and the woman who was to become his third wife.[12]

The larger point behind this crisis, in which personal and communal echo each other, is that the contamination and ills of this culture of greed and corruption makes its inroads into all lives. All share, in various ways, in its ultimate moral vagrancy: the "big boys" who control the system, as well as its underdogs and victims. The artist/commentator, who had better keep his mouth shut, is certainly among the underdogs in this climate of crass, philistine materialism:

> that I said: "Shabine, this is shit, understand!"
> But he get somebody to kick my crutch out of his office
> like I was some artist! That bitch was so grand,
> couldn't get off his high horse and kick me himself.
>
> (*CP*, 348)

Walcott the poet is thus provoked in righteous anger to serve as scourge of this society – like the Mighty Spoiler, a Trinidadian calypsonian of the 1940s and 1950s, whose mask he wears in "The Spoiler's Return".[13] Spoiler turned his special gift for loaded irony to trenchant social commentary,[14] and, in that poem, his ghost is summoned from hell to wage war against the "fat ones" of the Establishment. He returns, as in his famous calypso "Bed Bug", in the form of a bed bug whose bite is reserved for "all Power [which] has / made the sky shit and maggots of the stars" (*CP*, 435). The signature of the Spoiler calypso was his famous refrain "I want to fall", behind which lay the "groan" (Walcott's word) of the (social) consciousness that weighed on him. The poet of "The Schooner *Flight*", groaning like Spoiler in consciousness of the ills of the society, seeks a cleansing from the contaminations that have begun to poison its soul.

The integration of Walcott, both as poet and private individual, into the Shabine/Everyman figure is thus complete. Answering directly to this is the complex portraiture and role of Maria Concepcion, the woman in Shabine's life. She moves between realistic and metaphoric/symbolic planes, in a dynamic that corresponds to the two interrelated complements of the external, social self and the interiorized, poetic self fused in Shabine/Walcott. Maria Concepcion is thus present both as Shabine's flesh-and-blood mistress and as muse figure, featuring, in fact, as a fluid presence between the two. On the deepest level, however, she functions as muse, engaging a visionary, spiritual dimension in Shabine's dream journey through Caribbean waters, which is the core of the narrative. As such, she represents Walcott's vision and hope for the wholeness of a people. We get our first glimpse of her as Shabine gets ready to leave Trinidad. To Shabine, in that troubled parting, she is a kind of sleeping beauty, her "dreamless face" suggestive, as in the fairy tale, of a beauty unready to be awakened in the ill climate of the times:

> I blow out the light
> by the dreamless face of Maria Concepcion
> to ship as a seaman on the schooner *Flight*.
> . . . .
> I pass me dry neighbour sweeping she yard
> as I went downhill, and I nearly said:
> "Sweep soft, you witch, 'cause she don't sleep hard,"
> but the bitch look through me like I was dead.
>
> (*CP*, 345)

These early lines provide a striking example of the rich poetic use to which Walcott is able to put the speaking, dialect voice in the poem. They are supple, capturing the mixture of feelings and sentiments he experiences as he is about to take flight from Trinidad, from the compassion and tenderness with which he blows out the light, the raw anger bristling in the expletives aimed at an oblivious "dry neighbour sweeping she yard", and the hints of a keen anguish moving beneath it all. Expressive of the simultaneous pain and love of this departure, the lines – indeed the whole, justly celebrated passage[15] – tell of his attachment to his people and their landscape, and a deeply cherished ideal of their wholeness and creative being. It is this ideal that is embodied in the image of Maria Concepcion. Maria Concepcion features, as in this opening passage, especially strongly as an embodiment of landscape, bearing close resemblances to Anna as muse figure in *Another Life*. She serves as his guiding light in his journey across the waters; and, in the epiphany at the journey's end, Shabine/Walcott will awaken to the realization of Maria Concepcion in the light/life that irradiates the landscape.[16]

Shabine's story unfolds in a well-constructed plot comprised of eleven sections, which fall basically into two parts. The first four sections deal with the occasion of his departure from Trinidad, depicting the conditions and factors that presage his desire for flight. The other seven sections enact his sea odyssey on the *Flight*. The first part, as identified above, giving us a résumé of the crisis of the society, serves something of an expository function vis-à-vis the sea journey. Some of the fundamental problems and issues with which it deals are directly engaged, as discussed above, in the significance of the protagonist's identification as "red nigger"/"Shabine", as well as his characteristic circumstances. The latter brings into the foreground, for example, the immediate, contemporary ills of materialistic, oil-boom Trinidad. Walcott extends from the focus on this crisis to a wider, inclusive survey of the failures and misdirections that have marked the course of Caribbean society since it assumed the responsibility of self-government. This Caribbean-wide focus also occurs in "The Spoiler's Return". Characteristically, his purpose is to embrace the entire region "from Monos[17] to Nassau", Trinidad thus becoming representative of the Caribbean. It is the opportunity, in effect, for a diagnostic overview of the peculiar disabilities and failures, political and sociological, from which the Caribbean suffers at this juncture, leaving it open to the kind of disintegration exemplified by Trinidad.

Walcott targets the black radicalism of the period, spearheaded by the Black Power movement of Trinidad itself.[18] The latter, the one attempt at militant activism during the period (apart from the Rastafarian movement of Jamaica), has failed, in Walcott's view, to contribute to any progressive, revolutionary direction. Black radicalism represents an ideology and political alternative he continues to reject, as we saw above, as no less racist and retrogressive than that of the white imperialist system of colonial times. Taking a close-up look at the armies of idlers, the ranks of the unemployed malingering along the inner haunts and streets of the city, he paints this bleak, despairing picture of the only variety of revolution the society seems capable of producing in its present state. There is as much pathos as grim irony in this picture:

> on Frederick Street the idlers all marching
> by standing still, the Budget turns a new leaf.
> In the 12:30 movies the projectors best
> not break down, or you go see revolution. Aleksandr Blok
> enters and sits in the third row of pit eating choc-
> olate cone, waiting for a spaghetti West-
> ern with Clint Eastwood and featuring Lee Van Cleef.
>
> (CP, 351)

It is from these very ranks of the socially depressed that the Black Power movement had drawn its would-be guerrillas in the time of its uprising (early 1970s). Earlier lines in the passage have already evoked a poignant epitaph for these young men, each fatally drawn to the illusory power of struggle in the hills of the Northern Range, and the futile waste of their easy death at the hands of the police who brutally hunted them down.[19]

> Young men without flags
> using shirts, their chests waiting for holes.
> They kept marching into the mountains, and
> their noise ceased as foam sinks into sand.
> They sank in the bright hills like rain, every one
> with his own nimbus, leaving shirts in the street,
> and the echo of power at the end of the street.
>
> (CP, 351)

The alternatives readily available to them are such substitute, compensatory fantasies as spaghetti westerns, providing an outlet for the pressures and anger waiting to explode. Walcott invokes, as presiding genius of the scene, the Russian writer Aleksandr Blok, who wrote in "The Twelve" about the small band of Russian rebels in the Bolshevik army intent on an anarchic rampage of their own.[20] Like the twelve in that story, the young men of this scene are irrevocably alienated, divorced from all ties or allegiance to the surrounding environment, and representing a constant threat of anarchy. Their plight is a sad indictment of a society deeply locked in the system of inherited social injustice from which it was meant to be delivered, and improvident of means and direction.

The crisis of alienation thus focused in the plight of the socially depressed (it lies behind the enervation and ill-temper we have met in Shabine) takes its toll in the kind of psychic disorder documented in Shabine's traumatic breakdown in "Raptures of the Deep". This kind of mental breakdown was quite common among the vagrants mentioned above. Many of these vagrants had, in fact, walked out of the nearby mental hospital to inhabit the city's pavements. It is with their level of desolation and psychological disorder that Walcott identifies in the experience that sends the protagonist to the mad-house. In this spell of psychic derangement, Shabine/Walcott's schizophrenic "raptures" are those of the dissociated self, plunged into an inner chaos where all that is human is abominated. Typically in Walcott, it is a place of howling demons (see "Moon"),[21] lacerating in sensibility. Thus he is traumatized by surreal hallucinations of "God / like a harpooned grouper bleeding . . . " (*CP*, 349); and women become to him nothing more than "spiky cunts / bristl[ing] like sea-eggs [where he] couldn't dive" (*CP*, 350). Naturally, too, the demons of private guilt and remorse are part of the chaos – so that Walcott's own marital problems surface here. This is the anatomy of the peculiar sickness of a society which is death to the individual spirit – an inner destitution whose first and conspicuous victims are the terminally deprived and dispossessed; a condition to which, however, the better circumstanced and more privileged are no less susceptible. Walcott penetrates these depths right through to the residue of historical dread buried in the unconscious. The shadow of ancestral calamity and void returns, reflected in the image of a spectral Caribbean sea laden with the dead of the middle passage – "their bones / ground white from Senegal to San Salvador" (*CP*, 349). Thus, as endorsed by his personal testimony in "Raptures of the Deep", individual and communal, private and public are wholly interfused in this concern with the crisis and deliverance of a society.

Shabine's sea odyssey (sections 5–11) is primarily an interior journey into the depths of consciousness, symbolized as a descent into submarine depths. Walcott employs a composite technique: multiple, corresponding modes and images are working in concert within the underlying metaphor of sea odyssey. Interior journey is enacted as dream-vision/hallucination, or descent into the surreal territory of the unconscious. Thus the middle passage returns to Shabine in a hallucinatory vision of "a rustling forest of ships" ("Shabine Encounters the Middle Passage"); and, in the aboriginal setting of Dominica (where "they still have Caribs"),[22] he descends into the primordial terrors of the unconscious in an experience of dream-nightmare ("Maria Concepcion and the Book of Dreams"). Walcott's role as poet questing on behalf of the tribe/society, and the collective dimension represented by Shabine/Walcott are simultaneous in the progress and substance of the journey. The journey traces a historical itinerary: it revisits the main landmarks of the region's history, moving through re-encounters with the middle passage ("Shabine Encounters the Middle Passage"), the colonial experience ("The Sailor Sings Back to the Casuarinas"), back into the setting of prehistory, in aboriginal times ("Maria Concepcion and the Book of Dreams") and also incorporates childhood memories from the personal history of the poet himself. This historical itinerary is also made to coincide with the geographical. Thus the journey starts from the more developed island of Trinidad in the south; proceeds upwards to Barbados, appropriate as site of the re-encounter with the colonial heritage; then to the more primal settings of the smaller islands to the north – St Lucia, as site of Walcott's native roots, and Dominica, home of a community of aboriginal Caribs. Retraced in that historical itinerary is the spiritual history of a people. Essentially retrospective in dynamic, the interior process of this odyssey is rediscovering, reclaiming, and regrounding self in a consciousness and identity whose potentiality is already there from what has been traversed in the region. Repeating many of the fundamental values affirmed in *Another Life,* this odyssey reaches its culmination in the naked, existential travail of the self – the life-death struggle, "leap-fall" of the "crossing" necessary for deliverance ("Maria Concepcion and the Book of Dreams" and "Out of the Depths").

Shabine's first encounter is with the middle passage, as starting point of the region's history. The encounter occurs in a hallucinatory experience: a "rustling forest of ships" takes shape out of the visual effects of coiling mist and fog on the early morning sea. This is another of the outstanding pieces of image-making in Walcott, woven out of his original blend of lyrical, painterly and meditative modes. Shabine experiences what he describes, in his native idiom, as "horrors but beautiful". A phantasmal procession of ships floats through the *Flight,* reflecting hazy impressions of skeletal crew and rusted weaponry. A special feature in that apparition is the passage of the great European admirals "Rodney, Nelson, de Grasse", who dominated the stage of history during that time (seventeenth and eighteenth centuries). They now appear in ghostly silhouette, leaving only the sounds and echoes of their once heroic passage:

> and high on their decks I saw great admirals,
> Rodney, Nelson, de Grasse, I heard the hoarse orders
> they gave those Shabines, and the forest
> of masts sail right through the *Flight,*
> and all you could hear was the ghostly sound
> of waves rustling like grass in a low wind
> and the hissing weeds they trailed from the stern;
>
> (*CP*, 352)

The meaning of that apparition consists in that "all you could hear". In the hoarseness of their orders to their subordinate(d) Shabines, we hear the cravings of these naval heroes, men unappeased and time-wearied, exposing the nakedness of their need and anxieties. In the sounds of waves "rustling like grass in a low wind" are the strains of the endless, restless motion of their quests, with the hissing threat of danger, peril – the archetypal snake motif is subtly evoked in "hissing weeds" – always in their trail. What endures as the residual core of all human action, then, is the nakedness of the human spirit and its endless craving and questing, in error or right-mindedness, always stalked by adversity. Time's action thus exposes this common, binding condition of great admirals and subordinate Shabines alike. Like the muse of timeless history at Rampanalgas, "the rustling forest of ships", elegiac in its rhythms and cadences, recovers the mythic truth of all the voyages as the one human odyssey, universal through time. This is one of the places where Walcott's profound lines in "The Star-Apple Kingdom" apply – "a hymn ascending to earth from a heaven inverted / by water" (*CP*, 386).

Out of these essentials of all the voyages (as a single, repeating human odyssey) crystallizes this original and powerful visual image of the human world in time – an endless water wheel, with every bucket (ship, age, epoch, culture) flowing into and turning in its cycle:

> slowly they heaved past from east to west
> like this round world was some cranked water wheel,
> every ship pouring like a wooden bucket
> dredged from the deep; . . . .
>
> (*CP*, 352)

It is an image which tells, too, how the dead generations/ancestors make themselves heard down the centuries (as in the case of the howl of the "intricately swivelled Babel" of *Another Life*). Both in the domestic imagery used here, and in the natural features and properties/effects of the "rustling forest of ships", Walcott remains, characteristically, close to elementals, and to the "prime simplicities" of culture. The ordinary, rustic wooden bucket and cranked water wheel describing "this round world" are all of a piece with the natural imagery of water, waves, wind and weeds out of which the rustling forest of ships is conjured. This vision and its meanings are being mediated through the powerful metaphoric conception of the sea/water as guardian of time/memory. The sea/water is the guardian of time/memory both as the destination/repository of the ruins of all the histories; and as it finally mirrors the timeless imprints of human endeavours in their translucent "nothingness", "commemorat[ing] nothing".[23] (The "sea as history" conceit, which finds its classic expression in "The Sea Is History"[24] of this volume, has one of its earliest expressions here.) In the light of this total epiphanic experience, Shabine begins with his memory revolving on this existential bond with "all sailors before him", tacitly pledging himself to this order of awareness in his own undertakings as a quester.

Seen through the lens of time, the middle passage yields this wider universal awareness. This perspective on history-in-time is, as we have seen, seminal in Walcott's multiple approach to history;[25] and it is positioned at the head of the journey for an important reason. It enables an awareness that will guard the protagonist, in his quest through memory, against seeing the action of history strictly in terms of conquest and defeat, of hero and victim – that is, in terms of the Manichaean duality bred of the false muse of history as achievement. Its philosophical perspective precedes, therefore, as a forearming, a right orientation, serving to free the consciousness for the journey ahead. It is the kind of freedom that enables a deeper seeing of history as, in Walcott's words, neither "a creative [n]or culpable force".[26] Underlining this, Shabine/Walcott, aiming his polemics at the current directions of black radicalism, makes this provocative, mocking response to the apparition of the slave ships:

> Next we pass slave ships. Flags of all nations,
> our fathers below deck too deep, I suppose,
> to hear us shouting. . . .

> (*CP*, 353)

Walcott thus continues his rejection of the ideological focus on the victimhood of a past of slavery. In "The Star-Apple Kingdom" the Manley protagonist begins his meditative sojourn through the region's past with the same kind of philosophical perspective on the action of history. The experience is, significantly, identified as his "baptism".

The next two stages of the journey retrace major stages in Walcott's own artistic quest for a native identity. This autobiographical route itself registers some of the seminal constituents and aspects of the process of Caribbean identity. The autobiographical register thus stands, as in *Another Life,* as testimony of the collective biography; projecting, at the same time, Walcott's own credo about the true directions and process of a native identity. Moreover, consistent with the structure and form of the poem, the autobiographical content actively embraces the communal. The latter is represented by the crew who share in the experience of the journey, and come into the foreground at various points. The communal on the wider regional level is also being embraced, in the movement through the English-speaking Caribbean, as the journey proceeds from Trinidad upwards through the smaller islands of the Eastern Caribbean.

Thus the first landfall occurs in Barbados, where "The Sailor Sings Back to the Casuarinas". This is, for Walcott as Shabine, a retrospective encounter with the issue of the heritage of the colonizer's language, as the main medium of a legacy of inferiority and culture of imitation that proved the main obstacles to a native naming and self-acceptance. That issue has been the crux of Walcott's own artistic struggle. This reality comes back to him as he responds to the sight of the casuarinas growing on the low hills of the island. The casuarinas become the occasion of a confessional moment and rediscovery. In earlier times (his divided childhood), the more common name "casuarinas"[27] had stamped these trees as inferior copies, consigned to yearning, aspiring to the classic status of "cypresses", deemed to be the more "real" name/metaphor/identity enshrined in the colonizer's "superior" culture. He has since gained, however, an understanding of the existential, humanizing necessity that is the root of all naming; and a recognition, therefore, of the wholeness and integrity of different names in their respective settings:

> But cedars, cypresses, or casuarinas,
> whoever called them so had a good cause,
> watching their bending bodies wail like women
>
> . . . .
>
> Once the sound "cypress" used to make more sense
> than the green "casuarinas," though, to the wind
> whatever grief bent them was all the same,
> since they were trees with nothing else in mind
> but heavenly leaping or to guard a grave;

(CP, 353)

In that light, he now fully celebrates the more common name "casuarinas" – which means, in Walcott, the affirmation of a truly indigenized, naturalized consciousness. It is also typical of the mature Walcott that, starting with the freer philosophical perspective on the middle passage, he should thus proceed to give priority to this area of the ongoing struggle of history in language as the main battlefront in the effort to overcome the surviving negations of the colonial experience. Sidelining the issues of race and the claims of a past of victimhood, he zeroes in here on the humanizing bond of naming as an ultimate value in the claiming of self, and this includes, for him, the peculiar accents of a sensibility in its local habitation, as well as the mythic. The present poem endorses this on an important level in its resourceful, experimental use of a native creole to obtain the full range and flexibility of the West Indian tongue. But the section is, especially, one of his most lucid statements about that struggle with language for the ex-colonized:

> but we live like our names and you would have
> to be colonial to know the difference,
> to know the pain of history words contain,
> to love those trees with an inferior love,

(CP, 353–54)

Serving as a timely reminder of this seminal source of native difference, the comment also underscores the residual relevance of language as a focal area of self-realization.

The next scene of re-encounter is Walcott's native St Lucia: "The *Flight* Anchors in Castries Harbour". In this strongly personalized section, Walcott celebrates his awakening to love and to the gift of poetry in his native land. The celebration is addressed to the woman of his first love, the Anna of *Another Life*, and the landscape as one. In a spirit of thanksgiving, he pledges to return the gift of his poetry to Anna/St Lucia. It is an act of acknowledgment of his lasting debt to these origins, where, falling in love with Anna, poetry and landscape, "life began" (*CP*, 186). The poetry of this section recaptures afresh the lyrical joy of awakening to the wonder of creativity, as the roots of generative being and possibility. The latter is also the message being extended to the wider community from this personal recovery. We have, in these lines, another example of the felicity with which Walcott is able to distil the lyrical joy of that recovery in the tone and idiom of the creole voice: "When the stars self were young over Castries, / I loved you alone and I loved the whole world" (*CP*, 354).

Following immediately on this affirmation, Shabine/Walcott gets involved in a fierce, head-on defence of his poetry in "Fight with the Crew". In the person of Vincie, a likely migrant sailor on the Trinidadian schooner, the insensitivities of the rabble, its mockery of poetry, is brutally attacked. (Vincie comes from the neighbouring island of St Vincent.) Vincie, though, is of the common run of hecklers typical of the society: "but he keep reading, 'O my children, my wife,' / and playing he crying, to make the crew laugh" (*CP*, 355). His offence is not as grievous as those of the purveyors of false (revolutionary) doctrines dealt with elsewhere, and so:

> There wasn't much pain,
> just plenty blood, and Vincie and me best friend,
> but none of them go fuck with my poetry again.
>
> (*CP*, 355)

Making full use of the raw, expletive force of the dialect, Walcott gives notice of his commitment to an all-out fight in the cause of poetry – the cause of Imagination/consciousness itself, so deeply imperiled in the present climate of the society.

Charting, through Walcott's own artistic struggle, the representative course of Caribbean history, the journey has, effectively, been recovering the pains and gains of what has gone into the native experience. This recovery itself is the means of an important advance. It is a garnering of some of the strengths and values realized in that past experience, which must serve to bolster and equip the beleaguered self in its passage through the ordeals and travail necessary for healing and regeneration. We arrive at this culmination point in the next two stages of the journey. "Maria Concepcion and the Book of Dreams" and "Out of the Depths" enact the experience of travail undergone by Shabine/Walcott in this flight/odyssey, exploring the kind of consciousness and struggle necessary for the challenge of self-liberation facing the individual and community alike. The generic metaphor of descent into the (sea-) depths of self comes into the foreground in both these sections. In "Maria Concepcion and the Book of Dreams" this becomes specific in a descent into the dream territory of the unconscious, whose hallucinatory, surreal images open onto mythic frontiers. Here Maria Concepcion, as presiding muse/anima,[28] features as seer/local gardeuse, seeking to read the dreams of destiny.

A fundamental feature of that dream experience is that it takes place in the aboriginal territory of the Caribs. This enactment, recovering close connections with the world of the Caribs, signifies, importantly, the encounter with the aboriginal. Like the opening vision of history-in-time, the return to the aboriginal is a vital facet of Walcott's multidimensional, expansive search for an alternative idea of history. Accordingly, for the quester, it marks an important frontier of reckoning and discovery. This is the eclectic, assimilative Walcott at his best, drawing together a complex of converging elements and ideas in a movement that is at once narrative and dialogic discourse. Located in actual Carib territory, the experience cues into an episode from Wilson Harris's fiction (*The Whole Armour*) for an act of identification which claims the Caribs as ancestors. He is, at the same time, on his own ground in this territory of the Caribs: he has already made an original and classic reclamation of their ancestry in mythologizing the leaping Caribs of Grenada. He stakes this claim of ancestry, as we have seen, in one essential paradigm. These aboriginals represented an imagination in organic contact with elemental and existential necessity; one grounded, therefore, in the powers and vulnerabilities of the natural. The narrative takes on a polemical angle for this entry into Carib territory, resuming the Walcottian attack on the materialist-imperialist constructions of the Western/European concept of historic time as they have travestied these native truths of the imagination. The core event of the narrative, the night-time descent into the dream territory of the unconscious, is prefaced by a sceptical reflection on the idea of history as progress. The sound of a jet screeching overhead triggers a casual exchange about progress, to provoke Shabine's bitter contention: "Progress is history's dirty joke." Walcott actually frames the dream experience within the polemics of this issue. With its implicit allusion to the original clash between prehistoric Caribs and historic Europeans, between their two contrasting epistemologies, the total experience is projected, on an important level, as a refutation of the conventional view of history as evolutionary progress.

The dream-vision follows a ritual process, answering in intensity and extremity to the horrors and tribulations that have presaged the need for cleansing and regeneration. It begins with the traumatic torments of Shabine/Walcott's own conscience and sins: thus the smells of burning children surface from Walcott's guilt-ridden preoccupations with his marital problems. He is forced to taste of his own inner disintegration in the sense of a self reverting back to vegetal process in the depths of the forest. Thus the eating of the "brains of mushrooms, the fungi / of devil's parasols under white, leprous rocks; / . . . leaf mould in leaking forests" (*CP*, 356). The will to resistance and survival is presaged in that very extremity. In this dynamic,

Shabine is gaining entry into knowledge of the dual poles of his being, its utter nakedness on the one hand, and its inner potentialities and resources of power on the other, organically and indivisibly linked. It is precisely at the point of arrival at this will to resistance and survival that he is transported back to a visionary identification with the ancestral Caribs. Walcott assimilates a specific episode from Harris's *Whole Armour*, returning to the theme of journey through the interior (see the "Guyana" sequence). On the run through the interior forests of Guyana, the protagonist Cristo has a hallucinatory experience of joining the earlier Caribs, who are in desperate flight from the European soldiers during the early stages of their historical encounter.[29] Like Cristo "running" in ancestral company, Shabine's course takes him through purgatorial rigours of terror and risk ("the blades of balisier sharper than spears" [*CP*, 356]); to the capacity for exercise of native wit/intelligence necessary for the safety and survival of the self (the camouflage of painted bird, which is also there in Harris). The life-and-death race through the forest, like the camouflage device, signals the power to outwit, outpace, and thereby avoid falling prey to, the enemy within and without – mirror images of each other. This is followed in the dream by a sleep of extinction (death to the old self) from which, awakening as to a new birth, Shabine glimpses this fresh vision of progress in a numinous image: "an iguana as still as a young leaf in sunlight" (*CP*, 356). The image is revelatory of the immanence and timelessness of life/creation in its elementals. A lyrical rounding off of the polemical context of this section, it urges consciousness of this deeper reality of timelessness that must temper our presumption of the march of progress in successive time.

This dream experience is also, however, a prophecy of the live experience of travail that lies ahead in this odyssey. It leaves Shabine in a deep fit of distraction, to be further disturbed by portentous dreams and omens. But, rising out of its prophetic power, he is possessed of fresh charges of fury to wage war against the malefactors and archenemies most intransigent in their betrayal of the times. He delivers the full blast of this fury against the "big boys" of the Establishment, reaching here the climax of his militant purpose to be their scourge and conscience. Confident of the native powers of poetry/imagination as an ultimate weapon, of its natural authority in the service of life itself, he calls their apocalypse:

> All you see me talking to the wind, so you think I mad.
> Well, Shabine has bridled the horses of the sea;

> you see me watching the sun till my eyeballs seared,
> so all you mad people feel Shabine crazy,
>
> . . . .
>
> and all you best dread the day I am healed
> of being a human. All you fate in my hand,
> ministers, businessmen, Shabine have you, friend,
> I shall scatter your lives like a handful of sand,
> I who have no weapon but poetry and
> the lances of palms and the sea's shining shield!

(CP, 357–58)

Walcott's experiment with the dialect in this passage is especially effective and far reaching in its achievement. The power of his rhetoric remains strongly grounded in the grassroots tone, idiom and imagery of the dialect. It is the very force of this grassroots medium that recovers the voice of the Old Testament prophets, attesting to the elemental and primal powers of their own declamatory rhetoric against the tyrants of their times. One with that of these ancient predecessors, Walcott's poetic fury – rendered in the voice of Shabine as ordinary man – is also indistinguishable from that of the street prophets of his own setting. They all echo each other, emanating from the same perennial source.

The journey comes to its ultimate testing place in the life-and-death struggle of the storm at sea ("Out of the Depths"). Realistic content converges dramatically with the underlying metaphoric mode in the presentation of the storm. The experience captures graphically the concrete realities of the Caribbean storm, its turmoil and terror. Inner, mythic action is as strongly represented, evoked in such archetypal imagery as that of Leviathan, of the "drowned sailor in her *Book of Dreams*" (a sign foretold by Maria Concepcion), and allusions to the Crucifixion. Shabine continues to bear the central burden of discovery as quest figure, but the entire crew share in the total experience, the individual and communal visibly interconnected in this final phase of the struggle. Thus the narrative focuses on both Shabine and the captain of the crew in defining the process and values entailed in its resolution. All that has been gained so far in knowledge of the self – the merging of the existential self and the self shaped by history – contribute towards a consciousness ready to face the ordeal. Shabine, however, reaching his own private terror and extremity in that storm, is driven back to find refuge in further, deeply embedded reserves of strength. He returns instinctively to the memory of his "family safe home", and to a childhood of strongly nurtured spiritual strengths. Walcott's personal biography surfaces here. He recalls the Methodist chapel[30] – a powerful presence in Walcott's religious upbringing in St Lucia – and its sounds and hymns of worship. Alive with the Protestant spirit, they were hymns in which faith and the will to resistance pitted themselves against the surviving disadvantages and privations of their peculiar past. What Walcott specifically invokes here are the tenacious roots of a native tradition of spiritual purpose and resistance nurtured at the levels of family and close community – a tradition which, fading and even jettisoned on the highways and byways of "progress" and modernization, is an indigenous product of the earliest, essentially provincial background of the Caribbean people:

> Then a strength like it seize me and the strength said:
> "I from backward people who still fear God."
> Let Him, in His might, heave Leviathan upward
>
> . . . .
>
>   and that was the faith
> that had fade from a child in the Methodist chapel
> in Chisel Street, Castries, when the whale-bell
> sang service and, in hard pews ribbed like the whale,
> proud with despair, we sang how our race
> survive the sea's maw, our history, our peril,
>
>   *(CP*, 359)

It is a reiteration of his faith in the values generated and preserved at the grassroots level, expressed most strongly in his eulogy to Simmons. Erna Brodber, in *Jane and Louisa Will Soon Come Home* (1980), strikes similar chords in her return to childhood memories of "families walking bravely in fear"[31] – closely echoed in Walcott's "proud with despair".

The return to these resources signifies, on Walcott's part, faith in the capacity of the Caribbean people for a spiritual mettle that will resist their downhill slide. He goes on to give these potential resources and strengths their familiar, flesh-and-blood manifestation in the features of the captain steering the *Flight* through that storm. The image of the captain signals, in fact, the quality of leadership whose absence is being decried in this work. His courage and resilience under that duress is an inspiration to Shabine and the rest of the crew:

> beard beading with spray, tears salting the eyes,
> crucify to his post, that nigger hold fast

> to that wheel, man, like the cross held Jesus,
> and the wounds of his eyes like they crying for us,
> and I feeding him white rum, while every crest
> with Leviathan-lash make the *Flight* quail
> like two criminal . . .

(CP, 359)

Walcott works into his portrait motifs and insignia that deliberately echo the Christ of the Crucifixion undergoing his own "crossing". These motifs and insignia essentialize an archetype of Christianity truly indigenized in the region. We see this archetype personified in the captain's face, which is characterized by an earthiness, a thew and sinew that is very much of its grassroots setting. (Or, put another way, the captain's face says that Jesus, too, was a nigger.) The effects of this "naturalization" are fully carried in the sensibility and tenor of the creole medium: "And the noon sea get calm as Thy Kingdom come."

The regenerative vision follows the storm, extending celebratory overtures of healing and rebirth in section 11. Walcott the poet comes fully into the foreground for the lyrical evocation of the order of truth, according to his own faith, that upholds all creative being and struggle. It comes to epiphany in the features of a landscape irradiated with an immanent light and love. The apprehension of this signifies the realization of the truth ideal envisioned in Maria Concepcion. As in *Another Life and Sea Grapes*, that immanent light/love extends its ministry through the naturalistic world to the equally natural simplicities of the domestic, human sphere:

> Fall gently, rain, on the sea's upturned face
> like a girl showering; make these islands fresh
> as Shabine once knew them! Let every trace,
> every hot road, smell like clothes she just press
> and sprinkle with drizzle. I finish dream;
> whatever the rain wash and the sun iron:
> the white clouds, the sea and sky with one seam,
> is clothes enough for my nakedness.

(CP, 360)

Walcott ends on this note of prayerful hope, as much for his own personal maturity and serenity as for that of the community of islands to which he remains bound in love.

"The Star-Apple Kingdom"

This poem presents a novel departure in Walcott's engagement with politics in the region. It attempts, in fact, a singular treatment of the subject. Instead of the usual purpose of critical attack and denunciation, he undertakes here a sustained focus on political struggle as an important instrument of change in the region, and is concerned with its role and necessities in meeting the formidable challenge of self-development in the Caribbean in national times. He takes his cue from the situation of Jamaica under Michael Manley's regime from 1972 to 1980. Manley's attempt at democratic socialism was attended by a host of problems which, beginning with the severe austerity measures to which he was forced to resort, precipitated a collapse in the society. The case of Jamaica under Manley becomes the occasion of an intensive, meditative appraisal of sociopolitical conditions in the region, explored in close relation to their formative historical context. Jamaica's plight also becomes representative of the extreme difficulty of a materially impoverished, essentially powerless chain of islands attempting to deliver itself from the legacy of the past. The poem comprises Walcott's most conclusive statement on history and politics in the region, as these relate to the destiny of Caribbean society. Although not as well structured as "The Schooner *Flight*", it is, for the reasons cited above, the more significant of the two poems.

The poem attempts to construct a narrative around the ordeal faced by Manley in the crisis precipitated by his socialist experiment. For a right appreciation of the intent and achievement of the poem, we need to begin with an understanding of Walcott's treatment of biographical and historical material, especially in the portrait of the Manley figure at the centre of the narrative. His peculiar treatment is itself the axis of the poem's meaning. Essentially, he takes the external, practical realities of Manley's regime, and fictionalizes an inner process out of these; to project, in the fictionalized Manley of this inner process, the making of the kind of political intelligence that is necessary in the region.

The historical and factual realities are readily identifiable. Manley embarked on his socialist mission with a mandate from the poorer classes, and a commitment to the goal of redressing the chronic imbalances between Jamaica's rich and poor, in order to bring some measure of social justice to the "sufferers and victims" of the society, including the Rastafarians of the Kingston ghettoes.[32] (The Rastafarians are made representative of Manley's constituency, for reasons that will emerge later.) The first major reaction to his policies was the flight of middle-class and private sector capital, a setback from which he was never to recover. In the economic recession which ensued, he was forced to resort to austerity measures which brought severe hardship to the country, with the usual toll in social unrest and violence. Strong in his espousal of the socialist cause, Manley found himself increasingly dependent on external loans from capitalist agencies, notably the International Monetary Fund – an ironic and controversial position which for many summed up the hopelessness and failure of his leadership. The prescriptions of a hostile International Monetary Fund brought the country down to an intolerable standard of living, and it was under this pressure especially that the society finally collapsed. Another major factor contributing to this collapse was the destabilizing activities of the Central Intelligence Agency, which had promptly mounted guard against Manley's socialist effort and rhetoric, and his friendly relations with Cuba.[33] We get a résumé of most of these realities in the following portrait of Manley under siege. The portrait also makes reference to other critical problems that aggravated the situation: the wranglings between moderate and radical factions of Manley's party (the People's National Party); and the confusion and disorder of a society reflected in its starkly polarized reactions to his leadership:

> The soul, which was his body made as thin
> as its reflection and invulnerable
>
> . . . .
>
>   it entered a municipal wall
> stirring the slogans that shrieked his name: SAVIOUR!
> And others: LACKEY! he melted like a spoon
> through the alphabet soup of CIA, PNP, OPEC,
> that resettled once he passed through with this thought:
> I should have foreseen those seraphs with barbed-wire hair,
> beards like burst mattresses, and wild eyes of garnet,
> who nestled the Coptic Bible to their ribs, would
> call me Joshua, expecting him to bring down Babylon
> by Wednesday, after the fall of Jericho; yes, yes,
> I should have seen the cunning bitterness of the rich
> who left me no money but these mandates:
>
>   (*CP*, 389)

History has not yet made its final assessment of the real Manley or his political performance during that critical term of office. The question of that political performance aside, Manley achieved considerable stature on the Caribbean political scene for his other activities and contributions in the wider regional cause. The response to his death in 1997 was a measure of his impact as a Caribbean nationalist. A Caribbean delegation, which included Fidel Castro, was among the thousands who thronged his memorial service in Jamaica. Walcott's focus in the portrait precludes many of these other aspects of the wider, historical Manley. He featured, both in the Caribbean and internationally, as an advocate of Third World solidarity, and was an active member, along with figures like Indira Gandhi, of the Non-Aligned Movement which was its main platform. He was also a keen spokesman for African liberation. He had the distinction, moreover, of being among the special class of Caribbean politicians who pursued broad intellectual and cultural interests – a class epitomized by Eric Williams and C.L.R. James. Thus he combined his politics with a productive effort as a man of letters, writing a number of books on subjects ranging from the political and economic development of Jamaica, to West Indies cricket.[34] By all accounts, he was a rich personality of considerable range, and was also well equipped with charisma and the gift of oratory for his role as Caribbean politician. Never losing the polish of his privileged background, he turned quite readily on the platform into the gallery man who relished and played up to the title of "Joshua" conferred on him by the Rastafarian brethren.

On the substantive matter of his political experiment, there were, as earlier indicated, violently opposed reactions of full praise or outright condemnation. Among Jamaicans, this remains the case. The title of one of the many books reacting to the Manley regime sums up the situation: *Jamaica's Michael Manley: Messiah . . . Muddler . . . or Marionette.*[35] Carl Stone, the well-respected Jamaican scholar, pollster and columnist, saw a Manley whose socialist rhetoric was more radical than his quite moderate domestic, economic and social policies.[36] Turning to Walcott's poem, it is clear that he saw in Manley a leader genuinely committed to a national ideal and the goal of radical change in Jamaica. His Manley is a patriot whose socialist effort is motivated by the desire to redress the chronic problems of inequality in his society. Walcott attributes to him the dream of a national order based on self-reliance, equality and justice. Thus:

> that he wanted no other power but peace,
> that he wanted a revolution without any bloodshed,
> he wanted a history without any memory,

> streets without statues,
> and a geography without myth. He wanted no armies
> but those regiments of bananas, thick lances of cane,
> and he sobbed, "I am powerless, except for love."
>
> (*CP*, 388)

It is precisely from this testing combination of material powerlessness and love-power that Walcott begins to fictionalize the internalized process of the Manley persona who is the protagonist of the poem. Thus his Manley, facing this powerlessness amid a sea of troubles, is engaged in an introspective/meditative experience which represents the main movement of the narrative. His passage through that internal process, and what he achieves as a result, contains the essential meaning of the poem. Briefly, the experience comprises the following. Under duress from his failed effort, he is forced back into self for a journey inward and backward. It is a journey which takes him through the territory of the shared, collective unconscious of a people. From the total experience he gains an understanding of the nature and complexity of Caribbean society, and a deeper insight into its crisis and revolutionary challenge. He advances towards maturity in enlightened choice and inwardly grounded struggle informed by that understanding. Necessarily, the peculiar meanings and emphases of the process come from Walcott's own perceptions and understanding of Caribbean identity and destiny. But the relationship between Walcott and the Manley persona is different from that between himself and Shabine in "The Schooner *Flight*". There is not the functional merging of Walcott's persona (as poet and individual) into the fictionalized image of Manley as protagonist, such as we saw in the characterization of Shabine in "The Schooner *Flight*". Walcott's perspectives do come to the fore at certain climactic points. But what we see here is the logic of the Walcott imagination informing that of the fictionalized persona, intended to represent the struggle of the rooted politician as one with that of his necessary brother and kindred spirit – the rooted artist. The characterization of Manley takes its integrity from there.

As in "The Schooner *Flight*", the poem employs an innovative form which is a fundamental point of entry into its thematic purposes and perspectives. It combines a novelistic, narrative approach with metaphoric, poetic modes exploited to serve the interior/reflective content. Within that functional combination, the narrative has both a psychological and a visionary dynamic. The "plot" moves between the outer realism of Manley's Jamaica, and the inner setting of his responses to and engagement with it. This is reflected in the two main poles between which he moves: the sights, scenes and noises of the daytime world and its chaos, and the night-time world of sleep/dream; action on the conscious plane, and the inward plane of consciousness, or the unconscious. The interaction of these two modes comes to bear on the psyche of Manley in this trial by ordeal, a psyche and mind which, as we have noted, develops mainly through introspection.

Walcott makes use of a number of metaphors to present this interior action, which ultimately comprises a descent into the depths of self. Foremost is the metaphor of sleep/dream, representative of descent into the inward realms of consciousness, the territory of nightmare or dream-vision. The sleep/dream metaphor is, in some instances, associated with a moonlight motif, signifying the quality of visionary otherness, or hallucination. These metaphors and motifs are, in turn, inset and encompassed within the underlying metaphor of descent into the sea/submarine depths. The sea is also focused in this poem as the guardian, keeper of history and memory. As such, this underlying sea/underwater metaphor stands for the submerged reaches of conscious-ness, the repository of the residual content of history – which is at once individual and racial, personal and collective. Out of this idea develops a further, distinctly Walcottian conceit: the inversion of the terrestrial – the visible, tangible material of empirical history – into sea/water, to become history/memory reflected in its timeless dimension. The return to the history which lies buried at these levels thus opens onto existential frontiers. At the same time, the open narrative of this inward journey is anchored in close diagnostic scrutiny of the historical events and processes that pro-duced the region, its sociopolitical and cultural content. Walcott, then, manoeuvres a composite metaphoric structure to enact the inner action of the Manley odyssey. These metaphoric modes extend authentically from the language of the poem. Retaining a lyrical tone and texture throughout, it is a language which brings fresh light and life to the issues of politics and society.

The poem begins with a historical flashback to early colonial times as the background to the Jamaica of the present. The opening picture is of the landscape of a Jamaican countryside whose features still recall the pastoral, idyllic scenes of the early colonial order in its heyday. Almost as if wafted back by these scenes into the interior of one of the old colonial homes of that period, Walcott lights upon this painting: "Herefords at Sunset in the Valley of the

Wye". The painting presents the very model of the pastoral idyll which the British colonists tried to transpose onto the Jamaican landscape, along with the names of their home shires, which still survive around the island: the parishes of Trelawny, St David and St Andrew, for example. It will serve as the centrepiece in the effort to retrace the "sociological contours" of the Jamaican landscape from those times (postemancipation through to the 1860s), right down to the much-altered face of postcolonial Jamaica in the 1970s. Thus, taking its "gilt-edged" cue from "Herefords at Sunset in the Valley of the Wye", a picture-perfect image of the ancient pastoral returns:

> The mountain water that fell white from the mill wheel
> sprinkling like petals from the star-apple trees,
> and all of the windmills and sugar mills moved by mules
> on the treadmill of Monday to Monday, would repeat
> in tongues of water and wind and fire, in tongues
> of Mission School pickaninnies, like rivers remembering
>
> . . . .
>   and the cattle
> with a docile longing, an epochal content.
>
>   (*CP*, 383)

Although these "perfections" had diminished considerably by his time, a child of the privileged, half-white background of a Manley would have grown up amid surviving hints of that order and its appeal:

> And there were, like old wedding lace in an attic,
> among the boas and parasols and the tea-coloured
> daguerreotypes, hints of an epochal happiness
> as ordered and infinite to the child
> as the great house road to the Great House
> down a perspective of casuarinas plunging green manes
> in time to the horses, an orderly life
>
>   (*CP*, 383)

The images of a great house and its ambiance allude to Manley's background as the son of a father, Norman Manley, who had occupied the seat of government as prime minister of Jamaica.[37] Here, as elsewhere, Walcott specifically identifies the government house of both colonial and national times as the descendant of the great house of slavery days. He makes thereby an ironic comment on the traditions of power, its forms and trappings which survive from the original establishment to its counterparts in present times.

The portrait also includes allusions to the home, Drumblair,[38] where Manley's parents engaged in their much-loved pastime of rearing horses (deftly evoked in the "plunging green manes" of the casuarinas).

But a crucial part of Walcott's purpose is to turn the "epochal content" of this colonial pastoral to its reverse side; to zero in on the seeds of its own destruction, the contradictions and tensions which erupted into a violent backlash:

> Strange, that the rancour of hatred hid in that dream
> of slow rivers and lily-like parasols, in snaps
> of fine old colonial families, curled at the edge
> not from age or from fire or the chemicals, no, not at all,
> but because, off at its edges, innocently excluded
> stood the groom, the cattle boy, the housemaid, the gardeners,
> the tenants, the good Negroes down in the village,
> their mouths in the locked jaw of a silent scream.
>
> (*CP*, 384)

The "silent scream" resounds from the accumulated bitterness and outrage of those so excluded, as victims of the injustice and oppression upon which that pastoral was erected. The first major outbreak of this bitterness and outrage came in the postemancipation rebellions of the 1860s, beginning with the Morant Bay Rebellion (1865) which, involving much bloodshed and sacrifice, ushered in the winds of change.[39] The terror and threat of that change are conveyed in the imagery of the altered aspects of objects and features which, once part of the pastoral peace and order, now take on a surrealistic menace: the bulging, terrified eyes of the once-docile cattle; the caring benign figure of the nanny in white now shrivelled to a "chimerical, chemical pin speck" (*CP*, 384). The image of "the locked jaw of a silent scream" sounds the extremity of the violation that fuelled that rebellious outbreak, as well as its deep-seated need for release. It is an image whose resonances permeate and will explode again at an important climax in the text. But, as terrifying and sweeping as were the effects of that outbreak, it did not succeed in making radical changes – "a wind that blew all without bending anything". The politico-economic systems of the old order, its injustices and oppressions, remained basically the same. The contemporary scene of Manley's Jamaica, with its crises and turmoil, follows in unbroken succession from the Jamaica of the colonial pastoral, whose shards – now reduced to imitation porcelain replicas – still attest to that surviving link. Both epochs are indeed one.

This opening movement establishes the historical context of the troubled society of contemporary Jamaica, and, equally importantly, situates Manley the leader within that historical context. It is a Manley who begins with a childhood attachment to the colonial pastoral. The attachment echoes Walcott's own history of a divided childhood endemic in his colonial generation ("The Divided Child", *AL*). Manley has awakened from that childhood dividedness to adult consciousness of the legacy of ills and abuses that continue to afflict the majority of his country's people. The dream ideal of the earlier order has now been, effectively, transfused into his dream of a national transformation that will redress the plight of the depressed masses. The star-apple kingdom serves as the crowning symbol of this indigenized dream of a national transformation. Bearing a fruit known as the star-apple, the star-apple tree is indigenous to and especially common in Jamaica. As symbol, the star-apple kingdom comes with its own natural lyricism. The combination of star and apple motifs signifies aspiration to an upliftment that will provide for both the material needs of the Jamaican people and their enlightenment.

The narrative is presented in a sequence of section-paragraphs which will be numbered here for easy reference. The first two describe the historical context discussed above. Section 3, which follows, takes us straight to the portrait of Manley as political leader pursuing his socialist programme, and facing its failure to achieve his objectives. We see a Manley intent on a policy of thrift in implementing that programme. So scrupulous and stringent is his management that it would seem to extend even to the bare, elemental resources of the landscape:

> the flame trees obeyed his will and lowered their wicks,
> the flowers tightened their fists in the name of thrift,
> the porcelain lamps of ripe cocoa, the magnolia's jet
> dimmed on the one circuit with the ginger lilies

> (*CP*, 385)

Walcott's metaphoric hyperbole underlines the spartan resources with which Manley has to work, and the thrift that is sincerely geared to self-reliance and economic independence. It also hints at a determination which will resort to authoritarian measures if need be. But the crux of the situation is that, despite his sincerity and determination, Manley remains unable to deliver the most immediate demands and expectations of his mandate, namely, to change the desperate and destitute conditions of the ghettoes of Kingston. Walcott paints a graphic picture of the stark and desolating extremes of life in these ghettoes, the stronghold of Jamaica's Rastafarians. Its characteristic images of shacks, torrents of dust, rocks, rags ("crucified by cactus") and refuse describe the raw, violent abrasiveness of conditions in that setting. The sounds and pressures of that life are what echoes from the famous "dread beat" of Rastafarian music. The latter, with its looming threat, overshadows and virtually takes over the city to make a "jukebox of Kingston". To the ears of Manley facing the chronic plight of these ghettoes, the strains of this dread beat are the exact opposite of the harmonious rhythms of his pastoral childhood environment. The euphonious vowels of that earlier period are now replaced by the harsh consonantals of "Rock stone. Rock stone" – a remarkable fusion of the sound and visual quality of this ghetto environment.

The reality of this failure is the affliction that sets Manley off on his inner meditative sojourn. It presages his first dream/sleep experience, initiating the process of the inward/backward looking effort through which he will advance. The dream experience and its complex of related images, as noted above, combine psychological and visionary levels. On the psychological level, we see the Manley protagonist repairing from the chaos of the day-time world, back into the deeper buried realms on the other side of consciousness, where there is cessation of action and of the temporal. This is the area, too, of the naked and defenceless self, specifically identified here with the condition of power-lessness on the other side of power. The motif which expresses this harks back to Gabriel Garcia Marquez's *The Autumn of the Patriarch* (1976): "poleaxes the tyrant to a sleeping child" (*CP*, 386). In this work, which Walcott acknowledges as a strong influence in deepening his view of Caribbean politics, Marquez negotiates a double image of the patriarch as a powerful despot of gargantuan abuses, and as a defenceless sleeping figure shorn of all the trappings of his status. The territory of dream/sleep is also the realm of the visionary. Walcott employs the overarching metaphor of descent into the sea/submarine depths to mediate the core visionary content of this dream/sleep experience. Effectively, what Manley perceives in this submerged, underwater realm is an inversion of the terrestrial recorded images of history, now dissolved into their timeless dimension. The vision is the equivalent of "the rustling forest of [the] ships" of the middle passage in "The Schooner *Flight*", and repeats the Walcottian idea of history seen through the lens of time.

The history first encountered here is national history, answering to Manley's immediate concern with the destiny of the nation. Imbued with the apparitional otherness of moonlight, scenes and images from the landmarks of Jamaica's earlier history delineate themselves in an underwater mirage. They are now reflected as mere silhouettes and imprints: their former substance, its final emptiness, parodied in the shapes and forms of the sea's flora and fauna. This is what Walcott calls, in *Omeros,* the sea's "parodic architecture".[40] His portraiture of this parodic architecture combines the pictorial, decorous appeal of scene-painting with effects of the revelatory. Pirates, buccaneers, the gowned ladies of the ancient pastoral – all the traditional subjects of imperial history – are among the images that take shape. Especially prominent are images of the historic fate of Port Royal, which was "swallowed by water" in the famous earthquake of 1692, at the height of its prosperity.[41] There are echoes of its drowned choirs, caught by the earthquake in the middle of Sunday service; a crab "climbs the steeple" of the inverted cathedral:

> and he hears, in the sleep of his moonlight, the drowned
> bell of Port Royal's cathedral, sees the copper pennies
> of bubbles rising from the empty eye-pockets
> of green buccaneers, the parrot fish floating
> from the frayed shoulders of pirates, sea-horses
> drawing gowned ladies in their liquid promenade
> across the moss-green meadows of the sea;
> he heard the drowned choirs under Palisadoes,
> a hymn ascending to earth from a heaven inverted
> by water, a crab climbing the steeple,

(CP, 386)

The case of Port Royal makes the most telling point about a history inverted by/in water. The voices of its drowned choirs echo from the depths of time in the miraculous line cited earlier in this chapter: "a hymn ascending to earth from a heaven inverted / by water". The line captures the essence of the elegiac burden that permeates Walcott's vision of history seen through the lens of time, sounding the spiritual depths of the renewed humanity that informs it. Typically, the narrative turns readily from this visionary level to take a polemical thrust at those who remain prisoners of the traditional view of history as solely a record of successive, cumulative events. As Manley resurfaces from this submarine dream, the scholars at the Institute of Jamaica seem trapped in its artificial aquarium of archival history, in slavish concern with the succession of historic moments recorded as Jamaican history: 'Jamaica was captured by Penn and Venables, / Port Royal perished in a cataclysmic earthquake" (*CP*, 387). As in "Muse of History at Rampanalgas" this view of history is debunked as sterile, an academic exercise incapable of breaking through to any liberating vision. The latter point is underscored in this forceful oxymoron: "bubbles like ideas which he could not break" (*CP*, 387).

As in the case of Shabine, then, the Manley figure begins his meditative sojourn with a philosophical perspective on history. It serves likewise as a forewarning against the values of history seen as cumulative, epic achievement, with its Manichaean opposition between hero and victim. For those who come from an absurd and disastrous past, especially, that is a road of bitterness and despair; and given his responsibility to lead the quest for some revolutionary possibility, Manley must avoid that road. This philosophical encounter, serving as his baptism, thus equips him for the next stage of his interiorized effort, a major confrontation with the region's history. The latter engages him in an extended, speculative analysis of the sociopolitical and cultural context of the Caribbean past (section 5). The Hispanic and English-speaking Caribbean come into focus as one essential zone of the wider South American configuration in terms of which Walcott sees the region ("Guyana V: A Map of the Continent"). The Hispanic Caribbean also places Manley within the ambit of his socialist path, and his identification and allegiance with Castro's Cuba.

Manley's revisitation of the past of this environment is, first, a trenchant diagnostic review of the politics of imperialist oppression and the culture it bred. Second, it zeroes in from this to a penetrative analysis of the legacy of a history of violence and violation on the psyche of the peoples of the region. Walcott's voice is very much present in the incisive, satiric mode of its discourse. The attack comes to bear on the role of Christianity, the imperial religion, as the most influential instrument of the system of imperial oppression and exploitation.[42] It served that function by entrenching a culture of servitude in prayer, under the aegis of which the atrocities and violations perpetrated on the victims of the system were virtually absolved:

> if it gave tongue
> to the tortures done in the name of the Father,
> would curdle the blood of the marauding wolf,
> the fountain of generals, poets, and cripples
> who danced without moving over their graves
> with each revolution; . . .

(CP, 388)

This tradition of violence has left its pernicious influence on the native psyche. A violated psyche, thus conditioned, stands in constant danger of falling prey to an ethos of violence in its bid for revolt. Hispanic America, on the whole, represents the case history of that syndrome: coming from a background of extreme and persistent brutality, it sets the pace in a tradition of militant armed struggle. This ethos and environment of violent struggle will remain a troubling, haunting presence for the Manley figure, not merely because of his identification with Castro's path. Walcott also focuses on the rising tide of violence among the poorer classes – Manley's own constituency – as political tribalism set in with increasing hardships in the society. It was this violence that forced Manley to resort to martial law in 1976. Ultimately, though, the exploration of this psyche and its past means, for the Manley figure, that a deeper empathy with the cause of the dispossessed masses of the region; it also means that a wider understanding must guide his judgement in the choice of a viable revolutionary route.

The metaphoric power that fuels Walcott's anger and invective shows to full effect in this section. This is one of the points where his own authorial voice merges with that of his protagonist. The analysis penetrates to the core ill of this hegemony of the imperial religion. The doctrine of sin, guilt and expiation legitimized the suffering and abuses visited on the oppressed, virtually displacing the transgression of the oppressor onto the oppressed, as it conditioned the latter to a life of prayer in expiation for wretchedness. This ironic comment identifies the huge hoax: "and a people were absolved / of a history which they did not commit" (*CP*, 387). A sequence of images emphasizes the deep entrenchment of that culture of expiatory servitude, and its stranglehold in shaping the character and condition of the region in prerevolutionary times. Thus the Caribbean, insignificant in size and status, amounted to a "baptismal font", used for the business of recruiting souls into the fold; a baptismal font, also, where the ills of poverty were appeased and sanctioned by the hypocritical pieties of clerics "wash[ing] the feet of paupers". The image of the baptismal font is carried in the more richly loaded one of the Caribbean as "elliptical basin":

> Before the coruscating façades of cathedrals
> from Santiago to Caracas, where the penitential archbishops
> washed the feet of paupers (a parenthetical moment
> that made the Caribbean a baptismal font,
> turned butterflies to stone, and whitened like doves

the buzzards circling municipal garbage),
the Caribbean was borne like an elliptical basin
in the hands of acolytes, . . .

(CP, 387)

The elliptical/oval shape of the Caribbean area coincides with its elliptical/parenthetical status, that is, its marginal condition, insignificance and powerlessness in the global scheme of things. "Basin" itself is the final reductive denominator describing its total condition as a lowly, utilitarian object associated with the functions of serving and servitude. Especially effective too is the image of the emblematic rosary, repeating its circular route from the Hispanic coast through the chain-beads of the islands in endless recitation. "Knees turned to stone" describes the condition of a people immured in that tradition of religious servitude. Its relentless fixity continues unabated amid the glaring contradictions: changing eras with unchanging systems of exploitation, against which the futile sacrifice of a succession of lone revolutionaries is unable to prevail. As the review traces the movement into capitalist times, dominated by the North American presence and its peculiar corruptions, the details evoke the case of Cuba. The dread backlash of the stranglehold of that tradition exploded in the armed (guerrilla) revolution of contemporary Hispanic America, which is equally relentless in its militarist ideology. The muse who comes to tempt the poem's Manley in his dream arises out of this climate, and represents its strange and bitter fruit. She announces herself in this way: "Let me in, I'm finished with praying, I'm the Revolution. / I am the darker, the older America" (*CP*, 388).

Section 6 goes on to paint a portrait of this muse of revolution. A singular, outstanding achievement in this text, it carries a core aspect of Walcott's message on the question of revolutionary direction in the region. The terrifying, dread image of the muse of revolution, presented in the guise of a woman, pictures the face of the ethos of persistent, armed revolutionary struggle:

She was as beautiful as a stone in the sunrise,
her voice had the gutturals of machine guns
across khaki deserts where the cactus flower
detonates like grenades, her sex was the slit throat
of an Indian, her hair had the blue-black sheen of the crow.
She was a black umbrella blown inside out
by the wind of revolution, La Madre Dolorosa,
a black rose of sorrow, a black mine of silence,

> . . . .
>   her Caesarean was stitched
>   by the teeth of machine guns, . . .
>
>   (*CP*, 388)

Walcott extends in this woman-muse figure the ruling passion and moving spirit of the revolution. As such, her horrifying features reflect the revolted bitterness of the revolutionaries against the ravages of the past, of "the(ir) heart grown brutal".[43] She is, in effect, a goddess of unfeelingness, remorseless destruction, and dread. There is also an existential dimension into which Walcott taps, along with the psychological, in the creation of his muse figures. On this existential level, the muse as female lover is the object of desire as aspiration to creativity and completeness (as in the case of Makak, whose white goddess is an "image of his longing"). All the qualities and attributes that define the dynamic and aesthetic of this desire are invoked in this muse figure – the lyrical, the erotic, the libidinal, and the biological/physical. But – and herein lies the crux of the matter – all these qualities and attributes are shockingly transvested, displaced onto the sights, sounds, scenes and effects of warfare and gun power. Thus her appeal consists in hardness, unfeelingness (her beauty like "a stone in the sunrise"); her music in the violent rhythms of machine guns. Bloodlust has virtually taken over from the sex drive in what is perhaps the most unsparing image in Walcott: "her sex was the slit throat / of an Indian". Most shocking and brutal of all is the image of her birthing process replaced by a violent disembowelment typical of the scenes of carnage: "her Caesarean was stitched / by the teeth of machine guns". A perversion of the birthing process, this epitomizes the extremes of a process of "uncreation" that is the end product of this ethos of armed struggle. The muse of revolution presents, in fact, a travesty of woman in what emerges as an apotheosis of gun power.[44]

In her deep destructiveness, however, the muse of revolution also bears a doleful, tragic aspect. She is La Madre Dolorosa, a black rose of sorrow, reflecting the inevitable joylessness and gloom overshadowing the whole. Walcott's muse figure has the complexity and depth of the human psyche she embodies, with all its varying facets and contradictions. Travesty though she is, she is no monster: there are still hints and chords that sound the human susceptibilities that have now turned so brutal. Thus, as image of the revolutionaries' longing, she is "transfixed by arrows from a thousand guitars". A most important aspect of her total meaning, moreover, is the image of the

Caribbean woman contained in her portrait.[45] Remaining focused on the brutalizing past that accounts for this muse of revolution, Walcott begins his projection of the figure from the reality of the Caribbean woman as arch-victim and underdog in a society of victims and underdogs. As such, the Caribbean woman serves as the genuine archetype and bearer of the legacy of violation in the region. Thus the muse of revolution bears the Caribbean woman's experience of the worst extremes of the ravages of the past – as "raped wife, empty mother, Aztec virgin" (*CP*, 388). Deeply sensitive and responsive to the feminist cause in this text, he goes on, in fact, to represent in this muse figure the collective historical plight of the women of the region: she is one of a "flowing black river of women" (*CP*, 394). This "flowing black river of women" embraces counterparts from different parts of the Caribbean: the peasant women of Haiti as archetypes of the wretched of the Caribbean earth, bearing baskets down "the haemophilic red hills of Haiti" (*CP*, 394); or the women of Latin America, in whom the muse figure finds her strongest likeness. These Latin American counterparts, who "carried the penitential napkins / to be the footbath of dictators . . ." (*CP*, 388), are archetypes of bondage and servitude to a patriarchal religious establishment, reminiscent of Joyce's description of Ireland as "the scullery maid of Christendom".

But it is, as we have seen, the remorseless, terrifying face she assumes as apotheosis of that ethos of revolution that bears the substance and brunt of Walcott's message. Walcott's portrait highlights a total abnegation and travesty of all womanly and humanly attributes in that ethos of revolution. His portrait warns that such a travesty of the humanizing properties – traditionally associated with the feminine side of our natures – must leave us bereft of all the healing and generative capacities necessary for our survival. He gives us an apocalyptic (even futuristic, for the Caribbean) image of that tragedy, which speaks universally to all the trouble spots where resistance has become a career of violence. Finally, the portrait intends a clear indictment of an ideology of retaliatory militant power as a viable revolutionary path. Just as the image of the muse of revolution is poised between terror and pity, this indictment is balanced by Walcott's empathy with its fatal lure for those who have come from a history of brutalization – a concern which precedes and is an integral part of his meaning in this climax. But from Walcott's perspective, the past of brutalization and the ideology of violent revolution are both to be decried as Janus faces of the same thing. The alternative, as reflected in sections 5 and 6, is a revolution directed towards and always in touch with a humanistic goal.

This is the spectre which surfaces out of the Manley protagonist's penetrative analysis of the region's past and its legacy of victimization. It surfaces to trouble the consciousness of a careworn Manley: "Now she stroked his hair / until it turned white . . ." (*CP*, 388). But, committed to his goal of a better society, he is sensitive to the dangers and perils of this muse. She will, as we have seen, continue to haunt him as the crises of his regime increase, and she remains a central figure in his drama to the very end. But it is at this stage, against the extreme danger of what she offers, that his own vision is crystallized. It comes over as a *cri de coeur*:

> but she would not understand
> that he wanted no other power but peace,
> that he wanted a revolution without any bloodshed,
> he wanted a history without any memory,
> streets without statues,
> and a geography without myth. . . .

> (*CP*, 388)

The ideal, however, is in sharp contrast to harsh actuality, taking him back to the enormity of the challenge he faces as leader of a beleaguered society. Returning to this day-time world, the reflective Manley has a moment of clairvoyance into his destiny in a heritage of national struggle. He discovers in that moment a binding sense of spiritual kinship with the Maroons – the ancestral freedom-fighters of Jamaica – and George William Gordon, one of the martyrs of the struggle.[46] What follows is a pragmatic appraisal of the barrage of problems closing in on him from all sides. For this full-scale survey, the focus is on the far more critical, tragic second term of the Manley regime (1976–80). He closely documents both the external and the internal factors involved. (This is the account from which we cited earlier in this piece.) The external factors represent a particularly severe combination of adverse forces. There is, as identified above, the stranglehold of the International Monetary Fund and its punishing conditionalities; economic hardship is further exacerbated by the exorbitant prices set by the Organization of Petroleum Exporting Countries during the energy crisis; and there is also the increasingly vicious destabilizing campaign of the Central Intelligence Agency, playing a major role in fomenting the political tribalism and internecine violence that became rife during this period. Add to this the divisions within his own party (the

People's National Party), and we have the formula for an overpowering, mixed brew in which Manley is totally consumed. Another felicitous conceit registers that effect:

> he melted like a spoon
> through the alphabet soup of CIA, PNP, OPEC,
> that resettled once he passed through with this thought:

(CP, 389)

But, despite the crushing weight of these external pressures, the most affecting and demoralizing problems have their sources in the native failings and shortcomings of the society. There is the importunity of the Rastafarians, representative of his own constituency, who look to him for overnight achievement of their millennial expectation of a society purged of the inequities and injustices that favour the privileged classes, the "Babylon" of their world. Treating a few peculiar features of their physiognomy and lifestyle to his unique combination of decorous wit and irony, Walcott conveys the full impact of the ethos and personality of this religious-cum-political group. They are "seraphs with barbed-wire hair", whose dreadlocks signal the threat of militant violence that comes side by side with their strongly held spiritual faith. Fuelled by the smoking of their holy weed (*ganja*/marijuana), their "wild eyes of garnet" are possessed of their dream of deliverance. Their matted locks also resemble the burst mattresses of the destitute living conditions in their shanties.

But if the importunity of the desperate Rastafarians is a major source of misgiving, the far more grievous and disabling factor is the material disadvantage to which he has been abandoned by the "cunning bitterness of the rich" who, fleeing with their capital (to the safe haven of Miami), have left him bereft of the money to meet the basic needs of the country. Striking rock bottom here, Manley takes this hard ironic measure of his true mandate (section 8). The material wherewithal of that mandate amounts to very little indeed, comprised of the bare elemental endowments of air, sea, sky and the land itself, now strained by an ailing bauxite industry. Some of these bare, elemental resources are, furthermore, fraught with geopolitical dangers (Miami-based anti-Cuban spies plying the Caribbean waters). The only sustaining, countervailing factor is the love that binds him to its naked, disadvantaged landscape. The latter is, as always in Walcott, the surest investment.

Confronting these hard facts, Manley arrives at a critical juncture of recognition. The recognition is marked by a climactic, prophetic, spiritual signal. The image of his father suddenly materializes, imprinted on the clouds like a portent of the destiny to which he is called in this ordeal. It is a portent much more pregnant in its intimations than the earlier moment of spiritual kinship with the ancestral freedom-fighters of Jamaica's past. To appreciate its positive import, we need to pay close attention to the references and subtle play of allusions which invoke the substance and spirit of the older Manley. The face which takes shape from the clouds "in a photographic wind" captures his demeanour and spirit in what proved the historic, testing case of his political career: his calling, in 1961, of the Jamaican referendum on the West Indian Federation. That referendum resulted in the demise of the federation (1958–62), and the subsequent defeat of his own party, which suffered the further disappointment of watching the government of Bustamante, his arch-rival, usher Jamaica into an independence pioneered and piloted by Norman Manley himself. Despite the political pressures that had forced him to call the referendum, Norman Manley had also been and remained a leading champion of Federation. The face in this apparition (there will be another appearance) shows the resolve and fortitude with which he met the tragic necessity of the historic "no" of the Jamaican people to that referendum. It was an inevitable "no", arising out of factors and attitudes embedded in the history and geography of the Caribbean islands.[47] Manley's resolve in the face of that necessity, and his acceptance of its outcome, showed the courage of compromise and a quality of wisdom rare in a politician. They are strengths which take on, in Walcott's hands, a philosophical dimension. The latter is registered in the play on the epithets "first" and "last". "First" and "last" allude factually to the referendum; at the same time, they denote the alpha and omega of mortal limitations, to finally reflect the existential frontiers of political struggle, as testing to the human spirit as any sphere of human endeavour:

> the mouth of mahogany winced shut,
> the eyes lidded, resigned
> to the first compromise,
> the last ultimatum,
> the first and last referendum.

(CP, 390)

The father's image thus flashes across the consciousness and conscience of his son as tutelary guide, forecasting a testing and arduous destiny. Walcott has struck here upon a happy coincidence between the mythic and the biographical in this visitation of the son by the spirit of the father.[48]

Before proceeding with the narrative, we need to pay special attention to two important emphases in the foregoing account of the problems of the Manley regime. Walcott's close, comprehensive documentation of both the external and internal factors involved bears important statements about his concern with the struggle for development in Caribbean society. With respect to the external factors, he is especially focused on the Jamaican crisis as the representative case history of the precarious position of the small island states of the Caribbean, strapped for resources, and at the mercy of the larger economic and political forces of the international order. He describes the Jamaican ordeal in a phrase which shows his keen sensitivity to the magnitude of this problem for the Caribbean: "a government groaning uphill" (*CP*, 392). Turning to the internal factors, he directs an important message towards the society. If it is the responsibility of the leadership to bear the burden of its people's weaknesses, it is equally the case that the people must carry a significant measure of the responsibility for change. Here, and more explicitly in the concluding movements of the poem, he makes the point that the onus of political maturity must be shared by both the leadership and the wider society.

We have met, in Walcott's Manley, the kind of leader who has the historical sense and vision to see the destiny of his own country within the context of the Caribbean as a whole. From the desperate, near-hopeless situation his own revolutionary effort has provoked at home, he turns to a reflective review of directions in the surrounding Caribbean. The Hispanic Caribbean has already featured for reasons examined above; now it is the rest of the English-speaking Caribbean, culturally and politically much closer, that comes into the fore-ground. Manley is greeted by an equally dismal scenario. This is Walcott's opportunity for a trenchant, critical review of the political and economic directions of the English-speaking Caribbean since the break-up of the fed-eration. The review (section 10) takes its cue from the reference to Norman Manley's role in the federation in the preceding section. (Walcott uses this linking device for the transition from one section-paragraph to the next throughout the poem's discourse.) It is an eloquent satiric portrait of the economic concept and model of progress that characterizes this area in national times. It focuses the tenuous, largely ineffectual economic union between "seven prime ministers", which replaced the federation as a unifying arrangement.[49] The latter arrangement, explicitly targeted as a mere sham, serves as the ironic backdrop to the materialistic scramble that is the order of the day.

The scenario that unfolds is dominated by an endless chain of sell-outs, which is as usual led by the politicians, and extending right through the ranks of the wider society (as in the case of Shabine's Trinidad). So that it reflects, as a whole, a society constantly selling out and underselling itself; and consigning itself to persistent impoverishment, as it barters and fritters away its native bounty and potentiality, material and human. In another brilliantly executed conceit, the sea serves as a metaphor for this native bounty, embracing the prime assets of the Caribbean islands – such traditionally exploited resources as their strategic location and the attractions of a tourist industry; and, more crucially in Walcott, the innate, natural sources of human power to which its people can lay claim. Historically, the precedent for these sell-outs of the sea was set by the imperial powers. During World War II, Britain leased a number of bases in the islands to the United States in exchange for a contingent of warships. A deft allusion recalls this deal: "the same conglomerates who had rented the water spouts / for ninety-nine years in exchange for fifty ships" (*CP*, 390). Walcott's sea metaphor is amazingly apposite and loaded, enriched by his own blend of lyricism and satire:

> One morning the Caribbean was cut up
> by seven prime ministers who bought the sea in bolts—
> one thousand miles of aquamarine with lace trimmings,
> one million yards of lime-coloured silk,
> one mile of violet, leagues of cerulean satin—
> who sold it at a markup to the conglomerates,
>
> . . . .
> who retailed it in turn to the ministers
> with only one bank account, who then resold it
> in ads for the Caribbean Economic Community,
> till everyone owned a little piece of the sea,
>
> (*CP*, 390)

Characteristically, the satire cuts simultaneously in all directions – at the neocolonial, capitalist system of multinationals that overshadows the region; at the prevailing breed of venal politicians who serve the multinationals for their own acquisitive ends; and at the wider society, cashing in on the materialistic spoils for its own consumerist, individualistic ends. The portrait also includes an ironic glance at the cosmetics culled from these spoils, proffered by the different groups, in the manner of Trinidad, as claims to their separate identities: "from which some made saris, some made bandannas" (*CP*, 390). The final image is of the residual, hapless condition of these islands as mere tourist trinkets, and small-time retail outlets for the capitalist market. It is an incisive statement on the futility of this materialistic route.

In this kind of environment, Manley is in a veritable wilderness (but for his friendship with Cuba), as the situation deteriorates to the point where he, like the historical Manley, is forced to call a state of emergency. This state of emergency, called in June 1976, and lasting an entire year, was one of the worst spells of political turbulence that have troubled Jamaica in modern times. Nearly six hundred people were detained, and statistics for the casualties of the rampant violence ran into the hundreds. Manley had imposed martial law specifically to deal with an upsurge of political violence in the ghettoes of Kingston, where the masses of victims and sufferers had become split into bitterly opposed factions of the two parties. Political allegiances in the ghettoes, fuelled by poverty and unemployment, were also exploited by the machinations of the Central Intelligence Agency (working in collusion with the Opposition), as earlier noted. It was, as Darrel Levi notes, mainly a matter of the "cannibalism of the poor by the poor",[50] erupting into such horrendous incidents as the Orange Street massacre.[51] Walcott captures the chaos and terror which enveloped Kingston during this time, closely reproducing the web of events and effects in their nightmarish climate. There was the increased busyness of the spies of the enemy intelligence over the rumours of a Cuban takeover, and the tension and unrest generated by that rumour; the hysteria of the terrified middle classes, under constant threat of violence from the ghettoes (their "white paranoia" is ingeniously set like an ill flower beside the bougainvillea of "astonishing April" which adorned their suburban gardens); and the motorcycle gangs, the advance guards of the political tribes dealing violence and dread.

The Manley protagonist has reached the zero point of his crisis in this state of emergency. Forced to resort to the draconian measures of absolute force, he is now a far cry from the visionary who cherished the ideal of a "revolution without bloodshed":

> Now a tree of grenades was his star-apple kingdom,
>
> . . . .
>
> he felt his fist involuntarily tighten
> into a talon that was strangling five doves,

(CP, 391)

But, internally, he is a man traumatized by this choice and an unmanageable situation. From here on, in fact, the narrative focuses on the psychological and spiritual process of an experience in which his patriot's love, and its original purpose, are being sorely tested. We see a Manley caught between despair and bitterness, on the one hand, and an anger that, with its deeper roots in love, strives to refuel his purposive will towards his responsibility. It becomes a struggle to find the right groundings for a love capable of meeting a formidable challenge.

A deep and instinctual response in that struggle is his yearning for retreat from the chaos and outrage of the day-time world into a realm of solace. He is drawn back into a state of inwardness where, now sobered from the ardours and dream-driven anxieties of his earlier idealism ("the sleep after love"), he seeks release from the absurdities of the world of action and time (section 12). That retreat is thus described as a sleep of oblivion from the action of history. But this is no escapist flight; it "wipes out history" for the Walcottian return to the condition of nakedness where the self is open to the organic principles and properties of being that it shares with wider, external nature. It is the Walcottian return to the primal sphere of prehistory/the aboriginal, where one is in the presence of either the primordial (the opening sequence of chapter 22, *AL*), or the pristine ("Anna Awaking", *AL*). The traumatized Manley has repaired, then, to a place of "mineral" nakedness which resembles and echoes the features of his primal landscape, and he is sensitive to the healing and recreative properties of that state. It represents a moment of respite when he can reconnect with the signals of the generative and nurturing in the natural bounties of the landscape, in the pristine, tropical lushness and peculiar fragrance of its country environs. This is enacted in a passage which recalls both the lyricism and the dynamic of "Anna Awaking":

> whose flesh smells of cocoa, whose teeth are white
> as coconut meat, whose breath smells of ginger,
> whose braids are scented like sweet-potato vines
> in furrows still pungent with the sun.

> (*CP*, 391)

The figure of a woman takes shape out of these images, here in the country likeness of a girlhood Anna (one of the many faces of woman in this poem). Her figure accentuates both the sensuous/erotic and the nurturing/mothering properties inherent in these organic origins. It is, in fact, the generative, integrative and supportive properties of these natural [re]sources that have been perverted in the woman-muse of revolution. Manley's retreat to the "sleep that wipes out history" echoes the several instances in *Another Life* where the self returns to the nakedness of the "child without history", to reground and reorient itself through and in its rapport with the primal signals of nature in landscape.

Thus he advances from the recreative intimations of this retreat to the recognition, in the next movement, of the native landscape as the true nurturing mother of "us all, / her history-orphaned islands . . . ". (The phrase "history-orphaned" is one of several echoes from Brathwaite's *Mother Poem* [1977], which becomes an important context at this point.) This identity of landscape as nurturing mother is represented in the figure of the Caribbean mother, who comes into the foreground as the personification of the land-scape: that is, she is the human substantiation of the native condition as it moulds and shapes its products. Walcott's treatment of the woman figure – it is pertinent to observe at this point – is one of the outstanding features of this poem, giving testimony of his progressive response to the contemporary climate of gender consciousness. The Caribbean woman/mother figure is a positive counterpart to the woman-muse of revolution. While the latter is a psychic expression of the woman factor brutalized and perverted, the image here is of a Caribbean woman/mother in the flesh. In this portrait he recognizes the Caribbean mother as a carrier of identity. These recognitions mark a definitional climax in the narrative.

The Caribbean mother figure is at once a strongly realistic presence, and a race-containing symbol encompassing all the characteristic features of a landscape of elementals stamped by the influences and effects of history. Her total image combines the residual marks of a history of dispossession, and native strengths forged out of that reality. Significantly, Walcott goes to the working class for this image, representing thereby the native condition at its reduced, grassroots level. His peasant/housemaid mother is marked by the hardship and toil of her underprivileged background, and its ways and means of survival. She is habituated to striving at the level of bare necessities to provide and care for her offspring, and looking to religious faith for refuge in her troubles. Out of these very efforts of caring and providing and their trials, however, she has developed her own reserves of resilience and resistance. Her mettle has been forged, especially, in what is the most testing experience of mothering at the lowest rungs of underprivilege and privation – the experience of giving birth to lives doomed to defeat and failure. Thus she "is the head-tie mother, the bleached-sheets-on-the-river-rocks mother, / . . . her sons like thorns, / her daughters dry gullies that give birth to stones" (*CP*, 392). Stretched to deep reaches of creative will in the face of such odds, she stands out as a figure who has been forced to find her "underground resources" – to echo another phrase from Brathwaite's *Mother Poem* – and to become anchored in them. Walcott's portrait also pays close attention to what has been taken from the tradition of the colonizer into this characteristic identity. The "t'ank you parson" attitudes of the subordinate notwithstanding, she has taken possession of its religious tradition, invested it with her own innate resources of a faith which sounds again the oceanic depths of the race's "crossing of water" – "in the deep Atlantic heave of her housemaid's hymn" (*CP*, 392).

There are obvious resemblances, as earlier indicated, between Walcott's figure and Brathwaite's earlier portrait of the Barbadian mother as embodiment of the peculiar configuration of his landscape – the bare naked properties of its physical setting (of waterless limestone), and the sociohistorical oppressions it has had to endure. Certain specific allusions show that Walcott intends an intertextual cross-reference to Brathwaite's poem in this section. Walcott, though, has his own emphases in his definitions of the identity borne by the Caribbean mother as landscape. Characteristically, in this respect, he emphasizes her relationship to the historied, classical tradition of the colonizer. Thus, in earlier times (the childhood of Walcott's generation), she was the servant in the great house (lasting symbol of the colonial heritage of the ruling, privileged class) polishing such sacred objects of colonial tradition as "the plaster figure / of Clio, Muse of history" (*CP*, 392). This reflects the reverential, aspiring awe the subordinate developed towards such objects of tradition.

Walcott represents in this emblematic image the common colonial background that has left an ex-colonized peoples worshippers of history according to the lights of the Old World Western tradition. The susceptibility, his context also suggests, extends from the lowly station of the housemaid right through to the artist of more privileged circumstances – like himself. His perspective in this image is on the complex, ambiguous hold of the colonizer's tradition which moves the native to yearn for the higher things of the spirit, binding him or her, at the same time, to the tragic flaws of the epic-heroic muse of that tradition. This is the complex he analysed in "The Divided Child" (*AL*). His comment on our late coming to landscape as nurturing mother must be seen in the context of this concern with the native's early colonial bondage to the older muse of history:

> But now she held him, as she holds us all,
> her history-orphaned islands, she to whom
> we came late as our muse, our mother,
>
> (*CP*, 392)

Still tied to the epic muse of history as achievement, the Caribbean people have been slow in coming to the recognition of their true roots in the native condition of their landscape/setting; they have tended to look to history from the traditional viewpoint, instead, for their definitions of identity. Walcott takes his cue from the Brathwaite of *Mother Poem*, who extends from this emphasis on history (*The Arrivants*) to embrace landscape. This may seem like shades of his early quarrel with Brathwaite as poet of "epic" history;[52] but the observation is, finally, confessional, and makes an incisive statement regarding the region as a whole – a statement, perhaps, more of hope than reality.

It is with the reality embodied in the image of the Caribbean woman-mother as the human face of nurturing landscape that the Manley protagonist reconnects for the creative bonding that will renew his purpose to face the chaos of his political dream turned nightmare. This creative bonding means a fresh recovery of the roots of identity and an integration into these roots: "But now she held him, as she holds us all, / her history-orphaned islands" (*CP*, 392). Most importantly, it is a bonding which takes him closer to the grassroots life of the country, opening him up to a deeper capacity for identification with the masses he is committed to deliver – effectively, therefore, bridging the residual gap between the privileged Manley and the poorer classes. Like the sine qua non of a mature historical consciousness, this identification of the leadership with the grassroots is an important part of Walcott's total statement in the poem. The resolutions of the poem define themselves, in fact, in terms of the possibility of an enlightened consciousness shared by Manley and this segment of the society, represented by the "men with barbed-wire beards" (*CP*, 395). The bond with landscape thus marks a climactic advance in Manley's meditative sojourn, renewing a commitment now firmly grounded in the consciousness of the patriot as native son of the soil:

> the shower crowned him and he closed his eyes,
> he was a bride under lace, remarrying his country,
> a child drawn by the roars of the mill wheel's electorate,
> those vows reaffirmed; . . .
>
> (*CP*, 393)

Rendering this fresh awakening from the "sleep after love", section 14 is suffused with the lyrical and celebratory spirit of this bond with landscape. Thus there are stirrings of hope and release as he returns to face the day-time world and its chaos: "the palms unclenched their fists, / his eyes opened the flowers" (*CP*, 392) by contrast with the Manley of the state of emergency, who felt a despotic fist "involuntarily tighten / into a talon that was strangling five doves" (*CP*, 391).

The signal which signs and seals this advance towards maturity follows immediately after this "remarrying [with] his country". It is the union with the spirit of his father, whose image had earlier visited him as a portent of the arduous destiny to which he was called. The legendary father with whose spirit the son's blends is the Norman Manley whom history has adjudged – despite the shadow of his ill-fated referendum – a rare, true model of the Caribbean statesman. Here, in the fictionalized context of the ripening of the younger Manley, Walcott adds his own endorsement, and holds him up as an ideal of the kind of mettle and wisdom necessary for mature leadership in the region. Norman Manley was the founding father of the nation, and among the first to adopt the values and strategies of democratic socialism in the struggle against the colonial system, accommodating them strictly to the circumstances of his own country. Though his first loyalty was to Jamaica, he was also a committed federationist. Among West Indian politicians, moreover, he holds the record as a model of integrity.[53] The novelist Vic Reid, who has written to date the most thorough biography of his political career,[54] sums up the man and his achievement thus:

> His generation would not be walking about when much of the mores would change; . . . But his resistance to the formulae of his own time was real, and in areas, mildly wild; and it made others put up with his By-God bridge bidding, and his sometimes loneliness. For he was the very best they had, and he was very, very good.[55]

Manley's political career, though, far from being a success story, was characterized by many serious difficulties and defeats. In his thirty-odd years of political service (for which he had sacrificed a brilliant career as a lawyer) his party occupied the seat of government for only seven years (1955–62). The portrait that emerges is of a patriot who endured a number of failures, disappointments and compromises without ever losing the commitment and will to struggle for the larger cause of national emancipation. It is in this very capacity of the older Manley that Walcott finds and affirms the quality of leadership necessary in the region.

The son's spirit ripens towards that of his father in a scene rendered in the uniquely naturalistic/domestic modes of the Walcott epiphany since *Another Life* (as in the irradiated "green simplicities" at the end of "The Schooner Flight"). It is a familiar moment of the waking day, and its ordinary, domestic images and effects are imbued with a quality of radiance reminiscent of the similarly familiar scene of "Anna Awaking":

> he dressed, went down to breakfast,
> and sitting again at the mahogany surface
> of the breakfast table, its dark hide as polished
> as the sheen of mares, saw his father's face
> and his own face blent there, . . .

(CP, 393)

The mythic undertones of that union are quietly sounded in the contained lyricism of the passage. These familiar details of the breakfast scene are, at the same time, carefully chosen, recognizable emblems and insignia associated with the Manley family. The surface of polished mahogany evokes the famous sculptures of Edna Manley, outstanding in her own right; the "sheen of mares" alludes to the horses reared and enjoyed by the Manleys at Drumblair. Horses have assumed the status of a kind of heraldry in the personal stories of the Manleys. They inspired Edna Manley's celebrated sculpture "Horse of the Morning", the title echoed in Vic Reid's biography of Norman Manley, *The Horses of the Morning*. Typically, too, Walcott celebrates in these naturalistic motifs of mahogany and horses, the products and emblems which root the talents and creativity of these gifted parents in the elementals of their native landscape. Reflecting and framing the face of the older Manley, they connote properties which immortalize the durable value of his virtues, and affirm the lasting glow of his shining example.

Walcott's fictionalized Manley, his understanding and acceptance of his onerous commitment deepened in his passage through this ordeal, now takes a full-scale and intensive appraisal of the Caribbean region to which he belongs. Walcott's own perspectives are very much present in those of his protagonist for this concluding testimony on the identity and destiny of the region. The appraisal begins with a pragmatic review of its material reality in the global, international scheme of things. The image, at that immediate level, is of a tiny chain of islands, consigned to their obscure, insalubrious place in the backyard of the major imperialist powers, past and present:

> What was the Caribbean? A green pond mantling
> behind the Great House columns of Whitehall,
> behind the Greek façades of Washington,

> *(CP,* 393)

That forlorn image of their historical, geopolitical reality leads right back, in true Walcottian fashion, to a reflection on the geography and origins of these islands in natural history. They come from one common geological source in the Caribbean seabed, the subterranean bond that underlies their primary identity as one archipelago. Surfacing from that bond, they appear on the face of the sea like a trail of turtles that have mounted each other to engender the numerous, tinier islets in tow, presenting altogether the sad aspect of a fragile, hapless trek in the open Atlantic.

It is in response to this hapless image of the chain of islands – on both the international and the cosmic map – that the Walcott/Manley consciousness is touched into a profound empathy with the natural pull of its peoples back through "magnetic memory" to their ancestral sources:

> they yearned for Africa,
> they were lemmings drawn by magnetic memory
> to an older death, . . .
>
> . . . .
> Yes, he could understand their natural direction

> *(CP,* 393)

The discourse comes to a critical juncture at this point: the question of the place of Old World ancestries in the shaping of a native identity, to which Walcott returns again and again. It is important to get the perspective in this reflection right. Consistent with the narrative context of Jamaica as case history, the particular ancestry identified is the Africa of the black masses of sufferers and victims, represented in this text by the Rastafarians; it is also the representative ancestry of the black majority of the Caribbean people, to which Walcott belongs. But Walcott is making a point which applies to all the peoples of the various diasporas that comprise the Caribbean setting, given the prevailing ideological tendency to give primacy to Old World, parent ancestries in staking the claim to separate ethnic identities. (See chapter 22, *AL.*) He reiterates his firmly held belief that the route through rehabilitation of these parent ancestries, or, in effect, the consolidation of their legacies in the New World environment, offers no panacea or salvation: "they were lemmings drawn by magnetic memory / to an older death".[56] This older death (the New World has developed its own) alludes to the chronic failings of Old World systems and traditions, which were themselves the source of the breakdowns that presaged the diasporas into the New World.

It is as if the contemplation of the final futility of this "magnetic pull" backwards brings Walcott's protagonist face to face with the formidable challenge of a truly liberating change, confronting him anew with the failings within the society that aggravate the problem. The pain and frustration provoke a deeply troubled consciousness to the imploding outcry of a "silent scream". That silent scream, echoing a powerful motif encountered earlier in the poem, becomes a resounding climax to the narrative. It is an inner outcry presaged by the perception of the radical leap necessary to redirect the consciousness of a people to their "second birth". For the Manley persona undergoing and comprehending its awsome imperative, it is a leap equal in the urgency of its agony and its power to the postemancipation upheaval which had initiated the change from the earlier extremes of colonial oppression:

> He cried out at the turtles as one screams at children
> with the anger of love, it was the same scream
> which, in his childhood, had reversed an epoch
> that had bent back the leaves of his star-apple kingdom,
> made streams race uphill, pulled the water wheel backwards
>
> (CP, 394)

That very outcry, at the same time, breaks into the light of that leap into a liberating consciousness (like the whitening flash of the leaping Caribs) – revealing its spiritual possibilities and imperatives.

Manley arrives at the culmination of his journey to maturity in the realization of the core truths comprehended in this leap. Importantly, it is enacted as a collective maturity shared by the leader and his society/constituency, binding them together. The final section (15) presents these resolutions. The narrative takes on a complex, allegorical ordering which links Manley, the Rastafarians ("the men with barbed-wire beards"), and the "woman in black" (the figure of the muse of revolution), who resurfaces at this point. That muse figure, as we saw earlier, represents the call of the victims and sufferers to an ethos of armed resistance and reprisal; and as such, she has remained a lurking, troubling presence for Manley – like "a bat that hung day and night / in the back of his brain" (*CP*, 389). The muse figure appropriately reappears here in the role of intermediary/conduit between him and the "men with barbed-wire beards". As it reaches them through her ears/muse, what they as under-dogs hear in that cry are the harsh, disruptive strains of outrage and violence: "the pitched shriek of silence". But the leap in consciousness consummated in that silent scream attains to a revelatory moment which bears the opposite of the disruptive, destructive signals of the "pitched shriek of silence". The silence it reaches is the silence of a deep, numinous moment of enlightenment, which, like Eliot's glimpse of timelessness in *Four Quartets,* comes only in rare flashes when the veil is lifted:

> Star-apples rained to the ground in that silence,
> the silence was the green of cities undersea,
> and the silence lasted for half an hour
> in that single second, a seashell silence, resounding
> with silence, and the men with barbed-wire beards saw
> in that creak of light that was made between
> the noises of the world . . .

(CP, 394–95)

The movement of thought in this passage is complex, combining the rationale of the bond between Manley and the Rastafarians, and the visionary intima-tions of this moment of enlightenment. To misunderstand it is to miss the resolution and meaning of this important poem. It represents, first, the vision of "another life"/light which Manley as leader would share with his society, his own enlightenment simultaneously embracing that of the society – its constituency of sufferers and victims – he would see thus enlightened. So that it is the Rastafarians, arch-representatives of the suffering and its answering "dread", that come into the foreground as the special recipients of the vision of the earthly kingdom, and its moment of upliftment.

The other feature vital to our understanding of the whole is that the meaning of this enlightenment turns on a paradoxical dynamic similar to that of the illuminatory flash of the leaping Caribs. The leap which gives access to that "creak of light" is simultaneous with what is sounded in its resounding, silent scream – the awesome reality of becoming grounded in the conditions of our earthly destiny, its wounds and afflictions; just as, with "one scream of bounding lace", the Sauteurs' leap into light was simultaneously their "fall" in purposive surrender to the burden of mortality. The "creak of light" that breaks from that other quality of silence signals a ripening of consciousness, intimated in the somewhat enigmatic line: "Star-apples rained to the ground in that silence". It is the bountiful raining to ground of star-apples – the symbol of the millennial dream of a national transformation – the ripening/falling of that dream into a terrestrial vision at one with the deeper harmony of this numinous silence (carrying also the lingering echoes of becoming grounded in the paradoxical realities of our earthly condition). What is glimpsed in that "creak of light" is the miracle of the creative, organic life-principle and its elation, immanent and alive in the surrounding natural world, and continuous through our own human sphere in our native bond with the natural. It means, especially for those among the most dispossessed of the earth, the perception of the natural inheritance of this innate creative capacity on one's own native ground – that is, of the ultimate sources of empowerment within the self. Walcott himself puts the message this way in *Remembrance,* commenting on the theme of obscurity and achievement in Gray's "Elegy": "it doesn't matter where you're born, how obscure you are, that fame and fortune are contained within you. Your body is the earth in which it springs and dies. And it's the humble people of this world . . . that he's concerned about" (*Remembrance and Pantomime,* 86–87).

Reaching the consciousness of the "humble" and dispossessed, the deep harmony of the silence of this "creak of light" suspends the noises so prevalent in their world to illuminate, in the process, a related truth: that the noises also confound the world of those on the other side of advantage and privilege. Walcott inserts his testimony of the insidious bond between oppressor and oppressed, and the radical nakedness that links us across all divides, as he makes a global survey of the chronic divisions that characterize our world. The paired opposites of these divisions all, finally, coincide:

> . . . and the men with barbed-wire beards saw
> in that creak of light that was made between
> the noises of the world that was equally divided
> between rich and poor, between North and South,
> between white and black, between two Americas,
> the fields of silent Zion in Parish Trelawny,
> in Parish St David, in Parish St Andrew,
> leaves dancing like children without any sound,
> in the valley of Tryall, and the white, silent roar
> of the old water wheel in the star-apple kingdom;

(CP, 395)

This vision, with its deep lyricism, is invoked in terms of the Rastafarian dream of Zion as promised land, symbolic of their yearning for the peaceable kingdom and its plenitude. Here, however, the vision of the earthly kingdom is given its local habitation and name, and existentially grounded. Finally, the realizations and meanings contained in this epiphany are extended as the truer path to self-achievement, as against the futilities of the ideology of militancy, or the pull back to Old World ancestries.

We return, at the end of this epiphany, to the concrete, domestic setting where Manley, sitting down at the breakfast table, had seen his father's face reflected in his own. Resurfacing from the inwardness of his culminating vision back to the real-life scene, he now faces the break of a new day with a smile (by contrast with his earlier recoil from daylight and its avalanche of noises). Wearing that smile, his features and demeanour show a refreshed spirit, as he "crack[s] the day open and [begins] his egg", – settling down to the work of the day with all its difficulties. (As Walcott himself would observe, the break of day, the breaking of the egg, and breaking-the-fast of the preceding night rhyme and echo each other for one essential meaning.) The allegoric ordering of the triangular relationship between Manley, the Rastafarians, and the muse of revolution remains operative. That smile, signal of the rekindling of his spirit and purpose, is subtly reflected in the features of the muse figure:

> and the woman's face, had a smile been decipherable
> in that map of parchment so rivered with wrinkles,
> would have worn the same smile with which he now
> cracked the day open and began his egg.

> (*CP*, 395)

The hints of the play of that smile in her time- and pain-worn features signify a humanizing change – an easing of the bitterness, and the dread of the terrifying, unfeeling visage she has worn until now. It is in the spirit of this deeply internalized smile, with its modulations of a residual elegiac wisdom, that a now truly mature and ripened Manley renews his commitment to his difficult task and its ongoing struggle as he faces another day. Walcott, in placing the moment within the domestic scene, deftly suggests the day-to-day struggle, the ordinary, "unheroic" pace the effort must entail. His Manley, beginning with the familiar act of cracking his breakfast egg, settles down to another day's task – much as Walcott the artist, overcoming the inroads of each night's despair at the difficulty of love's labour, must return to the task of writing with each new day, refreshed in its elation.

Notes

Chapter 1

1. See Rei Terada, *Derek Walcott's Poetry: American Mimicry* (Boston: Northeastern University Press, 1992), 10.

2. Derek Walcott, *Collected Poems: 1948–1984* (New York: Farrar, Straus and Giroux, 1986), 127.

3. Terada, *American Mimicry*, 219.

4. Derek Walcott, "The Figure of Crusoe", in *Critical Perspectives on Derek Walcott*, ed. Robert Hamner (Washington, DC: Three Continents Press, 1993), 36.

5. Derek Walcott, "The Antilles: Fragments of Epic Memory", in *What the Twilight Says* (New York: Farrar, Straus and Giroux, 1998), 70.

6. William Baer, ed., *Conversations with Derek Walcott* (Jackson: University of Mississippi Press, 1996), 58.

7. Interestingly, the phrase "don't leave on the earth" is echoed in the epigraph to *Dream on Monkey Mountain* (*Dream on Monkey Mountain and Other Plays* [New York: Farrar, Straus and Giroux, 1970; London: Jonathan Cape, 1972]), which is repeated by Makak in the play: "If the moon is earth's friend, / how can we leave the earth?" The quotation is taken from an unidentified Noh play.

8. Octavio Paz, *The Bow and the Lyre*, trans. Ruth L. Simms (Austin: University of Texas Press, 1973), 218.

9. Walcott, "The Muse of History", in *What the Twilight Says*.

10. See ibid., 39; and "Laventille", *CP*, 85.

11. Edward Baugh, "The West Indian Writer and His Quarrel with History", *Tapia* 7, no. 8 (20 February 1977): 6–7.

12. James Livingston, cited in Robert Hamner, *Derek Walcott* (New York: Twayne, 1993), 64.

13. Walcott, "What the Twilight Says: An Overture", in *What the Twilight Says*.

14. In addition to Baugh's "The West Indian Writer", see the following: Lloyd Brown, "Caribbean Castaway, New World Odyssey: Derek Walcott's Poetry", *Journal of Commonwealth Literature* 11, no. 2 (December 1976): 149–59; R.D.E. Burton, "Derek Walcott and the Medusa of History", *Caliban* 3, no. 2 (1980): 3–48; Michel Fabre,

" 'Adam's Task of Giving Things Their Name': The Poetry of Derek Walcott", *New Letters* 41, no. 1 (Fall 1974): 91–107.

15. There is very little on "the pain of history" in this chapter, however.

16. John Thieme, *Derek Walcott* (Manchester: Manchester University Press, 1999), 92.

17. Terada, *American Mimicry*, 60.

18. See interview with Frank Birbalsingh, entitled "The Sea Is History", in *Frontiers of Caribbean English Literature*, ed. Frank Birbalsingh (London: Macmillan Education, 1996).

19. See analysis of "The Sea Is History" in Terada, *American Mimicry*, 168–71.

20. Terada, *American Mimicry*, 170.

21. Ibid., 171.

22. Thieme, *Derek Walcott*, 92.

23. Ibid., 93.

24. Antonio Benítez-Rojo, *The Repeating Island*, 2d edition, trans. James Maraniss (Durham: Duke University Press, 1996), 4.

25. Thieme, *Derek Walcott*, 184.

26. See Terada's commentary on Helen Vendler's critical response to Walcott in *American Mimicry*, 44–46.

Chapter 2

1. Walcott, "Twilight", 8, 27.

2. Walcott won a Rockefeller award (1958) which enabled him to study theatre at Circle in the Square, New York, under José Quintero.

3. "A Sea-Chantey" won the Guinness award for poetry in 1961.

4. See the following: Keith Alleyne, review of *Epitaph for the Young, Bim* 3, no. 11 (December 1949): 267–72; Frank Collymore, "An Introduction

to the Poetry of Derek Walcott", *Bim* 3, no. 10 (June 1949): 125–32.

5. Derek Walcott, "Leaving School", *London Magazine* 5, no. 6 (1965): 13.

6. Walcott, "Leaving School", 9.

7. See "A Letter from Brooklyn", in *CP*.

8. "Elegy" first appeared as "In My Eighteenth Year", in *25 Poems* (Port of Spain, Trinidad: Guardian Commercial Printery, 1948; Bridgetown, Barbados: Advocate, 1949).

9. Walcott, "Leaving School", 10.

10. Derek Walcott, "Meanings", *Savacou* 2 (September 1970): 51.

11. See "Prelude" in Derek Walcott, *In a Green Night* (London: Jonathan Cape, 1962).

12. Walcott, "Twilight", 27.

13. These lines inspired the title of George Lamming's first novel *In the Castle of My Skin* (London: Michael Joseph, 1953).

14. Derek Walcott, "Sambo Agonistes", *Bim* 4, no. 15 (1951): 210.

15. See Derek Walcott, *Epitaph for the Young* (Bridgetown, Barbados: Advocate, 1949), Canto III, and "Margaret Verlieu Dies", in *Poems* (Kingston, Jamaica: Kingston City Printery, 1951).

16. The theme finally evolves into Makak's dream of the white goddess in *Dream on Monkey Mountain*.

17. In hindsight the phrase "dream of reason", taken from Goya, carries the sardonic echoes of the original. But Walcott is, first, recalling the early time when this "dream of reason" represented a genuine ideal.

18. C.L.R. James, "Here's a Poet Who Sees the Real West Indies", review of *In a Green Night, Trinidad Guardian*, 6 May 1962, 5.

19. First cited in the blurb on the dust jacket of *In a Green Night*.

20. See Revd C. Jesse, "The Great Castries Fire", in *Outlines of St Lucia's History* (Castries, St Lucia: St Lucia Archaeological and Historical Society, 1970), 51 ff.; and Derek Walcott, "Leaving School", *London Magazine* 5, no. 6 (1965): 4–5.

21. Dylan Thomas, *Collected Poems 1934–1953* (London: J.M. Dent and Sons, 1988).

22. Cited in editor's "Notebook", *Bim* 7, no. 26 (January–June 1958): 65.

23. John Figueroa, "Some Subtleties of the Isle: A Commentary on Certain Aspects of Derek Walcott's Sonnet Sequence, *Tales of the Islands*", *World Literature Written in English* 15, no. 1 (April 1976): 195–219.

24. *Bim* 7, no. 26 (January–June 1958): 67–70.

25. For a description of *kélé*, see Harold Simmons, "Notes on Folklore in St Lucia", in *Iouanaloa: Recent Writing from St Lucia*, ed. Edward Brathwaite (Castries, St Lucia: Department of Extra-Mural Studies, St Lucia, 1963), 45–47.

26. See Figueroa, "Some Subtleties of the Isle", 222.

27. Ibid., 191.

28. Walcott left St Lucia for university in Jamaica in 1950.

29. "Tales, Chapter X" reappears in its entirety in *Another Life* (*CP*, 257).

30. This motif of aerial flight reappears in "The Gulf" (*The Gulf and Other Poems* [London: Jonathan Cape, 1969]), and "The Light of the World" (*The Arkansas Testament* [New York: Farrar, Straus and Giroux, 1987]).

31. John Donne, "For Whom the Bell Tolls", *Devotions Upon Emergent Occasions* 7 in *Selected Prose* (Oxford: Clarendon Press, 1967), 100–101.

32. Thomas Traherne, *Centuries of Meditation* (London: Dobbel, 1908).

33. Joan Bennet, *4 Metaphysical Poets* (Cambridge: Cambridge University Press, 1964), 6.

34. Stewart Brown, "The Apprentice", in *The Art of Derek Walcott*, ed. Stewart Brown (Bridgend, Wales: Dufour, 1991), 30.

35. Joan Bennet, *4 Metaphysical Poets*, 5.

36. See Jesse, *Outlines of St Lucia's History*.

37. See the following works on the history of slavery in Jamaica: M. Craton and G. Greenland, *Searching for the Invisible Man: Slaves and Plantation Life in Jamaica* (Cambridge, Mass.: Harvard University Press, 1978); J.H. Parry, P.M. Sherlock and A. Maingot, *A Short History of the West Indies* (London: Macmillan, 1956).

38. C.L.R. James's *The Black Jacobins* was the source of Walcott's interest and inspiration to write about the Haitian revolutionary leaders. Despite the strong sociohistorical and Marxist approach in that book, his models for the Haitian heroes were drawn primarily from Elizabethan and Jacobean tragedy (Derek Walcott, *Henri Christophe: A Chronicle in Seven Scenes* [Bridgetown, Barbados: Advocate, 1952]). See his own comments in "Twilight", 11.

39. Walcott, "Twilight", 6.

Chapter 3

1. Daniel Defoe, *Robinson Crusoe* (Harmondsworth: Penguin, 1965).

2. Derek Walcott, "Walcott on Walcott", interview with Dennis Scott, *Caribbean Quarterly* 14, nos. 1 and 2 (March–June 1968): 81–82.

3. Walcott, "Twilight", 23.

4. Walcott, "Walcott on Walcott", 78.

5. Transcript of Walcott interview with Bill Moyers, *World of Ideas*, no. 137 (New York, Public Affairs Television Inc., 1 Nov. 1988), 3.

6. Walcott, "The Figure of Crusoe".

7. Michael McKeon, *Origins of the English Novel 1600–1740* (Baltimore: Johns Hopkins University Press, 1987).

8. Denis Donoghue, "Waiting for the End", review of *The Gulf, New York Review of Books* 16, no. 8 (6 May 1971): 27.

9. From Alejo Carpentier, *The Lost Steps* (Harmondsworth: Penguin, 1968), 66.

10. Derek Walcott, "The Caribbean: Culture or Mimicry?", *Journal of Interamerican Studies and World Affairs* 16, no. 1 (February 1974): 3–13. Also in Hamner, *Critical Perspectives*, 51–57.

11. Walcott, "Twilight", 13.

12. Ernst Cassirer, *Language and Myth*, trans. Susanne Langer (New York: Harper and Brothers, 1946), 84 ff.

13. Chinua Achebe's comment: "I have been given this language and I intend to use it." Cited in Gerald Moore, *The Chosen Tongue* (London: Longmans, Green and Co, 1969), xxiii.

14. J.A. Froude, *The English in the West Indies, or The Bow of Ulysses* (London: Longmans, 1888), 306. (The same passage also heads V.S. Naipaul's *The Middle Passage*.)

15. J.J. Thomas, *Froudacity: West Indian Fables by James Anthony Froude* (London: T.F. Unwin, 1889).

16. Rhoda Reddock, ed., *Ethnic Minorities in Caribbean Societies* (St Augustine, Trinidad: Institute of Social and Economic Research, University of the West Indies, 1996).

17. Walcott, "The Figure of Crusoe", 12–13.

18. The poem has echoes of the confessional, manic turmoil of Robert Lowell in "Night Sweat" (Robert Lowell, *Selected Poems* [London: Faber, 1965]).

19. Walcott, "Metamorphoses", in *The Gulf and Other Poems*.

20. Derek Walcott, *Ti-Jean and His Brothers* in *Dream on Monkey Mountain and Other Plays* (New York: Farrar, Straus and Giroux, 1970; London: Jonathan Cape, 1972).

21. Claude McKay, *Selected Poems* (New York: Bookman Associates, 1953).

22. Derek Walcott, interview by author, 8 July 1974.

23. See Derek Walcott, "The Schooner Flight" (*The Star-Apple Kingdom* [New York: Farrar, Straus and Giroux, 1979]), and *Omeros* (New York: Farrar, Straus and Giroux, 1990).

24. He returns to this concern about giving his native St Lucia nothing in "The Light of the World" (*Arkansas Testament*). There, however, it is a misgiving reconciled and a "nothing" seen in a positive light.

25. Garth St Omer's four novels are *A Room on the Hill* (London: Faber and Faber, 1968); *Shades of Grey* (London: Faber and Faber, 1968); *Nor Any Country* (London: Faber and Faber, 1969); and *J-, Black Bam and the Masqueraders* (London: Faber and Faber, 1972).

26. It is still the Walcott of "Prelude", the opening poem of *In a Green Night*:

I with legs crossed along the daylight, watch
The variegated fists of clouds that gather over
The uncouth features of this, my prone island

(CP, 3)

27. Ted Hughes, "Hawk Roosting", in *Lupercal* (London: Faber and Faber, 1960).

28. "Tarpon" won the Boreston Mountain Poetry Award for "a best poem" of 1963.

29. Walcott was engaged in extensive reviewing as art critic for the *Trinidad Guardian* during this period, and did several pieces on Harris's work.

30. William Henry Hudson, *Green Mansions* (1904; reprint, New York: Watts, 1966); Denis Williams, *Other Leopards* (London: Heinemann, 1963); Alejo Carpentier, *The Lost Steps* (Harmondsworth: Penguin, 1968).

31. Wilson Harris, *Palace of the Peacock* (1960; reprint, London: Faber and Faber, 1988); *The Far Journey of Oudin* (London: Faber and Faber, 1961); *The Whole Armour* (London: Faber and Faber, 1962); *The Secret Ladder* (Faber and Faber, 1963); *Heartland* (London: Faber and Faber, 1964). Subsequent references to *Palace of the Peacock* refer to the 1988 edition and appear parenthetically in the text.

32. Wilson Harris, "History, Fable and Myth in the Caribbean and Guianas", *Caribbean Quarterly* 16, no. 2 (June 1970): 32.

33. One needs to note, however, that apotheosis in Harris has its distinct, liberating accesses in its insistence on fluidity/openness and continuous risk between "opposite" states – between void and plenitude, wound and beatitude – as a means of breaking free of the fixed absolutes of older epistemologies.

34. *Dream on Monkey Mountain,* Walcott's major statement play, is being written about the same time as *The Gulf and Other Poems.* A great deal of the experience and meanings of that play informs this journey through the interior.

35. In *Eternity to Season* (Georgetown, Guyana: Master Printery, 1954), it is also Harris's task to recover "the lost concept, man".

36. See Lloyd Brown, *West Indian Poetry* (London: Heinemann, 1984), 133 ff. Brown emphasizes this personal odyssey as the core of Walcott's achievement as a poet.

37. Walcott is probably prompted to this climax for his protagonist – the contemplation of the leap down the waterfall – by the legend of Kaieteur Falls. According to the legend, Kaie, an Amerindian chief, plunged down the waterfall in his corial as an act of human sacrifice. He sought thereby to placate the god Makonaima, and earn for his tribe relief from a spell of severe attacks by the warring Caribs. See A.J. Seymour's poem "The Legend of Kaieteur", in *Selected Poems* (Guyana: B.G. Lithographic Co., 1965).

38. Malcolm Schofield and Martha Craven Nussbaum, eds., *Language and Logos: Studies in Ancient Greek Philosophy* (London: Cambridge University Press, 1982), 5–7.

39. Joseph Brodsky, "On Derek Walcott", *New York Review of Books* 30, no. 17 (10 November 1983): 39–41.

40. See n. 32 above.

41. Jorge Luis Borges, "Tlön, Uqbar, Orbis Tertius", in *Labyrinths* (Harmondsworth: Penguin, 1971), 42.

42. Walcott, interview by author, 8 July 1974.

43. Derek Walcott, "An Incident, an Epiphany" (typescript [essay written on a Borges incident which took place at a conference of Latin American writers], 1972).

44. Gordon Rohlehr, "Withering into Truth", review of *The Gulf and Other Poems, Trinidad Guardian,* 10 December 1969.

45. The present version of the line comes from *The Gulf and Other Poems*: "love or literature". In *Collected Poems* it reads: "love of literature".

46. For poems that repeat this theme, see Derek Walcott, "Cold Spring Harbour" (*The Gulf and Other Poems*), and "God Rest Ye Merry, Gentlemen" (*The Castaway* [London: Jonathan Cape, 1965]).

Chapter 4

1. See the following works on the Black Power uprising in Trinidad: Raoul Pantin, *Black Power Day* (Port of Spain, Trinidad: Hatuey Productions, 1990); Lloyd Best, *Black Power and National Reconstruction* (Port of Spain, Trinidad: Tapia House, 1974).

2. These essays were first published as follows: "What the Twilight Says", in *Dream on Monkey Mountain and Other Plays,* 3–40. "The Muse of History", in *Is Massa Day Dead?,* ed. Orde Coombs (New York: Doubleday Anchor, 1974), 1–27. All references to these essays are from *What the Twilight Says.*

3. Walcott, "Twilight", 4. *Another Life* also opens with this image of twilight.

4. Walcott, "Twilight", 11.

5. Derek Walcott, interview with Raoul Pantin, "Any Revolution Based on Race Is Suicidal", *Caribbean Contact* 1, no. 8 (August 1973): 14, 16.

6. Walcott, "Twilight", 9.

7. Ibid., 16.

8. Walcott, "Muse", 40.

9. See chapter 3, n. 9.

10. Aimé Césaire, "Memorial for Louis Delgrès", in *Ferraments* (Paris: Seuil, 1960).

11. The quality of lyricism in both these poets differs from Walcott's. While lyricism in Neruda and Césaire is charged with a spirit of resistance, Walcott tends more towards the numinous.

12. See "A Far Cry From Africa" (*Green Night*). The bond with Africa is intensively explored in *Omeros.*

13. Walcott, "Twilight", 9.

14. Walcott, "Muse", 45.

15. See *Another Life, CP,* 167.

16. Walcott, "Muse", 47.

17. The early poem "Bronze" (*Green Night*) is a classic projection of Walcott's concept of the renewal and meeting of the Old World ancestors in the primal territory of the New World.

18. Walcott, "Muse", 64.

19. The term first appears in "Homecoming: Anse La Raye" (*The Gulf and Other Poems*); and Dunstan St Omer/Gregorias is hailed as a "black Greek" in the concluding lines of *Another Life.*

20. See this comment in Walcott's review of the 1984 reissue of *Beyond a Boundary*: "In his long life Mr James has arrived, through this book, at a calm center. His calm is that of a meridian between two oceans, two cultures, even between radical and conservative politics, without mere neutrality" (*New York Times Book Review,* 25 March 1984, 35).

21. See Walcott's discussion of the personality of Trinidad in "On Choosing Port of Spain", in *David Frost Introduces Trinidad and Tobago,* ed. David Frost (London: André Deutsch, 1975).

22. See Walcott, "Muse", 49, and "Twilight", 8.
23. Wilson Harris, "History, Fable and Myth".
24. Tales of Ti-Jean also occur in the French Caribbean islands and Louisiana (United States).
25. In her book *Divine Horsemen* (New York: McPherson, 1970), Maya Deren rightly recognizes the predominance of the African religious intelligence, and the assimilation of other religious traditions, notably the Christian, in the composition of Vodun. She focuses, though, on the New World process at work in this indigenous form, especially the translation of African ancestral worship into the ritual of making the dead serve the living (in rites of atonement before release), and its culmination in the possession ritual. This characteristic adaptation and its unique achievement, Deren recognizes, met the urgent necessity for spiritual empowerment to overcome the extremes of bondage and oppression.
26. Gordon Rohlehr, *Pathfinder* (Port of Spain, Trinidad: G. Rohlehr, 1981), 46.
27. Edward Brathwaite, "Jazz and the West Indian Novel", in *Roots* (Havana: Casa de las Americas, 1986), 55–110.
28. Gordon Rohlehr, "Possession as Metaphor: Lamming's *Season of Adventure*", *Journal of West Indian Literature* 5, nos. 1 and 2 (August 1992): 25. Also in Gordon Rohlehr, *The Shape of that Hurt* (Port of Spain, Trinidad: Longman, 1992), 66–96.
29. Walcott, "Muse", 43.
30. Ibid., 37.
31. Dates of publication for the three works later published as *The Arri-* *vants* are as follows: *Rights of Passage* (Oxford: Oxford University Press, 1967); *Masks* (Oxford: Oxford University Press, 1968); and *Islands* (Oxford: Oxford University Press, 1969).
32. Walcott, "Muse", 43.
33. See Patricia Ismond, "Walcott versus Brathwaite", *Caribbean Quarterly* 17, nos. 3 and 4 (December 1971).
34. Derek Walcott, " 'Rights of Passage': Drama in Itself", *Trinidad Guardian,* 25 April 1973: 5.
35. Walcott, "Muse", 53.
36. Walcott, "Twilight", 29.
37. Ibid., 16.
38. See the section on *The Star-Apple Kingdom* in chapter 6.
39. See Derek Walcott, "Tropic Zone", in *Midsummer* (New York: Farrar, Straus and Giroux, 1984).
40. Walcott, "Muse", 40.
41. Walcott, "Twilight", 35.
42. The "long hot summers" describe a period of black uprising in the United States from 1965 to 1968. See Harvard Sitkoff, *The Struggle for Black Equality 1954–1980* (New York: Hill and Wang, 1981).
43. The motif makes an early appearance in "We, Being all Islands in Air" (*25 Poems*).
44. Walcott first explores this image of the sea as amnesiac divide in *The Castaway.* See "Laventille".
45. The following comment appears in an extract from "American without America" (unpublished book-length essay), Walcott Collection 1957–81: Poetry and Prose, University of the West Indies Library, St Augustine: "As for the South I looked at it in an intellectual arrogance, as a sea of stupidity where Negroes had the privilege of contemptuous servility. An endemic flaw that no art could re-

deem, not Faulkner's novels. . . . I did not trust any art that could absorb or dramatise prejudice." (Entry dated 2 June 1980.)

46. Walcott, "Any Revolution Based on Race", 16.

47. See tributes to Ché Guevara in "Che" and "Elegy" (*The Gulf and Other Poems*).

48. Walcott's most searching analysis of militancy as ideology occurs in the portrait of the muse of revolution in "The Star-Apple Kingdom" (*CP*, 388–89).

49. The quarrel with North America for its betrayal of the dream of "democratic vistas" is reiterated throughout the corpus. An early expression of this occurs in "A Village Life" (*The Castaway*), and he returns to it in 1988 in a television interview with Bill Moyers (*World of Ideas*).

50. So far, Robert Hamner seems to be the only critic who sees "Elegy" as beginning with a response to Che Guevara's death. See Hamner, *Derek Walcott*, 73.

51. Walt Whitman's "When Lilacs Last in the Dooryard Bloom'd" (*Leaves of Grass* [New York: Bantam, 1983]) is an elegy on the death of Abraham Lincoln.

52. Walcott shows this appreciation of Kennedy's effort in "The Gulf" as, flying out of Texas, he looks down on Love Field. Kennedy's assassination, which occurred on his drive from that airport, acquires emblematic significance in the poem as a "wound" received on "Love Field".

53. Walcott's "whispering, rag-bound feet" seems to be a reference to the Trail of Tears, although he speaks of the Cheyennes instead of the Cherokees, who were the tribe concerned.

54. These same insights and views inform his diagnosis of North American society in *Omeros*.

55. See the following for a historical account of the Trinidad carnival: Errol Hill, *The Trinidad Carnival: Mandate for a National Theatre* (1972; reprint, London: New Beacon, 1997).

56. See reference to this practice in Orlando Patterson, *The Sociology of Slavery* (London: Mac Gibbon and Kee, 1967), 205.

57. Gordon Rohlehr, "Withering into Truth", *Trinidad Guardian*, 13 December 1969, 8. Rohlehr cites "Mass Man" as an example of "the vexed question of Walcott's stature as a sensitive commentator on the West Indian scene".

58. Rohlehr, "Withering into Truth", 8.

59. Walcott, "On Choosing Port of Spain", 22.

60. Walcott, chapter from "American without America".

61. Walcott, "On Choosing Port of Spain", 22.

62. Walcott, "The Caribbean: Culture or Mimicry?", 9.

63. See also Hill, *Trinidad Carnival*.

Chapter 5

1. Robert Lowell, letter to Derek Walcott, 19 February 1973, Walcott Collection 1957–81: Correspondence – Letters 1959–80, University of the West Indies Library, St Augustine.

2. Edward Baugh, *Derek Walcott: Memory as Vision: "Another Life"* (London: Longman, 1978).

3. The earlier prose version of *Another Life* is designated MS One – the designation used throughout the present text. It is lodged at the University of the West Indies Library, Mona, Jamaica.

4. See Edward Baugh, "The Poem as Autobiographical Novel: Derek Walcott's *Another Life* in Relation to Wordsworth's 'Prelude' and Joyce's 'Portrait'", in *Awakened Conscience: Studies in Commonwealth Literature,* ed. C.D. Narasimhaiah (New Delhi: Sterling Publishers, 1978), 226–35.

5. These lines first appear in MS One.

6. See closing lines of *Another Life*.

7. Walcott indicated this to the author (undated casual conversation). It is also borne out in his review of *The Gift*: "A Great Russian Novel", *Trinidad Guardian,* 19 April 1964, 15.

8. This is illustrated in the young writer's biography of Chernyshevski, the representative communist ideologue of the Russian Revolution. In reproducing it, the "author" departs from the facts of that hero's ending to create a fiction which manifests what was most real about that Chernyshevski and his fate.

9. The comment on autobiography as "supreme fiction" appears in MS One, chapter 1, 9.

10. Robert Lowell, letter to Derek Walcott, 7 August 1973, Walcott Collection 1957–81: Correspondence – Letters 1959–80, University of the West Indies Library, St Augustine.

11. Paul Breslin, " 'I Met History Once, but He Ain't Recognise Me': The Poetry of Derek Walcott", *Tri-Quarterly* 68 (Winter 1987): 179.

12. M.M. Bakhtin, "Epic and Novel", in *The Dialogic Imagination* (Austin: University of Texas Press, 1981), 14–17.

13. See MS One, 49.

14. See the following work: Raymond P. Devas, *A History of the Island of Grenada 1498–1796* (Grenada: Carenage Press, 1974).

15. For a description of the Fighting Fifth see Baugh, *Memory as Vision,* 12. B.H. Easter, *A Guide to Morne Fortune, St Lucia* (Castries, St Lucia: St Lucia Archaeological and Historical Society, 1966), 6.

16. See MS One, chapter 1, "Verandahs".

17. Thomas Craven, *A Treasury of Art Masterpieces: From the Renaissance to the Present Day* (New York: Simon and Schuster, 1939).

18. George Campbell, *First Poems* (Kingston, Jamaica: City Printery, 1945).

19. Walcott, "Leaving School", 6.

20. Caravaggio's *The Conversion of St Paul* appears in Craven, *Treasury of Art Masterpieces*.

21. The motto depicted on the Old Badge of St Lucia: "A Safe Harbour for Ships".

22. His native protagonists in *Omeros* also have parallels in Homer's *Iliad*.

23. In MS One, chapter 1, he makes this response to Craven's book: "there was his heaven! / the visible emanation [sic] of his soul".

24. MS One, chapter 1, 3.

25. Walcott has also exploited the "metaphysical" irony of this inversion in "Negatives" (*The Gulf and Other Poems*).

26. Walcott, "Leaving School", 11.

27. See the following for an account of the life and achievement of St Omer: Father Patrick Anthony, "The Silent Revolution", *Caribbean Contact* 5, no. 5 (August 1977); Caroline Popovic, "Hail Mary", *Caribbean Beat* 13 (Spring 1995): 54–58.

28. The most outstanding of these is the altarpiece at the Roseau Valley church, celebrated in Walcott's poem of the same name (*Sea Grapes*).

29. MS One, 49. Walcott writes: "How many others did I know who were, to write stupidly, self-combustible, who could ignite their imaginations at will? Even if the fuel were liquor?"

30. Cited in Angela Livingstone, ed., *Pasternak and Creativity* (Cambridge: Cambridge University Press, 1985), 148.

31. Entitled "The Act of Painting" in MS One. See Baugh, *Memory as Vision*, 39.

32. See *CP*, 262 (*Another Life*, chapter 18).

33. See Clara Rose de Lima, "Painting and the Shadow of Van Gogh", in *The Art of Derek Walcott*, ed. Stewart Brown (Bridgend, Wales: Dufour, 1991), 171–90.

34. Van Gogh is reputed to have been working on *Crows Over the Wheatfield* at the time that he shot himself.

35. The cliffs were named La Morne des Sauteurs after their historic leap.

36. Walcott, "Twilight", 4.

37. See Easter, *A Guide to Morne Fortune*.

38. See Jesse, *Outlines of St. Lucia's History*; H.H. Breen, *St Lucia: Historical, Statistical and Descriptive* (London: Frank Cass, 1970); Sir Frederick Treves, *The Cradle of the Deep* (London: Smith, Elder and Co., 1908).

39. James A. Williamson, *The History of the British Empire and Commonwealth: a History for Senior Forms* (1908; reprint, London: Macmillan, 1964).

40. See David B. Gaspard, "The Most Noxious of Our Islands", *Voice of St Lucia*, Independence supplement, 18 February 1979, 44.

41. Allister Macmillan, ed., *The West Indies* (1912; reprint, London: W.H. and L. Collingridge, 1938), 408.

42. Lamming also deals with the Sauteurs incident in *Of Age and Innocence* (London: Michael Joseph, 1958), 96–99.

43. See Baugh, *Memory as Vision*, 44: "the heart nonetheless will yearn for examples of heroism in the past."

44. See Baugh's comment on Walcott's transference of this ritual of "combing his hair" from the example of the Spartans preparing for Thermopylae (*Memory as Vision*, 46).

45. Walcott, "Leaving School", 11.

46. See "The Great Castries Fire", in Jesse, *Outlines of St Lucia's History*.

47. Walcott, "Leaving School", 11.

48. Ibid., 10.

49. Walcott, "Walcott on Walcott", 78.

50. Walcott, "Leaving School", 11.

51. See Ronald Hingley on Akhmatova in *Nightingale Fever: Russian Poets in Revolution* (London: Weidenfeld and Nicolson, 1982).

52. This motif bears echoes of Matthew Arnold's "To Marguerite". Walcott began MS One with a verse from Arnold's poem which sounded this theme of separation/"estrangement".

53. Walcott makes the following entry in his memos: "not time, but art that falls in love with Time" (Walcott Collection 1957–81: Diaries, Memo Books, University of the West Indies Library, St Augustine).

54. See Walcott, *Omeros*.

55. Paolo Milano, ed., *The Divine Comedy* in *The Portable Dante*, trans. L. Binyon (Harmondsworth: Penguin, 1975), 541–42.

56. This motif of "litheness" also appears in *Another Life*, chapter 8 (*CP*, 191); and *Another Life*, chapter 15 (*CP*, 239).

57. See chapter 3, n. 38.

58. "Oddjob, a Bull Terrier" (*Sea Grapes*) deals with this theme of love "blest / deepest by loss".

59. Chapter 22, i–vi was first published in the *New Yorker* (28 October 1972, 36–37) as "The Muse of History at Rampanalgas".

60. See Walcott, MS One entry titled "Pompes Funèbres", dated 8 May 1966.

61. Walcott, MS One, "Pompes Funebres".

62. Simmons was a member of the St Lucia Historical and Archaeological Society.

63. Walcott, "Leaving School", 10.

64. *Noa Noa* (1894) is Paul Gauguin's account of his personal life and experience as an artist in the Polynesian islands.

65. Vincent Van Gogh, *Dear Theo*, ed. Irving Stone (New York: Doubleday, 1937). *Dear Theo* also haunts this exile.

66. Walcott, MS One, "Pompes Funèbres" (entry dated 8 May 1966).

67. Sören Kierkegaard, *Fear and Trembling* and *The Sickness Unto Death*, trans. Walter Lowrie (New York: Doubleday, 1954), 151.

68. See Harold Simmons, "Notes on Folklore in St Lucia".

69. Walcott repeats an earlier sketch of Simmons presented in Book One, chapter 1 (*CP*, 147).

70. "Msieu Harry Simmons" was their respectful way of addressing him in the French creole.

71. See n. 50 above.

72. The slum, Conway, has since been razed and the area is now the site of modernized public buildings.

73. The banana industry is the mainstay of the island's economy.

74. See Walcott, *Dream,* the "Guyana" sequence, and "Air".

75. At the time of this author's visit (April 1996) the "small red shop" was in a state of disrepair and barricaded with galvanize sheets. According to the villagers it had been in existence and owned by the same Chinese family for over a hundred years.

76. See these lines in "Guyana VI: A Georgetown Journal": "the precise exhilaration / with which the heron's foot pronounces 'earth' ".

77. After the indentured East Indians, a small contingent of Chinese came into Trinidad to meet the demand for labour created by the emancipation of the African slaves (beginning in 1838). See Walton Look Lai, *The Chinese in the West Indies, 1806–1995* (Kingston, Jamaica: The Press, University of the West Indies, 1998).

78. This linking of the methods of conventional history with the principle of accountancy also appears in "On Choosing Port of Spain", where he writes: "There is nothing exciting about the stock-taking of merchants, and the history of Port of Spain is possibly as interesting as some Portuguese retailers calculations on brown paper, the penny-pinching inventory of creoles" (p. 21).

79. Saltfish was brought into the West Indies as cheap fare to feed the slaves.

80. Derek Walcott, "Reflections on Omeros", in *The Poetics of Derek Walcott: Intertextual Perspectives*, ed. Gregson Davis, *South Atlantic Review* 96, no. 2 (Spring 1997): 237.

81. See "Guyana V: A Map of the Continent": "between them curl the vigorous, rotting leaves" (*CP*, 118).

82. Walcott makes this comment in MS One, 45: "As botanists make no distinctions of beauty in the anatomy of

plants, the poet, a natural scientist, makes no distinctions in the beauty of humankind."

83. See Paul Breslin in a paper entitled "Shabine Among the Fishmongers: Derek Walcott and the Suspicion of Essences" (typescript, 1995).

Chapter 6

1. A phrase from "Return to D'Ennery, Rain" (*Green Night*).
2. Edward Baugh, "The Poet's Fiction of Self: Perspectives for Viewing 'The Schooner *Flight*'" (paper presented at the fourteenth annual Conference on West Indian Literature, 1995). Also published as "The Poet's Fiction of Self", in Davis, *The Poetics of Derek Walcott: Intertextual Perspectives*.
3. An Eastern Caribbean creole word for bribery, fraud and corruption.
4. Patricia Ismond, "Walcott's Later Drama: From *Joker* to *Remembrance*", *Review of International English Literature* 16, no. 3 (July 1985): 89–101.
5. The Nobel committee quoted from this poem in its citations on Walcott's achievement. It is also the main poem singled out by Seamus Heaney for an article on Walcott: "The Language of Exile", *Parnassus: Poetry in Review* 8, no. 1 (Fall–Winter 1979): 5–11.
6. "Shabine" is a French creole word used in many of the Eastern Caribbean islands with a French colonial legacy.
7. See Victor Questel, review of *The Star-Apple Kingdom, Trinidad Guardian*, 3 June 1978, 9. Questel writes: "Now the mulatto and the Shabine have never been exactly one and the

same thing. The mulatto is half-white and respectable, while the Shabine is a "red-nigger", the term has derogatory connotations." (NB: 'Questel' is misspelt 'Quesnel' in this review.)

8. Mervyn Morris, "*The Fortunate Traveller*" in *The Art of Derek Walcott*, 110.
9. Baugh, "The Poet's Fiction of Self".
10. O'Hara seems a deliberate echo of the name of John O'Halloran, an influential minister of finance in the Eric Williams government during the late 1960s and early 1970s. O'Halloran's name was associated with political corruption for his alleged involvement in a number of rackets.
11. Victor Questel also makes the plight of the vagrant a central theme in a play entitled *Two Choices,* written in September 1981. (Performed in Jamaica in 1982, and in Trinidad in 1986.)
12. Walcott married Norline Metivier in 1982.
13. "The Spoiler's Return", which appears in *The Fortunate Traveller* (1981), falls outside the chronology of what we have designated as the Caribbean phase. It stands out in this transitional volume, however, as a fully Caribbean poem.
14. For commentary on the Mighty Spoiler, see Gordon Rohlehr, *Calypso and Society in Pre-Independence Trinidad* (Port of Spain, Trinidad: G. Rohlehr, 1990), 428–523.
15. Heaney, "The Language of Exile", 6–7.
16. See Walcott, "Anna Awaking", *Another Life*.
17. One of a number of small islands off the northwest coast of Trinidad, used mainly as holiday resorts.

18. The National Joint Action Committee, a group in the vanguard of the Black Power movement, survives as the main exponent of an Africanist ideology.

19. During the Black Power uprising (1970), the militants repaired to the mountains of the Northern Range (adjoining the densely populated east-west corridor), seeking to use it as a guerrilla stronghold.

20. Aleksander Blok, *The Twelve and Other Poems*, trans. Jon Stallworthy and Peter France (London: Eyre and Spottiswoode, 1970).

21. Walcott, "Moon", in *The Gulf and Other Poems*, 12.

22. For information on the Carib community in Dominica see Rhoda Reddock, ed., *Ethnic Minorities in Caribbean Society* (St Augustine, Trinidad: Institute of Social and Economic Research, University of the West Indies, 1996).

23. Walcott, *Omeros*, 297: "because this is the true element, / water, which commemorates nothing in its stasis".

24. See commentary on "The Sea Is History" in chapter 3.

25. See discussion on the muse of history in chapter 5.

26. Walcott, "Muse", 37.

27. I am indebted to a reader of the manuscript who has pointed out that "casuarina" is the Latinized version of the name for that tree, which originates from Australia. From Walcott's argument in the text, however, it is clear that "casuarina" was for him, as for most West Indians, the more indigenized name/sound (by contrast with "cypress", for example).

28. Mary L. Alexander, " 'The Woman Within': A Quest for Masculine Wholeness in Derek Walcott's 'The Schooner *Flight*' " (paper presented at the fourteenth annual Conference on West Indian Literature, Antigua, March 1995).

29. Harris, *The Whole Armour* and *The Secret Ladder* (London: Faber and Faber, 1973), 121–23.

30. Ned Thomas, "Obsession and Responsibility", in *The Art of Derek Walcott*, ed. Stewart Brown (Bridgend, Wales: Dufour, 1991), 95.

31. Erna Brodber, *Jane and Louisa Will Soon Come Home* (London: New Beacon, 1980), 14.

32. The Rastafarians, who originate from the black depressed segments of Jamaican society, are a religious-cum-militant group who believe in the divinity of Haile Selassie of Ethiopia, and repatriation to Africa. For a brief account of the Rastafarians and their movement, see M.G. Smith, Roy Augier and Rex Nettleford, *The Rastafari Movement in Kingston, Jamaica* (Kingston, Jamaica: Institute of Social and Economic Research, University of the West Indies, 1960).

33. For analyses of Manley's experiment, see Darrel E. Levi, *Michael Manley: The Making of a Leader* (London: André Deutsch, 1989); Evelyn Huber Stephens and John D. Stephens, *Democratic Socialism in Jamaica* (London: Macmillan, 1986).

34. Manley's books include *Up the Down Escalator* (Washington, DC: Howard University Press, 1987); *A Voice at the Workplace* (London: André Deutsch, 1975); *The Politics of Change* (London: André Deutsch, 1974).

35. Christopher Arawak, *Jamaica's Michael Manley: Messiah . . . Muddler . . . or Marionette* (Miami: Sir Henry Morgan Press, 1980).

36. Carl Stone, "Running Out of Options in Jamaica", *Caribbean Review* 15, no. 3 (Winter 1987): 10.

37. Norman Manley was prime minister of Jamaica from 1955 to 1962.

38. Rachel Manley, *Drumblair* (Kingston, Jamaica: Ian Randle Publishers, 1996).

39. For a fictional account of the Morant Bay Rebellion, see Vic Reid, *New Day* (1949; reprint, London: Heinemann, 1973).

40. Walcott, *Omeros*, 296.

41. C.V. Black, *The Story of Jamaica* (London: Collins, 1965).

42. From the earliest, St Lucian phase of his career, institutionalized religion has been a primary target of protest in Walcott. See *Sea at Dauphin* (written *circa* 1952).

43. The phrase is taken from Peter Costello's title *The Heart Grown Brutal* (Dublin: Gill and Macmillan, 1977).

44. Lemuel A. Johnson, "Abeng: (Re) Calling the Body in (to) Question", in *Out of the Kumbla*, ed. Carole Boyce Davies and Elaine Savory Fido (Trenton, NJ: Africa World Press, 1990), 132. Johnson makes the following comment on the muse figure: "The female body is thus called into service as the vessel in which the body politic is (man)-made and (woman)-unmade."

45. See Patricia Ismond, "Woman as Race-Containing Symbol in Walcott's Poetry", *Journal of West Indian Literature* 8, no. 2 (April 1999): 83–89.

46. See Parry, Sherlock and Maingot, *A Short History of the West Indies*, 212–14.

47. Ibid., 260–63; Vic Reid, *The Horses of the Morning* (Kingston, Jamaica: Caribbean Authors Publishing Co., 1985), 262.

48. Another meeting between the son and the ghost of his father occurs in *Omeros*.

49. A free-trade arrangement known as Carifta came into existence between the English-speaking islands of the Eastern Caribbean in 1968. It evolved into the Caribbean Economic Union (1973), the purpose of which was to establish economic integration and functional cooperation within the region.

50. Levi, *The Making of a Leader*, 175.

51. The occupants of a block-long tenement were destroyed by a fire set by a group of fifty well-organized gunmen. Levi observes in a note on the incident that some confusion exists about the political affiliation of the Orange Street residents (Levi, *The Making of a Leader*, 171, and n. 22, chapter 16).

52. Walcott, "Muse", 43–44.

53. Rex Nettleford quotes Arthur Lewis's comment on Norman Manley: "When Mr Manley, the Prime Minister of Jamaica, went into politics he was a rich lawyer; when he left office 25 years later, he had to sell the old family home in order to provide for himself and his wife. West Africa will solve its economic problems when it starts to produce this kind of politician, but not till then." See Nettleford, *Manley and the Politics of Jamaica* (Kingston, Jamaica: Institute of Social and Economic Research, University of the West Indies, 1971), 5.

54. For another notable biography of Norman Manley, see Philip Sherlock, *Norman Manley* (London: Macmillan, 1980).

55. Reid, *The Horses of the Morning*, 377.

56. Lemmings are a species of small rodents from polar climes, vast numbers of which are drowned in mass migrations through the seas.

Bibliography

Primary Sources: Works by Derek Walcott

Poetry and Plays

25 Poems. Bridgetown, Barbados: Advocate, 1949; Port of Spain, Trinidad: Guardian Commercial Printery, 1948.

Epitaph for the Young: XII Cantos. Bridgetown, Barbados: Advocate, 1949.

Poems. Kingston, Jamaica: Kingston City Printery, 1951.

Henri Christophe: A Chronicle in Seven Scenes. Bridgetown, Barbados: Advocate, 1952.

In a Green Night: Poems 1948–1960. London: Jonathan Cape, 1962.

Selected Poems. New York: Farrar, Straus and Giroux, 1964.

The Castaway. London: Jonathan Cape, 1965.

The Gulf and Other Poems. London: Jonathan Cape, 1969. Published as *The Gulf: Poems*. New York: Farrar, Straus and Giroux, 1970.

Dream on Monkey Mountain and Other Plays. New York: Farrar, Straus and Giroux, 1970; London: Jonathan Cape, 1972.

Ti-Jean and His Brothers in *Dream on Monkey Mountain and Other Plays*. New York: Farrar, Straus and Giroux, 1970; London: Jonathan Cape, 1972.

Another Life. London: Jonathan Cape; New York: Farrar, Straus and Giroux, 1973.

Sea Grapes. London: Jonathan Cape, 1976.

The Joker of Seville and O Babylon! New York: Farrar, Straus and Giroux, 1978; London: Jonathan Cape, 1979.

The Star-Apple Kingdom. New York: Farrar, Straus and Giroux, 1979.

Remembrance and Pantomime. New York: Farrar, Straus and Giroux, 1980.

The Fortunate Traveller. New York: Farrar, Straus and Giroux, 1981; London: Jonathan Cape, 1982.

Midsummer. New York: Farrar, Straus and Giroux; London: Faber and Faber, 1984.

Collected Poems 1948–1984. New York: Farrar, Straus and Giroux; London: Faber and Faber, 1986.

Arkansas Testament. New York: Farrar, Straus and Giroux, 1987.

Omeros. New York: Farrar, Straus and Giroux, 1990.

The Bounty. New York: Farrar, Straus and Giroux, 1997.

Tiepolo's Hound. New York: Farrar, Straus and Giroux, 2000.

Essays, Publications in Periodicals, Other

"The Poetry of George Campbell". *Public Opinion* (Jamaica), 20 July 1957, 7.

"A Great Russian Novel". Review of *The Gift* by Vladimir Nabokov. *Sunday Guardian,* 19 April 1964, 15.

"The Figure of Crusoe". Typescript of lecture delivered at the University of the West Indies Open Lecture Series, St Augustine, Trinidad, 27 October 1965.

"Leaving School". *London Magazine* 5, no. 6 (1965): 4–14.

"Walcott on Walcott". Interview with Dennis Scott. *Caribbean Quarterly* 14, nos. 1 and 2 (March–June 1968): 77–82.

"Meanings". *Savacou* 2 (September 1970): 45–51.

"What the Twilight Says: An Overture". Originally published in *Dream on Monkey Mountain and Other Plays,* 1–40. New York: Farrar, Straus and Giroux, 1970.

"An Incident, an Epiphany". Typescript, 1972.

"The Caribbean: Culture or Mimicry?" *Journal of Interamerican Studies and World Affairs* 16, no. 1 (February 1974): 3–13.

"The Muse of History". Originally published in *Is Massa Day Dead?* edited by Orde Coombs, 1–27. New York: Doubleday Anchor, 1974.

"On Choosing Port of Spain". In *David Frost Introduces Trinidad and Tobago,* edited by David Frost, 14–23. London: André Deutsch, 1975.

"Any Revolution Based on Race Is Suicidal". Interview with Raoul Pantin. *Caribbean Contact* 1, no. 8 (August 1979): 14, 16.

Review of *Beyond a Boundary* by C.L.R. James. *New York Times Book Review,* 25 March 1984, 35.

World of Ideas, no. 137. Interview with Bill Moyers. Public Affairs Television Inc., New York, 1 November 1988.

"Caligula's Horse". In *After Europe,* edited by Stephen Slemon and Helen Tiffin, 138–42. Sydney: Dangaroo Press, 1989.

The Antilles: Fragments of Epic Memory. New York: Farrar, Straus and Giroux, 1992.

Conversations with Derek Walcott, edited by William Baer. Jackson: University Press of Mississippi, 1996.

"The Sea Is History". In *Frontiers of Caribbean Literature in English,* edited by Frank Birbalsingh, 22–28. London: Macmillan Education, 1996.

"Reflections on *Omeros*". *The Poetics of Derek Walcott: Intertextual Perspectives,* ed. Gregson Davis, *South Atlantic Review* 96, no. 2 (Spring 1997): 229–46.

What the Twilight Says. New York: Farrar, Straus and Giroux, 1998.
Another Life. MS One (prose version). University of the West Indies, Mona, Jamaica. N.d.
Walcott Collection 1957–81: Poetry and Prose; Correspondence; Diaries and Memo Books. University of the West Indies Library, St Augustine, Trinidad.

Secondary Sources

Anthony, Fr. Patrick. "The Silent Revolution". *Caribbean Contact* 5, no. 5 (August 1977): 10–11.

Baugh, Edward. *Derek Walcott: Memory as Vision: Another Life.* London: Longman, 1978.

———. "Metaphor and Plainness in the Poetry of Derek Walcott". *Literary Half-Yearly* 11, no. 2 (1970): 47–58.

———. "The West Indian Writer and His Quarrel with History". *Tapia* 7, no. 8 (20 February 1977): 6–7.

Bobb, June. *Beating a Restless Drum: The Poetics of Kamau Brathwaite and Derek Walcott.* Trenton, NJ: Africa World Press, 1998.

Breslin, Paul. " 'I Met History Once but He Ain't Recognize Me': The Poetry of Derek Walcott". *TriQuarterly* 68 (Winter 1987): 168–83.

Brodsky, Joseph. "On Derek Walcott". *New York Review of Books* 30, no. 17 (10 November 1983): 39–41.

Brown, Lloyd. "Caribbean Castaway New World Odyssey: Derek Walcott's Poetry". *Journal of Commonwealth Literature* 11, no. 2 (December 1976): 149–59.

———. *West Indian Poetry.* London: Heinemann, 1984.

Brown, Stewart, ed. *The Art of Derek Walcott.* Bridgend, Wales: Dufour, 1991.

Burton, R.D.E. "Derek Walcott and the Medusa of History". *Caliban* 3, no. 2 (1980): 3–48.

Fabre, Michel. " 'Adam's Task of Giving Things Their Name': The Poetry of Derek Walcott". *New Letters* 41, no. 1 (Fall 1974): 91–107.

Figueroa, John. "Some Subtleties of the Isle: A Commentary on Certain Aspects of Derek Walcott's Sonnet Sequence in *Tales of the Islands*". *World Literatures Written in English* 15, no. 1 (April 1976): 190–228.

Goldstraw, Irma E. *A Bibliography of Published Poems 1944–1979.* St Augustine, Trinidad: University of the West Indies, 1979.

Hamner, Robert D., ed. *Critical Perspectives on Derek Walcott.* Washington: Three Continents Press, 1993.

———. *Derek Walcott.* New edition. New York: Twayne, 1993.

Heaney, Seamus. "The Language of Exile". *Parnassus: Poetry in Review* 8, no. 1 (Fall–Winter 1979): 5–11.

Ismond, Patricia. "Derek Walcott: The Development of a Rooted Vision (Poetry and Drama)". PhD thesis, University of Kent, Canterbury, 1974.

———. "Self-Portrait of an Island: St Lucia Through the Eyes of its Writers". *Journal of West Indian Literature* 1, no. 1 (October 1986): 59–73.

———. "Walcott's Later Drama: From *Joker* to *Remembrance*". *Review of International English Literature* 16, no. 3 (July 1985): 89–101.

———. "Walcott versus Brathwaite". *Caribbean Quarterly* 17, nos. 3–4 (December 1971): 54–71.

———. "Woman as Race-Containing Symbol in Walcott's Poetry". *Journal of West Indian Literature* 8, no. 2 (April 1999): 83–89.

James, C.L.R. "Here's a Poet who sees the Real West Indies". Review of *In a Green Night. Sunday Guardian,* 6 May 1962, 5.

Johnson, Lemuel A. "Abeng: (Re) Calling the Body in (to) Question". In *Out of the Kumbla,* edited by Carole Boyce Davis and Elaine Savory Fido, 111–42. Trenton, NJ: Africa World Press, 1990.

King, Bruce. *Derek Walcott and West Indian Drama.* Oxford: Clarendon Press, 1992.

Livingston, James. "Derek Walcott: Poet of the New World". Paper delivered at the annual Conference of the National Council of Teachers of English, Las Vegas, Nevada, 26 November 1971.

Morris, Mervyn. "*The Fortunate Traveller*". In *The Art of Derek Walcott,* edited by Stewart Brown, 101–11. Bridgend, Wales: Dufour, 1991.

———. "Walcott and the Audience for Poetry". *Caribbean Quarterly* 14, nos. 1–2 (March–June 1968): 7–24.

Popovic, Caroline. "Hail Mary". *Caribbean Beat* 13 (Spring 1995): 54–58.

Review of *Another Life. Booklist* 70 (1 September 1973): 25.

Review of *Another Life. Choice* 10 (September 1973): 986.

Review of *Another Life. Virginia Quarterly Review* 51 (Spring 1975): lviii.

Rohlehr, Gordon. "Withering into Truth: A Review of Derek Walcott's *The Gulf and Other Poems*". *Trinidad Guardian,* 10 December 1969.

Taylor, Patrick. *The Narrative of Liberation.* Ithaca: Cornell University Press, 1989.

Terada, Rei. *Derek Walcott's Poetry: American Mimicry.* Boston: Northeastern University Press, 1992.

Thieme, John. *Derek Walcott.* Manchester: Manchester University Press, 1999.

Wilson-Tagoe, Nana. *Historical Thought and Literary Representation in West Indian Literature.* Gainesville: University of Florida Press, 1998.

General

Achebe, Chinua. *Hopes and Impediments: Selected Essays 1965–1987.* London: Heinemann, 1988.

Aristotle. *Poetics.* Trans. Malcolm Heath. Harmondsworth: Penguin, 1996.

Ashcroft, Bill, Gareth Griffiths, and Helen Tiffin. *The Empire Writes Back*. London: Routledge, 1989.

Bakhtin, M.M. *The Dialogic Imagination*. Translated by Caryl Emerson and Michael Holquist. Austin: University of Texas Press, 1981.

Baudelaire, Charles. *Les Fleurs du Mal*. Translated by Richard Howard. Boston: David R. Godine, 1982.

Benítez-Rojo, Antonio. *The Repeating Island*. Translated by James Maraniss. Durham: Duke University Press, 1996.

Bennet, Joan. *Five Metaphysical Poets*. 3d ed. London: Cambridge University Press, 1964.

———. *Four Metaphysical Poets*. Cambridge: Cambridge University Press, 1964.

Best, Lloyd. *Black Power and National Reconstruction*. Port of Spain, Trinidad: Tapia House, 1974.

Borges, Jorge Luis. *Labryinths: Selected Stories and Other Writings*. Harmondsworth: Penguin, 1981.

Brathwaite, Edward. *The Arrivants: A New World Trilogy*. Oxford: Oxford University Press, 1973.

———. *Mother Poem*. Oxford: Oxford University Press, 1977.

———. *Roots*. Havana: Casa de las Americas, 1986.

Breen, H.H. *St Lucia: Historical, Statistical and Descriptive*. London: Frank Cass, 1970.

Brodber, Erna. *Jane and Louisa Will Soon Come Home*. London: New Beacon, 1980.

Browne, T. *The Works of Sir Thomas Browne*. London: Faber and Faber, 1954.

Campbell, George. *First Poems*. Kingston, Jamaica: City Printery, 1945.

Carpentier, Alejo. *The Lost Steps*. Harmondsworth: Penguin, 1968.

Carrington, Lawrence. *St Lucian Creole: A Descriptive Analysis of Its Phonology and Morpho-Syntax*. Hamburg: Helmut Buske, 1984.

Cassirer, Ernst. *Language and Myth*. New York: Harper and Brothers, 1946.

Césaire, Aimé. *The Collected Poetry*. Translated by Clayton Eshelman and Annette Smith. Berkeley: University of California Press, 1983.

Craven, Thomas, ed. *A Treasury of Art Masterpieces: From the Renaissance to the Present Day*. New York: Simon and Schuster, 1939.

Defoe, Daniel. *Robinson Crusoe*. 1719. Reprint, Harmondsworth: Penguin, 1965.

Deren, Maya. *Divine Horsemen*. New York: McPherson, 1970.

Devas, Raymund. *A History of the Island of Grenada 1498–1796*. Grenada: Carenage Press, 1974.

Donne, John. *Selected Prose*. Oxford: Clarendon Press, 1967.

Easter, B.H. *A Guide to Morne Fortune, St Lucia*. Castries, St Lucia: St Lucia Archaeological and Historical Society, 1966.

Eliot, T.S. *The Use of Poetry*. London: Faber and Faber, 1933.

———. *Collected Poems 1909–1962*. London: Faber and Faber, 1974.

Froude, James A. *The English in the West Indies or the Bow of Ulysses*. London: Longmans, 1888.

Gaspard, David B. "The Most Noxious of Our Islands". *The Voice of St Lucia*, Independence supplement, 18 February 1979, 44.

Gilkes, Michael. *Wilson Harris and the Caribbean Novel*. Port of Spain, Trinidad: Longman Caribbean, 1975.

Glissant, Edouard. *The Ripening*. Translated by J. Michael Dash. London: Heinemann, 1985.

———. *Caribbean Discourse*. Translated by J. Michael Dash. Charlottesville: University Press of Virginia, 1992.

Grimshaw, Anna, ed. *The C.L.R. James Reader*. Oxford: Blackwell, 1992.

Harris, Wilson. *Eternity to Season*. Georgetown, Guyana: Master Printery, 1954.

———. *Palace of the Peacock*. 1960. Reprint, London: Faber and Faber, 1988.

———. *The Far Journey of Oudin*. London: Faber and Faber, 1961.

———. *The Whole Armour*. London: Faber and Faber, 1962.

———. *The Secret Ladder*. London: Faber and Faber, 1963.

———. *Heartland*. London: Faber and Faber, 1964.

———. "History, Fable and Myth in the Caribbean and the Guianas". *Caribbean Quarterly* 16, no. 2 (June 1970): 32.

Hill, Errol. *The Trinidad Carnival: Mandate for a National Theatre*. 1972. Reprint, London: New Beacon, 1997.

Hingley, Ronald. *Nightingale Fever: Russian Poets in Revolution*. London: Weidenfeld and Nicolson, 1982.

Homer. *The Iliad*. Translated by Robert Fitzgerald. London: Collins Harvill, 1985.

———. *The Odyssey*. Translated by A.T. Murray. Revised George E. Dimock. Cambridge, Mass.: Harvard University Press, 1995.

Hudson, William. *Green Mansions*. 1904. Reprint, New York: Watts, 1966.

Hughes, Ted. *Lupercal*. London: Faber and Faber, 1960.

———. *Selected Poems 1957–1981*. London: Faber and Faber, 1982.

James, C.L.R. *Beyond a Boundary*. 1963. Reprint, London: Hutchinson, 1976.

Jesse, Revd C. *Outlines of St Lucia's History*. Castries, St Lucia: St Lucia Archaeological and Historical Society, 1970.

Joyce, James. *Portrait of the Artist as a Young Man*. Harmondsworth: Penguin, 1992.

———. *Ulysses*. Harmondsworth: Penguin, 1992.

Kierkegaard, Sören. *Fear and Trembling* and *The Sickness Unto Death*. Translated by Walter Lowrie. New York: Doubleday, 1954.

Knight, Franklin W. *The Caribbean: The Genesis of a Fragmented Nationalism*. New York: Oxford University Press, 1990.

Lamming, George. *In the Castle of My Skin*. London: Michael Joseph, 1953.

———. *Of Age and Innocence*. London: Michael Joseph, 1958.

———. *The Pleasures of Exile*. London: Michael Joseph, 1960.

————. *Season of Adventure*. London: Michael Joseph, 1960.

Lever, J.W. *The Elizabethan Love Sonnet*. London: Methuen, 1966.

Levi, Darrel E. *Michael Manley: The Making of a Leader*. London: André Deutsch, 1989.

Livingstone, Angela, ed. *Pasternak and Creativity*. Cambridge: Cambridge University Press, 1985.

Look Lai, Walton. *The Chinese in the West Indies, 1806–1995*. Kingston, Jamaica: The Press, University of the West Indies, 1998.

Lovelace, Earl. *The Dragon Can't Dance*. London: André Deutsch, 1979.

Lowell, Robert. *Selected Poems*. London: Faber, 1965.

Macmillan, Allister, ed. *The West Indies*. 1912. Reprint, London: W.H. and L. Collingridge, 1938.

Malraux, André. *Psychology of Art*. Translated by Stuart Gilbert. 3 vols. New York: Pantheon, 1949, 1950.

Manley, Michael. *The Politics of Change*. London: André Deutsch, 1974.

————. *Up the Down Escalator*. Washington, DC: Howard University Press, 1987.

Márquez, Gabriel Garcia. *The Autumn of the Patriarch*. New York: Harper and Row, 1976.

Marvell, Andrew. *Andrew Marvell: The Complete English Poems*. Edited by Elizabeth Story Donno. New York: St Martin's Press, 1972.

Mbiti, John. *African Religions and Philosophy*. New York: Doubleday, 1970.

McKay, Claude. *Selected Poems*. New York: Bookman Associates, 1953.

McKeon, Michael. *Origins of the English Novel 1600–1740*. Baltimore: Johns Hopkins University Press, 1987.

Milano, Paolo, ed. *The Divine Comedy*. In *The Portable Dante,* translated by L. Binyon. Harmondsworth: Penguin, 1975.

Nabokov, Vladimir. *The Gift*. Harmondsworth: Penguin, 1980.

Naipaul, V.S. *The Middle Passage*. London: André Deutsch, 1962.

————. *The Mimic Men*. London: Penguin, 1969.

Neruda, Pablo. *Selected Poems*. Translated by Anthony Kerrigan et al. Harmondsworth: Penguin, 1975.

Nettleford, Rex. *Manley and the Politics of Jamaica*. Kingston, Jamaica: Institute of Social and Economic Research, University of the West Indies, 1971.

Pantin, Raoul. *Black Power Day*. Port of Spain, Trinidad: Hatuey Productions, 1990.

Parry, J.H., P.M. Sherlock, and A. Maingot. *A Short History of the West Indies*. London: Macmillan, 1956.

Pasternak, Boris. "Safe Conduct". In *Prose and Poems,* edited by Stefan Schimanski, 11–126. London: Ernest Benn, 1959.

Patterson, Orlando. *The Sociology of Slavery*. London: MacGibbon and Kee, 1967.

Paz, Octavio. *The Bow and the Lyre*. Translated by Ruth L.C. Simms. Austin: University of Texas Press, 1973.

Pound, Ezra. *The Cantos of Ezra Pound*. London: Faber and Faber, 1964.

Reddock, Rhoda, ed. *Ethnic Minorities in Caribbean Societies*. St Augustine, Trinidad: Institute of Social and Economic Research, University of the West Indies, 1996.

Reid, Vic. *New Day*. 1949. Reprint, London: Heinemann, 1973.

———. *The Horses of the Morning*. Kingston, Jamaica: Caribbean Authors Publishing Co., 1985.

Rewald, John, Frances Weitzenhoffer, and Irene Gordon. *Studies in Post Impressionism*. New York: Harry N. Abrams, 1986.

Rohlehr, Gordon. *Calypso and Society in Pre-Independence Trinidad*. Port of Spain, Trinidad: G. Rohlehr, 1990.

———. *The Shape of that Hurt*. Port of Spain, Trinidad: Longman, 1992.

St Omer, Garth. *A Room on the Hill*. London: Faber and Faber, 1968.

———. *Shades of Grey*. London: Faber and Faber, 1968.

———. *Nor Any Country*. London: Faber and Faber, 1969.

———. *J-, Black Bam and the Masqueraders*. London: Faber and Faber, 1972.

Schofield, Malcolm, and Martha Craven Nussbaum, eds. *Language and Logos: Studies in Ancient Greek Philosophy*. Cambridge: Cambridge University Press, 1982.

Seymour, A.J. *Selected Poems*. Guyana: BG Lithographic Co., 1965.

Shakespeare, William. *The Tempest*. In *Riverside Shakespeare*, edited by G. Blakemore Evans. Boston: Houghton Mifflin, 1974.

Sherlock, Philip. *Norman Manley*. London: Macmillan, 1980.

Simmons, Harold. "Notes on Folklore in St Lucia". In *Iouanaloa*, edited by Edward Brathwaite, 41–49. Castries, St Lucia: Department of Extra-Mural Studies, 1963.

Sitkoff, Harvard. *The Struggle for Black Equality 1954–1980*. New York: Hill and Wang, 1981.

Smith, M.G., Roy Augier, and Rex Nettleford. *The Rastafari Movement in Kingston, Jamaica*. Kingston, Jamaica: Institute of Social and Economic Research, University of the West Indies, 1960.

Stephens, Evelyn Huber, and John D. Stephens. *Democratic Socialism in Jamaica: The Political Movement and Social Transformation in Dependent Capitalism*. London: Macmillan, 1986.

Thomas, Dylan. *Collected Poems 1934–1953*. Edited by Walford Davies and Ralph Maud. London: J.M. Dent and Sons, 1988.

Thomas, J.J. *Froudacity: West Indian Fables by James Anthony Froude*. London: T.F. Unwin, 1889.

Traherne, Thomas. *Centuries of Meditation*. London: Dobbel, 1908.

Warner-Lewis, Maureen. *Guinea's Other Suns*. Dover, Mass.: Majority Press, 1991.

Whitman, Walt. *Leaves of Grass*. New York: Bantam, 1983.

Williams, Denis. *Other Leopards*. London: Heinemann, 1963.

Yeats, W.B. *Selected Poetry*. Edited by Timothy Webb. Harmondsworth: Penguin, 1991.

Index